The World of the Civil War

Recent Title in
Daily Life Encyclopedias

The World of Ancient Rome: A Daily Life Encyclopedia
James W. Ermatinger

1 ARTS TO FAMILY LIFE AND GENDER ROLES

The World of the Civil War

A Daily Life Encyclopedia

Lisa Tendrich Frank, Editor

GREENWOOD™

An Imprint of ABC-CLIO, LLC

Santa Barbara, California • Denver, Colorado

Library of Congress Cataloging-in-Publication Data

The world of the Civil War : a daily life encyclopedia / Lisa Tendrich Frank, editor.
    pages cm. — (Daily life encyclopedias)
  Includes bibliographical references and index.
  ISBN 978-1-4408-2978-9 (alk. paper) — ISBN 978-1-4408-2979-6 (EISBN)
1. United States—History—Civil War, 1861–1865—Social aspects—Encyclopedias.
2. United States—Social life and customs—1783–1865—Encyclopedias.   I. Frank, Lisa Tendrich.
  E468.9.W753   2015
  973.7003—dc23   2014046268

ISBN: 978-1-4408-2978-9
EISBN: 978-1-4408-2979-6

19 18 17 16 15   1 2 3 4 5

This book is also available on the World Wide Web as an eBook.
Visit www.abc-clio.com for details.

Greenwood
An Imprint of ABC-CLIO, LLC

ABC-CLIO, LLC
130 Cremona Drive, P.O. Box 1911
Santa Barbara, California 93116-1911

This book is printed on acid-free paper ∞

Manufactured in the United States of America

For Daniel, Noah, and Shayna, with love

Contents

Family Life and Gender Roles, 209

Science and Technology, 625

Preface

As much as the Civil War era was about battles and freedom, warfronts and home fronts, enslaved African Americans and the "peculiar institution" of slavery, it was also about much more. *The World of the Civil War: A Daily Life Encyclopedia* explores these experiences through more than 230 entries that have been organized into ten interrelated categories—Arts; Clothing, Fashion, and Appearance; Economy and Work; Family Life and Gender Roles; Food and Drink; Housing and Community; Politics and Warfare; Recreation and Social Customs; Religion and Beliefs; and Science and Technology. These categories and the related entries they include provide the context and background for the military narratives that most commonly get retold as the history of the Civil War. They, along with a series of related primary documents, allow these two volumes to reveal the multilayered meanings of the nation during the war.

Arts. The entries in the Arts section highlight the ways that nineteenth-century Americans interpreted the events around them and understood their world. These entries cover topics that include literature, newspapers, dance, music, and photography. Each of these aspects of nineteenth-century life reveals elements of what it was like to live during the Civil War.

Clothing, Fashion, and Appearance. This section allows readers to better visualize how nineteenth-century Americans looked. Their dress, although varied by age, class, race, and region, had similarities. Fashion magazines like *Godey's Ladies Book* dictated much of the style of the time. War, too, shaped people's sense of fashion; shortages led to the reuse of old styles as well as a dependence on homespun.

Economy and Work. Nineteenth-century America had a varied landscape and economy. Although rural farms and plantations dominated the Southern slaveholding economy, factories and urban areas proved dominant in the North. The Economy and Work section offers insight into the various ways that people worked and survived during this period. Entries on the work of seamstresses, artisans, factory workers, farmers, and others show how different people's lives could be from each other. In addition, this section contains entries on war-specific work. Camp followers found positions as laundresses, cooks, and prostitutes. Sutlers sold their wares to the soldiers. In addition, women on their respective home fronts took jobs for the Confederate and U.S. governments.

Family Life and Gender Roles. The fourth section explores how family and gender shaped the ways nineteenth-century Southerners and Northerners saw the world around them. This section highlights the ways that these aspects of life affected and were affected by men and women, children and adults, free people and enslaved people. From childhood, Americans were taught to understand things in a way that was specific to their region and sex. Girls were dressed like and taught to behave like their mothers. Fathers taught young men to hunt, run the farm, and participate in male culture. Race affected families as well. Enslaved African American were often sold away from their blood relations and had to form kinship networks within their plantation group.

Food and Drink. The entries on food and drink in this section illuminate the different types of nourishment that people ate and drank based on their class, race, culture, and region. Some of the differences in food resulted from the availability of certain items in specific regions, such as watermelon in the South. Others owed their prominence to cultural ideas about how to prepare it. The Civil War forced many people to change their dietary habits in response to shortages of antebellum staples. Coffee and sugar shortages, for example, led many Americans to seek out creative substitutes for items that resembled these luxuries. Food shortages also led to bread riots, especially in urban areas around the Confederacy.

Housing and Community. The entries in this section examine the types of buildings and people that made up communities in the Confederacy and the Union. With its rural focus, the Confederacy had more farms and plantations than did the more urbanized Union, whose cities had row houses, factories, and marketplaces. This section also explores how the Civil War disrupted families and communities. The wartime destruction of houses and threats to civilians forced many people to leave their homes and become refugees in other communities.

Politics and Warfare. Nineteenth-century Americans both shaped and were shaped by the politics and warfare of their era. Debates over slavery dominated the political arena and ultimately led to war. Civilians could not escape from the problems of the war. In the South, backyards frequently became battlefields. In addition, sieges and bombardments brought the battle directly to many people.

Recreation and Social Customs. Even with a war going on around them, people in the Union and the Confederacy found ways to relax and maintain some sense of normalcy. Entries in this section describe the ways in which nineteenth-century Americans entertained themselves. During the war, balls, fund-raising bazaars, theatrical shows, concerts, and sporting events continued to play a role in people's lives.

Religion and Beliefs. The section details the various spiritual ideas and rituals that governed the lives of nineteenth-century Americans. Faith played a prominent role in helping all people, regardless of race, age, region, or religion. As Americans dealt with the deadliest war their country had known up to that time, they turned to faith and religion to make sense of it. Some participated in religious revivals within the military, and others renewed their faith on the home front. Those on the home front as well as on the battlefield dwelt on ideas about the afterlife, crafted eulogies for the deceased, and otherwise mourned the loss of their soldiers. Many Americans even interpreted the war itself as a divine act of judgment.

Science and Technology. The nineteenth century saw advancements in technology and medicine, some of which are detailed in this section. Several of these advances, such as more accurate firearms and bullets, increased Civil War casualties. Others made it possible for doctors to treat battlefield wounds. There were also significant advances in transportation that allowed for the movement of people and troops as well as for the transport of food and military supplies.

Written by more than 100 scholars and period specialists, and aimed at high school and college students, as well as interested general readers, these entries have several valuable features. Each entry has a "See also" line listing cross-references to other related entries in these volumes identified by topic section. Each entry also concludes with a bibliography of additional print and electronic information resources. Some entries also contain sidebars, which offer more in-depth information on an interesting related topic. The entries in these volumes are supplemented with an Introduction that puts the Civil War period into context, a Chronology of major Civil War events, a Bibliography of important general information resources, and 15 primary documents from the Civil War period. Each document has a brief introduction that puts the document into context and provides an assessment of its importance. A detailed subject index helps readers access information in the entries.

Taken together, these ten topical sections of entries along with their accompanying documents and many other features reveal how the Civil War shaped all of American society. Indeed, between 1861 and 1865, more than 600,000 soldiers lost their lives, four million enslaved people obtained their freedom, and the United States resolved the issue regarding the ability of states to legally withdraw from the Union. These volumes demonstrate that the Civil War was much more than a dramatic four-year military and political struggle. It was a cultural, social, and economic experience that affected all aspects of the United States, and it was a campaign whose legacies and memory continue to shape the nation today.

Introduction

When Abraham Lincoln met author Harriet Beecher Stowe in 1862, he reportedly said, "So you're the little woman who wrote the book that made this great war!" By personalizing the horrors of slavery and publicizing them to the nation, Stowe's *Uncle Tom's Cabin* increased support for the abolitionist movement, outraged many slaveholders, and otherwise helped push the nation toward war. That an author of fiction could play such an important role in the era's defining moment should remind us that the Civil War (1861–1865) was more than a series of battles and that its history was shaped by people other than soldiers and politicians. Americans of all occupations and backgrounds—racial, economic, social, and regional—shaped and were shaped by the sectional conflict. One cannot tell the history of the war without understanding the nation and people that were at war.

For a few generations, scholars have sought to understand the history of the United States from the perspective of the common man and woman. Rather than focusing solely on presidents and generals or elections and military campaigns, they have tried to understand life as Americans lived it. The resulting social history asks different questions than does traditional military history and also clarifies and modifies much of what we once knew about the most significant events in the nation's history. The Civil War is no exception. Presidents Abraham Lincoln and Jefferson Davis certainly shaped the era, but understanding the experience of war also requires an examination of common soldiers, enslaved families, religious institutions, recent immigrants, cattle herders, cotton planters, artists, poets, refugees, women, and engineers.

The Civil War, like all wars, required that families and entire communities mobilize for a cause larger than themselves. Soldiers came from every community and seemingly all households. Some families resisted this expectation and asked for exemptions for their loved ones or prayed that once enlisted their loved ones would not be gone for long. Some families protested the drafts; others took to the streets to vent their anger about food shortages and inflation. In other instances, families were totally supportive and encouraged their sons and husbands to enlist in their respective armies. Tales abound of Confederate and Union women who shunned men who shirked their duty by refusing to enlist. Countless other families experienced the disruption of war, as their communities were cut off by blockades, invaded by enemy soldiers, or evacuated.

Even the experiences of enlisted soldiers revealed that the war was more than the summation of battles. Although one cannot tell the history of the war without an understanding of military campaigns, the experiences of soldiers require that we also understand the foods that they ate on the campaigns, the introduction of the Minié ball and other new wartime technologies, and the diverse uniforms that they wore. Most soldiers spent more time gambling, eating, and drinking than they did fighting. They worried about their fates and about the families they left behind, even as their own safety was at risk. They prayed and wrote letters home.

For the men, women, and children who spent the war years on the home front, the Civil War also shaped their daily lives in ways that went beyond waiting to hear news about the battles and the fates of their loved ones. The creation of Civil War armies required the support of everyone on the home front. This mobilization included, but was not limited to, the enlistment of soldiers. Both the Union and Confederate governments asked their citizens to send soldiers and otherwise sacrifice on behalf of the war effort. Some Americans willingly sacrificed comforts and necessities for the Union or Confederacy; others struggled to balance their personal needs with those of their nation. Some women helped to outfit the soldiers with homemade uniforms. Even children joined in the efforts to raise regiments and support the soldiers. The war also determined what fabrics and other materials could be used and what styles of clothing would be worn. Wartime shortages forced white Southerners and others to use homespun fabric for their clothes. Women's stress on the importance of sacrifice for their nation often gave men an example to follow.

Perhaps more importantly, the Civil War was arguably the most transformative four-year period in African American history. For starters, the war affected free African American families in the North in many of the same ways that it did other families—although the enlistment of black soldiers and the need to deal with food shortages and others sacrifices often hit African American communities harder than it did others. For the vast majority of the nation's African American population—the four million men and women who were enslaved when the war began—the Civil War constituted the turning point in the nation's history. On the eve of the secession crisis, most enslaved African Americans lived in the American South. There, they sustained the region's agricultural strength as cotton became what Alexander Stephens called the "cornerstone" of the Confederacy. When the war ended, the nation's tangled dependence upon with slavery abruptly came to an end. Former slaves became freedmen, voters, and potential landowners. Emancipation, though, hardly ended the struggle over the meaning of freedom. The South would remain tied to cotton and agriculture in general, and the generations that followed would continue to invent new ways of disenfranchising African Americans and maintaining white supremacy. The scars of slavery and emancipation continue to haunt the nation.

Lisa Tendrich Frank

Chronology

December 1833	American Anti-Slavery Society forms in Philadelphia.
July 1840	Abby Kelley is elected to the board of the American Anti-Slavery Society. Debate over the role of women results in the formation of a separate American and Foreign Anti-Slavery Society.
July 1848	Lucretia Mott, Elizabeth Cady Stanton, and other women's rights supporters hold a convention at Seneca Falls, New York, and issue a "Declaration of Sentiments."
September 1850	Congress passes a series of bills known as the Compromise of 1850.
June 1851	*The National Era* begins publishing in serial form Harriet Beecher Stowe's *Uncle Tom's Cabin; or, Life Among the Lowly*.
December 1851	First American Young Men's Christian Association (YMCA) opens in Boston, Massachusetts.
April 1853	Harriet Tubman begins bringing other slaves to freedom through the Underground Railroad.
May 1854	Congress passes Kansas-Nebraska Act. Escalating violence—"Bleeding Kansas"—begins between proslavery and antislavery settlers in the territory.
May 1856	Massachusetts senator Charles Sumner delivers "Crime Against Kansas" speech.
	John Brown and his sons kill five proslavery men during a raid on Pottowatomie Creek.
November 1856	Proslavery Democrat James Buchanan is elected president of the United States.
March 1857	Supreme Court makes *Dred Scott v. Sanford* ruling.
May 1857	Elizabeth and Emily Blackwell open New York Infirmary for Women and Children.

August 1857	Panic of 1857 begins.
June 1858	Abraham Lincoln delivers "House Divided" speech.
August 1858	First transatlantic telegraph cable is completed.
	Abraham Lincoln and Stephen A. Douglas engage in their first debate in Ottawa, Illinois.
October 1858	Lightweight sewing machines by Isaac Singer are first available.
April 1859	In Philadelphia, Union workers call for an eight-hour work day.
October 1859	Abolitionist John Brown leads a raid on the federal arsenal at Harper's Ferry, Virginia.
February 1860	Jefferson Davis asks U.S. Senate to pass slave codes for the territories.
March 1860	Shoemakers in Lynn, Massachusetts, march for higher wages.
April 1860	Pony Express mail service between Missouri and California begins.
	Democratic Party splits over slavery.
	Anna Dickinson delivers "The Rights and Wrongs of Women" at a Quaker meeting.
May 1860	Former members of the Whig and American Parties create the Constitutional Union Party.
November 1860	Abraham Lincoln is elected president of the United States.
December 1860	South Carolina secedes.
January 1861	Kansas is admitted to the Union under its antislavery constitution.
	Mississippi, Florida, Alabama, Georgia, and Louisiana secede.
	Harriet Jacobs (Linda Brent) publishes *Incidents in the Life of a Slave Girl*.
February 1861	Texas secedes.
	At a convention in Montgomery, Alabama, seceded states form Confederate States of America and elect Jefferson Davis as president.
March 1861	Abraham Lincoln is inaugurated as president of United States.
April 1861	Confederates capture Fort Sumter in South Carolina.
	Lincoln calls for 75,000 soldiers and orders naval blockade of Confederate seaports.
	Virginia secedes.

	Lincoln orders all executive branch civilian employees to take Loyalty Oath.
	Riots erupt in Baltimore, Maryland.
	Dorothea Dix is appointed Superintendent of Female Nurses for the Union Army.
May 1861	Arkansas and North Carolina secede.
	U.S. Congress creates Department of Agriculture.
June 1861	Western counties in Virginia form West Virginia.
July 1861	U.S. Congress authorizes the enlistment of 500,000 soldiers.
	Confederate and Union armies face each other for the first time at Battle of Bull Run (Manassas).
August 1861	Lincoln declares Confederate States to be in a state of insurrection.
	U.S. Congress passes first Confiscation Act.
	U.S. Congress passes first federal income tax.
	U.S. Secret Service arrests Rose O'Neal Greenhow as a Confederate spy.
September 1861	Sally Louisa Tompkins becomes a commissioned Confederate officer in order to keep Robertson Hospital open in Richmond, Virginia.
	Reverend L. C. Lockwood opens a Sunday school for freed slaves at Fortress Monroe, Virginia.
	American Missionary Association opens the first school for freedpeople.
October 1861	First transcontinental telegraph line is completed.
	Lincoln suspends the writ of habeas corpus.
November 1861	Lincoln appoints George B. McClellan to replace General Winfield Scott as head of the U.S. Army.
January 1862	Port Royal Experiment begins on the Union-occupied Sea Islands in South Carolina.
	Union's first ironclad steamer (the *Monitor*) is launched in Long Island, New York.
February 1862	Jefferson Davis suspends the writ of habeas corpus.
	Julia Ward Howe publishes "The Battle Hymn of the Republic."
March 1862	Confederate ironclad *Merrimac* and Union ironclad *Monitor* fight to a draw.
	Peninsular Campaign begins.
	U.S. Congress passes Impressment Act.
April 1862	Battle of Shiloh is fought.

	Forces commanded by Admiral David Farragut capture New Orleans.
	U.S. Congress abolishes slavery in the District of Columbia.
	Confederacy passes its first Conscription Act.
May 1862	U.S. Congress enacts Homestead Act.
	Union general Benjamin Butler takes command of occupied New Orleans and issues General Order Number 28, the "Woman Order."
	Union general David Hunter frees slaves in Georgia, South Carolina, and Florida. Lincoln revokes the order.
	Confederate navy worker, slave Robert Smalls, navigates the *Planter* from Charleston Harbor into Union lines where he surrenders it.
June 1862	Virginian Robert E. Lee assumes command of Confederate Army.
July 1862	U.S. Congress passes second Confiscation Act.
	U.S. Congress issues Ironclad Oath.
	Lee and McClellan face each other at the Seven Days' Battle.
	General Henry Halleck takes control of the Union Army.
	Confederate spy Belle Boyd is imprisoned at Old Capitol Prison.
	U.S. Congress passes the Morrill Land Grant Act.
August 1862	Confederate soldiers defeat Union Army at the Second Battle of Bull Run (Manassas).
September 1862	Lee's Army of Northern Virginia invades the North. On the deadliest day of fighting, 26,000 soldiers die at the Battle at Antietam.
	Lincoln issues preliminary emancipation proclamation.
October 1862	Jefferson Davis amends draft law, exempting those who own 20 or more slaves.
	Southerners organize Protestant Episcopal Church of the Confederate States of America.
December 1862	Confederates defeat Union forces at Battle of Fredericksburg.
	Ulysses S. Grant issues General Order Number 11, expelling Jews from his area of operation in the hopes of ending war profiteering. He revokes the order after a few weeks.
	Louisa May Alcott begins work at Union Hospital in Washington, D.C.

January 1863	Emancipation Proclamation goes into effect.
	General Ulysses S. Grant takes control of Army of the West.
	Recruitment begins for Massachusetts 54th Infantry Regiment, the first African American regiment.
February 1863	U.S. Congress passes National Banking Act.
March 1863	Habeas Corpus Act gives government the authority to imprison an individual indefinitely without charging that person.
	Women in Salisbury, North Carolina, riot in response to shortage of salt and flour.
	U.S. Congress passes Conscription Act.
April 1863	Women in Richmond, Virginia, protest wartime shortages with a "Bread Riot."
	Battle of Chancellorsville begins.
	Union's conscription policy goes into effect.
May 1863	Lee defeats Hooker at Chancellorsville.
	National Women's Loyal League meets for first time.
	Louisa May Alcott begins to publish *Hospital Sketches* in serial form.
	Confederate general Thomas "Stonewall" Jackson dies in Virginia from friendly fire.
June 1863	Lee invades Pennsylvania.
	General George G. Meade becomes Union commander of the Army of the Potomac.
	Residents of Vicksburg, Mississippi, evacuate to avoid Union shelling.
July 1863	Union Army defeats Lee at the Battle of Gettysburg.
	Grant's Union forces capture Vicksburg and take control of Mississippi River.
	Draft riots in New York City, Boston, Massachusetts, Holmes County, Ohio, and elsewhere across the Union.
August 1863	Confederate William C. Quantrill and 450 supporters raid Lawrence, Kansas.
September 1863	Confederates win Battle of Chickamauga.
October 1863	Lincoln calls for national day of thanksgiving to be held in November.
	Grant takes control of all western theater operations.
	United States Sanitary Commission holds successful sanitary fair in Chicago.
November 1863	Lincoln delivers "Gettysburg Address."
	Grant repels Confederate siege at Chattanooga, Tennessee.

January 1864	Confederacy enacts conscription law that requires enlistment of all white males between the ages of eighteen and forty-five.
February 1864	National Women's Loyal League brings petition to Congress demanding abolition of slavery.
March 1864	Grant takes control of all armies of the United States.
	General William T. Sherman assumes control of Union forces in the West.
	Women protest for peace in High Point, North Carolina.
April 1864	United States Sanitary Commission's three-week fundraising fair in New York raises $1 million.
	Bread riot takes place in Savannah, Georgia.
	Nathan Bedford Forrest and his Confederate cavalry capture Fort Pillow, Tennessee. They murder African American soldiers who are trying to surrender.
May 1864	Forces under Grant and Lee fight each other at the Wilderness and Spotsylvania.
June 1864	Confederates win Battle of Cold Harbor.
	Grant begins nine-month siege of Petersburg, Virginia.
	U.S. Congress passes Internal Revenue Act.
	Arlington is established as national cemetery.
September 1864	Sherman captures Atlanta and evicts all civilians from the city.
	Bread riots occur in Mobile, Alabama.
October 1864	Union general Philip H. Sheridan defeats Jubal Early's troops in Shenandoah Valley.
	Nevada becomes 36th state.
November 1864	Lincoln defeats McClellan in presidential election.
	Sherman's troops burn Atlanta and begin March to the Sea.
December 1864	Sherman captures Savannah, Georgia.
January 1865	Freed slaves obtain control of the Sea Islands between Jacksonville, Florida, and Charleston, South Carolina.
	Sherman marches through South Carolina.
	Confederacy's largest fund-raising bazaar is held in Columbia, South Carolina.
February 1865	Confederate peace commissioners meet with Lincoln and Secretary of State William Seward in Hampton Roads, Virginia.
	Sherman captures Columbia.

March 1865	Grant defeats Lee at Battle of Petersburg.
	Davis signs bill allowing African American enlistment in Confederate Army.
	U.S. Congress creates Freedmen's Bureau.
April 1865	Confederate forces evacuate from Richmond, Virginia.
	Lee surrenders to Grant at Appomattox Courthouse, Virginia.
	John Wilkes Booth assassinates Lincoln at Ford's Theater in Washington, D.C.
	Confederate Joseph E. Johnston surrenders to William T. Sherman at Durham Station, North Carolina.
	Andrew Johnson becomes president.
May 1865	General O. O. Howard becomes head of the Freedman's Bureau.
	General Edmund Kirby-Smith surrenders to General E. S. Canby in New Orleans, Louisiana.
July 1865	Mary Surratt, David E. Herold, Lewis Paine, and George A. Atzerodt are hanged for their involvement in Lincoln's assassination. Four other conspirators are sentenced to prison.
August 1865	Convention in Jackson, Mississippi, repeals secession and outlaws slavery.
October 1865	Convention in Savannah, Georgia, repeals secession and outlaws slavery.
November 1865	Mississippi passes first Black Code. Other Southern states follow with similar codes.
December 1865	Congress ratifies Thirteenth Amendment, abolishing slavery.
	Ku Klux Klan forms in Pulaski, Tennessee.
March 1866	Congress enacts Civil Rights Act of 1866.
May 1866	Susan B. Anthony and Elizabeth Cady Stanton organize Eleventh National Women's Rights Convention in New York City.
	Jefferson Davis is indicted for treason against United States.
June 1866	Congress approves Fourteenth Amendment, guaranteeing citizenship rights to all men born and naturalized in the United States.
July 1866	Race riot takes place in New Orleans.
	U.S. Congress passes the Freedmen's Bureau bill.

March 1867	Thaddeus Stevens proposes freedpeople receive forty-acre plots of land. Congress votes down this plan.
	Congressional Reconstruction Acts divide South into five militarily controlled districts.
July 1868	Fourteenth Amendment is ratified.
November 1868	Ulysses S. Grant is elected president.
February 1869	Congress passes Fifteenth Amendment preventing states from denying voters the right to vote on the basis of race, color, or previous condition.
April 1871	Congress passes Civil Rights Act of 1871 (Ku Klux Klan Act).
June 1872	Congress abolishes Freedman's Bureau.
March 1875	Civil Rights Act of 1875 guarantees African Americans receive equal treatment in public facilities.
November 1876	Rutherford B. Hayes is elected president.
April 1877	President Hayes removes last federal troops from South Carolina, formally ending Reconstruction.
May 1881	Civil War nurse Clara Barton forms American Association of the Red Cross.

ARTS

INTRODUCTION

Nineteenth-century Americans turned to the arts to understand and interpret the growing crisis and the Civil War. In the public realm, literature, music, visual arts, and theater allowed Northerners and Southerners to interpret events and influence others. Privately, many turned to diaries, letters, and other artistic expressions to deal with the everyday wartime problems they had to face.

The written word proved particularly powerful during the Civil War era. Novels such as *Uncle Tom's Cabin* highlighted the problems of slavery and the approach of war. Some even credit the novel's author, Harriet Beecher Stowe, with helping to push the nation toward war. In the Confederacy, words also held sway. August Jane Evans's *Macaria* vehemently defended the "peculiar institution" and the Confederate cause. Wartime themes also carried over to the stage. Others used wartime theater productions to escape their daily worries, if only briefly.

Poetry also allowed Northerners and Southerners to express their attitudes about the war, death, and other topics. In the North, poet Walt Whitman published poems that highlighted war themes. He also composed poems on the nation's reaction to Abraham Lincoln's assassination.

In addition, newspapers in both North and South contributed both to the information about the war and to the rumors about battles and results. After the war, some journalists became novelists who focused on Civil War topics. During the war, magazines, especially those in the North, offered political commentary on wartime events through articles and cartoons. They also offered advice on how to deal with wartime shortages and commented on fashion.

Portraits, by an artist or a photographer, became especially valuable to nineteenth-century Americans. The death of so many men on the battlefields led to an increased desire to have an image of a loved one. In addition, growing advances in the field of photography allowed Americans to see what the carnage of battle looked like. In particular, photographer Mathew Brady took photographs of battlefields after battles. He also photographed military leaders; these images often allowed civilians and soldiers to feel like they knew those figures.

In the private sphere, many Northerners and Southerners began keeping diaries to chronicle the momentous events around them. They also sent detailed letters to family members and friends describing the events in their areas, news of family and friends, and hopes for the future.

Slaves also created written accounts of their bondage. The nineteenth century saw the publication of many slave narratives. Frederick Douglass, who also did speaking tours promoting the cause of abolition, wrote the most prominent autobiographical account by an escaped slave.

Patriotic music and songs helped keep up morale on the home front, encourage support of the war causes, and keep military units in time with each other. The South's most famous patriotic song was "Dixie," a tune that glorified slavery and the world it created. Northerners reveled in "The Battle Hymn of the Republic."

So, too, did some find artistic outlets in flags for local military units. The flags, usually made by a community's women, were presented to the soldiers during an elaborate ceremony. Women's creativity in designing the flags helped the men on the battlefield remember those at home and the reasons they were fighting.

ART

The Civil War shaped the field of visual culture in America without being its direct subject matter. In addition to painting, illustration, sculpture, and other forms of art that captured the events, the Civil War was the first war to be extensively photographed from start to finish. The majority of Americans had to wait until the 1880s to see any of the photographed images from the war, as photography was a new medium in the era. Publications such as *Harper's Weekly* featured the illustrations of several prolific artists, some who became known as special artists. These special artists worked for the press to capture life on the battlefield and its surroundings in their art. In general, it was through the work of Civil War artists and photographers that the people of the United States and Europe were given images of the war.

The Civil War was the subject of many paintings. Although there were not any grand manner historical paintings that emerged from the Civil War, a group of American artists made contributions to genre painting that depict scenes from everyday life. These artists produced hundreds of history paintings. Optimistic art critics at the time had hoped the Civil War would give the art world the opportunity to generate great American grand manner history painting. However, very few

American artists felt the need to depict the conflict. The narrative conventions of grand manner history painting failed to adequately address the Civil War, as did the associational interpretive strategies of landscape painting.

Many prints and paintings depicted particular battles in the Civil War. During the war, however, very few artists actually drew battle scenes. Artists sketched scenes of camp and the quiet moments of soldier's daily life in the army, mostly for the reason that few artists were close enough to witness the actual battles that the soldiers fought. Arthur Lumley (1837–1912), a landscape painter and illustrator, was the first of the artists sent to the Army of the Potomac by an illustrated newspaper to cover the Civil War. Edwin Forbes (1839–1895) was one of the few artists to cover the entire war.

Throughout the war, *Harper's Weekly* sent numerous artists, including Winslow Homer (1836–1910), to the battlefront to cover the action. The war impacted Homer's work. His aesthetics acknowledged that translating the war into painting meant breaking almost entirely with the accepted conventions of genre and grand manner history painting.

Many artists' work in relation to the conflict has been overlooked until very recently. For example, Eastman Johnson (1824–1906), Frederic Church (1826–1900), Sanford Gifford (1823–1880), Timothy H. O'Sullivan (1840–1882), Alexander Gardner (1821–1882), George Barnard (1819–1902), Conrad Wise Chapman (1842–1910), and Julian Scott (1846–1901) were among the American artists and photographers who incorporated the Civil War into their artworks. George Caleb Bingham (1811–1879) most dramatically used African American types in his controversial painting *Order No. 11*. William Sidney Mount (1807–1868) painted more works of African Americans than any other artist from the Civil War period in America. Among other recognized artists who produced artworks based on the Civil War, or who were highly active during the period of American history, are Edward Lamson Henry (1841–1919), Theodore Kaufmann (1814–1896), Thomas Nast (1840–1902), Augustus Saint-Gaudens (1848–1907), William Aiken Walker (1838–1921), Granville Perkins (1830–1895), William D. Washington (1834–1870), Dennis Malone Carter (1820–1881), Constant Mayer (1829–1911), George Cope (1855–1929), David Blythe (1815–1865), John Quincy Adams Ward (1830–1910), William Wells Brown (1814–1884), William Notman (1826–1891), Robert S. Duncanson (1821–1872), Thomas Moran (1837–1926), Lilly Martin Spencer (1822–1902), Edmonia Lewis (1844–1907), and Thomas Satterwhite Noble (1835–1907).

James Walker's (1819–1889) large painting, *The Battle of Gettysburg*, showed some of the battle's bloodshed and confusion during General George Pickett's catastrophic charge. David Blythe also depicted the drama of Gettysburg in a classic war painting in 1863. Eastman Johnson, in a *Ride for Liberty—The Fugitive*

Slaves, March 2, 1862, depicted a tense moment for a black family as they fled for Union lines with the intent to achieve freedom.

In 1866, a full year after the war ended, Homer painted *Prisoners from the Front*, the Civil War painting that would define his career for years. It was received well and to much critical acclaim when first displayed. The artwork was widely reviewed for its depiction as a painting about Northern triumph over a dismayed South.

Amid the aftershocks of President Abraham Lincoln's assassination, the National Academy of Design in New York City opened its doors for its spring exhibition, after a delay in deference to Lincoln's death. Artworks displayed included an 1863 painting by Sanford Gifford, *The Coming Storm*. In 1863, the National Academy of Design's spring exhibition included New York painter Henry Peters Gray's (1819–1877) artwork *America in 1862*, an allegorical image featuring a personification of America breaking the chains of a kneeling slave with one hand and giving the slave a sword with the other, and sculptor John Quincy Adams Ward's *The Freedman*, a plaster statuette inspired by the recent Emancipation Proclamation.

Some artist themselves saw active duty during the Civil War, such as James Hope (1818–1892), who enlisted in the Union Army and participated in numerous battles. In the years immediately following the war, he gained a reputation as a painter of battle scenes.

Dustin Garlitz

See also: *Arts: Harper's Weekly*; Newspapers, Northern; Newspapers, Southern; Photography; Portraiture; *Economy and Work*: Artisans; Slavery

FURTHER READING

Boime, Albert. *Art in the Age of Civil Struggle, 1848–1871*. Chicago: University of Chicago Press, 2007.

Conn, Steven. "Narrative Trauma and Civil War History Painting, or Why are These Pictures So Terrible?" *History and Theory* 41 (2002): 17–42.

Conn, Steven, and Andrew Walker. "The History in the Art: Painting the Civil War." *Art Institute of Chicago Museum Studies* 27:1 (2001): 60–81, 102–103.

Giese, Lucretia Hoover. " 'Harvesting' the Civil War: Art in Wartime New York." In Patricia M. Burnham and Lucretia Hoover Giese, eds. *Redefining American History Painting*. New York: Cambridge University Press, 1995, pp. 64–81.

Grossman, Julian. *Echo of a Distant Drum: Winslow Homer and the Civil War*. New York: H.N. Abrams, 1974.

Harvey, Eleanor Jones. *The Civil War and American Art*. New Haven, CT: Yale University Press, 2012.

Kaufman, Will. *The Civil War in American Culture*. Edinburgh, Scotland: Edinburgh University Press, 2006.

National Gallery of Art. *The Civil War: A Centennial Exhibition of Eyewitness Drawings.* Washington, DC: National Collection of Fine Arts, 1961.

Neely, Mark E., Jr., and Harold Holzer. *Mine Eyes Have Seen the Glory: The Civil War in Art.* New York: Orion Books, 1993.

Neely, Mark E., Jr., and Harold Holzer. *The Union Image: Popular Prints of the Civil War North.* Chapel Hill: University of North Carolina Press, 2000.

Neely, Mark E., Jr., Harold Holzer, and Gabor S. Boritt. *The Confederate Image: Prints of the Lost Cause.* Chapel Hill: University of North Carolina Press, 1987.

Savage, Kirk. "Molding Emancipation: John Quincy Adams Ward's *The Freedman* and the Meaning of the Civil War." *Art Institute of Chicago Museum Studies* 27:1 (2001): 26–39, 101.

"BATTLE HYMN OF THE REPUBLIC"

The words to the "Battle Hymn of the Republic," by Julia Ward Howe (1819–1910), first appeared in the *Atlantic Monthly* magazine in 1862. Originally a song to support the Union war effort, it continues in the twenty-first century to be sung as a patriotic hymn in America.

Speculation still abounds concerning the original source of the melody for the song known today as the "Battle Hymn of the Republic." The chorus's melody was used as a camp meeting song in the 1850s, "Say Brothers Will You Meet Us." For the hymn, "Mine Eyes Have Seen the Glory," *The Methodist Hymnal* of 1966 cites the musical source as an American Camp Meeting tune, with Julia Ward Howe as the author of the text. The roots for its other texts and melody lie in the abolitionist fervor expressed by John Brown (1800–1859), who became famous due to the raid he led on United States Armory and Arsenal at Harper's Ferry in western Virginia, in 1859. Future Confederate general Robert E. Lee led the troops who arrested Brown, who was subsequently executed. The song was sung principally by Union troops and sympathizers during the Civil War, but was revived many times with altered text during the temperance movement and the labor movement of populism in the 1880s.

The text to "John Brown's Body" was printed on broadsides in 1861. It began with verses that repeated "John Brown's body lies a mouldering in the grave, /His soul's marching on!" Subsequent verses speak to the martyrdom of Brown ("He's gone to be a soldier in the army of the Lord"), and revenge against the Confederate president ("They will hang Jeff Davis on a tree!"). "John Brown's Body" was also called "John Brown's baby has a cold upon his chest." Yet another version, "Glory! Glory! Hallelujah!," published by Oliver Ditson of Boston in 1862, substituted the name Ellsworth for John Brown, which was shrunk into a smaller font. Elmer Ephraim Ellsworth (1837–1861), a member of Abraham Lincoln's campaign staff, became the first well-known Civil War death on May 24, 1861, during a raid on Alexandria, Virginia. The tune, a well-known nineteenth-century camp-meeting and revival hymn, has been variously attributed to William Steffe (1830–1890), Thomas Brigham Bishop, and Frank E. Jerome, but none of these is substantiated as the creator of the tune. Steffe did compose band arrangements, many of which were subsequently edited by modern arrangers such as Morton Gould.

In 1862, Julia Ward Howe wrote her words to the *Battle Hymn of the Republic*, beginning with "Mine eyes have seen the glory of the coming of the Lord." It was edited to match the tune of *John Brown's Body* around 1863. During the Civil War, Howe's lyrics were reprinted in several Union songbooks. "Battle Hymn of the Republic" took on a more sacred attitude than earlier versions of the tune, extolling righteousness, judgment, and Christ's birth and holiness in its subsequent verses; many hymnals today across denominations include this hymn.

"John Brown's Body" was sung as a cheer by Union troops, including by those under the command of General William Tecumseh Sherman, during his March to the Sea (1864). The original tune, "John Brown's Body," also became a pastiche, a melody with altered text. One of the early renditions was a campaign song by the Copperheads, called the "White Soldiers' Song," which began with the line, "Tell Abe Lincoln that he'd better end the war." The text of the fifth verse, "Tell Abe Lincoln of Antietam's bloody dell," harkens to a chant sung a hundred years later during the Vietnam War against President Lyndon Johnson: "Hey, hey, LBJ, how many kids did you kill today?" Word of Lincoln's assassination took more than a week to reach the West Coast. On April 24, 1865, in a memorial service aboard the ship *Constitution*, near San Francisco, four Italian singers sang the "Battle Hymn"; Louis Moreau Gottschalk (1829–1869), a famous pianist and composer of the day, accompanied the singers, and had performed in Washington, D.C., with the Lincolns attending.

The wounds of the Civil War were still present in the 1872 reelection campaign of President Ulysses S. Grant. The melody, part of the song "Hurrah! Hurrah! For Grant and Wilson," laid scorn upon Horace Greeley and Copperheads. Later versions of the song were employed by the temperance movement, the presidential election of 1892 between Grover Cleveland and Benjamin Harrison, and even by socialists in 1900. In addition, "Battle Hymn" eventually became a tune sung during the protests of the 1960s against the Vietnam War, and by those favoring civil rights. It was also sung at the second inauguration of President Barack Obama in January 2013.

On June 4, 1892, *Western Rural*, a weekly agricultural newspaper published in Illinois, printed one such rendition or pastiche, by Nellie Booth Simmons, entitled the "Battle Hymn of Labor": "Since the slowly moving cycles of the nation first began, / Has the world been curs'd and sadden'd by selfishness of men, / And the student of the people can but count his saying true, / That the many toil and struggle for the pleasure of the few." This version was part of the populist and labor movement of the late nineteenth century. In its many varied melodies, harmonies, and texts, the tune of "John Brown's Body" still evokes revolution.

Ralph Hartsock

See also: *Arts*: Music, Nonmilitary; *Housing and Community*: Nationalism, United States

FURTHER READING

Bernard, Kenneth A. *Lincoln and the Music of the Civil War*. Caldwell, ID: Caxton, 1966.
Cornelius, Steven H. *Music of the Civil War Era*. Westport, CT: Greenwood Press, 2004.
Randall, Annie Janeiro. "A Censorship of Forgetting: Origins and Origin Myths of Battle Hymn of the Republic." In Annie J. Randall, ed. *Music, Power, and Politics*. New York: Routledge, 2005, pp. 5–24.
Sanders, Paul D. *Lyrics and Borrowed Tunes of the American Temperance Movement*. Columbia: University of Missouri Press, 2006.
Silber, Irwin. *Songs America Voted By*. Harrisburg, PA: Stackpole Books, 1971.

BRADY, MATHEW B. (ca. 1823–1896)

Photographer Mathew Brady produced many of the images that we now associate with the Civil War. His battlefield photos gave those on the home front a glimpse into the horrors of war.

It is believed that Mathew Brady was born in 1823 in the vicinity of Lake George, New York, to Andrew and Julia Brady. Very little is known about his childhood, other than that he was raised in a poor, working-class family. Despite his humble beginnings, he became renowned as a photographer although it is now known that a significant number of the photographs credited to him were actually the work of the employees at his photography studio. He is best remembered for the photographs that his studio produced during the Civil War.

In the early 1840s, Brady was taught by Samuel F. B. Morse how to produce daguerreotypes, which was an early type of photograph. Brady subsequently opened the Daguerrean Miniature Gallery in New York City in April 1844. He quickly established himself as one of the leading photographers in the city by exhibiting his work at the American Institute's Fair, where he won the top prize in 1844, 1845, 1846, 1849, and 1857.

Photograph of Mathew Brady with his photography wagon in Petersburg, Virginia, ca. 1864. Photographer Mathew Brady and his team captured thousands of images of Civil War battlefields. (Library of Congress)

By 1845, Brady had in his New York studios begun producing portraits of famous people that he hoped to eventually publish in a series of books. To further the project, he opened a studio in Washington, D.C., which gave him access to many politicians. In 1850, he published a book of portraits entitled *The Gallery of Illustrious Americans*, which included images of luminaries such as Andrew Jackson, Henry Clay, John C. Calhoun, and Zachary Taylor. The book proved a financial failure. The studio in Washington, D.C., closed soon thereafter. In 1858, Brady opened another studio in Washington, D.C., which he named Brady's National Photographic Art Gallery. The manager of the new gallery was Alexander Gardner, who subsequently produced some of the more famous images that were credited to Brady. It was common practice during that period for the owner of photography studios to have all of the photographs produced by his employees credited to him. Nonetheless, Gardner left Brady's employ in 1862 and opened his own studio. Many of Brady's other talented but uncredited photographers, such as Timothy O'Sullivan, joined Gardner at his gallery.

The establishment of Brady's National Photographic Art Gallery situated Brady and his employees to effectively chronicle the Civil War. Even before warfare erupted, Brady's respective studios had made portraits of most of the members of the U.S. Congress, many of whom subsequently left their posts to join the Confederate States of America. As a result, Brady had relatively recent photographs of many of the major leaders of both sides of the Civil War. Brady also got to photograph Abraham Lincoln during the presidential campaign of 1860. His relationship with Lincoln and other politicians in the United States enabled Brady to have many of his photographers embedded with Union troops. Although the technology of the day did not enable the photographers to take pictures of actual combat, they were able to document the grisly aftermath of many battles. Brady displayed many of the early Civil War photographs in his gallery at the corner of Broadway and Tenth Street in New York City, where the general populace was exposed to the horrors of war being faced by their loved ones in the field.

Although the Civil War enabled Brady to gain immense fame, it also set the stage for his financial ruin. During the war, Brady purportedly spent nearly $100,000 chronicling the conflict. He mistakenly expected to recoup his expenses during the war by selling copies of his photographs in the New York and Washington, D.C., galleries. That strategy resulted in him struggling to secure the financing necessary to pay his many employees by 1864. To alleviate his financial difficulties, he tried to sell approximately 7,000 negatives from the Civil War era to the New York Historical Society but was unable to finalize a deal. In 1869, he offered to sell them to the U.S. Congress but was rejected. Brady subsequently was forced in 1872 to file for bankruptcy. It wasn't until 1875 that Brady finally found a buyer, and he sold his collection of negatives to the U.S. government for $25,000. That collection is now housed at the National Archives in Washington, D.C. The sale of the negatives enabled him to finally settle debts with his creditors that stemmed from the Civil War.

By the late 1880s, Brady's health had begun to obviously decline. He lost his wife Julia, whom he had married in 1850, in 1887. Her death led to a bout of depression accompanied by serious alcohol abuse. During this period, Brady was still able to earn a living as a photographer, although he actually was taking very few photographs. He had become a celebrity that people came to hear as he regaled them with stories about photography during the Civil War. In 1895, he suffered a broken leg in a traffic accident in New York City. The injury ultimately led to his death on January 15, 1896. He was buried in Arlington National Cemetery.

John R. Burch, Jr.

See also: *Arts*: Photography; *Politics and Warfare*: Casualties

FURTHER READING

Sullivan, George. *In the Wake of Battle: The Civil War Images of Mathew Brady*. Lakewood, NJ: Prestel Publishing, 2004.

Trachtenberg, Alan. *Reading American Photographs: Images as History, Mathew Brady to Walker Evans*. New York: Hill and Wang, 1989.

Zeller, Bob. *The Blue and Gray in Black and White: A History of Civil War Photography*. Westport, CT: Praeger, 2005.

DANCE

During the Civil War, Americans danced for social, religious, martial, theatrical, and popular entertainment purposes. The variety of dances reflected the many cultural groups that spread across the continent. For much of the nineteenth century, European Americans had ambivalent attitudes toward dance; many religious leaders railed against the sinful potential of dance, but some advocated for regulated dancing as a healthy means of channeling physical desires.

Although influenced by contact with other cultural groups, European Americans often looked to Europe for both theatrical and social dance styles. Social dance for the middle and upper classes included the many ballroom dances explained in widely circulated dance and etiquette manuals. Some social dance styles were quite complex and necessitated lessons from a dancing master. Ballroom dance was part of maintaining social status, as well as a means to exclude those seeking upward mobility. It was also part of physical well-being and courtship. Initially considered scandalous in the early nineteenth century for the intoxicating whirling motion and sense of individual abandon, the waltz remained popular during the Civil War. Although the waltz required an intimate face-to-face embrace with a single partner, most other ballroom dance styles involved changing partners by moving in and out of formations in lines and patterns. Such dance styles included the Virginia Reel, quadrilles, and square dances. These social dances allowed for meeting and mingling with many people. Knowing not only how to do the dances well but also the appropriate etiquette of a ball or casual dance at home was an essential part of showing good breeding, taste, marriageability, and social power.

Blending elements of European dance styles with West African dance aesthetics, African American slaves and freedmen continued social and religious dances such as the Ring Shout. Because some Protestant sects considered dancing sinful, and further defined dance as crossing and/or picking up the feet, a shuffling motion characterized the religious Ring Shout dance. Long before the Civil War, slaveholders banned drumming due to its martial associations. But the enslaved people drew from West African dance traditions and developed ways of making music with the body—"Patting Juba," or slapping the thighs, arms, and chest and stomping the feet. For social purposes, slaves and freedmen also danced in figures and patterns inspired by French Quadrilles, English and American square dances, and reels.

Native American dancing included a variety of religious and social dances. Across the continent, the number of different tribes and dance styles was vast. For example, the Plains tribes reorganized in the wake of forced migration and population decline. Different tribes reformulated various dance rituals, including a variety of religious vision-inducing dances later known as the sun dance. Travelers such as Henry A. Boller wrote reports of their observations of ceremonies and dances, including many animal and bird dances. Visiting the Hidatsa of the Missouri River, Boller reported on a ceremony in which men dressed as bulls performed a stamping dance, followed by men and boys streaming forth and scattering, representing antelopes. In some dance styles, the dancers added to the music through the use of ankle bells; during the Civil War, sleigh bells became popular. In a tumultuous time of change, dance provided religious communion and social cohesion.

Community building through movement was also important for soldiers during the war. Along with impromptu dancing to pass the time, soldiers on both sides of the war danced in the form of military drill. Moving together in time helped to create a sense of solidarity and community, as it also provided combat training and physical fitness. A few key German immigrants contributed to the war with physical training skills honed in the Turner Gymnastics movement, which tied physical conditioning with involvement in political causes.

Although European governments funded the training of professional dancers in the early nineteenth century, the U.S. government did not yet consider theatrical dance an essential element of national identity. Demand for ballet soared during the 1840s Romantic ballet craze, then waned from the 1850s until just after the Civil War. Thus, a few individual American-born dancers such as George Washington Smith (1825–1899) characterized theatrical dance during the 1860s. Visiting foreign dancers such as Italian mime and ballet choreographer Domenico Ronzani (1800–1868) met with only a lukewarm response.

Spurred on by the popularity of African American minstrel entertainer and tap dance pioneer Master Juba (William Henry Lane, c. 1825–c.1852) and white troupes such as Christy's Minstrels in the 1840s and 1850s, minstrel shows continued to be America's major popular entertainment during the Civil War. Many of the minstrel performers were Irish immigrants who blackened their faces with burnt cork and mocked the songs, dances, and dialect of African American slaves. However, racial issues in minstrelsy were even more complicated; African

Americans also performed in blackface minstrelsy, even more so after the Civil War. Minstrel shows also dealt with contemporary issues such as immigration and urbanization. Minstrelsy continued to be popular, sometimes included as a part of circus performance.

At the end of the Civil War, a series of serendipitous events occurred that led to the production of the most influential nineteenth-century American theatrical spectacle: *The Black Crook* (1866). In the 1865–1866 New York City theater season, a production of the ballet-pantomime *La Biche au Bois* was about to open, complete with imported European performers and sets designed for impressive theatrical tricks. However, the theater burned down just before the show opened. William Wheatley of Broadway's Niblo's Garden bought the sets and the dancers' contracts, hoping to insert them into a melodrama he had previously purchased called *The Black Crook*. This hodgepodge of spectacular sets, costumes, and voluptuous dancers had a thin plot, but it dazzled audiences. The show enjoyed a long run on Broadway, went on tour, and had several revivals. Some scholars consider *The Black Crook* to be the first major American musical. Despite the difficulties of war, or perhaps because of them, Americans continued to dance and watch dance entertainment during the Civil War.

Kathaleen Boche

See also: *Arts*: Theater; *Economy and Work*: Rural Life, Northern; Rural Life, Southern; Urban Life, Northern; Urban Life, Southern; *Family Life and Gender Roles*: Immigrants; *Politics and Warfare*: Morale; *Recreation and Social Customs*: Concerts; Dances and Balls; Military Drills; Theatrical Productions

FURTHER READING

Aldrich, Elizabeth. *From the Ballroom to Hell: Grace and Folly in Nineteenth-Century Dance*. Evanston, IL: Northwestern University Press, 1991.

Boller, Henry A. *Among the Indians: Eight Years in the Far West, 1858–1866*. Philadelphia: T. Ellwood Zell, 1868.

Emery, Lynn Fauley. *Black Dance: From 1619 to Today*. 2nd rev. ed. Hightstown, NJ: Princeton Book Company, 1972, 1988.

Freedley, George. "The Black Crook and the White Fawn." In Paul Magriel, ed. *Chronicles of the American Dance: From the Shakers to Martha Graham*. Reprint ed. New York: Da Capo Press, 1978 (1948), pp. 65–79.

McNeill, William H. *Keeping Together in Time: Dance and Drill in Human History*. Cambridge, MA: Harvard University Press, 1995.

Moore, Lillian. "George Washington Smith." In Paul Magriel, ed. *Chronicles of the American Dance: From the Shakers to Martha Graham*. Reprint ed. New York: Da Capo Press, 1978 (1948), pp. 139–188.

Toll, Robert C. *Blacking Up: The Minstrel Show in Nineteenth-Century America*. New York: Oxford University Press, 1974.

DIARY WRITING

Civil War diaries provide invaluable information about daily life in the wartime United States. Individuals from all walks of life kept diaries, although it was easier for members of the upper class to do so. Northerners and Southerners, soldiers and civilians, as well as men and women often recorded their daily activities and thoughts in journals. In the postwar period, some people published the diaries that they had kept during the war. Others, perhaps those who did not keep journals, wrote reflections of the war after 1865 and published these accounts. Countless numbers of diaries were never published: they may have been lost, donated to archives for historical research, or remain in the possession of the diarist's descendants.

Southern women on the home front frequently kept diaries chronicling their wartime experiences. Many recognized, and mentioned in their journals, that the events about which they were writing had historical significance. At the outset of the conflict and before the war began, women expressed their anxieties about national and regional concerns. Then and once the war began, they made repeated allusions to Union and Confederate political and military leaders conveying a keen awareness of the contemporary political landscape. In particular, they were eager to learn the outcome of each battle. At the same time, white female diarists also discussed familial affairs, mainly worrying about the welfare of their husbands and sons on the front lines.

Women's diaries also reflect the difficulties faced on the home front. The financial and logistical administration of the household was a major theme in women's diaries. Under conditions of extreme scarcity and inflation, women struggled to acquire food and basic goods to ensure their survival and that of family members on the home front. They were also concerned about the security of their homes and families, from both Union invasion and slave insurrection. Despite these fears, many elite white Southern women were devoted to the Confederate cause and expressed their fervent patriotism within the pages of their diaries. Several of these diaries have become canonical in Civil War studies, including one about the life of Baton Rouge native Sarah Morgan. Most of the existing Southern women's diaries were written by wealthy, often slaveholding, white women because elite women were educated, had access to material resources such as pens and paper, and had the time to habitually write in their diaries. Lower-class white women and slaves on the home front, for the most part, did not possess these luxuries and left few written records.

Perhaps the most famous Civil War diarist was Mary Boykin Chesnut, the wife of South Carolina's U.S. senator James Chesnut. During the Civil War, he became the aide to Confederate president Jefferson Davis and a brigadier general in the Confederate Army. Chesnut spent most of the war in Charleston, and she provided astute commentary on the political and social developments of the

South as the war progressed. Historians laud her diary for its historical acumen and literary talent. Four versions of her diary have been published since its initial publication in 1905. Historian C. Vann Woodward's 1981 edition, *Mary Chesnut's Civil War*, won the Pulitzer Prize for history in 1982.

Diaries of Union women are far scarcer than those of their Confederate counterparts. However, the diary of Maria Lydig Daly, the wife of a New York City judge, conveys the experiences of her life in the wartime Union. Daly records her opinions on military leaders, Dorothea Dix, Mary Todd Lincoln, and others. She also comments on the plight of Union soldiers and the desire to help them.

Female nurses served in both Union and Confederate hospitals. Some of these women kept diaries of their work in the hospitals, illustrating the daily operations of their respective medical systems. In their diaries, Confederate nurses Phoebe Yates Levy Pember and Kate Cumming not only describe their individual roles as nurses, but also critically comment on the personnel and health policies of the overarching Confederate Medical Department. Likewise, from the Union, the nursing diaries of Hannah Ropes and Harriet Eaton depict caretaking North of the Mason-Dixon Line. Louisa May Alcott, the famed author of *Little Women* (1868), first published *Hospital Sketches* in 1863 based on her service as a Union nurse.

Soldiers also kept diaries during the war, depicting life on the battle front and in military camps. These diaries tend to focus on the brutal conditions of warfare and the degraded physical conditions of their allocated provisions such as clothing, shoes, and food and the resulting illness. Although many of the personal papers and letters of key military officers, such as Union general Ulysses S. Grant and Confederate general Robert E. Lee, were preserved, there is much less primary source material relating to the lives of lower-level conscripts and enlisted soldiers, namely privates. Diaries of Union and Confederate privates address a dearth in the historiography: the wartime lives of the lower classes. The diary of Confederate private Sam Watkins as well as that of Union private Elisha Hunt Rhodes exemplify this collection of diaries.

Civil War diaries detail everyday life in the war-torn Union and Confederacy. Diaries are not objective accounts, but they are valuable sources that offer a personal glimpse of how those who lived through the Civil War experienced it. Diaries are mediated through editorial and publisher interventions as well as through an individual diarist's personal and political agenda. Additionally, if the diary was drafted or revised after the war's conclusion, themes of memory, myth, and legacy are inserted into the narrative. Nevertheless, if one acknowledges these issues of legitimacy and authenticity while examining diaries, they remain a fruitful and rich terrain of study for the Civil War period.

Kristen Brill

See also: Arts: Letter Writing; *Clothing, Fashion, and Appearance*: Shortages, Clothing; *Family Life and Gender Roles*: Young Women; *Food and Drink*: Food, Shortages; Food, Soldiers; *Religion and Belief*: Lost Cause; *Science and Technology*: Nursing

FURTHER READING

Bunkers, Suzanne, and Cynthia Huff, eds. *Inscribing the Daily: Critical Essays on Women's Diaries*. Amherst: University of Massachusetts Press, 1996.

Chesnut, Mary. *Mary Chesnut's Civil War*. Edited by C. Vann Woodward. New Haven, CT: Yale University Press, 1981.

Daly, Maria Lydig. *Diary of a Union Lady, 1861–1865*. Edited by Harold Earl Hammond. Lincoln: University of Nebraska Press, 2000.

Faust, Drew Gilpin. *Mothers of Invention: Women of the Slaveholding South in the American Civil War*. Chapel Hill: University of North Carolina Press, 1996.

Kagle, Steven E. *Early-Nineteenth Century American Diary Literature*. Boston: Twayne Publishers, 1986.

Morgan, Sarah. *Sarah Morgan: The Civil War Diary of a Southern Woman*. Edited by Charles East. Athens: University of Georgia Press, 1991.

Schultz, Jane E. *Women at the Front: Hospital Workers in Civil War America*. Chapel Hill: University of North Carolina Press, 2004.

"DIXIE"

"Dixie," the short title for the popular song, "I Wish I was in Dixie's Land," began as a tune written for a minstrel program in New York. It became popular as a Southern anthem during the Civil War, but was also sung with varied texts by abolitionists, and later, those advocating temperance. At the request of Dan Bryant (1833–1875), the leader of the Bryant's Minstrels, Daniel Decatur Emmett (1815–1904) composed the tune and words for this blackface troupe. The original lyrics by Emmett included, "I wish I was in de land ob cotton, / Old times dar am not forgotten, / Look away! Look away! Look away! Dixie land."

Emmett, a native of Ohio, and a musician with abolitionist leanings, played banjo and sang in the Bryant's Minstrels and Virginia Minstrels. He had previously been a drummer in military ensembles. His first song for the minstrel troupe in 1858 was "The Land of Freedom" or "I Ain't Got Time to Tarry." In 1859 he composed both the music and lyrics for the song "Dixie," a tune sung by both sides in the Civil War. The music was first heard on April 4, 1859, in New York. Emmett remembered that the first phrase was one sung by his mother when he was a young child. However, African Americans recognized portions of the tune as a wedding tune, both in the Northern and in the Southern states.

Shortly after the first performance, Firth, Pond & Co. of New York bought the rights from Emmett, and published several versions in 1860, and in subsequent years. Numerous other publishers, such as Oliver Ditson of Boston, joined, either printing new editions or distributing to their regions the Firth editions. An arrangement for piano, by Edgar Porter, used the title, "Dixon's Line." Its popularity spread quickly, and several variations upon the theme were also composed. It was performed in burlesque and minstrel shows as far west as Chicago, St. Louis, and New Orleans.

This popularity also crossed the political spectrum. At a reception in December 1860 for outgoing president James Buchanan, a band played "Dixie," and then "Yankee Doodle." During secession talks in Charleston, South Carolina, later in December 1860, a band played the tune between speeches. In February 1861, Jefferson Davis was being inaugurated in Montgomery, Alabama, the first Confederate capital. Bandleader Herman Frank Arnold (1837–1927) arranged "Dixie" as a Southern quickstep for the ceremony. Despite the popularity of the song in the South, U.S. President Abraham Lincoln enjoyed the tune as well.

Philip P. Werlein (1812–1885), a Bavarian immigrant who settled in New Orleans, was known as the first Southern publisher of Dan Emmett's "Dixie" in 1860. Werlein published editions of Dixie that attributed the music to J. C. Viereck. He also continued to publish several songs that spoke to the South during the Civil War, such as Flora Byrne's "President Jefferson Davis Grand March." Firth and Pond issued a corrected edition of "Dixie," which Werlein also sold. Werlein also issued an edition, "I Wish I was in Dixie's Land," which was composed by Emmett, and arranged by Viereck.

Beginning in 1860, Armand Edward Blackmar (1826–1888) issued more Confederate music than any other publisher in New Orleans, including early editions of "Dixie," "The Bonnie Blue Flag," and "Maryland! My Maryland!" Like Emile Johns's and Louis Grunewald's, a substantial portion of Blackmar's business was publishing, but he also sold music from other publishers and musical instruments.

Early in 1862, as Farragut's soldiers lowered the Confederate flag in New Orleans, a crowd marched to the river, led by a woman with a Confederate banner and a fifer playing the "Bonnie Blue Flag" and "Dixie."

The tune of "Dixie" was employed in the propaganda of both sides. Union troops sang "Dixie" due to its Northern origins; abolitionist Fanny Crosby (1820–1915) supplied text to a version entitled "Dixie for the Union." In the midst of the close combat of the Civil War, Union troops would sing George Root's "Battle Cry of Freedom." A Confederate soldier would answer by singing "Dixie."

The Union singer responded by singing another song with words about hanging Jeff Davis from a sour apple tree. Some freed slaves in Georgia recognized the tune, "Dixie," when played by the bands that accompanied U.S. General William Tecumseh Sherman in his march to the sea in 1864. Union bands performed the piece as they captured the Confederate capital of Richmond, Virginia, in 1865. One day after General Robert E. Lee surrendered to General Ulysses S. Grant in Appomattox, Virginia, Lincoln spoke at the White House, and requested that the band play "Dixie."

But not everyone was happy to hear "Dixie," mainly because some felt that the song lacked dignity. Andrew Bowering, bandleader in Lee's Army of Northern Virginia, played the tune only when it was mandatory. Similar sentiments were expressed by diplomat Henry Hotze (1833–1887) as well as by the Arkansas poet who became a brigadier general, Albert Pike (1809–1891).

The tune, however, served to inspire numerous other songs that partially shared the same title, such as the "Dixie Polka" (1860), "Hard Time in Dixie (1864), and "Dixie Doodle" (1865). At the time of Emmett's death, no fewer than 37 people had claimed the authorship of "Dixie."

Ralph Hartsock

See also: *Arts*: Music, Nonmilitary

FURTHER READING

Abel, E. Lawrence. S*inging the New Nation: How Music Shaped the Confederacy, 1861–1865*. Mechanicsburg, PA: Stackpole Books, 2000.

Cornelius, Steven H. *Music of the Civil War Era*. Westport, CT: Greenwood Press, 2004.

Emmett, Dan D. *I Wish I Was in Dixie's Land*. New York: Firth, Pond & Co, 1860a.

Emmett, Dan D. *I Wish I Was in Dixie's Land*. New Orleans: P.P. Werlein, 1860b.

Hearn, Chester G. *When the Devil Came Down to Dixie: Ben Butler in New Orleans*. Baton Rouge: Louisiana State University Press, 1997.

Nathan, Hans. *Dan Emmett and the Rise of Early Negro Minstrelsy*. Norman: University of Oklahoma Press, 1962.

Sanders, Paul D. *Lyrics and Borrowed Tunes of the American Temperance Movement*. Columbia: University of Missouri Press, 2006.

DOUGLASS, FREDERICK (1818–1895)

Frederick Douglass was the leading spokesperson for American blacks during the nineteenth century. Born a slave, Douglass became a noted author and orator. He devoted his life to the abolition of slavery and the fight for black rights.

Frederick Augustus Washington Bailey was born a slave in Tuckahoe, Maryland, in 1818. Despite state laws against it, he was taught to read and write as a child. After being sold and traded to several different owners, he escaped from slavery at age 20, got married, and adopted the surname Douglass. He quickly became active in the abolitionist movement. After making an ad lib speech at the Massachusetts Antislavery Society in 1841, Douglass began to speak frequently on behalf of abolitionism. He eventually did a three-year long speaking tour through many Northern cities. His powerful oratorical style, which combined humor and indignation, showed audiences the many tribulations of slavery and built public support for the abolitionist battle.

Photograph of editor, orator, and abolitionist Frederick Douglass, the foremost African American leader of the nineteenth century and an advocate for women's suffrage. After Douglass escaped from slavery in 1838, he began giving public lectures about the horrors of slavery and published his autobiography. During the Civil War he continued to push for the abolition of slavery and he was instrumental in raising an African American regiment to fight for the Union. (Library of Congress)

In 1845, Douglass published his autobiography, *Narrative of the Life of Frederick Douglass, An American Slave*. Written to bolster the cause of abolitionism, this influential story told of his resistance against bondage and his fight to gain his freedom. In the book he also identified his "owner." The book became a national runaway success. However, the details it revealed forced Douglass into exile in England for two years to evade arrest by slave hunters. British supporters paid for Douglass's freedom so that he could once again live free in the United States. Although he recognized the necessity for his purchase to ensure his safety in the United States, Douglass did not like being purchased.

Douglass returned to the United States in 1847 and settled in Rochester, New York. Once there, he started the

North Star, an abolitionist paper. On the masthead appeared the slogan, "Right is of no sex. . . . Truth is of no color . . . God is the Father of us all, and we are all Brethen." Douglass's offspring helped issue the paper.

As the abolitionist cause gained support in the 1850s, Douglass became more directly involved with the Underground Railroad. Harriet Tubman and other Underground Railroad conductors habitually stayed at Douglass's home as they headed toward Canada with other freedom-seeking slaves. He also continued to travel and give antislavery speeches. His most famous speech, "The Meaning of July 4th for the American Negro," was given in Rochester, New York, on July 5, 1852. Throughout the decade the issue of slavery continued to color American politics. In the notorious *Dred Scott* decision of 1857, the Supreme Court ruled that blacks had no privileges under the Constitution. This verdict enraged Douglass, as it also deepened the national debate over slavery.

Slavery divided the nation in the 1860 presidential election. When Abraham Lincoln was elected president in 1860, he promised to restrict slavery's development without interfering in slavery where it existed. In response to Lincoln's election, 11 Southern states, all built on a slave economy, voted to leave the United States and form their own nation. Douglass welcomed the Civil War as an occasion for a moral crusade to free enslaved people and establish a true democratic system. During the Civil War, Douglass traveled around the United States calling on Lincoln to instantly end slavery and to enlist black troops in the Union Army. After Lincoln issued the Emancipation Proclamation on January 1, 1863, Douglass helped enlist African Americans for the Union Army and especially for the 54th Massachusetts.

Douglass continued to advise Lincoln throughout the Civil War. In this role, Douglass pushed for constitutional alterations that would end slavery and give African Americans a lawfully guaranteed place in the public. After the war ended, Douglass saw these objectives achieved: the Thirteenth Amendment banned slavery, the Fourteenth Amendment gave citizenship to every person born in the United States, and the Fifteenth Amendment guaranteed the right to vote to all men regardless of color.

At the end of the Civil War, Douglass assumed numerous positions. In 1877, President Rutherford Hayes selected Douglass as his federal marshal in Washington, D.C. In 1889, Douglass became minister to Haiti, a post he occupied for two years. The 1890s saw Douglass return to public speaking to denounce the lynching of African Americans and the Jim Crow laws that continued to segregate African Americans in the former Confederate States. Douglass died on February 20, 1895.

Gerardo Del Guercio

See also: Arts: Literature, Northern; Newspapers, Northern; Slave Narratives; *Economy and Work*: Slavery; Urban Life, Northern; Urban Life, Southern; *Family Life and Gender Roles*: Free Blacks; Slave Families; *Housing and Community*: Slave Life; *Politics and Warfare*: Abolitionists; 54th Massachusetts Infantry; *Recreation and Social Customs*: Fourth of July; Political Speeches; *Religion and Belief*: Reformers

FURTHER READING

Blight, David W. *Frederick Douglass' Civil War: Keeping Faith in Jubilee.* Baton Rouge: Louisiana State University Press, 1991.

Del Guercio, Gerardo. *The Fugitive Slave Law in* The Life of Frederick Douglass, an American Slave *and Harriet Beecher Stowe's* Uncle Tom's Cabin*: American Society Transforms Its Culture.* Foreword by Robert T. Tally, Jr. Lewiston, NY: The Edwin Mellen Press, 2013.

Douglass, Frederick, *Frederick Douglass on Slavery and the Civil War: Selections from His Writings.* Edited by Philip Foner. Mineola, NY: Dover Publications, Inc., 2003.

McFeeley, William S. *Frederick Douglass.* New York: W.W. Norton, 1991.

Oakes, James. *The Radical and the Republican: Frederick Douglass, Abraham Lincoln, and the Triumph of Antislavery Politics.* New York: W.W. Norton, 2008.

FLAGS, CONFEDERATE

Throughout its short history, the Confederacy had many flags. Although varied, these flags served as a powerful and unifying symbol of nationalism for white Southerners. For Confederates, the national flags flown from 1861 to 1865 represented both an ideological connection to the Confederacy and a commitment to the defense of their homes from invasion. The battle flags of the various Confederate armies represented both national loyalty to a cause and a unit's pride. The flags were often emblazoned with names of battles and, over time, became a symbol of courage and dedication. Battlefield accounts are filled with stories of soldiers who willingly sacrificed themselves to keep their battle flag aloft or prevent its capture. In the last days of the war, soldiers often hid their battle flags or tore them up and distributed the pieces to prevent them from being surrendered.

On February 4, 1861, delegates from the six seceded states—South Carolina, Mississippi, Florida, Georgia, Alabama, and Louisiana—met in convention at Montgomery, Alabama, to write a constitution for the Confederate States of America. Four days later the state delegates had adopted the document. With the

The First flag of the Confederate States of America, the "Stars and Bars," was adopted on March 4, 1861. Over the course of the war the Confederacy adopted three different official flags. (Ridpath, John Clark, *Ridpath's History of the World*, 1901)

establishment of a sovereign country, they needed a national flag. A special committee was formed to design the flag. One flag had been quite popular among Southerners. Called the Bonnie Blue flag, it was a rectangular flag of blue with a large single five-pointed star in the center. The flag committee, however, decided to work from the basic design and colors of the U.S. flag. The committee replaced 13 red and white stripes with two red bars and one white bar. The blue field remained the same and, harkening back to the American Revolution and the first U.S. flag, the committee used a circular pattern of seven stars (Texas joined the Confederacy on March 5). This flag, called the Stars and Bars, was first raised in the new capital of the Confederacy, Montgomery, Alabama on March 4, 1861.

Three days after the Confederate bombardment of Fort Sumter on April 12, President Abraham Lincoln declared the seceded states in rebellion and called for 75,000 volunteers for military action. This call brought Tennessee, North Carolina, Arkansas, and Virginia into the Confederacy. Although sympathetic to the Confederacy, Missouri and Kentucky remained in the Union; both states however raised units to defend the Confederacy and had unofficial representation in the

Confederate government. As a result of these events, the Stars and Bars was modified over time to include 13 stars in the circular pattern.

The Stars and Bars proved to be a problem for military commanders on the battlefield. Because it so closely resembled the U.S. flag, especially when furled or veiled by the smoke of battle, commanders lost track of their units and soldiers could not distinguish friend from foe. The confusion that reigned during the first major battle of the war near Manassas, Virginia, on July 21, 1861, led Generals P.G.T. Beauregard and Joseph E. Johnston, who both commanded Confederate forces during the battle, to develop a design for a distinctive flag that could be easily recognized on the battlefield. The design adopted in late 1861 and presented to the units of the Confederate Army in Virginia was a square red flag with a blue diagonal cross, known as the cross of St. Andrew, within which were arranged 13 white five-pointed stars.

Beauregard continued to use a variation of this battle flag in later commands. In 1862, before the battle of Shiloh, Beauregard presented to the army battle flags with a design that he preferred over the one adopted in Virginia. These flags had 12 six-pointed stars. In 1863, when he took command of the defense of Charleston, South Carolina, Beauregard issued battle flags that had resembled the Virginia battle flag of 13 five-pointed stars. Johnston in 1863 also adopted a modified Virginia battle flag for his army, but this flag was rectangular and had 12 five-pointed stars. In 1863, the Confederate Navy adopted as its ensign the rectangular version of the battle flag, but with 13 five-pointed stars.

In reaction to public opinion that expressed a dislike of the Stars and Bars, the Confederate Congress addressed the creation of a new national flag in 1863. In May, a new flag appeared. It was a white rectangular flag with the blue square field of the old Stars and Bars replaced with the Virginia battle flag of 13 five-pointed stars. The flag's first significant presentation was during the funeral for General Thomas J. "Stonewall" Jackson on May 12, 1863, when the new flag covered the coffin of the Confederate hero. However, this flag had problems as well. The flag, as adopted by the Congress, was twice the length of its width. This size prevented the flag from being fully visible when flown, creating the image of a surrender flag.

In late 1864, artillery officer Major Arthur L. Rogers submitted a third design. This flag, with a more standard length of two-thirds the width, had a larger battle flag design, which was three-fifths of the width of the flag. Its most distinguishing characteristic was the vertical red bar extending along the width at the end of the flag, reminiscent of the flag of France. The new flag was officially adopted by the Confederate Congress on March 4, 1865, but was never produced. By April 2, the Confederate government began evacuating the capital of Richmond, Virginia, and effectively ceased to exist within a month.

Today, many mistake the rectangular 13-star battle flag flown by the Confederate Navy and by some units in the western theater of war as the Confederate national flag. Both the Confederate battle flag and the national flags of the Confederacy are potent with symbolic memory and, therefore, remain a reflection of Confederate collective national identity that cannot be effaced from American life.

Keith Dickson

See also: *Arts*: Flags, United States; *Housing and Community*: Nationalism, Confederate; *Politics and Warfare*: Morale; *Religion and Belief*: Lost Cause

FURTHER READING

Bonner, Robert E. *Colors and Blood: Flag Passions of the Confederate South*. Princeton, NJ: Princeton University Press, 2002.

Coski, John M. *The Confederate Battle Flag: America's Most Embattled Emblem*. Cambridge, MA: Harvard University Press, 2005.

Devereaux, Cannon D. *The Flags of the Confederacy: An Illustrated History*. Gretna, LA: Pelican Publishing, 1988.

Rollins, Richard. *"The Damned Red Flag of the Rebellion": The Confederate Battle Flag at Gettysburg*. Redondo Beach, CA: Rank and File Publishers, 1997.

FLAGS, UNITED STATES

The Star Spangled Banner that flew over Fort Sumter in the early morning hours of April 12, 1861, held 33 stars in the blue canton representing the 33 states. It also had 13 alternating red and white stripes representing the original 13 colonies. The design of stars on the Fort Sumter flag was in the shape of a diamond pattern both symbolizing and announcing that the men in the fort were on garrison duty. The diamond garrison flag had become an unofficial army tradition since 1845. The Flag Act of 1818 never designated a particular pattern on the canton, and by 1861 the two most common patterns of stars were in rows or ovals.

Flags represented sacred symbols of common cause, hearth and home, liberty and freedom. Usually presented by the governor of the state, the mayor of the city, or the women of the town who made the flag, the ceremony to present the colors to the unit was filled with patriotic fanfare. The expectation was that the flag would return home safely after the war. This hope meant that soldiers would die protecting their flags, and indeed, tens of thousands did.

The flag itself was often made of silk with a yellow fringe. Flagstaffs were close to 10 feet in height with a brass finial and blue and white intermixed cords and tassels. Army regulations in 1863 allowed regiments to embroider in silver, on the center stripe of the national flag, the name of battles in which "they have borne a meritorious part." During the Civil War there was no established flag etiquette that explained why, in many Mathew Brady and Alexander Gardner photographs, national flags were seen draped over tents, used as desk covers, and sometimes touching the ground. The custom of flying a flag at half-mast was established by the war, but not the custom of draping a flag over a coffin.

A color sergeant and guards were officially designated by each regiment to carry and keep the flag in their hands, not the enemy's. When the color bearer fell wounded or dead on the battlefield, it was the job of other comrades nearby to lift and carry the standard forward, often only to be wounded or killed as well. Thus, many died attempting to safeguard their flags.

It was during the Civil War that the national flag became celebrated as "Old Glory." The nickname was attributed to a retired naval shipmaster named Stephen Driver who displayed his brig's flag after Union forces liberated Nashville, Tennessee. He was given permission by the commanding officer to fly his flag on the state capitol building. Driver's efforts so moved the Sixth Ohio Volunteer Infantry that the regiment adopted the nickname "Old Glory."

In addition to military tradition and the powerful symbolism of flags, these objects served a critical tactical purpose. Flags were used as designated points on which to guide an attack or form a defense. They helped officers identify where particular units were on the battlefield, and they marked the location of regimental, brigade, division, and corps headquarters to facilitate communications among the chain of command.

Each infantry regiment was authorized to have two different flags or colors, the national flag and the regimental flag. Most regimental flags were blue with the national eagle emblazoned in the center. Beneath the eagle was a scroll with the regiment's name and number. The flag was often fringed in yellow. Pennsylvania and New Jersey regiments often used the national flag with the state coat of arms in the blue canton.

Artillery flags had a yellow field with crossed cannons in the center, and cavalry regiments had a blue field with the national coat of arms in the center, beneath which was a scroll painted with the regiment's name and number. Each cavalry company also had a swallowtail guidon. The guidon could be rectangular, but many had a triangular portion removed from the pennant, which made it as swallow-tailed. The top half of the flag was red and the bottom half was white, with the company's letter and U.S. appearing on the flag.

Brigades, divisions, and corps developed a series of complicated "designating flags" to provide quick identification for officers and couriers. For example, the Army of the Potomac adopted a series of headquarter flags recognizable by shapes: swallowtail for corps, rectangles for divisions, and triangles for brigades. The Army of the Potomac's commander from June 1863 to the end of the war, Major General George Gordon Meade, adopted as his headquarters' flag a swallowtail design with a golden eagle set within a silver wreath in a plain magenta field. By 1863 the U.S. Army had also adopted badge identifications for each corps. For example, the first corps was a disc, the second corps a trefoil, the 11th corps a crescent moon, the 14th corps an acorn, and the 17th corps an arrow. Thus corps headquarter flags were designated by a blue guidon with the corps insignia in white with the corps number in the middle of the insignia in red. The United States Colored Troops adopted a blue flag with an inner white square inside of which was a red shield and the letters USCT.

Naval vessels also flew a large Stars & Stripes called an ensign. Nine sizes of ensigns corresponded to a ship's class. In addition, commissioning pennants, signal flags, designating flags, and jacks were featured as part of an array of naval banners. The Union Naval jack looked like the canton of the national flag and was hoisted onto the jack-staff (flagstaff) of the ship. Located at the ship's bow (front end) the Union naval jack was flown at anchor or in port.

During the Civil War two stars were added to the "Stars and Stripes." Following the established custom of sewing a new star to the flag on the Independence Day succeeding Congress's approval of statehood, on July 4, 1861 a 34th star was added for Kansas, and on July 4, 1863, a 35th star was added for West Virginia. Nevada entered the Union on October 31, 1864, but was not represented by a star until July 4, 1865. West Virginia gained recognition to the United States on June 20, 1863 and Nevada on July 4, 1864.

Thomas Army

See also: *Arts*: Flags, Confederate; *Housing and Community*: Nationalism, United States; *Politics and Warfare*: Morale

FURTHER READING

Cannon, Devereaux D., Jr. *The Flags of the Union: An Illustrated History*. Gretna, LA: Pelican Publishing, 1994.

Revised United States Army Regulations of 1861 with an Appendix Containing the Changes and Laws Affecting Army Regulations and Articles of War to June 25, 1863. Washington, DC: U.S. Government Printing Office, 1863.

Whitman, Walt. "Walt Whitman to Louisa Whitman, April 10, 1864." Familytales. www.familytales.org/dbDisplay.php?id=ltr_waw7190. Accessed July 30, 2014.

HARPER'S WEEKLY

Founded in 1857 by Fletcher Harper (1806–1877) of the Harper & Brothers Publishing Company, *Harper's Weekly* was the preeminent illustrated American news periodical of the Civil War era. Most newspapers of the time had few, if any, illustrations. During the war years *Harper's Weekly*, and its main rival *Frank Leslie's Illustrated Newspaper*, were the most important sources of visual imagery of the war with depictions of battle scenes, maps, and pictures of military and political leaders.

January 3, 1863, *Harper's Weekly* cover by Thomas Nast showing Santa Claus distributing gifts to soldiers in camp. Founded in 1857 by Fletcher Harper, the magazine employed several artists, including Nast, Theodore R. Davis, Alfred R. Waud, and Winslow Homer. The magazine became one of the most important sources of visual imagery of the war. (Library of Congress)

Joining the company's established literary and current events magazine *Harper's Monthly*, Fletcher Harper's new magazine quickly became successful. Before the Civil War, *Harper's Weekly* avoided controversy and kept to a conservative and family-oriented outlook as opposed to what was considered the sensationalism of *Leslie's Illustrated*. In the Confederate States, the only counterpart to *Harper's Weekly* was the *Southern Illustrated News* of Richmond. Because of the scarcity of skilled labor and printing equipment, the Southern paper struggled to produce a limited number of new pictures.

During the early months of the war, *Harper's Weekly* serialized Charles Dickens's new novel *Great Expectations*. With an eye toward keeping his Southern subscribers, Harper made sure that his newspaper took a neutral stance on slavery. Once the war began, however,

Harper's Weekly evolved into a patriotic and pro-Union periodical that strongly supported the Lincoln administration and the doctrine of emancipation. When George W. Curtis became editor in 1863, he further tilted the tone of the newspaper toward Lincoln.

Photography of the 1860s did not lend itself to publication. High-speed reproduction of photographs was not possible without the halftone process, which came into widespread use only in the late nineteenth century. Long exposure times for film meant that any movement resulted in blurred images, so that photos of battlefield action were impossible. Instead, pictorial weeklies relied on wood-engravings, a form of fine-quality woodcut illustrations. Drawings were copied onto hard end-grain boxwood blocks. Then, the white areas were cut away with artists' tools, leaving lines that resembled pen and ink drawings when printed.

To speed production, large illustrations were cut into numerous separate blocks and handed to different engravers. A two-page image might be cut into as many as 40 pieces. Then, the blocks were reassembled and a master artist would finish cutting the final details so that the joints in the printing blocks were barely detectable. Multiple copies of the newspaper's pages of woodcuts and type were created by the electroplate process. Thus, several presses could print the same pages simultaneously, enabling high press runs. At the outbreak of the war, weekly circulation had reached about 120,000. Interested readers could purchase back copies of earlier issues. Occasionally, sales of a particular issue could eventually number several hundred thousand.

Artists working for the magazine included Theodore R. Davis, Alfred R. Waud, Winslow Homer, and the prominent cartoonist Thomas Nast. Homer became known during the war for his drawings of life in Union Army camps. In addition to his important postwar political cartoons, Nast's work for *Harper's Weekly* included what many believe to be the first modern depiction of Santa Claus. In the image printed in the January 3, 1863 issue, Santa Claus hands presents to Union soldiers in camp. He appears in the expected white beard and fur-trimmed clothing, although his jacket and trousers are patterned with the Union's stars and stripes.

Harper's Weekly sent its art correspondents, called "special artists," to the front lines or other places where important news events were expected. The artists made quick sketches of battles, scenes, and incidents, sometimes adding explanatory notes for the newspaper engravers, who carefully filled in details and textures such as foliage, waves, or masonry. War artists lived a dangerous life among the troops and shared their privations and perils. Theodore Davis was wounded twice during the war, and on another occasion had a sketchbook shot out of his hand.

It would take several days for a special artist's drawing to be rushed to New York and converted into a finished woodcut. In the case of the July 1–3 1863 Battle of Gettysburg, an image of Union commander Major General George G. Meade appeared on the cover of the July 11 issue. However the first images of the battle itself, by Alfred R. Waud, were in the July 25 issue.

Working from photographs from the studios of Mathew Brady and other eminent photographers, *Harper's Weekly* engravers also made portraits of the war's military and political leaders that were far more widely seen than the originals. Battle and campaign maps were another important offering of *Harper's Weekly*.

For their work, artists in the field were usually paid their expenses and a fee for each printed drawing. Homer, for instance, was paid $60 for large two-page images. Some artists could go for several weeks or more without having a drawing chosen for publication. Coverage of one battle might be crowded out by other battles and events that followed, and many drawings were never used during the war.

The single-copy price of the magazine rose from five cents in 1861 to ten cents by the war's end in April 1865. With other national periodicals, *Harper's Weekly* was popular in army camps and the troops could buy them from sutlers or newspaper vendors, although often at twice the cover price.

Harper's Weekly remained a politically and culturally influential periodical for some years after the end of the war. Its importance slipped after the advent of magazine photography, but publication continued until 1916. For the Civil War years, *Harper's Weekly* and its competitors left behind a rich legacy of pictorial imagery that continue to have a major impact on modern-day impressions of the war.

David A. Norris

See also: *Arts*: Art; Brady, Mathew B. (ca. 1823–1896); Newspapers, Northern; Newspapers, Southern; Photography; Serial Novels

FURTHER READING

HarpWeek (digital versions of *Harper's Weekly* issues from 1857 to 1912). www.harpweek.com. Accessed July 30, 2014.

Kennedy, Robert C. "Censorship, Racism, and the Antebellum Press: *Harper's Weekly* Reports Harper's Ferry." In David B. Sachsman, S. Kittrell Rushing, and Debra Reddin van Tuyll, eds. *The Civil War and the Press*. New Brunswick, NJ: Transaction Publishers, 2000, pp. 63–74.

Library of Congress. Prints & Photographs Online Catalog. http://www.loc.gov/pictures. Accessed July 30, 2014.

Starr, Louis M. *Bohemian Brigade: Civil War Newsmen in Action*. New York: Alfred A. Knopf, 1954.

LETTER WRITING

Letter writing during the Civil War was such an extended phenomenon that it led to the emergence of a new epistolary genre, the "soldier letter." The conflict gave a significant boost to letter writing, which until then had not been a very widespread occupation in America if compared to Great Britain, for example. Letter writing fulfilled a fundamental role: first, letters communicated detailed battlefield reports to headquarters or politicians; second, families got in touch with their soldier family members, thereby receiving firsthand testimonies on their war experiences.

Although the telegraph was widely used by the army and by journalists to give the latest information about the warfront, soldiers and their families relied mainly on letters. Letter writing played a fundamental role in providing civilians with accurate information on what was happening on the battlefield. Letters constituted a more trustworthy source of information than newspapers, as the latter were often propagandistic, especially in the South. Personal letters were so detailed and thorough that sometimes they inadvertently disclosed information the army would want to keep secret.

As the Northern blockade caused serious shortages of supplies in the South, paper became scarce and extremely expensive. As a result, letters were often written using previous letters, writing in the spaces not used on the original missive. Whatever scraps of paper the writer could get hold of also made do as stationery, such as bills, newspapers, and old documents, to name a few. Every space on the paper was utilized, with writers often criss-crossing their words with more words.

Because of the importance of letters to soldiers, charities often provided them with free stationery. Special attention was paid to envelopes, also called "covers." Although sometimes they were done without, there was a wide range of manufactured envelopes that featured patriotic scenes. Some printers sold envelopes especially made for a given army regiment, printing a list of that regiment's battles on the outside of the envelope.

Acknowledging that mail was vital for troops' morale, in 1862 U.S. president Abraham Lincoln created a new government post to control the army mail. To ensure soldiers' access to correspondence, Union post offices were set up next to camps or forts, with mail officers following armies to provide them with constant mail service. Additionally, in 1864 the United States decided to give soldiers free mail, with no need to put stamps on their letters—a measure not adopted by the Confederacy. Letter writing was a popular pastime for soldiers. Scholars estimate that each regiment sent approximately 600 letters a day. Keeping up a correspondence with soldiers was regarded as a patriotic duty and another of the tasks that women on both sides of the conflict took on as part of their contribution to the war effort. Even magazines and newspapers urged women to write letters to men at the battlefront. In addition, some soldiers placed personal ads in newspapers seeking pen friends, as did Union soldier Edwin Lybarger, whose correspondence was later compiled as *Wanted—Correspondence: Women's Letters to a Union Soldier*. Families also sent soldiers care packages that included food, stationery, and writing materials.

Because education in rural America was scarce, spelling or grammar mistakes in letters were common. Many soldiers had serious difficulties penning letters and sought the help of more literate comrades. Letter writing was especially important for women because, other than being a patriotic duty to keep the troops' spirits up, it provided women with an opportunity to further their education. In any case, women understood the importance of their letters to the morale of the troops. As a result, women's Civil War letters often gloss over the problems civilians were suffering at home and instead focus upon cheering up the men or provoking their patriotism.

One of the most well-known and often reprinted letter written during the Civil War is the one that Lincoln sent to Lydia Bixby of Boston, dated November 21, 1864. In the Bixby letter, Lincoln wrote to Mrs. Bixby, a widow, to comfort her after he received reports of the deaths of her five sons who were all fighting for the Union. In reality, three of her children survived the war. As a result, controversy has surrounded the letter, as it is not clear whether Lincoln wrote it himself. Some claim that it was written by his secretary. Scholars also question if Bixby was aware of her children's survival and was trying to fraudulently claim benefits or a pension from the government. Moreover, Bixby was suspected of having a house of ill repute and of being sympathetic to the Confederate side up to the point that she may have persuaded one of her surviving sons to desert from the Union Army and join the Confederate forces instead.

Numerous compilations of letters written during the Civil War have made their way into print throughout the years. Although women were devout correspondents, fewer Civil War women's letters have been preserved than have men's. Often women's letters were carried by soldiers and lost over the course of the war hardships, whereas soldiers' letters were dutifully preserved by their addressees, as women cherished and treasured their men's letters.

M. Carmen Gomez-Galisteo

See also: *Arts*: Diary Writing; *Family Life and Gender Roles*: Young Women; *Politics and Warfare*: Morale; *Science and Technology*: Education, Northern; Education, Southern

FURTHER READING

Bailey, L. E. "'So Pleasant to Be a School Maam': The Civil War as an Educational Force for Women." *Advancing Women in Leadership Journal* 29:11 (2009): 1–15.

A FUGITIVE SLAVE'S LETTER TO HIS WIFE

By dividing people from their families, the Civil War became a great impetus to letter writing. However, soldiers were not the only people to write letters to their loved ones with news of their welfare and whereabouts. Reproduced here, with the original spelling, are excerpts from a letter written in January 1862 by a fugitive slave from Maryland to his wife.

> My Dear Wife it is with grate joy I take this time to let you know Whare I am I am now in Safety in the 14th Regiment of Brooklyn this Day I can Adress you thank god as a free man I had a little truble in giting away But as the lord led the Children of Isrel to the land of Canon So he led me to a land Whare freedom Will rain . . . Dear you must make your Self content I am free from al the Slavers Lash . . . . I am With a very nice man and have All that hart Can Wish But My Dear I Cant express my grate desire that I Have to See you I trust the time Will Come When We Shal meet again And if We don't met on earth We Will Meet in heven Whare Jesus ranes . . . . Dear Wife I must Close rest yourself Contented I am free I Want you to rite to me Soon as you Can . . . Direct your letter to the 14th Regiment New York . . . Uptons Hill Virginea . . . Your Affectionate Husban Kiss Daniel For me
>
> *John Boston*
> *Give my love to Father and Mother*

FURTHER READING

Letters Received, Series 12, Adjutant General's Office, Record Group 94. National Archives, Washington, DC.

Culpepper, Marilyn. M. *Women of the Civil War South: Personal Accounts from Diaries, Letters and Postwar Reminiscences*. Jefferson, NC: McFarland, 2004.

Gooding, James Henry. *On the Altar of Freedom: A Black Soldier's Civil War Letters from the Front*. Amherst: University of Massachusetts Press, 1999.

Wakeman, Sarah Rosetta. *An Uncommon Soldier: The Civil War Letters of Sarah Rosetta Wakeman, Alias Pvt. Lyons Wakeman, 153rd Regiment, New York State Volunteers*. Edited by Lauren Cook Burgess. New York: Oxford University Press, 1996.

LITERATURE, NORTHERN

Americans North and South shared a common literary canon before the Civil War. However, the Civil War highlights a change in American literature, both in terms of the differences between the regions regarding literary taste and in terms of a change in production and interpretation.

Much had changed with regard to American letters during the second half of the nineteenth century. The common school movement had raised literacy levels, especially in the North where it took hold earlier, and had introduced students to important works of history and literature. Increased literacy rates served to enliven the American publishing industry, which in 1834 produced fewer than 500 titles. With increased literacy, by 1862 American publishing houses produced more than 4,000 titles. The first American "dime" novels, like *Malaeska, the Indian Wife of the White Hunter* by Ann Stephens, were published in 1860. Civil War soldiers provided a large market for such works. Soldiers on both sides sought relief from long periods of inactivity. In addition, because they were freed from agricultural and industrial labors, these men actually had leisure time to spend reading.

The Bible remained the best-selling book in the United States and wartime organizations like the U.S. Christian Commission distributed more than one million Bibles to soldiers on both sides. Whereas the Bible as a whole possessed universal appeal to Americans on both sides of the Mason-Dixon Line, Northerners and Southerners interpreted Scripture quite differently. The advent of the Free Will theology in the North emphasized those Scriptural tenets that promoted individual growth, reform, and perfectionism. In the hierarchically ordered South, however, Old Testament scripture that advocated that Christians accept and work within their station proved more meaningful.

Likewise, Charles Dickens's novella *A Christmas Carol* was widely read in both North and South but to different acclaim. Whereas Northerners interpreted the book to infer redemptive qualities inherent in all human beings, Southerners saw the problems of the protagonist Ebenezer Scrooge and indeed that of his society as stemming from the alienation wrought by industrialization and wage labor. Such evils, Southerners were quick to note, they had conscientiously avoided through an ordered, agrarian society, in which individuals possessed a moral responsibility to protect and care for neighbors, family, and slaves. Surprisingly, Victor Hugo's *Les Miserables*, published in 1862, proved to be the most popular book during the entire war period on both sides of the Mason-Dixon Line, despite Hugo's abolitionist sympathies.

The Northern states had witnessed a literary renaissance in the early decades of the nineteenth century that was not paralleled in the South. Emerging from the oppressive constraints of Calvinist Puritanism, the New England states produced such authors as Nathaniel Hawthorne, Herman Melville, and Ralph Waldo Emerson. Emerson, a lapsed minister, celebrated individualism and human potential and initiated what would become the Transcendentalist movement. Hawthorne and Melville, on the other hand, explored the darker aspects of the human condition. Hawthorne's masterpiece, *The Scarlet Letter*, published in 1850, explored the oppression of his Puritan ancestors through the character Hester Prynne and surmised the innate depravity of man. Melville, a contemporary and personal friend of Hawthorne, published *Moby Dick* in 1851. In it, Melville mined the depths of human existence similarly but contextualized his search within the author's own personal experiences on whaling expeditions. He concluded similarly in the depravity of man but blamed God, as creator, for man's depravity.

Darker still, Mary Shelley and Edgar Allen Poe initiated the American gothic genre, an offshoot of Romanticism, in which stories blended elements of science fiction, mystery, and romanticism. Poe's most famous works, including *The Fall of the House of Usher*, undertook to examine man's fascination with death in its various forms. Generally considered the first work of science fiction, Shelley's *Frankenstein; or the Modern Prometheus* investigated resurrection and reanimation through the eyes of Dr. Victor Frankenstein who unravels his tale in epistolary fashion to another scientist whom Dr. Frankenstein identifies as similarly ambitious and destructive.

Other American authors similarly made a mark on the literary landscape. James Fenimore Cooper wrote such adventure tales as *The Deerslayer, The Pathfinder*, and *The Last of the Mohicans*. His books were all set in an American landscape that predated the establishment of the American state at around the time of the French and Indian War. Through his books Cooper crafted a mythology common to both North and South. Contrastingly, Harriet Beecher Stowe's antislavery novel *Uncle Tom's Cabin* proved incredibly popular in the North selling over 300,000 copies in just one year. Stowe portrayed the evils and brutality of slavery though she herself had never visited a plantation in the South nor had any personal experiences with slavery.

Mark A. Panuthos

See also: *Arts*: Literature, Southern; Newspapers, Northern; Serial Novels; Slave Narratives; *Uncle Tom's Cabin; Politics and Warfare*: Camp Life; *Recreation and Social Customs*: Leisure Time; *Science and Technology*: Education, Northern

FURTHER READING

Fahs, Alice. *The Imagined Civil War: Popular Literature of the North and South, 1861–1865*. Chapel Hill: University of North Carolina Press, 2001.

Percy, Walker. *Signposts in a Strange Land*. New York: Farrar, Straus, and Giroux Publishers, 1991.

Sizer, Lyde Cullen. *The Political Work of Northern Women Writers and the Civil War, 1850–1872*. Chapel Hill: University of North Carolina Press, 2000.

Volo, Dorothy Deneen, and James M. *Daily Life in the Civil War*. Westport CT: Greenwood Press, 1998.

Wiley, Bell Irvin. *The Life of Billy Yank*. Baton Rouge: Louisiana State University Press, 1952.

Wiley, Bell Irvin. *The Life of Johnny Reb*. Baton Rouge: Louisiana State University Press, 1952.

Wyatt-Brown, Bertram. *The Literary Percys: Family, Gender and the Southern Imagination*. Athens: University of Georgia Press, 1994.

LITERATURE, SOUTHERN

The primary goal of Civil War era Southern literature was to undermine what Southern authors perceived as a pernicious image of the South put forward by Northern newspapers, abolitionist tracts, and novels. Instead, Southern authors presented a benevolent picture of slavery based on the image of the master as a paternal figure for his child-like slaves, picturing the "peculiar institution" as an intrinsic characteristic of the genuine Southern lifestyle. Despite the diversity of the South that included a Creole culture of Louisiana that had little to do with the refinement of North Carolina, Southern writers managed to convey a homogeneous picture of the South, erasing or ignoring regional differences while promoting nationalistic feelings in the process. Plots often revolved around questions of virtue or honor, as exemplified by the Code of Honor that ruled Southern gentlemen's behavior, offering a vision of gentleness and good manners in the face of the Yankees' rudeness and lack of refinement.

In the antebellum period, Charleston, South Carolina, and Virginia rivaled as the literary center of the South. Because Southern authors often modeled their novels after British ones, echoes of Elizabethan and Byronic literature are present. George Tucker, the main Southern author of the 1820s, followed English novels, most notably Samuel Richardson's *Clarissa*, after which he modeled *The Valley of the Shenandoah* (1824). Tucker also wrote *The Partisan Leader* (1836), which advanced the possibility of a guerrilla war in Virginia. Southern writers also emulated Northern authors. For example, John Pendleton Kennedy's *Swallow Barn* (1832) mimicked Washington Irving's style. Kennedy also wrote the romantic novels *Horse Shoe Robinson* (1835) and *Rob of the Bowl* (1838). Later, Kennedy, who was married to the daughter of a Baltimore manufacturer, changed sides and became anti-Southern in his writing, as evidenced by his *Letters of Mr. Paul Ambrose on the Great Rebellion in the United States*. In poetry, English-born Edward Pinkney wrote *A Serenade Written by a Gentleman of Baltimore* (1823),

Rodolph (1825), and *Poems* (1825). The scarcity of his poetic production was no obstacle for his being heralded as the exemplification of the Old South in the 1820s.

Because he was raised in Virginia, Edgar Allan Poe has been regarded as a Southerner although he did not deal with specifically Southern topics. He authored, among other works, *Tamerlane and Other Poems* (1827), *Al Aaraaf, Tamerlane, and Minor Poems* (1829), *Poems* (1831), *The Narrative of Arthur Gordon Pym* (1838), and *Tales of the Grotesque and Arabesque* (1840). A friend of Poe, poet Thomas Holley Chivers, wrote *Nacoochee* (1837), *The Lost Pleiad and Other Poems* (1842), and *Eonchs of Ruby* (1850). The latter was very controversial since Chivers was accused of plagiarizing the late Poe, whereas Chivers claimed that Poe had plagiarized him.

From 1830 onward, Southern literature revolved around contradicting the writings by abolitionists such as Wendell Phillips and William Lloyd Garrison. After the publication of Harriet Beecher Stowe's *Uncle Tom's Cabin* caused a significant increase of support for the abolitionist cause, Southern authors produced dozens of works to offer a dramatically different picture of slavery. The works resulting from this reaction were known as "anti-Tom" literature, which was, curiously enough, often produced in Philadelphia. Examples of this subgenre include Mary H. Eastman's *Aunt Phillis's Cabin* (1852). Another popular "anti-Tom" author was William Gilmore Simms. Simms's earlier works were romantic novels portraying life at the frontier, the American Revolution, or South Carolina history, such as *The Kinsmen* or *Guy Rivers* (1834), a novel about gold miners. He went on to publish anti-Tom novels, such as *The Sword and the Distaff*. His marriage into a planter family made Simms present a positive and idealized image of slavery in the South, which he saw as a Greek democracy. However, Southern literature could not match the popularity or effectiveness of *Uncle Tom's Cabin*, John Greenleaf Whittier's abolitionist poetry, or Ralph Waldo Emerson's and Henry David Thoreau's denunciation of slavery.

John Beauchamp Jones's novel, *Wild Southern Scenes* (1859), is remarkable for dealing with an imagined Civil War fought over slavery. Once the actual war began, Henry Timrod and Paul Hamilton Hayne, who did not serve in the army, turned to writing patriotic poetry. In contrast, poet Sidney Lanier fought and was taken prisoner near the end of the war. John Esten Cooke, captain of the cavalry, was the author of romances inspired by his war experiences, such as *Surry of Eagle's Nest* (1866). Margaret Junkin Preston, Stonewall Jackson's sister-in-law, wrote a narrative poem, *Beechenbrook* (1865), about women's sufferings. The plight of Southern abolitionists was also recorded, as for example in Alabama politician Jeremian Clemens's *Tobias Wilson* (1865).

A very popular Southern author during the war was Augusta Jane Wilson Evans. A fervent Southern patriot who devoted herself to the task of being a Confederate propagandist, she broke her engagement with a pro-Union New Yorker. Although she served as a nurse, her main contribution to the war effort was *Macaria; or, Altars of Sacrifice* (1864), about Southern women's war sacrifices. Copies of *Macaria* were burned in Tennessee, but its Northern edition reached best-selling figures. Her next novel, *St. Elmo* (1866), met an extraordinary success, selling 1 million copies in four months and inspiring a parody. Her works were sentimental, Victorian-style novels, very much in vogue with the literary tastes of the period. Although not quite as popular, Confederate Sally Rochester Ford's *Raids and Romance of Morgan and His Men* (1863) was published in the North, too.

After the war, the authors of Southern literature devoted all of their efforts to defending the Lost Cause, with *The Conquered Banner*, published on June 24, 1865, as the first example. This moonlight-and-magnolia subgenre was characterized by its apology of slaveholding and the glorification of the South. Critical voices such as those of African American author Charles W. Chesnutt rose against the sentimentalization of the South, but Civil War–themed novels have continued being written into the present. Stephen Crane, born in 1871, described the war scenes so accurately in *The Red Badge of Courage* (1895) that rumors had it that he was a Civil War veteran.

M. Carmen Gomez-Galisteo

See also: *Arts*: Literature, Northern; *Macaria; or, Altars of Sacrifice;* Slave Narratives; Theater; *Politics and Warfare*: Abolitionists; *Religion and Belief*: Lost Cause

FURTHER READING

Carby, Hazel V. "The Canon: Civil War and Reconstruction." *Michigan Quarterly Review* 28:1 (1989): 237–244.

Fahs, Alice. *The Imagined Civil War: Popular Literature of the North and South, 1861–1865*. Chapel Hill: University of North Carolina Press, 2001.

Harwell, Richard B. "Gone with Miss Ravenel's Courage: or Bugles Blow So Red. A Note on the Civil War Novel." *The New England Quarterly* 35:2 (1962): 253–261.

Wilson, Edmund. *Patriotic Gore: Studies in the Literature of the American Civil War*. New York: W.W. Norton., 1962; 1994.

MACARIA; OR, ALTARS OF SACRIFICE (1864)

Augusta Jane Evans published *Macaria; or, Altars of Sacrifice* in the midst of the Civil War. The novel offered Southern women a model of female sacrifice during wartime.

Augusta Jane Evans Wilson (1835–1909) was one of the most celebrated writers of nineteenth-century America. She wrote nine novels over her lauded 52-year literary career, only one of which failed to become a best seller. Her most commercially successful novel, *St. Elmo* (1866), even rivaled the popularity of Harriet Beecher Stowe's classic *Uncle Tom's Cabin* (1852). Evans began her prolific literary career with the publication of *Inez: A Tale of the Alamo* in 1855. She would go on to publish *Beulah* (1859), *Macaria* (1864), *St. Elmo* (1866), *Vashti* (1869), *Infelice* (1875), *At the Mercy of Tiberius* (1887), *A Speckled Bird* (1902), and *Devota* (1907).

Evans was the first of eight children, born on May 8, 1835, in Columbus, Georgia. Although born into an elite Southern family, Evans faced hardships as her family soon descended into financial ruin. Following the depression of 1839, they left Columbus in 1845 and eventually relocated to Mobile, Alabama. Her family remained in poverty until she started publishing novels; according to Rebecca Grant Sexton, her first two novels were written to secure the finances of her family. On December 2, 1868, Evans married a wealthy former planter and Confederate colonel Lorenzo Madison Wilson. She moved to his estate, Ashland, also in Mobile. After 23 years of marriage, her husband died in 1891. On May 9, 1909, Wilson died of a heart attack in Mobile.

Her third novel, *Macaria; or, Altars of Sacrifice*, became a best-selling novel of the Confederacy. *Macaria* was regarded as an extremely effective propaganda text, and it was printed both in the Confederacy and in the Union. By 1865, it had sold more than 20,000 copies in the South. Evans herself was a fervent Southern patriot, even breaking off an engagement with a Northerner, James Reed Spalding, with the outbreak of war. The novel follows the lives of two young Southern women during the Civil War, Irene Huntingdon and Electra Grey. Evans believed literature should provide moral instruction; the self-sacrifice and Christian virtue of the female protagonists are presented as archetypes for her female readership to emulate in the context of war. Both Irene and Electra refused proposals of marriage so that they could completely dedicate themselves to the Confederate war effort. They subsumed their individual identities and desires into the collective republican Confederate project. Considering the severe conditions of hardship and suffering on the Southern home front, women's service and commitment to the Confederacy was absolutely essential in maintaining the war effort.

One of the major themes of the novel is marriage. Evans rejected the traditional nineteenth-century marriage plot, including the later Reconstruction era reconciliation novel trope of marriage; both of the female protagonists, Irene and Electra, reject their respective marriage proposals and devote themselves to the Confederacy. This valorization of self-sacrifice was a model for Confederate women to try and achieve; women should wholeheartedly dedicate their lives to the republic. Moreover, the rejection of an unhappy marital union can be seen as a metaphor for the Confederacy's rejection of an unviable union with the North. The title itself, *Macaria*, references the Greek heroine—the daughter of Hercules who sacrificed herself to save Athens from invasion.

Although the novel rarely discusses slavery, it mirrors the antebellum plantation novel genre in its valorization of the Old South and the Southern way of life. Women's labors for the war effort in the setting of the plantation are lauded frequently, in particular the production of homespun goods and nursing endeavors. Evans was a nurse during the war; she trained with the famed Confederate nurse Kate Cumming. This experience may account for Evans's focus on women's nursing in the text. Although Evans advocates for women's active role in the war effort, she adheres to the cult of domesticity in her prescription of labors associated with the home and femininity: primarily sewing, food distribution, nursing, and fund-raising.

Furthermore, the novel also comments on the erosion of both antebellum masculinity and the privilege and leisure of the planter class with the advent of war. By 1864 over half of Southern white men were wounded or dead and women had to adapt to a changing world. The novel attempts to come to terms with this loss as it empowers single women on the home front to sustain the Confederate mission. Death and the process of memorialization resonate throughout the novel, linking the health of the nation to the health of the individual. Keen to ensure the accuracy of these descriptions of battle and death, Evans frequently corresponded with General P.G.T. Beauregard during the war.

Augusta Jane Evans's *Macaria* was a paramount text in circulating and fortifying the Confederate nationalist message. An ardent Southern patriot herself, Evans centralized women's contribution to the war and the importance of sustaining women's sacrifice and commitment to the Confederacy in the latter years of the war. During and after the war, *Macaria* was a foundational novel, amalgamating issues of domesticity, single womanhood, and self-sacrifice to increase popular support of and participation in the Confederate war effort.

Kristen Brill

See also: *Arts*: Literature, Southern; *Clothing, Fashion, and Appearance*: Homespun; Women's Dress, Confederate; *Science and Technology*: Nursing

FURTHER READING

Ayres, Brenda. *The Life and Works of Augusta Jane Evans Wilson, 1835–1909*. Surrey, UK: Ashgate Publishing Company, 2012.

Baym, Nina. *Woman's Fiction: A Guide to Novels by and About Women in America, 1820–1879*. Ithaca, NY: Cornell University Press, 1978.

Evans, Augusta Jane. *Macaria; or, Altars of Sacrifice*. Edited with an Introduction by Drew Gilpin Faust. Baton Rouge: Louisiana State University Press, 1992.

Faust, Drew Gilpin. *Mothers of Invention: Women of the Slaveholding South in the American Civil War*. Chapel Hill: University of North Carolina Press, 1996.

Fidler, William Perry. *Augusta Evans Wilson*. Tuscaloosa: University of Alabama Press, 1951.

Sexton, Rebecca Grant, ed. *A Southern Woman of Letters: The Correspondence of Augusta Jane Evans*. Columbia: University of South Carolina Press, 2002.

Stevenson, Louise L. *The Victorian Homefront: American Thought and Culture, 1860–1880*. New York: Twayne, 1991.

MUSIC, MILITARY

Military music during the Civil War was conveyed in several ways. Some of the music was inspired by leaders of the armies or navies of the Union and Confederacy. Other tunes allowed singers and soldiers to revel in the uniforms they wore. Some were used for propaganda, particularly in the close range that nineteenth-century combat required. In addition, each regiment had its musical details, most often a drummer, bugler, and fifer as field musicians, with several other brass and percussion instrumentalists in the bands.

Soldiers, both Union and Confederate, had a limited knowledge of melodies, as did the society at large. Thus, many texts were used for each tune. These were usually pastiches, but there were imitations and parodies as well.

There were two primary categories of military musicians. Field musicians—fifers, buglers, and drummers—traveled with the unit. They performed coded commands for the soldiers, and signaled the beginning and end of each day. Soldiers also heard music from bands. Bands usually included brass and percussion instrumentalists; woodwind instruments appeared less frequently. Bands performed marches for drills and exercises, and songs of home, country, love, and family. These included arrangements of Henry R. Bishop's *Home, Sweet Home*. Some music motivated, such as John Stratton's arrangements of *Hail Columbia*, and *Hail to the Chief*. Often the duties of these two groups overlapped. Musicians also doubled as medical staff to transport the wounded and assist surgeons.

Fifers, buglers, and drummers were generally younger than those serving in the regular infantry. In many cases, they were adolescent boys from ages 12 to 18, but some who were even younger than 12 also served as musicians. Music served as a code, either by rhythm or by melodic sequence. Tunes most often heard from field musicians were "Reveille" and "Taps," both ceremonial tunes. Most of these field musicians learned their craft by rote, maintaining rigorous schedules that

Photograph of the Elmira Cornet Band, Thirty-Third Regiment, of the New York State Volunteers, July 1861. Military regiments often included a band, with a drummer, bugler, and fifer for field musicians, and sometimes several other brass and percussion instrumentalists. Field musicians entertained the soldiers, but more importantly they performed coded commands to indicate the beginning and end of each day and they played marches during drills and exercises. (Library of Congress)

included much practice and several rehearsals. The fife is a small transverse instrument, in which the performer blows air across an opening in the rosewood. Each had six to eight holes, but no keys. The bugle, a small brass instrument, with a sonority similar to that of the trumpet, consisted of a tube approximately five feet long, coiled to about 15 inches in length. Trumpets and cornets usually have valves, while the standard bugle has no valves. Field drums, also known as snare drums, were about 16 inches in diameter and 10 inches deep.

Two orders from the U.S. War Department exerted the major influence upon the composition of field ensembles and bands. General Order 48 (July 1, 1861) presented guidelines used by regiments for their musicians. There were 2 principal musicians per regiment, with up to 20 allowed as field musicians. Up to 24 were permitted in brass bands for regular regiments, but up to 16 in the cavalry. Estimates vary as to how many musicians served the Union; Lord and Wise estimate that by the conclusion of 1861, 28,000 musicians performed in 618 bands, with an average of 23 members each. The War Department was said to invest $4 million that year. By the time of the Lee's surrender, there were over 32,000 drums, 21,000 bugles, and 15,000 trumpets for the Union. However, when Congress determined that expenses exceeded benefits, budgets for music were reduced. Subsequently, General Order 91 (July 29, 1862) reduced band leaders' compensation, reassigned regimental bands to the brigade level, and eliminated up to 300 bands.

During the Civil War, Patrick Gilmore (1829–1892) emerged as one of the most respected band directors. A cornetist and composer who was Irish by birth, Gilmore led the Boston Brigade Band beginning in 1859. He renamed it the Gilmore Band and performed promenade concerts in Boston and on tour in Virginia and North Carolina. Francis Scala (ca. 1819–1903), another influential military conductor, led the United States Marine Band from 1855 to 1871. Originally founded in 1798 as a field band, the Marine Band was officially elevated to a concert band by Congress in 1862. Members performed mainly in Washington, D.C., for official military ceremonies, as well as for presidential inaugurations and at other events as a concert or dance band. The Dodworth family included trombonist Thomas Dodworth (1790–1876) and three sons, Allen, Harvey, and Thomas, who conducted bands in New York. Harvey Dodworth (1822–1891) had directed the 13th New York Regiment Band since the 1830s, and took the baton of the Dodworth Band during the Civil War.

The Confederacy also employed field musicians and bands, and had a wealth of tunes including "The Bonnie Blue Flag," "Beauregard's March," "Dixie," and "Marseillaise." During the funerals of Southern officers, bands would play the "Dead March," an arrangement from George Frederic Handel's oratorio, *Saul*. The most notable playing of this arrangement was at the funeral procession for General Thomas "Stonewall" Jackson in May 1863.

Another influence on music that grew during the Civil War was the interchangeability of mechanical parts. This advance affected the ability of not just musicians but also soldiers. Manufacturers of musical instruments created parts that could be used on several instruments.

Music served to discipline soldiers, comfort them with songs of home, and motivate them during battle. It even found use in propaganda. During the battles in which there was close proximity between the opposing sides, Union soldiers would sing songs such as "Battle Cry of Freedom." A Confederate responded with "Dixie" to which the Union soldier sang the pastiche of "John Brown's Body," with text that advocated hanging Jeff Davis from a sour apple tree.

Ralph Hartsock

See also: *Arts:* "Battle Hymn of the Republic"; "Dixie"; Music, Nonmilitary; *Recreation and Social Customs:* Concerts

FURTHER READING

Abel, E. Lawrence. *Singing the New Nation: How Music Shaped the Confederacy, 1861–1865*. Mechanicsburg, PA: Stackpole Books, 2000.

Bruce, George B., and Dan D. Emmett. 1862. *The Drummer's and Fifer's Guide*. New York: Firth, Pond & Co., 1862

Bufkin, William A. "Union Bands of the Civil War: (1862–1865): Instrumentation and Score Analysis." Thesis, Louisiana State University, 1979.

Carder, P. H. *George F. Root, Civil War Songwriter: A Biography*. Jefferson, NC: McFarland & Co., 2008.

Cornelius, Steven H. *Music of the Civil War Era*. Westport, CT: Greenwood Press, 2004.

Hazen, Margaret Hindle, and Robert M. Hazen. *The Music Men: An Illustrated History of Brass Bands in America, 1800–1920*. Washington, DC: Smithsonian Institution Press, 1987.

Library of Congress, Music Division. *Band Music from the Civil War Era*. 2000. http://memory.loc.gov/ammem/cwmhtml/cwmhome.html. Accessed January 23, 2013.

Lord, Francis A., and Arthur Wise. *Bands and Drummer Boys of the Civil War*. New York: Da Capo Press, 1979.

MUSIC, NONMILITARY

Numerous forms and genres of music flourished before, during, and after the Civil War. These included popular music, blackface minstrelsy, spirituals, and songs of the Underground Railroad. Some ballads took on political connotations. Serious music included operas, symphonies, fantasies based on known classical music, and the accompaniments to musicals. Music was also performed in a wide variety of locations and events, including at theaters, concert halls, and sanitary fairs. Several major ensembles performed during the two presidential inaugurations of Abraham Lincoln (1861, 1865), Lincoln's speech commemorating the Battle of Gettysburg (1863), and the lengthy funeral for the assassinated leader (1865).

Music, including blackface minstrelsy, was an integral part of American culture. In both Northern and Southern communities, this type of music provided entertainment for white men and women. Thomas Dartmouth Rice (1808–1860), "Daddy Rice," had first appeared in a performance as "Jim Crow" in 1832. Other minstrel singing groups also flourished. George N. Christy (1827–1868), Edwin Pearce Christy (1815–1862), Dan Bryant (1833–1875), Harry Macarthy (1834–1888), and Daniel Decatur Emmett (1815–1904) led some of the best-known minstrel singing groups. Songs by Stephen Foster were particularly popular with many of these singers.

Other popular music also thrived during the Civil War. In the North, several composers created songs to encourage enthusiasm for the cause. Inspired by patriotism, the words of J. Cullen Bryant's poem "We Are Coming Father Abram,

300,000 More" (1862) were set to music by Patrick Gilmore (1829–1892), Luther Orlando Emerson (1820–1915), Augustus Cull, and Charles William Glover (1806–1863). Gilmore's most famous tune, however, was "When Johnny Comes Marching Home" (1863). Another popular songwriter, George F. Root (1820–1895), inspired many with his compositions, which included "The Battle Cry of Freedom" (1862) and "Tramp! Tramp! Tramp!" (1864). Root also owned a publishing firm in Chicago that had influence far beyond that city.

In addition there arose an antiwar movement in the North, partially influenced by the descriptive poetry and prose of Walt Whitman and the photography of Mathew Brady. Music expressed this sentiment as well. "All Quiet Along the Potomac Tonight" (1862), by John Hill Hewitt (1801–1890), expressed the sentiment of grief for the war. "When This Cruel War Is Over" (1863) by Henry Tucker (1926–1882) expressed similar emotions.

The Underground Railroad, a loosely organized clandestine network, assisted fugitive slaves in search of freedom from the slave-bound South on their way to the North, as far as Canada. Music was not only a cultural aspect of the Underground Railroad, but it was also a means of communication and a code. One of the primary songs related to the Northern constellation of Ursa Major (the Great Bear). Those African Americans trying to escape slavery learned the song "Follow the Drinking Gourd," that symbolized the Big Dipper, a portion of Ursa Major. The spiritual "Go Down Moses" was a reference to Harriet Tubman (1820–1913), a leading "conductor" on the Underground Railroad. Spirituals such as "Swing Low, Sweet Chariot," "The Gospel Train," and "Wade in the Water" referred directly to the Underground Railroad.

Lincoln's inauguration on March 4, 1861, in Washington, D.C., provided a public venue for several military and civilian ensembles to perform. Musical personnel varied from regiment to regiment. Harvey Dodworth (1822–1891) conducted the 71st New York Regimental Band in patriotic concerts. The repertoire ranged from the popular favorites of the day and blackface minstrelsy to arrangements of excerpts from operas by Giuseppe Verdi. Professor L. F. Weber led a band with 45 members at the president's post-inauguration party. His repertoire included waltzes and polkas by Johann Strauss (1804–1849) and Joseph Lanner (1801–1843). The director of the United States Marine Band, Francis Scala (ca. 1819–1903), composed the "Inauguration March." Although the president enjoyed the sound of "Dixie," bands played popular tunes such as "Yankee Doodle," and ceremonial favorites such as "The Star Spangled Banner" and "Hail to the Chief."

In November 1863, the United States Marine Band, along with the Second United States Artillery Band, went by train to the site of the summer's major battle, Gettysburg. Two other ensembles, the Fifth New York Artillery Band and Adolph Birgfield's Band of Philadelphia, joined them there. The opening musical work of the program, composed by Birgfield, was a dirge entitled "Homage d'un Heros."

In spite of the war, opera thrived in cities. New York performances of 1862 included Giuseppe Verdi's *La Traviata* and *Il Trovatore*, Vincenzo Bellini's *Norma* and Christoph Willibald Gluck's *Orefo ed Euridice*. Other urban bastions of classical music were Philadelphia and Washington, D.C. In the Union capital, the Colored American Opera company presented the operetta, *The Doctor of Alcantara*, by Julius Eichberg.

Three Southern cities were cultural centers in the Civil War: New Orleans, Louisiana; Macon, Georgia; and Savannah, Georgia. Here music became an expression of rebellion. Antebellum New Orleans, with a population of 60,000, developed as a cultural center for opera production. Whites, free blacks, and enslaved people attended performances at the St. Charles Theatre and the French Opera House. Although Giacomo Meyerbeer's *Dinorah* was performed in 1861, the capture and occupation by Union troops in 1862 delayed other operas in New Orleans until after the war.

Popular music also flourished in the Confederacy, even after the occupation by the Union. Songs such as "Dixie" and "Maryland, My Maryland" were published and sung widely. New Orleans had a robust music publishing industry led by Philip P. Werlein, Louis Grunewald, and A. E. (Armand Edward) Blackmar (1826–1888). Blackmar published several editions of "The Bonnie Blue Flag," sometimes known as the "Marseillaise of the South." When Union general Benjamin Butler occupied New Orleans, he confiscated all music from Blackmar's publishing house. When Butler ordered that anyone singing or even whistling "The Bonnie Blue Flag" would be fined $25, Blackmar obliged the general by whistling the melody as he was escorted to jail. Foremost in Georgia music publishing was John Schreiner and his son Hermann. They formed Shreiner & Son in 1860, and expanded to Savannah soon after. The firm published over 100 works during the Civil War.

The United States Sanitary Commission, founded in 1861, was charged with providing medical care and sanitation for the Union troops. Sanitary fairs were held in several locations in the North to finance this commission. Benefit concerts were an integral part of these fairs.

Ralph Hartsock

See also: *Arts*: "Battle Hymn of the Republic"; "Dixie"; Music, Military; *Recreation and Social Customs*: Concerts; Fairs and Bazaars; Sanitary Fairs

FURTHER READING

Abel, E. Lawrence. *Singing the New Nation: How Music Shaped the Confederacy, 1861–1865*. Mechanicsburg, PA: Stackpole Books, 2000.

Bernard, Kenneth A. *Lincoln and the Music of the Civil War*. Caldwell, ID: Caxton Printers, 1966.

Cornelius, Steven H. *Music of the Civil War Era*. Westport, CT: Greenwood Press, 2004.

Hudson, J. Blaine. *Encyclopedia of the Underground Railroad*. Jefferson, NC: McFarland & Co., 2006.

Lawson, Melinda. *Patriot Fires: Forging a New American Nationalism in the Civil War North*. Lawrence: University of Kansas Press, 2002.

Library of Congress, Music Division. *Band Music from the Civil War Era*. 2000. http://memory.loc.gov/ammem/cwmhtml/cwmhome.html. Accessed January 23, 2013.

Library of Congress, Music Division. *Music for the Nation*. 2000. http://memory.loc.gov/ammem/mussmhtml/mussmhome.html. Accessed January 23, 2013.

Thomas, Jean W. "Music of the Great Sanitary Fairs: Culture and Charity in the American Civil War." Ph.D. Dissertation, University of Pittsburgh, 1989.

NEWSPAPERS, NORTHERN

During the Civil War, newspapers throughout the North—many of which featured reports directly from the battlefield—were more widely distributed than ever before. They consequently shaped the public's wartime experience to a greater extent than papers had during any previous conflict. Newspaper coverage of the war often included details of individual battles and military campaigns, political coverage, editorials, eyewitness accounts of events, and for the first time illustrations drawn either on site or based on photographs. Some of the larger newspapers, like those in New York, Boston, and Chicago, sent reporters to stay close to military field headquarters and relay news and sometimes opinion about what was happening on the front lines. The reporters would send information to their papers via telegraph or, when not available, via courier. This practice created the first war correspondents in American history. The sheer volume of information relayed by the war correspondents, combined with its increasingly personal and solemn nature, greatly impacted Northern opinion of the conflict and of war in general.

Printing illustrations in a newspaper in the 1860s was a time-intensive process requiring the work of several artists and as many skilled wood engravers. Published pictures were considered timely if they appeared two to three weeks after the events that they depicted occurred. Three illustrated newspapers served the Northern public during the Civil War: *Harper's Weekly, Frank Leslie's Illustrated Newspaper*, and the *New York Illustrated News*. In the early months of the war, the shortage of skilled sketchers quickly became apparent. In response, *Harper's* and *Leslie's* offered free subscriptions to soldiers who sent in sketches, and both paid generously for printed illustrations. Although most illustrations from early in the war reflected a certain romanticism about army life and battlefield heroics, as the war entered its first winter and Union officers prepared for a spring campaign, more illustrations began to highlight the complexities and hard labor of modern

Photograph of the *New York Herald's* wagon in the field near Bealton, Virginia, in August 1863. Newspapers played a vital role during the Civil War, serving as lightning rods for public opinion and informing both the public and government leaders alike. Newspaper coverage of the war often included details of individual battles and military campaigns, political coverage, editorials, eyewitness accounts of events, and illustrations drawn either on site or based on photographs. (Library of Congress)

warfare. As fighting continued through a second year, some illustrations became more graphic, like those by Henri Lovie for *Frank Leslie's Illustrated* depicting the brutality of the war in the West.

Founded in 1857 by Fletcher Harper of the famed Harper and Brothers publishing family, *Harper's Weekly* was the most popular of the three illustrated papers with a circulation of 300,000 and an estimated readership of half a million. During the Civil War, its stories and illustrations from the front lines were so detailed that Secretary of War Edwin Stanton once tried to suspend publication of the paper because the reports were aiding the enemy.

Wartime papers faced censorship because of the details they offered. Early on, the Lincoln administration realized that newspapers could be an effective way for those against the war to feed information to the Southern states or to encourage their resistance. In response, the administration adopted a number of wartime measures intended to limit such activities. As in a case involving the *Philadelphia Enquirer*, commanding officers were to be notified if a reporter sent incorrect or false information about troop numbers, readiness, location, or battle performance.

Reporters, as non-enlisted civilians, had no legal right to be with army in camp or in battle but rather were there by permission of the military. Therefore, the military had the right to determine if the reporters should be allowed to send information to their respective newspapers as well as the right to censor such reports. War correspondents fell within the jurisdiction of military courts and were thereby subject to court martial before a tribunal for any attempt to subvert official review of their newspaper communications.

Tensions quickly developed between Northern newspapers and the Lincoln administration over the censorship of telegram dispatches between reporters and their papers. In August 1861, an agreement was reached whereby the government afforded facilities for reporters and regular access to proper information. In return, newspapers vowed not to publish any material that might give aid and comfort to the enemy. Still, some papers refused to be part of the agreement and continued to print forbidden information. Finally, Secretary of War Edwin Stanton, granted control of the telegraph wires by Lincoln, ordered that no telegraphic messages about military operations be sent without express permission by the War Department or commanding officers in the field. Newspapers that printed unauthorized information would be denied further use of the telegraphic wires and denied use of the railroads for delivering their papers.

Likewise, in 1861 the postmaster general acted to limit distribution of newspapers deemed to be hindering the success of the Union. Although some Northerners and members of Congress questioned the propriety of one executive of the government determining which newspapers were worthy of censorship, no one appears to have questioned the constitutionality of the government's right to deny access to the postal system for materials potentially injurious to the public's safety.

Not all papers supported the Northern war effort. Copperhead or Democratic newspapers in the North, such as the *Age* introduced in Pennsylvania in 1863, routinely criticized Lincoln and the war as well as supported the Southern argument that African Americans in the South actually benefited from the institution of slavery. In addition to editorials railing against the Lincoln administration and Republicans in Congress, these newspapers frequently printed stories designed to counter any public sympathies roused by abolitionists. The Copperhead press often recounted cases of free blacks attacking or raping white women in the North. They also frequently reprinted accounts of brutality by black Union troops published in Southern newspapers, such as the *Richmond Enquirer*. Such stories routinely highlighted the blackness and inherent cruelty of the African American aggressors versus the innocence, education, and mildness of their white victims.

Kathleen Gronnerud

See also: Arts: Newspapers, Southern; Photography; Serial Novels; *Housing and Community*: Nationalism, United States; *Recreation and Social Customs*: Political Speeches

FURTHER READING

Beckett, Ian F. W. *American Civil War—The War Correspondents*. Gloucestershire, UK: Sutton Publishing Ltd., 1993.

Bracken, Donagh. *Words of War: The Civil War Battle Reportage of the New York Times and the Charleston Mercury and What the Historians Say Actually Happened*. Palisades, NY: History Publishing Company, 2007.

Thompson, William Fletcher, Jr. "Illustrating the Civil War." *The Wisconsin Magazine of History* 45: 1 (Autumn 1961): 10–20.

NEWSPAPERS, SOUTHERN

Newspapers were the most popular reading material and source of information for most nineteenth-century Americans. Between 1825 and the eve of the war, the number of newspapers had quadrupled; in 1860 there were 3,725 newspapers for a population of 31,443,000, and 80 percent of daily newspapers were classified as political in nature. The number of newspapers in America was twice that of Britain and accounted for one third of all the world's broadsides. Many cities had two papers or more, even those with just a few thousand residents.

Within hours of the first shot on Fort Sumter on April 12, 1861, telegraph wires carried the news to papers all over the South. Those newspapers that advocated secession were jubilant. Though some editorial writers were cautious or tried to warn readers of the dangers of secession, most Southern editors felt it was their duty to fashion public opinion to fight the growing opposition to slavery and to favor secession. Once the time for debate was over, most Southern newspapers fell in line with the Confederate cause or went out of business. For example, the editor of the anti-secession Richmond *Whig* was forced out of his job the day after the Union surrender at Fort Sumter.

Despite the numerous editors of Southern newspapers who saw their role as champions of and propagandists for the Southern cause, they were clearly outmatched by the sheer numbers, influence, and prestige of the Northern press. The North had four times the number of newspapers and twice the circulation of the South. Compared to the Richmond *Daily Dispenser*, with the South's largest readership and circulation of 30,000 during the war, the *New York Herald*, the North's largest newspaper, had a circulation of 77,000. New York was the newspaper center of America, boasting 17 daily papers in 1861. Only the larger Northern cities could afford the new technologies of the rotary steam-powered printing press and the stereotyping process, all of which increased production and distribution.

Almost immediately after the war began, the South began to lose resources, availability of news, and manpower. Hundreds of newspaper printers, mailing clerks, and reporters joined the military. As a result of this loss of manpower, in the first year of the war 40 newspapers in Virginia and 50 in Texas had to suspend publication. In Mississippi, only 9 of the 75 prewar newspapers were still in operation at the end of 1863. By June 1864, three-fourths of all the South's printers had seen active army service; half of those men died on the battlefield or were disabled by injury or disease. Editors could not adequately staff their newspapers, and by February 1864, daily Southern newspapers had dwindled to 35. By January 1865 there were fewer newspapers in the entire Confederacy than there had been in Virginia prior to the war.

Not only did the South's newspapers suffer tremendous attrition of workers, but they also faced war-created obstacles to production. Printing supplies had previously come from the North and from Europe, so military blockades, the cutting of telegraph wires, and the halting of railroad, postal service, and river traffic greatly affected the Confederacy's access to ink and paper. The Confederacy had only 25 paper mills in five key states and only 5 percent of the nation's total newsprint production. The cost of paper led to drastic cuts in newspaper size: by 1862 all of the Richmond dailies were down to two pages. The Charleston *Courier*, for example, ended up 10 inches by 15 inches with only four columns to a page.

The ingredients used in manufacturing newspapers, such as glue, oil, and potash, became more and more costly as the war lengthened. The scarcity of printing paper forced newspapers to use whatever paper was available; sometimes colored paper, brown wrapping paper, and even wallpaper were used for newspapers. Ink was scarce as well, so bootblacking was often used as a substitute. Increased costs of supplies and labor were made worse by loss of two-thirds of advertising revenue. Many subscribers either did not pay their bills, or paid by bartering commodities such as chickens and butter.

In 1861, when the war began, papers on both sides predicted a short but conclusive end. Southern editors especially took pride in their mission to uphold public morale and feature stories of the heroic captains of the Confederacy. Some early victories were exaggerated to glorify the heroism of Southern men and women. Though most of the reporting on both sides was straightforward and reliable, the South almost relished its role as a victim of Northern aggression, referring to the Yankees as heinous murderers and rascals. As the war continued, Union forces seized more than 100 Southern cities and military authorities closed down newspapers or issued strict orders guiding publishing in occupied areas.

Some editors fled as Union armies advanced. A few were captured, had their property seized, or were put before military tribunals. A few were imprisoned, though there were no editors still jailed at the end of the war. Some newspaper operations were taken apart and moved to various cities to escape capture or destruction. The Memphis *Appeal*, moved so often that it was known as the "Moving *Appeal*."

Reporting the war was difficult and often hazardous. Hundreds of Southern reporters chronicled the war for little pay, and several were killed or captured. Working conditions were also difficult; reporters lived like soldiers and traveled with them. Long work days resulted in fatigue and illness. By 1864 and 1865, some of the editorial writers who had championed the Southern cause turned to disillusionment and defeatism. No Southern correspondent was on hand when Lee surrendered to grant at Appomattox Courthouse on April 9, 1865, and a Tennessee newspaper headline aptly summed up the feelings of most Southern newspaper writers by war's end: "The Agony Is Over."

Gary Kerley

See also: Arts: Newspapers, Northern; *Economy and Work*: Camp Followers; Rural Life, Southern; Urban Life, Southern; *Housing and Community*: Nationalism, Confederate; *Politics and Warfare*: Morale; Secession

FURTHER READING

Carter, Hodding. *Their Words Were Bullets: The Southern Press in War, Reconstruction, and Peace*. Athens: University of Georgia Press, 1969.

Cutler, J. Andrews. *The South Reports the Civil War*. Pittsburgh, PA: University of Pittsburgh Press, 1970.

Harris, Brayton. *Blue & Gay in Black & White: Newspapers in the Civil War*. Washington, DC: Batsford Brassey, Inc., 1999.

Reynolds, Donald E. *Editors Make War: Southern Newspapers in the Secession Crisis*. Nashville, TN: Vanderbilt University Press, 1970.

Risley, Ford. *Civil War Journalism*. Santa Barbara, CA: Praeger, 2012.

Sachsman David, S. Kittrell Rushing, and Roy Morris, Jr., eds. *Words at War: The Civil War and American Journalism*. West Lafayette, IN: Purdue University Press, 2008.

PHOTOGRAPHY

Photography, though in its infancy in the mid-nineteenth century, has become central to understanding the nature and experience of the Civil War. Over the length of its duration, photographers took millions of images and chronicled the Civil War in all its detail, from mundane camp scenes to dramatic and sometimes horrifying battlefield landscapes. Never before had artists documented the atrocity of war so extensively or with such realism. Photography allowed Americans on the home front to follow the events of the Civil War as they happened, but it also put them face to face with the human tragedy and destructiveness of war.

Photography was a modern medium for a modern war; the technology of photography was barely 30 years old when the Civil War began. At that time, photographers most commonly employed the "wet plate" process of developing photographs by which they exposed a negative image on a glass or metal plate drenched with chemicals. They then printed the image on glass, metal, or paper to make an ambrotype, tin type, or carte de visite, respectively. Perhaps the most popular form of photography in the Civil War period, however, was the stereograph. Stereographs consisted of two like images printed side by side on a small

Photograph of dead from the Battle of Antietam, September 17, 1862. During the Civil War, photographers took millions of pictures including those that showed camp life, portraits of leaders and soldiers, and battle scenes. These photographs allowed Americans to see the devastation of war. (Library of Congress)

card which, when viewed through a special lens, formed one three-dimensional picture—a trick which produced a remarkable and exciting viewing experience for Civil War era Americans. In each of these forms, photographers captured images by the hundreds of thousands and the public, impressed by their novelty and by their perceived authenticity, eagerly consumed them.

Both sides of the conflict seized on the popularity of photography. In the South, however, shortages of manpower and materiel meant that the Confederacy spared few photographers from military service and that equipment became prohibitively expensive. As a result, Northern photographers took the vast majority of Civil War photographs. Most famous of these was Mathew Brady (1822–1896), who headed a team of talented photographers like Alexander Gardner (1821–1882) and Timothy O'Sullivan (1840–1882). These men captured some of the most enduring images of the Civil War.

For photographers in the field, like Brady and his associates, photographing the Civil War was an extraordinary experience, unlike anything seen in the profession before. In fact, many historians consider these photographers to be the predecessors of modern photojournalists. They followed the major armies on campaigns, hauling mobile dark rooms and wagonloads of equipment. Though these photographers were always at the scene of action, the length of time required to expose a negative, usually several seconds, meant that they could not effectively capture combat scenes. As a result, they often only photographed static scenes—posed portraits, landscapes, and the aftermath of battle. The static scenes were no less affective.

Despite the limitations of their equipment, however, battlefield photographers did not shy away from shocking subject matter. They often took pictures of horribly wounded and dead soldiers. In some instances, they took these images for use as medical records; the photographs helped medical professionals understand the wounds inflicted on soldiers and they could also record the most successful methods of treatment. Perhaps the most famous photographs of the Civil War, however, are those of its dead, especially those taken by Gardner in the aftermath of Antietam. Though not the first war in which photographers captured dead soldiers, the American Civil War was nevertheless the first war in which photographers publically exhibited and sold these images.

Indeed, the easy accessibility of Civil War battlefield photographs to the public on the home front was an important shift in the availability of information. For the first time, even Americans far removed from the battlefield could see the war firsthand, almost simultaneously with the battles themselves. In public exhibitions as well as in newspaper stories, the photographs revealed the realities of the battlefield. Distance no longer spared civilians from witnessing its horrors either; the carnage was inescapably evident in the photographs. As a result, Americans had to come to terms with what it meant to look at battlefield photographs—especially those that depicted dead soldiers. The most common reaction was perhaps one of intense curiosity mixed with disgust. Photographs brought the horrors of warfare to civilian doorsteps.

Photographs came to mediate public knowledge of the war. Americans trusted photographs as indisputable evidence of actual events. In reality, however, any number of factors might distort their accuracy, including the moral position of the photographer, the censorship by officials, and the limitations of the photographer's equipment. In addition, some photographers deliberately staged their shots to get the most affective picture. For example, the photograph of the purported dead Confederate sharpshooter in the Devil's Den at Gettysburg represents perhaps the most famous instance of staging. In 1975, William Frassanito discovered that at least six photographs, taken in two entirely different locations on the battlefield, depicted the same body. Frassanito realized that the photographers had moved the body and posed it with a prop rifle on purpose to capture a more powerful image. Despite such hoaxes, however, Civil War photographs still serve as powerful evidence of the war and its world, demonstrating its impact both on the soldiers who fought it and on the nation itself.

Amy L. Fluker

See also: *Arts*: Brady, Mathew B. (ca. 1823–1896); Newspapers, Northern; Newspapers, Southern; Portraiture

FURTHER READING

Earle, Edward W., ed. *Points of View: The Stereograph in America—A Cultural History.* New York: Visual Studies Workshop, 1979.

Frassanito, William A. *Early Photography at Gettysburg.* Gettysburg, PA: Thomas Publications, 1995.

Moeller, Susan D. *Shooting War: Photography and the American Experience of Combat.* New York: Basic Books, Inc., 1989.

Trachtenberg, Alan. *Reading American Photographs: Images as History, Mathew Brady to Walker Evans.* New York: Hill and Wang, 1989.

Zeller, Bob. *The Blue and Gray in Black and White: A History of Civil War Photography.* Westport, CT: Praeger, 2005.

POETRY

During the Civil War period, Americans experienced a wide range of strong feelings as burning moral and political issues, factional enthusiasms and aversions, patriotic impulses, and emotional responses to military victories and defeats, along with the sympathetic regret for lost young lives and for places devastated by conflict, affected minds and often invited individuals to seek poetic comfort or consolation. Overwhelming as emotions were, the tremendous effusion of sentiment produced relatively little poetry the literary reputation of which has survived the changing tides of fashion and the diminishing memory of what Abraham Lincoln (1809–1865), something of a poet himself, called "this terrible war." However during the war, and in some cases long afterward, the resonance of the quantities of verse composed during this period or later by individuals who participated in this war thrilled an audience hungry to see a sublime aspect of the catastrophic events of the 1861–1865 struggle.

Of the Southern poets, the most durable in reputation was Georgian Sidney Lanier (1842–1881), a fine musician whose health seriously deteriorated during his incarceration in a federal prison late in the war. After his release from prison, he expressed his rhapsodic temperament in an elegy titled "The Dying Words of Stonewall Jackson," a poem that suggests a religious significance in the dying Confederate general's last feverish utterances. The poem, written by a young combat veteran, ex-prisoner-of-war, and disappointed Southerner, reveals intense nostalgia, hero-worship, and hope of otherworldly justification. Lanier's words are typical in their hyperbolic reverence and in their emotional conviction of the rightness of Jackson's cause.

Lanier's tone is not very unlike the famous anthem by New Yorker Julia Ward Howe (1819–1910), "Battle-Hymn of the Republic." In her marching song, Howe's fierce Puritanism enlists divine sanction against the sinners opposing the march of sacred justice, and there is certainly no room in these lines for doubt about which side God is on. Where Lanier suggests that Jackson's last words are now like stars (echoing, perhaps, Shelley's sonnet "To Wordsworth"), Howe's emotion is less complicated and more purposeful. After the war, she was to reflect less ferocity in a thoughtful poetic tribute to Confederate commanding general Robert E. Lee. Each poet felt exaltation and a kind of enthusiasm. Much other contemporary poetry of both North and South expresses similar emotions.

Another Confederate poet, the Catholic priest Father Abram Joseph Ryan (1838–1886), commemorated the fall of the South in a bitter elegy commanding that the flag of the Confederacy be furled, folded, and put away. In this poem, "The Conquered Banner," the narrator's distinct tone of reproach suggests that the ideals for which the banner stood have been betrayed and reminds the audience that the banner's "foes" are triumphing over this heroic symbol. This poem was highly popular and must have given some comfort to the many Southerners who admired it. Certainly there was no shortage of suspicion of betrayal as the war ended.

A few of the Northern poets published work that is still relatively compatible with twenty-first century poetic expectations. Among the flag-waving and the exercises in self-righteousness, hero-worship, and noble histrionics, Walt Whitman has remained popular. Although as moved as anyone by the emotional turbulence of the day, Whitman emerges in such brief sequences as "Bivouac on a Mountainside" and "Cavalry Crossing a Ford" as an alert observer of interaction between nature and the men engaged in the Civil War. As a pioneer of poetry not dependent upon emphatic rhyme and regular meter, Whitman stands out in retrospect. Though "O Captain! My Captain!"—one of his two poems on the death of President Abraham Lincoln—is written with attention to somewhat conventional form and rhyme, his longer elegy for Lincoln, "When Lilacs Last in the Door-yard Bloom'd," is shaped primarily by emotion and by passion for nature.

No less impressive than Whitman's original excursions are the restrained, rather knotty lyrics of Herman Melville (1819–1891). Melville's reservations about enthusiasm for war stand contrary to most of this period's effusions. In addition, Melville's relatively inconspicuous rhymes and laconic syntax contrast with the drumbeat poetics favored by his contemporaries.

Twenty-first-century critics of poetry value Civil War poetry for qualities less admired in the nineteenth century than in the era shaped by Pound, Eliot, and Stevens. However, among the sentimental, jingoistic, and ideologically obsessive poems produced by this devastating conflict of steel and of ideas, a critical intelligence occasionally is heard. These poems join company with the torrents of honest but often misguided emotion, sometimes only to express ambivalence but also at times to generate a philosophical lucidity which contrasts strikingly with the rhetorical excesses and delusive exaltations popular at this time.

Civil War poets include Abraham Lincoln (1809–1865), Emily Dickinson (1830–1886), Oliver Wendell Holmes (1809–1894), William Cullen Bryant (1794–1878), Ralph Waldo Emerson (1803–1882), Francis Bret Harte (1836–1902), John Greenleaf Whittier (1807–1892), Henry Wadsworth Longfellow (1807–1882), James Russell Lowell (1819–1891), Henry David Thoreau (1817–1862), and a host of others on the Union side, including African Americans James Madison Bell (1826–1902), Sarah Mapps Douglass (1806–1882), and Joshua McCarter Simpson (ca. 1820–1876). A similar host of bards composed verse of a Confederate inclination, though the names are generally less familiar. William Gilmore Simms (1806–1870), Henry Timrod (1828–1867), Paul Hamilton Hayne (1830–1886), Francis Orray Ticknor (1822–1874), and Catherine Ann Ware Warfield (1816–1877), along with Sidney Lanier and Father Ryan, represent the Southern faction.

Robert W. Haynes

See also: Arts: "Battle-Hymn of the Republic"; Literature, Northern; Literature, Southern; Whitman, Walt (1819–1892); *Politics and Warfare*: Surrender, Confederate; *Religion and Belief*: Eulogies

FURTHER READING

Barrett, Faith, and Cristanne Muller, eds. *Words for the Hour: A New Anthology of American Civil War Poetry*. Amherst: University of Massachusetts Press, 2005.

Boyes, John, ed. *Poetry of the Civil War*. New York: Gramercy Books, 2006.

McClatchy, J.D., ed. *Poets of the Civil War*. American Poets Project. New York: The Library of America, 2005.

Miles, Dudley H., ed. *Poetry and Eloquence of Blue and Gray*. Vol 9. *The Photographic History of the Civil War in Ten Volumes*. New York: The Review of Reviews Co., 1912.

Negri, Paul, ed. *Civil War Poetry: An Anthology*. Mineola, NY: Dover Publications, 1997.

PORTRAITURE

Portraiture refers to a particular form of art where the artist seeks to render the likeness of the subject, be it through painting, drawing, or photography. In the early nineteenth century, artists used various techniques, including realism, impressionism, and post-impressionism to depict their subjects.

During the Civil War, prominent men like Abraham Lincoln, Ulysses S. Grant, Jefferson Davis, Robert E. Lee and others had numerous portraits commissioned by artists, but one important invention of the mid-nineteenth century changed the way Americans experienced the war. Photography exposed both exceptional individuals and average citizens to much more information on the war. Soldiers' everyday lives became important parts of the historical record as photographers traveled with both armies to various locations. The carnage of war was also a subject captured by the new medium and struck at the hearts of men and women throughout the country. However, photography also changed the meaning of portraiture in the late 1800s. Politicians and upper-class individuals were not the only ones with the ability to have their portraits made by professional artists. Portrait photography allowed for the capture and quick dissemination of images of celebrities, cartes-de-visite, and death portraits. During the era of the Civil War, these images became everyday items in the homes of average Americans.

Although photographs of dead bodies on the battlefield became one of the most striking elements of the Civil War's legacy, photography was also and most often used to capture the likenesses of the numerous men and women who lived during the time. Mathew Brady was one of the most famous portrait-studio entrepreneurs of the nineteenth century. Beginning in the 1840s and lasting until his death in 1896, Brady was responsible for a collection of thousands of American portraits. Brady would later become involved in capturing battlefield scenes, but his initial success came from his thriving portraiture business. Brady was one of the first and most famous men who became involved early in the business as photography gained popularity in the mid-nineteenth century. He photographed many famous Americans, including Abraham Lincoln both before and during his presidency. In February 1864, Brady captured the image of Lincoln that currently appears on the $5 bill.

Carte de visite of an unidentified Civil War soldier, from Ball & Thomas' Photographic Art Gallery, Cincinnati, Ohio. Before they left for the battlefields, many Civil War soldiers had their portraits made so that they could commemorate their excitement and send their images to loved ones. Photography made it possible for people of all classes, not just the wealthy, to commemorate themselves or their loved ones in a portrait. (Library of Congress)

During the late 1800s, Americans scrambled to studios, like Brady's, for a chance to sit for their portraits. The process was often long and laborious as early technology necessitated that sitters remain perfectly still for lengthy amounts of time. Sitters were often obligated to wear metal apparatuses as a means of holding their poses for the acquired time span. Initially, photographers created portraits that were simply set to capture the likeness of their subjects without much artistic intent. However, with the growing popularity of the medium in the 1860s, photographers began to paint elaborate backgrounds to feature in their images and even began retouching negatives to make their subjects appear more pleasing.

Celebrities of contemporary theaters were some of the most significant customers of portrait photographers of the time. They sat in poses that mimicked their stage performances, and they used the images to promote themselves and the productions in which they appeared. These theater photographs allowed for more exposure to a larger audience in a shorter amount of time than had been possible in the past. It also allowed American citizens to form new connections to the people involved in entertainment.

One specific type of photograph also changed the nature of portraiture during the late nineteenth century. Carte-de-visite photographs were created using a technique first invented by a Frenchman in 1854. The photographer took eight images on one negative, thus allowing the subject to obtain eight different poses, then cut the piece into 4 × 2 ½ inch sections that were then mounted on pieces of cardboard. The universal size of these images (slightly larger than a modern business card) allowed people to collect the photographs into large, elaborate albums that preserved cartes-de-visite for numerous generations. Many Civil War soldiers, as they left for war, had their likenesses taken in this way by local photographers in an effort both to commemorate their excitement and to obtain images they could later send to loved ones.

Although celebrities' portraits and cartes-de-visite might seem similar to an average idea of portraiture, Americans (along with people in England and France) also practiced another type of photographic portraiture: postmortem photography. Today, most individuals would likely think of living persons as subjects of portraits. However, Americans of the late nineteenth century often had portraits commissioned of their deceased loved ones. These photographs might display one individual or entire families, including both dead and living members, or entire deceased families. Oftentimes, photographers posed their deceased subjects in ways that displayed their status, but the artists also sometimes positioned the dead in a manner to make them appear as if they were sleeping or even as if they were still alive. Much like they did with their living subjects, the photographers placed the individuals in metal contraptions to make them stand, and the artists sometimes painted open eyes onto the portrait prints.

Postmortem photography may seem odd or disturbing to contemporary Americas because of our particular views of illness, death, and dying, but Victorian Americans held different views of these subjects and photography became an important medium in completing their mortuary practices. First, due to the length of time subjects were expected to remain still, the dead were ideal for the new medium. However, and more importantly, Victorian Americans believed that retaining portraits of the deceased was an important way to memorialize their family members. In addition, due to high infant mortality rates, images of dead children might be the only mementos families had. Overall, postmortem and other types of portraiture allowed nineteenth-century Americans to experience their world differently and gave them a new visual medium that would continue to affect their lives for numerous generations.

Kelli Nelson

See also: *Arts*: Art; Brady, Mathew B. (ca. 1823–1896); Photography; *Religion and Belief*: Mourning

FURTHER READING

Codell, Julie. "Victorian Portraits: Re-Tailoring Identities." *Nineteenth-Century Contexts: An Interdisciplinary Journal* 34:5 (2012): 493–516.

Newhall, Beaumont. *The History of Photography from 1839 to the Present.* New York: Museum of Modern Art, 1982.

Panzer, Mary. *Mathew Brady and the Image of History.* Washington, DC: Smithsonian Books, 2004.

Ruby, Jay. *Secure the Shadow: Death and Photography in America.* Cambridge, MA: MIT Press, 1995.

QUILTS

During the nineteenth century, members of female antislavery societies used quilts to marshal collective action, express viewpoints, and remind men about the brutality, inhumanity, and evils of American slavery. Quilting gave artistic expression to the moral voice of women in mid-nineteenth century America.

It is estimated that more women than men belonged to antislavery societies before the Civil War, and women used their needlework to raise money for the abolitionist cause. Quilts were sold at church and county fairs with the express purpose of calling attention to the immorality of slavery. Quilts were made in support of the nation's first antislavery political party, the Liberty Party, and the names of familiar quilt patterns were changed to reflect the spirit of the movement: Job's tears became "Slave chain"; Jacob's ladder became the "Underground Railroad"; "North star" was named for the star escaped slaves followed to freedom. Quilts were both a public prayer and an effort to raise the level of public debate among men to include moral considerations.

Although there was little time left in their day, black slave women also quilted. These women used discarded scraps of cloth from the mistress of the plantation as well as pieces cut from gunny, feed, tobacco, rice, and sugar sacks. The inner layer of slave quilts was often filled with old blankets, slave clothing that could no longer be mended, and bits of wool and raw cotton. Quilting provided an occasion for slave women to gather late in the evening to socialize, to exchange information, and to rest from the unrelenting demands and trials of their daily lives.

Slave quilts were also made out of necessity. Blankets were scarce, clothing was meager for adults and deplorable for children, and environmental conditions were harsh. String quilts, in which strips of fabrics were sewn together, cut into blocks and made into quilts, were popular because the scraps of cloth alone were often too narrow to be worth using. Slave patterns, either learned from their mistresses or from each other, were most often used, but some made ingenious original patterns frequently based on elements from their environment. Oral tradition has it that quilts were used as a method of signaling along the Underground Railroad. However, historians have discovered little evidence to support the contention that quilt blocks held coded messages.

With the advent of the Civil War, many Northern women who had assisted with the Underground Railroad or who had been involved with antislavery societies, joined other benevolent organizations, or were a part of sewing circles, soon became members of soldiers' aid societies. The largest society, the United States Sanitary Commission (USSC), channeled volunteer contributions and supplies to the Union Army in an effort to provide clean linens, hospital bandages, clothing, socks, and blankets to soldiers. These soldiers often faced squalid conditions in camps and medical aid stations.

The Sanitary Commission's first fund-raising fair, organized by Mary Livermore and Jane Hoge of Chicago, opened on October 27, 1863, ran for three days, raised $78,000, and set off a chain reaction. In 1864 the New York metropolitan fair raised $1.2 million. The USSC estimated that at least 250,000 quilts were distributed during the war. Many of the quilts were made of cheap material and simply meant to keep soldiers warm.

Some women also sent their husbands and sons to war with a treasured family quilt. Many of these heirloom quality quilts that went to war were lost or destroyed during military campaigns or just fell apart as a result of hard use. The sacrifice women made in giving up family quilts or in the extra time they spent making quilts to sell at sanitary fairs or to ship to the battlefront did not go unnoticed. At the closing of the Washington Sanitary Fair on March 18, 1864, President Abraham Lincoln acknowledged women's hard work and sacrifice on behalf of the soldiers.

Southern women also organized relief efforts for the Confederacy and provided essential clothing and bedding for the Confederate Army. Unfortunately, women's resources at the start of the war were scarce, and by 1862 they were almost nonexistent. In 1861, the manufacture of textiles in the South was limited to a small number of factories principally in Georgia and South Carolina. With the Union Navy's blockade and the North's embargo all types of critical supplies for the war effort were choked off, including fabric of any kind. In time the few cotton mills in the South produced only coarse material such as sackcloth, and osnaburg.

Women in the Confederacy used homespun methods of manufacturing: knitting, carding, spinning, and weaving. Many of these skills were used during the antebellum period, but performed primarily by slave women. As a consequence, during the Civil War many white Southern women had to learn these skills from their black servants. As they managed their wartime households on their own, these white women also had to manufacture their own supplies, including making bedding and blankets for soldiers and their own families out of anything they could find. Some Southern women described making quilts and comforters from two homespun sheets lined with layers of newspapers. No makeshift Confederate quilts is known to have survived.

Thomas Army

See also: *Clothing, Fashion, and Appearance*: Homespun; Textiles; *Economy and Work*: Slavery; *Family Life and Gender Roles*: Aid Societies; Slave Families; United States Sanitary Commission; *Politics and Warfare*: Abolitionists

FURTHER READING

Gunn, Virginia. "Quilts for Union Soldiers in the Civil War." In Sally Garoutte, ed. *Uncoverings 1985*. Mill Valley, CA: American Quilt Study Group, 1986.

Horton, Laurel. "South Carolina Quilts and the Civil War." In Sally Garoutte, ed. *Uncoverings 1985*. Mill Valley, CA: American Quilt Study Group, 1986.

Kiracofe, Roderick. *The American Quilt: A History of Cloth and Comfort, 1750–1950*. New York: Clarkson Potter Publishers, 1993.

Lincoln, Abraham. *Speeches and Writings, 1859–1865: Speeches, Letters, and Miscellaneous Writings Presidential Messages and Proclamations*. Edited by Roy P. Basler. New York: Literary Classics of the United States, Inc., 1989.

SERIAL NOVELS

Serial novels, which were published in installments in sequential issues of a periodical publication such as a magazine or a newspaper, were extremely popular during the nineteenth century. Their popularity on both sides of the Atlantic contributed to the spread of literacy and the enlargement of the reading public. So widespread was this publication format that the standard practice was that novels were first serialized and later published in book format, because having one's work serialized was regarded as a sign of literary prestige and success.

Serial novels were popular in America and abroad. In England, Charles Dickens's novels and Arthur Conan Doyle's Sherlock Holmes stories first appeared in serialized form. In the United States, the first serial novels published were English novels or, if written by American authors, were largely derivative of English models. However, as time went by, American topics, characters, and situations were adopted. Among others, Herman Melville's and Henry James's works were serialized. Beginning on June 5, 1851, Harriet Beecher Stowe's *Uncle Tom's Cabin* was first published in the abolitionist periodical *National Era* over a 40-week period. The first novel by an African American writer, *Clotel; or, The President's Daughter: A Narrative of Slave Life in the United States* (first published in London in 1853) by fugitive slave William Wells Brown, was serialized in the *Weekly Anglo-African* in 1860–1861.

Printing innovations and better means of distribution as well as the increase in literacy rates favored the popularity of the serial novel. Serial publication offered authors the opportunity to get an extra source of income and a larger readership than did books, as not everybody could afford to buy books. The serial publication of their works enabled writers to make changes as they wrote and had a profound effect on their writing strategies. Writers wrote as the novel was being published—it was rare that a novel was serialized after having been completed—which meant that public sympathy or hatred for a given character weighed heavily. Often writers made decisions about the course their work would take based upon their readers' preferences and reactions. Thus, so as not to lose or alienate their readers, writers felt compelled to accommodate their audience's or editors' tastes, sometimes against their own preferences. Writers were careful to divide their works into chapters of similar length to meet the word count serial publication required.

Serial publication also affected reading practices. Readers did not perceive the work they were currently reading as a finished product, and indeed it was not, and felt that they might be entitled to have some say on the course of the novel or the future of certain characters. By reading a work over an extended period of time, readers felt close to characters. The plot of novels was a common topic of conversation at social gatherings.

The serial novel was intimately linked to democratic values because it allowed everybody to read current works, even if they could not afford to buy books. Moreover, democratic ideals called for a literate citizenship. Periodicals aimed at making this goal possible, as illustrated by the *Harper's New Monthly Magazine* issue of November 1859, which stated that "our firm conviction in this matter, as in politics, is that people may be trusted." Most magazines were published in the North, especially in New York, Philadelphia, and Boston. Some of the most well-known and best-selling periodicals in the antebellum period were the *Atlantic Monthly, Harper's Magazine, Harper's Weekly*, and the *Southern Literary Messenger*.

The *Atlantic Monthly*, founded in Boston in 1857, was a literature periodical but it also published abolitionist articles. Its founders included Harriet Beecher

Stowe, Ralph Waldo Emerson, Henry Wadsworth Longfellow, and James Russell, the latter serving as editor from 1857 to 1861. Julia Ward Howe's "Battle Hymn of the Republic" first appeared in the *Atlantic Monthly* (February 1, 1862). It was also the first to publish William Parker's slave narrative, "The Freedman's Story" (February–March 1866).

Harper's Magazine first came out in June 1850 as *Harper's New Monthly Magazine*. Extracts of *Moby Dick* by Herman Melville first appeared in the magazine in 1851 under the title "The Town-Ho's Story." Other notable contributors to the magazine were William Dean Howells, Jack London, and Mark Twain. Its heir, *Harper's Weekly: A Journal of Civilization*, first came out in New York in 1857. It became the best-selling journal during the Civil War, both in the North and in the South, which was no small feat for a journal published in New York. So as not to alienate its Southern readers, *Harper's Weekly* kept a mild position over slavery, which earned its being dubbed "Harper's Weakly" by its detractors. During the war, it printed war reports. Different from other publications, illustrations played an important role in *Harper's Weekly*. Political cartoonist Thomas Nast worked there for over 20 years until censorship and restrictions on his work from the new editor made him resign.

The *Southern Literary Messenger*, published from 1834 to 1864 in Richmond, Virginia, was unusual in that it was published in the South. It had a nationalistic component: featuring Southern fiction, nonfiction and poetry, to stimulate "the pride and genius of the south." Edgar Allan Poe, who served as staff writer, critic, and editor, prided himself on helping to increase the periodical's subscribers from 700 to 5,500. Excerpts from his only novel, *The Narrative of Arthur Gordon Pym*, were published in the magazine's pages. In addition, *Gertrude* by Nathaniel Beverley Tucker, a Southern legal scholar and advocate for states' rights, was serialized in the *Southern Literary Messenger* from 1844 to 1845.

The proliferation of magazines that published serial novels enriched the literacy of the nation. Serial novels shaped the reading public as those readers simultaneously shaped them.

M. Carmen Gomez-Galisteo

See also: *Arts: Harper's Weekly;* Literature, Northern; Literature, Southern; Slave Narratives; *Uncle Tom's Cabin*

FURTHER READING

Lund, Michael. *America's Continuing Story: An Introduction to Serial Fiction, 1850–1900*. Detroit, MI: Wayne State University Press, 1993.

Okker, Patricia. *Social Stories: The Magazine Novel in Nineteenth-Century America*. Charlottesville: University of Virginia Press, 2003.

SLAVE NARRATIVES

Slave narratives, firsthand testimonies written by a former slave narrating his or her life under slavery, escape from an owner, and the achievement of freedom, became popular reading material in the years leading up to the Civil War. Abolitionism was the most heatedly debated topic both prior to and during the Civil War. As a result, there was a great interest in the life and harsh working conditions of slaves in the South. Among other information sources or reading materials, readers felt a special predilection for slave narratives.

Teaching slaves to read and write was a punishable crime in the South, so most former slaves who authored slave narratives required assistance from others to effectively convey their experiences in written form. In addition, slave narratives were more often than not heavily edited and modified before they made their way into print. The genre soon became extremely popular, with dozens of accounts being published in the nineteenth century. As time went by and more slave narratives were published to meet the increasing demand, they became quite formulaic and included violent episodes so as to appeal to the public desire for sensationalism. Slave narratives often resorted to the use of biblical imagery, drawing parallelisms between biblical stories and slaves' trials and sufferings. *Pilgrim's Progress* also had a strong influence on the structure of the published slave narrative. It was common that they included a preface asserting the authenticity of the following narrative.

For obvious reasons, abolitionists used slave narratives to further their agenda. Slave narratives that sought readers' endorsement of abolitionism emphasized extreme physical abuse and brutal corporal punishments, hunger and starvation, sexual abuse, whippings, slave auctions, hard working conditions, the pain of slave families broken apart, mental anguish, a successful escape and often also a previous, failed attempt at escape.

However, not all slave narratives had as their main (or even sole) goal to gain support for the abolitionist movement, as some were written to give testimony of religious redemption. Slave narratives written with a religious goal downplayed the issue of slavery to emphasize, instead, the protagonists' journey from heathenism to their conversion to Christianity, such as *The Blind African Slave, Or Memoirs of Boyrereau Brinch, Nicknamed Jeffrey Brace* by Jeffrey Brace (1810; edited by Benjamin F. Prentiss).

Slave narratives constituted the first African American narrative genre in the United States. In them, one can see their efforts to negotiate an identity for themselves. Topics in slave narratives such as their identity search or "invisibility" among the white majority can still be perceived in the work of twentieth-century African American writers such as Ralph Ellison and Toni Morrison. Slave narratives are closely related to captivity narratives, accounts of European colonists who fell captive to the Native Americans during the colonial period and who later recorded their experiences to satisfy public curiosity and for the moral edification of their readers.

Some slave narratives were published in Canada, another possible destination for former slaves. Boston abolitionist Benjamin Drew compiled some in *The Refugee: Narratives of Fugitive Slaves in Canada Related by Themselves* (1856). John Brown, a slave who fled to England, published there *Slave Life in Georgia: A Narrative of the Life, Sufferings, and Escape of John Brown, a Fugitive Slave, Now in England* (1855).

The most well-known slave narratives of the period were those written by Frederick Douglass, William Wells Brown, and Harriet Jacobs. Douglass's master sent him to Baltimore, where he became literate. At age 21, he fled to Massachusetts and met abolitionist William Lloyd Garrison. Soon after he became one of the most recognized advocates for abolitionism. He authored *Narrative of the Life of Frederick Douglass, An American Slave* (1845), probably the most famous and often anthologized slave narrative. A decade later he published *My Bondage and My Freedom*. He toured the Northeast giving antislavery lectures.

Born in Kentucky but raised in St. Louis, Missouri, William Wells Brown fled to Ohio when he was 20 after having unsuccessfully tried to escape the year before with his mother. He got involved in abolitionist circles and became a regular orator in the lecture circuit, both in the United States and in Europe. His *Narrative of William W. Brown, a Fugitive Slave* (1847) was a best seller, second in popularity only to Douglass's narrative. When the Fugitive Slave Act requiring Northerners to return fugitive slaves to their owners was passed in 1850, Brown stayed in England. He would not return to the United States until 1854, after a British couple who had already bought Douglass's freedom also bought his freedom. Brown later authored *Clotel, or, The President's Daughter*, the first novel by an African American. First published in London in 1853 and later republished in America, during the 1860s Brown would write three other versions of *Clotel*. The novel centers on Clotel and her sister Althesa, Thomas Jefferson's children by a slave women. The novel shares certain features of the slave narrative genre such as the narration of an escape, which resembled the real escape of the Crafts, and was reminiscent of *Uncle Tom's Cabin* by Harriet Beecher Stowe.

Harriet Jacobs fled from her master's plantation to find shelter hidden in the attic of her grandmother's house for seven years until she was able to flee to the North. In Rochester, New York, she met Douglass, who encouraged her to make her experience known. The resulting work was *Incidents in the Life of a Slave Girl*, published in 1861, under the pseudonym "Linda Brent" and edited by Lydia Child. Its unique view into the damaging effects of slavery on a woman struck many chords with its Northern audience.

These prominent slave narratives as well as many others helped galvanize the Northern antislavery movement.

M. Carmen Gomez-Galisteo

See also: Arts: Literature, Northern; Literature, Southern; Newspapers, Northern; *Economy and Work*: Slaveholders; *Family Life and Gender Roles*: Slave Families; *Housing and Community*: Slave Quarters; *Politics and Warfare*: Abolitionists

FURTHER READING

Brown, William. W. *Narrative of William W. Brown, a Fugitive Slave. Written by Himself.* Chapel Hill: University of North Carolina, 2001. http://docsouth.unc.edu/neh/brown47/brown47.html. Accessed July 30, 2014.

Craft, William, and Ellen Craft. *Running a Thousand Miles for Freedom: The Escape of William and Ellen Craft from Slavery.* Athens: University of Georgia Press, 1999.

Douglass, Frederick. *Narrative of the Life of Frederick Douglass, An American Slave.* New York: Oxford University Press, 1999.

Jacobs, Harriet. *Incidents in the Life of a Slave Girl.* New York: W.W. Norton & Co, 2001.

Olney, James. "'I Was Born': Slave Narratives, Their Status as Autobiography and Literature." *Callaloo* 20 (1984): 46–73.

THEATER

During the Civil War, theatrical plays were more in demand than ever before, especially in the North. Productions staged during the war followed the pattern of the antebellum period, favoring the comedy of eccentric characters, the sensational play, and especially domestic melodrama. Shakespeare continued to be a favorite. In general, because the theater provided Civil War audiences with escape from their daily penuries and anxieties and had entertainment value, most theaters featured light plays.

American theater during the nineteen century was largely modeled after British drama and followed European models for the most part. However, it gradually incorporated American nationalism. Topics became distinctively American, dramatizing episodes in the recent American history, such as those used in Bronson Howard's *Saratoga*. Some plays dealt with American heroes, such as Frank Murdoch's *Davy Crockett* (1872). These were staged alongside European history plays such as Robert Montgomery Bird's *The Gladiator* and adaptations of Alexander Dumas's *The Count of Monte Cristo*, Robert Louis Stevenson's *Dr. Jekyll and Mr. Hyde*, and Mary W. Shelley's *Frankenstein*. The uniquely American *Uncle Tom's Cabin* had a dramatic adaptation that opened in September 1852 and had over 200 performances in New York.

Because drama dealt with contemporary concerns, white Americans' relationship with immigrants, Native Americans, and black slaves often appeared in plays. Characters were often stereotypical, such as the Yankee, the Indian, the Negro, and the Immigrant. Dion Boucicault's *The Octoroon; or, Life in Louisiana* (1859) depicted slavery and racism. Irish immigrants were the butt of the attack in *The Colleen Bawn* and *The Mulligan* and Chinese immigrants appeared in *A Trip to Chinatown*. *The Indian Princess; or, La Belle Sauvage* and *Metamora* dealt with Native Americans.

In the antebellum period, melodrama was the prevalent dramatic genre. Representative of the taste is *Francesca da Rimini*, a blank verse tragedy dealing with a fourteenth-century Italian woman. Melodramas featured stereotypical characters that were instantly recognizable by audiences. Mysterious locations such as Gothic castles gradually gave way to American locales and characters. Popular American melodramas of the period were *Leah the Forsaken, Under the Gaslight*, and *The Red Scarf*. Another favorite genre was the heroic play, which involved a character fighting for his freedom, reminiscent of the American Revolution.

Minstrel shows were very popular, too. They included parodies, slapstick comedy, and comic sketches, starring white actors whose faces were painted in black (blackface) and who displayed racist attitudes. Minstrel shows had a strong impact on popular music. Many of the songs became popular outside of the theater. In addition, minstrel shows' use of banjo later influenced the development of ragtime music. Their popularity reached its peak from the 1850s to the 1870s, although they were performed beginning in 1843 and continued until World War I. In New York during the 1850s there were 10 theaters that exclusively staged minstrel shows.

In the 1860s, Victorian burlesque was first introduced from England into America. It featured bawdy humor and sexual talk, with female performers playing male roles. The scandalous criticisms that it received provoked its move from theaters to saloons. Another change followed—male actors took over and the genre derived into scarcely dressed female singers and male comedians.

Temperance plays, a subgenre of melodramas whose plots revolved around the public denunciation of alcoholism, were very much in demand. Intended to move audiences to endorse temperance laws, they were most popular from the 1830s through the Civil War although they were staged and written until 1917. Examples include *The Drunkard; or, The Fallen Saved* by W. H. Smith (1844) and *The Drunkard* by P. T. Barnum (1850). Temperance plays portrayed the protagonist's destruction and the loss of his family, friends, and job because of his alcoholism. Although British plays were harsher on alcoholics, American temperance plays emphasized the possibility of redemption.

The Walnut Street Theatre in Philadelphia, founded in 1809, is the oldest American theater. Its first production, *The Rivals* (1812), was attended by President Thomas Jefferson. By 1800 theaters were scarce, being located mainly in the eastern seacoast and around New York City. The African Grove Theater, the third attempt to create an African American theater, opened in New York City in 1821 but closed down in 1823. The first play by an African American author opened there, *The Drama of King Shotaway*. William Wells Brown, a former slave, is considered the first African American playwright. He wrote *Experience; or, How to Give a Northern Man a Backbone* (1856) and *The Escape; or, A Leap for Freedom* (1858).

During the nineteenth century, there was a widespread negative social consideration of the theater and its actors. Actresses, in particular, were considered to be just a step higher than prostitutes. Dramatists of the period include James A. Herne, Bronson Howard, David Belasco, Clyde Fitch, and William Vaughn Moody as predecessors of later American drama. Because of ineffectual copyright legislation that favored piracy, dramatists were forced to become producers or actors to profit from the representation of their plays. Notable actor/dramatists or producer/dramatists include John Howard Payne, Dion Boucicault, and John Brougham. George Henry Boker, the author of 11 plays, met failure and lack of financial support, which resulted in his retirement from dramatic writing. He would not meet success until the production of *Francesca da Rimini* (first performed in 1855) in 1882, long after his retirement. It would not be until the postbellum period, with the rise of the traveling company, that dramatic authorship would be profitable. After the end of the Civil War, there was a boom of the theater, with actors receiving better social regard and higher salaries.

The most famous association of the theatrical world with the Civil War does not come from any theatrical achievement. On April 14, 1865, famed actor John Wilkes Booth shot U.S. president Abraham Lincoln during a performance of *Our American Cousin* at Ford's Theater. Booth's original plan had been to kidnap Lincoln on March 20, 1865, but Lincoln had not showed up, forcing Booth to change his plans.

The Civil War took quite a while to make its way onto the stage. It would not be until the 1880s that plays dealing with it appeared such as William Gillette's *Held by the Enemy* (1886) and *Secret Service* (1895) and Bronson Howard's *Shenandoah* (1889).

M. Carmen Gomez-Galisteo

See also: *Arts*: Literature, Northern; Literature, Southern; Slave Narratives; *Uncle Tom's Cabin* (1852); *Recreation and Social Customs*: Theatrical Productions

FURTHER READING

McConachie, Bruce A. *Melodramatic Formations: American Theatre and Society, 1820–1870*. Iowa City: University of Iowa Press, 1996.

Peterson, Bernard L., Jr. *The African American Theatre Directory, 1816–1960: A Comprehensive Guide to Early Black Theatre Organizations, Companies, Theatres and Performing Groups*. Santa Barbara, CA: ABC-CLIO, 1997.

Wilmeth, Don B., and Christopher Bigsby, ed. *The Cambridge History of American Theater: Beginnings to 1870*. New York: Cambridge University Press, 2006.

UNCLE TOM'S CABIN (1852)

Uncle Tom's Cabin; Or, Life Among the Lowly remains one of the most influential books in American literature. After its serialization in the abolitionist newspaper *National Era* (1851–1852) and publication as a novel (1852) it spurred a widespread push for the abolition of American slavery. The publication of the novel also made its author, abolitionist Harriet Beecher Stowe (1811–1896), a national celebrity. She became a spokesperson for the abolitionist movement. In addition, Stowe went on to write several more antislavery books, many of them in response to Southern critiques of her first antislavery novel.

Stowe was born in Litchfield, Connecticut, in 1811 to Roxana Foote and congregationalist minister Lyman Beecher. Born into a distinguished New England family—her brother, Henry Ward Beecher, followed in their father's footsteps to become a famous congregational preacher and her sister, Catharine Beecher, became an educational reformer who worked for women's rights—Stowe began her career writing stories for a Cincinnati literary club. Stowe was fortunate to have begun her career before writing had become sufficiently remunerative in the United States to allow men to dominate the profession.

The mother of seven children when she wrote *Uncle Tom's Cabin*, Stowe wrote about slavery with the keen eye of a mother. In particular, the 1849 death of her youngest child made her reflect upon the sting enslaved people endured when family members were sold away. She wanted her readers to understand the horrors of having a child taken away, whether by death or by slave owner. As a result, she decided to write a book about slavery and the damage inflicted upon families. Throughout the novel she highlighted the conflict between slavery and motherhood, appealing to women to end the system and its horrors.

The *National Era* published *Uncle Tom's Cabin* in serialized form between June 1851 and April 1852. Stowe based the book on accounts of runaway slaves which she had heard and read about in Ohio. She also based it on evidence of the conditions of enslaved people that she gathered while visiting Kentucky, a slave state. Although the book was a powerful condemnation of slavery and the South, it did not attract much attention until it was published as a novel in 1852.

Illustration from Harriet Beecher Stowe's *Uncle Tom's Cabin* (1852). The novel, first published in serial form, became a rallying point for abolitionists because it vividly portrayed the horrors of slavery, especially as they affected enslaved women and children. (Library of Congress)

Stowe was catapulted to international fame with the publication of *Uncle Tom's Cabin*. Thereafter, Stowe became one of America's best-paid and most famous writers. Following publication of the book she became a celebrity, speaking against slavery both in America and in Europe. She later published *A Key to Uncle Tom's Cabin* (1853), which documented the realities on which the book was based. It used evidence, often graphic, from Southern newspapers about slavery and enslaved people. Stowe published the *Key* to refute critics who tried to argue that the situations in *Uncle Tom's Cabin* were inauthentic and unrealistic. Stowe published a second antislavery novel, *Dred*, in 1856.

The publication of *Uncle Tom's Cabin* brought the issue of slavery home to millions of Americans. The story, which helped spur the abolitionist movement, was a dramatic—if somewhat patronizing—portrayal of the pain and heartbreak suffered by slaves throughout the South. It broke book sales records, selling over

500,000 copies in its first four years in print. A principal theme in Stowe's novel was the Fugitive Slave Act of 1850 which, among other things, added the stipulation that anyone who was found abetting a fugitive slave was obliged to return the escaped slave back to bondage or suffer a possible jail sentence and fine. Although *Uncle Tom's Cabin* did not start the war, it did bring into focus the severe brutality of slavery, and contributed to the divide growing between the North and the South in the 1850s.

Stowe's novel created such a controversy and had such a large impact on the move toward abolition that when she was introduced to President Abraham Lincoln in 1862, he is reputedly said to have greeted her with the words: "So you are the little woman who wrote the book that started this great war!"

Gerardo Del Guercio

See also: *Arts*: Literature, Northern; Serial Novels; Slave Narratives; *Economy and Work*: Slavery; *Family Life and Gender Roles*: Motherhood, Northern; Motherhood Southern; Womanhood, Northern; Womanhood, Southern; *Housing and Community*: Slave Life; *Politics and Warfare*: Abolitionists

FURTHER READING

Del Guercio, Gerardo. *The Fugitive Slave Law in* The Life of Frederick Douglass, an American Slave *and Harriet Beecher Stowe's* Uncle Tom's Cabin*: American Society Transforms Its Culture*. Lewiston, NY: The Edwin Mellen Press, 2013.

Jordan-Lake, Joy. *Whitewashing Uncle Tom's Cabin: Nineteenth-Century Women Novelists Respond to Stowe*. Nashville, TN: Vanderbilt University Press, 2005.

Scot, John Anthony. *Woman Against Slavery: The Story of Harriet Beecher Stowe*. New York: Thomas Y. Cromwell and Company, 1978.

Sizer, Lyde Cullen. *The Political Work of Northern Women Writers and the Civil War, 1850–1872*. Chapel Hill: University of North Carolina Press, 2000.

Stowe, Charles Edward. *The Life of Harriet Beecher Stowe: Compiled from Her Letters and Journals*. New York: Houghton, Mifflin, and Company, 1891.

Stowe, Harriet Beecher. *Uncle Tom's Cabin; or, Life Among the Lowly*. New York: Penguin Books, 1986 (1852).

White, Barbara A. *The Beecher Sisters*. New Haven, CT: Yale University Press, 2003.

WHITMAN, WALT (1819–1892)

Walt Whitman was already an established poet by the time the Civil War began. In May 1860, the third edition of his masterwork, *Leaves of Grass* (first issued in 1855), had been published. Although Whitman was not yet nationally famous or widely read, his poetry had attracted the attention of several literary luminaries.

Photograph of poet Walt Whitman. Whitman often visited wounded Union soldiers, bringing them gifts, reading to them, and helping them write letters to their loved ones. He immortalized his Civil War experiences in published newspaper articles, nonfiction collections of essays, and volumes of poetry. (Library of Congress)

Whitman could have maintained a respectable distance from the war and its unpleasantness, but instead chose to devote himself to the Union cause. From December 1862 through April 1866, Whitman made approximately 600 visits to hospitals, where he helped console and sustain the spirits of an estimated 100,000 men who were wounded or ill. Based in part on these first-hand experiences, Whitman wrote newspaper articles and poems that provide remarkably vivid impressions of the war, which marked a turning point in his life.

Born on Long Island, Whitman moved in 1841 to New York City, where he worked as a journalist and editor for more than one dozen local newspapers. When the war began in 1861, Whitman resided in Brooklyn, struggling to earn a living through limited royalties from *Leaves of Grass*, and from writing occasional articles in several newspapers. However, much of his time was spent in the company of the young, muscular men who drove horse-drawn stages throughout New York City. Although there is no solid evidence that Whitman was ever physically intimate with other men, he was obviously attracted to the stage drivers and even visited them in hospitals, when they suffered injuries resulting from the hazards of their profession.

Whitman's life in New York changed dramatically when he read a newspaper report in December 1862 that one of his younger brothers, George Washington Whitman (1829–1901), was wounded while serving as an officer with the 51st Regiment of New York Volunteers in the Battle of Fredericksburg. Whitman immediately traveled to Washington—where many of the wounded were taken—and then to Fredericksburg, Virginia, where he finally found his brother. Although his brother's wound was not life-threatening, Whitman was disturbed by the chaos and general lack of attention afforded the sick and wounded in the hospital wards he visited. Determined to help—and perhaps also motivated by the opportunity to sit by the bedsides of young men—Whitman decided to remain in Washington and devote himself to the task.

Through referrals from his publisher, Whitman found part-time work as a copyist, which meant that he duplicated letters, memoranda, and other paperwork for the Union Army for several hours each morning. Then his afternoons and evenings were spent visiting men in hospital wards around the city. When he could afford to do so, he brought them small gifts, such as candy, tobacco, fruit, reading materials, and articles of clothing, as well as writing supplies, so that they could correspond with their families. Because not all men were literate, Whitman often served as amanuensis, writing in his own hand the letters they dictated.

Although older historical sources occasionally refer to Whitman as a Civil War nurse or wound-dresser, he never formally held any such position—though he could and did assist medical nurses in their work. Rather Whitman's support was primarily emotional and spiritual: serving as an avuncular, comforting presence, sometimes even as the sick and wounded lay dying in hospitals where medical personnel did not yet understand the need for proper sanitation and disinfection.

As a professional poet and journalist, Whitman also used the hospital visits to gather firsthand material for his writings. For instance, several lengthy articles—filled with vivid descriptions of the hospital environments he visited—were published in the *New York Times*, such as "The Great Army of the Sick" (February 26, 1863) and "Washington in the Hot Season" (August 16, 1863). He wrote poems all during the war years, though they were not published until March 1865, when the first edition of *Drum-Taps* (with 53 poems) was issued. In contrast to *Leaves of Grass*, the poems of *Drum-Taps*—such as "A Sight in Camp in the Daybreak Gray and Dim" and "By the Bivouac's Fitful Flame"—were much more understated, almost minimalist in their realistic depictions of camp life and the rows of cots in hospital tents.

Whitman added 18 more poems for *Sequel to Drum-Taps*, published in October 1865, which included two of his best-known poems—"When Lilacs Last in the Door-Yard Bloom'd" and "O Captain! My Captain!"—both sorrowful elegies on the death of President Abraham Lincoln. Whitman also published two nonfiction accounts of his wartime experiences: *Memoranda During the War* (1875), a collection of essays that relied heavily on notes made during his hospital visits; and *Specimen Days* (1882), which was the closest Whitman ever came to writing an autobiography—borrowing many sections from *Memoranda During the War* to cover the Civil War years.

While visiting hospitals, Whitman often stayed awake all night to tend to patients, and presumably came in contact with cases of typhoid fever and malaria. His own health, both physical and emotional, certainly suffered as a result. In June 1864, Whitman was forced to return to Brooklyn for six months of convalescence and recuperation, before coming back to Washington in January 1865 and resuming his visits to hospitals, albeit less frequently. By the time the war ended, Whitman was in declining health, though not quite 46 years old. The book, *The Good Gray Poet: A Vindication*, published in 1866 by Whitman's friend William Douglas O'Connor, celebrated the poet's wartime service in the hospitals, noting how Whitman had worked so tirelessly and selflessly to soothe and console those in need that he turned gray in the process.

In 1873, Whitman suffered a paralytic stroke, which forced him to move from Washington into the home of his brother George in Camden, New Jersey. He died in Camden 19 years later.

James I. Deutsch

See also: *Arts*: Letter Writing; Newspapers, Northern; Poetry; *Science and Technology*: Hospitals; Nursing; Wounds, Treatment of

FURTHER READING

Epstein, Daniel Mark. *Lincoln and Whitman: Parallel Lives in Civil War Washington.* New York: Ballantine Books, 2004.

Genoways, Ted. *Walt Whitman and the Civil War: America's Poet During the Lost Years of 1860–1862.* Berkeley: University of California Press, 2009.

Morris, Roy, Jr. *The Better Angel: Walt Whitman in the Civil War.* New York: Oxford University Press, 2000.

Roper, Robert. *Now the Drum of War: Walt Whitman and His Brothers in the Civil War.* New York: Walker & Co., 2008.

CLOTHING, FASHION, AND APPEARANCE

INTRODUCTION

The elaborate dress worn by nineteenth-century Americans indicated a person's status, age, and position. Those on the Civil War home front dressed in ways appropriate to their station in life as well as to their loyalties. On the battlefield, soldiers' uniforms helped distinguish men by rank; they could also demonstrate where a regiment was from and whether it fought for the Union or the Confederacy.

Women's dress and fashion varied by region and class. When possible, many nineteenth-century women followed the fashions highlighted in *Godey's Ladies Book*. Even if they could not wear the styles shown in the magazine, they tried to imitate them in some way. Hoop skirts became commonplace. Well-to-do women wore jewelry to complement their fashions and show off their wealth. They also strove to keep up with personal hygiene.

Social situations also dictated the type of dress that people in the North and South could wear at particular times in their lives. Children in both regions dressed similarly, with casual loose fitting clothes for small children and dress modeled on that of adults as they grew older. When a woman was in mourning, she wore a widow's weeds in dark colors. Mourning dress became increasingly common as the war dragged on and more men died on the battlefield.

Wartime shortages, especially in the South, required that women of all classes make do with outdated dresses and rough fabrics. They wore dresses until they wore out, made new dresses or children's clothes from old dresses, and made dresses from homespun. For Southern women, the wearing of homespun, a rough homemade cloth, became a badge of patriotism and Confederate loyalty. Their use of material usually restricted to slaves was refashioned as a way to show defiance toward the Union.

Women in both North and South created sewing societies in their communities. These groups worked to make uniforms, undergarments, shirts, and socks for the soldiers at the front. These supplies were invaluable to the men on the

75

battlefield. In addition to producing goods for the soldiers, the societies helped women foster friendships and community bonds.

Although necessary to both war efforts, the uniforms created by women in sewing societies were not always identical to one another. The guidelines provided by each government as to what the uniforms should look like ensured that most soldiers on each side wore similar uniforms, but they were not perfectly matched. However, despite other variations most Union soldiers wore dark blue and most Confederates wore gray uniforms.

CHILDREN'S DRESS, CONFEDERATE

As a result of shortages during the Civil War, clothing for children, women, and men underwent numerous shifts. Families had to make do with old clothing as well as with homespun materials.

Ambrotype taken in 1862 or 1863 and labeled *Dora Allison, Little Miss Bonnie Blue, the light of the Confederacy* by photographer Charles R. Rees. Three- or four-year-old Dora Allison's fancy dress, shoes, and bonnet attest to her family's wealth. She also wears black mourning ribbons on her sleeves. (Library of Congress)

Throughout the nineteenth century, both young boys and girls dressed similarly. They commonly donned ankle-length pantalets, which were then topped by loose dresses or smocks reaching to the knees. The loose nature of the clothing made it easier for children to be active and play. The wardrobe of many children consisted of two outfits, one for Sundays and other special occasions and the other for everyday casual wear. As young girls grew older, their skirts grew in length and were often covered by pinafores, or white aprons covering the front of dresses from the shoulders to the shins. By the age of six, young boys switched from dressing similarly to girls to wearing pants; this practice was referred to as "breeching."

During the 1860s, sailor suits inspired by the Prince of Wales, Albert Edward, who wore a scaled-down version of a sailor suit of the Royal British Navy during a visit to the Channel Islands in 1846, became popular in the United States. During the Prince of Wales's visit to the Channel Islands, his portrait was painted and a set of engravings was made, which helped popularize the look in the United States. Throughout the Civil War, Zouave jackets were popular for young girls. The Zouave jacket was a colorfully braided, open front jacket influenced by the Zouaves, a name given to light infantry regiments in the French Army. Children of this era were commonly considered small versions of adults; therefore their clothing was similar to that of older men and women, albeit with restrictions due to wartime shortages.

Throughout the Civil War, cotton production in the South was at a virtual standstill. Wool production, however, continued to expand and was increasingly modernized in the North. Because of this reality, clothes in the South became extremely expensive. Toward the end of the war, bonnets for young girls in the South were essentially nonexistent. Clothing was commonly made from scraps or from previously used fabrics, and most items were handed down from child to child. Shoes were one of the most difficult items to acquire due to the increased use of leather for wartime activities, so many people considered a pair of shoes a prized possession.

Stylistically, children's clothing rivaled women's fashions in complexity and ornamentation. Some middle- and upper-class children were dressed in layers of clothing often constructed of impractical fabrics. Gauze, silk, wool, and taffeta were often suggested fabrics for children's dress in ladies' magazines. However, with the decrease in cotton production in the South, alternative fabrics came to dominate clothing production for women, men, and children. Printed fabrics tended to be small geometric or abstract designs, which allowed for the economical use of fabric since it was easier to match geometric prints, and resulted in less waste. Colorful braids or ribbons were popular trims for children and women's clothing. In rural areas, like those in the South, children's clothing was more practical and similar to that of their parents. Muslin and cotton (when available) were the fabrics of choice. The main difference between a woman's attire and that of a girl's was that a young girls' skirt was considerably shorter than a woman's, ending at mid-calf. Like her mother, a little girl wore a chemise, or shift, as the basic undergarment. By the age of seven, young girls began wearing a hoop under their skirts. This style was similar to older women's hoop skirts of the time, which were worn to extend the skirt of a woman's dress into the fashionable silhouette of the time.

Boys who worked for the Confederacy had a specific type of clothing. Early in the war, the Confederate Army used armored rams and gunboats, which necessitated the assistance of powder monkeys. Powder monkeys were boys as young as 12 who assisted navy men in loading guns aboard fighting vessels. Powder monkeys were outfitted in middies, a sailor inspired blouse, and flared trousers, which were patterned after sailor uniforms. Although photographs display a variety of details in the uniforms of powder monkeys, they commonly featured a yoke, a pattern piece fitted around the neck and shoulders, with a dropped-shoulder line across the chest, and a small panel or yoke at the neck. Black kerchiefs were also part of the uniform and were commonly tied in the front. The powder monkey's trousers were called slops and had a front fly and button down pockets, which buttoned onto the middy. The uniform was finished off with a sailor's tam, or hat, that was frequently the same color as the kerchief.

Young boys who went to war as drummers for Confederate infantry units also had a particular style of clothing. Often between the ages of 10 and 15, these boys' uniforms were usually like those of the men in their regiments. In the early years of the war, the drummers often wore state militia uniforms. Near the end of the conflict, drummers were commonly depicted wearing regulation Confederate uniforms and overcoats. Young men who served during the Civil War often struggled to secure child-sized shoes, socks, and shirts, which were difficult to procure due to their small size.

Jessica Schwartz

See also: *Clothing, Fashion, and Appearance*: Children's Dress, Union; Clothing, Style and Function; Fashion; Homespun; Hoop Skirts; Shortages, Clothing; Textiles; Undergarments; *Economy and Work*: Rural Life, Southern; Slaveholders; Urban Life, Southern; *Family Life and Gender Roles*: Childhood and Adolescence, Southern; Young Men; Young Women; *Politics and Warfare*: Blockades

FURTHER READING

Eubank, Phyllis G., and Keith Tortora. *Survey of Historic Costume: Fourth Edition.* New York: Fairchild Publications, Inc., 2005.

Gash, Lyn. *Victorian Clothes.* Sussex, UK: Wayland Ltd, 1993.

Harris, Priscilla Dalrymple. *American Victoria Costume in Early Photographs.* New York: Dover Publications, Inc., 1991.

Havelin, Kate. *Hoopskirts, Union Blues, and Confederate Grays: Civil War Fashions from 1861 to 1865.* Minneapolis, MN: Twenty-First Century Books, 2012.

Volo, Dorothy Denneen, and Volo, James M. *Daily life in Civil War America.* Westport, CT: Greenwood Press, 1998.

Worrell, Estelle Ansley. *Children's Costume in America 1607–1910.* New York: Charles Scribner's Sons, 1980.

CHILDREN'S DRESS, UNION

During the Civil War, clothing for women, men, and children was mostly dictated by which materials were available. In the Union, wool production increased during the war, while cotton production faltered in the Confederacy.

The uniforms of Union soldiers varied widely due to material shortages, but they were generally constructed in a shade of sky blue and were influenced stylistically by the French Army. Although the uniforms of Union soldiers influenced what young boys wore during the Civil War, the clothing of young girls and boys generally followed that of older women and men of the time. Wartime shortages also dictated the clothing worn by children.

The war also gave rise to various fads in children's clothing. These fads included Zouave jackets for young girls, sailor suits for young boys, and military influences in clothing for both young girls and boys. The Zouave jacket was a colorfully braided, open front jacket influenced by the Zouaves, a name given to light infantry regiments in the French Army. Sailor suits gained popularity in the United States during the 1860s after the Prince of Wales, Albert Edward, wore a scaled down version of a sailor suit of the Royal British Navy during a visit to the Channel Islands in 1846. During his visit to the Channel Islands, the prince's portrait was painted and a set of engravings made, thus easily disseminating the style in the United States. Another popular style was that of the Garibaldi shirt, which was worn with a full skirt that had a wide band of contrasting color material at the hem. The

Ambrotype of unidentified boy in Union Zouave uniform with a drum. Boys who served as drummers in the Union Army were furnished with clothes that mimicked those of soldiers in their unit. (Library of Congress)

Garibaldi shirt was a red wool shirt that referenced the Italian patriot Giuseppe Garibaldi, and was first popularized in 1860s. Young boys also wore the Garibaldi shirt with full pants, which were cut off at the knee. The Garibaldi shirt is considered the direct ancestor of the modern woman's blouse.

Those living within the Union often had access to a larger amount of products, which were available for trade or purchase, than did their Southern counterparts. Because of this availability of manufactured goods, children living in the Union often had more choices in clothing than those living in the Confederate States. However, in both the South and the North, wartime clothing was commonly made from scraps or previously used fabrics, and most items were handed down from child to child. Due to the wartime economy, shortages affected nearly everyone across the nation.

Through the analysis of period paintings and photographs, scholars have been able to discern information regarding the clothing of young boys who had an active role in the war. One folk painting by Estelle Ansley Worrell, depicts Major General William T. Sherman, a Union commander, and his troops marching through the Confederate state of Georgia. In this painting are two Union drummer boys wearing dark blue shirts, red trousers, tan gaiters (garments worn over the shoe and lower pant leg to provide personal protection) and red caps similar to those worn by Zouaves. These caps were red stocking caps with flat hard crowns and a cord with a tassel hanging from the center. The drums the boys carry are tan and painted with eagles, red metal strips, and black tension cords. This depiction of the young Union drummer boys provides insight into the uniforms worn by drummer boys in the Union Army. During the Civil War, young boys went to war as drummers for the Union. Photographs and paintings show these young boys to have been between the ages of 10 and 15. The drummer boys commonly wore uniforms similar to those of the men in their regiment. Early in the conflict, drummer boys often wore state militia uniforms. As the war progressed, the drummer boys wore regulation Union uniforms and overcoats.

Young girls often wore clothing similar in complexity and ornamentation to that of women's fashion of the time. During the 1860s, the prevailing silhouette for young girls and women consisted of a flat front and a fuller back. Cage crinolines, which helped support the voluminous layers of a woman's ensemble, became popular in the late 1850s and were still in use throughout the 1860s. Various styles of the cage crinoline were developed to accommodate the changing silhouettes. A single petticoat, or an undergarment worn under a skirt or dress, was often decorated with lace, embroidery, or small tucks and was placed over the hoop. Although young girls did not wear hoops like older women during the 1860s, their skirts did echo the popular style of wide, voluminous skirts. Throughout the war, the availability of fabrics dictated whether a young girl or woman's petticoat would be extensively or simply decorated. The neckline of a young girl's bodice was high during the 1860s and the widths of skirts increased throughout the decade, keeping in line with the styles of older women. The main difference between the skirt of a young girl and that of a woman's was that girls' skirts were considerably shorter, ending about mid-calf. As a girl grew in age, so too did the length of her skirts. By the age of 16, a girl's skirt rested around two inches above her ankle. Throughout the Civil War, women and young girls wore corsets, which were popular until the end of the nineteenth century. Although there was much disagreement regarding the effects of tight lacing and corsets, these elements of a woman's wardrobe remained in vogue for young women until the 1890s.

Jessica Schwartz

See also: *Clothing, Fashion, and Appearance*: Children's Dress, Confederate; Clothing, Style and Function; Fashion; Homespun; Hoop Skirts; Shortages, Clothing; Textiles; Undergarments; *Economy and Work*: Rural Life, Northern; Slaveholders; Urban Life, Northern; *Family Life and Gender Roles*: Childhood and Adolescence, Southern; Young Men; Young Women; *Politics and Warfare*: Blockades

FURTHER READING

Eubank, Phyllis G., and Keith Tortora. *Survey of Historic Costume: Fourth Edition*. New York: Fairchild Publications, Inc., 2005.

Gash, Lyn. *Victorian Clothes*. Sussex, UK: Wayland Ltd, 1993.

Harris, Priscilla Dalrymple. *American Victorian Costume in Early Photographs*. New York: Dover Publications, Inc., 1991.

Havelin, Kate. *Hoopskirts, Union Blues, and Confederate Grays: Civil War Fashions from 1861 to 1865*. Minneapolis, MN: Twenty-First Century Books, 2012.

Volo, Dorothy Denneen, and Volo, James M. *Daily Life in Civil War America*. Westport, CT: Greenwood Press, 1998.

Worrell, Estelle Ansley. *Children's Costume in America 1607–1910*. New York: Charles Scribner's Sons, 1980.

CLOTHING, STATUS AND POSITION

What people wore in the nineteenth century revealed their wealth and place in society. Dress could be used to highlight a person's wealth. It was also used to indicate a woman's marital status or widowhood as well as transitions from childhood to young adulthood. It further distinguished soldiers from civilians and slaves from free people.

With the exception of the dress of slaves, fashion trends proved remarkably similar through the United States during the late antebellum and early Victorian eras, across regional and class lines. Northern and Southern fashion tastes collectively lagged behind those of Europeans. Fashion plates or cut-out patterns appeared in American magazines two years after a fashion trend had caught on in Europe. Although the upper classes adopted European fashions first, the middle and lower classes also seized upon these fashions, albeit with different fabrics, dyes, and tailoring quality. Though there were variations across regional and economic class lines, American fashion between the late antebellum and early Victorian periods was remarkably consistent.

Clothing reflected status during the antebellum period primarily through colors and fabrics. Americans, regardless of class or region, preferred darker colors and generally stayed away from brighter colors, except in and around New Orleans. European influences shaped American tastes, but styles and cloth varied by region. From the 1840s through the Civil War, the styles preferred by the newly coronated Queen Victoria and Prince Albert set the tone for American fashion especially for men, though women often preferred French fashions when they were available. Although access to the materials and tailoring necessary to mimic those styles usually remained the prerogatives of upper-class Southerners and middle-to-upper–class Northerners, the general patterns and bodily accents penetrated to the lower and laboring orders as well.

Fashion preferences during the antebellum and Victorian periods usually derived from paintings, etchings, and references in literature. Most of these renderings depicted the upper and middle classes—those most capable of procuring the services of an artist and those most likely depicted in contemporary novels. In general, female fashions from the 1840s for the upper classes, North and South, tended to exaggerate female bodily dimensions by accentuating thin waistlines and more rounded hips. The only significant difference between the 1840s and 1850s was the tendency away from more cone-shaped dresses to those of a more bell-shaped design. Northern and Southern women generally shunned bright colors opting instead for whites and darker, though often shiny, greens, reds, and blues. All of these colors came from expensive dyes, so they exuded class status. Ordinary day clothes tended to mimic the fancier variety, though often with less bodice-structured dress diameter. Antebellum and early Victorian ladies generally preferred softer fabrics like cottons and silks as well as shoes or boots constructed of leather, suede or kid.

Throughout the 1850s and 1860s, hoop skirts decreased in diameter and became more ruffled to reveal either matching or contrasting underskirts, moving closer and closer to the "bustle design" of the late 1860s and 1870s. Little girls donned fashions similar to their mothers, except in two general areas. First, the skirts worn by young girls tended to stop about mid-calf. The more practical shorter skirt reflected the fact that children were likely to get clothing dirty by not picking up their skirts as they walked. Necklines also changed for children. Young girls tended to wear v-necks instead of collars that crested around the neck.

Male fashions tended to accentuate the more angular construction of the masculine anatomy. Longer coats were preferred in the 1840s, while waistcoats became the fashion trope of the years immediately preceding the Civil War. Men often included shoulder padding in their waistcoats, which fell to roughly belt-length. Pants tended to be cut to reveal thin waistlines and were constructed durably to suggest physical activities like horseriding. Like that of their female counterparts, men's fashion differed between North and South, by region and class. During the Civil War, waistcoats started hanging below the belt line as heftier waistlines suggested opulence. The clothing style of young boys was similar to that of older men until the introduction of the knickerbocker suit in the late 1840s.

Clothing among the enslaved people varied according to two criteria. First, the wealth and status of the master provided a good indication of the quality and styles worn by their slaves. Field hands wore a soft, durable cloth referred to as "negro cloth," which was designed to withstand the rigors of plantation labor. Second, field hands generally dressed in a utilitarian fashion, whereas house servants usually donned styles more similar to the master's family. In this case, male servants were usually provided with two or three suits per year, and females with as many as five outfits.

At war, uniforms between North and South proved so similar as to cause battlefield confusion. Often, Confederates simply wore uniforms that they had seized from federal arsenals or from prisoners of war. At the Battle of Bull Run (Manassas), Confederate troops fired upon a unit of their own because they were wearing uniforms of a sky-blue color. Uniforms for both North and South were made from wool, though as the war progressed, Confederates increasingly chose gray, black, or butternut. Federal troops, meanwhile, wore sky-blue trousers and dark blue jackets in an increasing effort to distinguish themselves from Confederate troops wearing what had been Union-issued uniforms. Whereas Confederate troops were oftentimes called upon to provide their own shoes, Union troops were issued a standard leather shoe for infantry and leather boots for cavalry. For officers, Federals were issued a uniform that differed slightly from those of enlisted men, and sometimes were provided an evening coat. Confederate officers either provided their own individually styled uniforms or wore standard-issue uniforms with some type of home-embroidered distinctiveness.

Mark A. Panuthos

See also: Clothing, Fashion, and Appearance: Children's Dress, Confederate; Children's Dress, Union; Clothing, Style and Function; Fashion; Homespun; Hoop Skirts; Jewelry; Men's Dress, Confederate Civilian; Men's Dress, Union Civilian; Mourning Clothes; Shortages, Clothing; Undergarments; Uniforms, Confederate; Uniforms, Union; Women's Dress, Confederate; Women's Dress, Union; *Economy and Work*: Rural Life, Northern; Rural Life, Southern; Urban Life, Northern; Urban Life, Southern

FURTHER READING

Dhalle, Kathy. "Bits of Blue and Gray: American Civil War Fashion." November 2001. http://www.bitsofblueandgray.com/nov2001.htm. Accessed July 31, 2014.

1860s Fashion Plates. Metropolitan Museum of Art Libraries. http://cdm16028.contentdm. oclc.org/cdm/search/collection/p15324coll12/searchterm/186*/field/title/mode/all/ conn/and/order/nosort. Accessed July 31, 2014.

Volo, Dorothy Deneen, and James M. *Daily Life in the Civil War*. Westport, CT: Greenwood Press, 1988.

Wiley, Bell Irvin. *The Life of Billy Yank*. Baton Rogue: Louisiana State University Press, 1952.

Wiley, Bell Irvin. *The Life of Johnny Reb*. Baton Rouge: Louisiana State University Press, 1952.

CLOTHING, STYLE AND FUNCTION

The function of clothing in the mid-nineteenth century served several purposes. It protected people from the elements and kept them warm. Clothing also satisfied the artistic expression of citizens as they adopted favorite styles, patterns, and colors. In addition, clothing sent social messages about power, influence, privilege, work, and gender.

In the mid-nineteenth century, Americans with considerable wealth wore Victorian-style clothing. Adopting the fashion trends from Great Britain, men wore knee-length frock coats for business and mid-thigh length sack coats for less formal occasions. They wore trousers made by a tailor or pants made in a factory instead of breeches. They also wore white shirts collared by cravats, neck cloths, and mufflers in various colors, but black satin was worn most often at the neck. The introduction of the lock-stitch sewing machine by 1850 made it possible to purchase ready-made shirts. Also available were partially made shirts which could be completed by a seamstress at home.

Vests and hats were common. Top hats made of wool or beaver pelt adorned the head of many a politician, businessman, minister, attorney, and undertaker. Stovepipe hats, made famous by President Abraham Lincoln, were just a taller version of the top hat. Most men wore them for style and warmth. Lincoln also wore his to store scrapes of handwritten papers. By 1860 middle-class men began to wear a melon-shaped, hard felt hat called a derby. Dress shoes were made of leather with elastic sides and a tab in the back allowing for more ease in pulling the shoes on the feet. Shoes for both right and left feet were the same.

Farmers and laborers wore shirts of coarse linen. Two shirts were often worn to prevent one from getting dirty and to mask body order. As was the Victorian custom, no man was seen in public with his shirt off. Coats were loose and straight and pants were made of cotton, wool, canvas, or denim. Checked vests were popular in greens, blues, and reds. The riding boots men wore were either turn-down boots or Wellingtons, which had a front that came up over the knee and a back lower in the bend of the knee. Boys wore knickerbockers and their jackets were occasionally cut away in front and fastened by a single button at the neck.

Wealthy women's daytime attire consisted of dresses with a solid bodice and long sleeves made in soft colors with patterns such as small flowers. During the war, with new clothing material hard to come by, often full-length skirts were paired with modest high collared blouses. Working women did not wear the so-called daytime dress, but instead while farming, cooking, cleaning, and raising children they wore what was called the camp dress. These were dresses made of sturdy cotton gathered at the waist while others hung straight down. Working women always wore aprons over the dresses to help them stay clean. Women's shoes came in several styles. Most common were front lace up boots and shoes either in a low or in a high heel. Embroidered shoes were also very popular. Girls wore stays instead of corsets with two rows of buttons. The lower row buttoned the drawers and the higher set buttoned a hoop skirt.

Unlike the daytime dress, an upper-class woman's evening gown was an elaborate creation. These dresses had design elements like tiered layered skirts or pagoda sleeves, and the gowns themselves were made of silk. The gowns had huge bell-shaped skirts, with off the shoulder necklines, and ribbons, bows, and piping adorned the dress. Petticoats, crinoline, corsets, and chemises were worn under the gown.

Another major function of mid-nineteenth century clothing was to identify people in mourning. Proper widows were expected to wear black mourning clothing for as long as three years. There was a complexity to etiquette rules that extended to mourning periods at the death of children, infants, parents, siblings, and other relatives. Emphasizing gender difference, men were expected to wear mourning black but for a much shorter period than women did. For example, widowers wore a black hatband or armband for only three months.

During the 1850s some women started to believe that their clothing reflected their subservient status in society. Elizabeth Smith Miller, cousin of women's rights organizer Elizabeth Cady Stanton, designed a new dress she called "Miller's Freedom Dress." With a skirt length just below the knees covering Turkish-style trousers, the dress did not gain in popularity, but it did capture the attention of some who argued that it clouded the traditional understanding of masculinity and femininity and that it was indecent.

Native Americans in the middle of the nineteenth century wore a mixture of traditional and Western-style clothing. The primary material available to them was leather. Animal hides used included deer, elk, big horned sheep, and bison. Beads, fringe, and the decorative placement of shells and feathers were used as ornamentation to symbolize family membership, position within the tribe, or great courage in hunting or battle. With little money or credit to purchase standard white people's clothing, and with increasingly limited natural resources available to make clothing, the Native American population often suffered from punishing exposure to the elements.

Like Native Americans, enslaved African American also suffered unspeakable hardships and cruelties, and a major contributor to their condition was inadequate clothing. Masters distributed clothing twice per year. Men generally received two cotton shirts, a pair of woolen or cotton pants, and a jacket every six months. Women received six yards of cotton shirting or woolen cloth, six yards of cotton drilling, a needle, thread, and buttons. The clothing was made of a burlap material that was quite rough. Children received less clothing than did adults. Enslaved people who worked in the plantation house were provided with better clothing than the field hands, but not necessarily in the elaborate style portrayed in later movies and novels. Most of their clothes were ill-fitting hand-me-downs from the white family. For enslaved people, shoes were a big problem. Shoes were made one size, and consequently, most enslaved people suffered with heel spurs, bunions, and ingrown toenails. All had to make due. Many of the clothes and all of the shoes slaves wore were manufactured in the North.

Thomas Army

See also: Clothing, Fashion, and Appearance: Children's Dress, Confederate; Children's Dress, Union; Clothing, Status and Position; Dress, Slaves; Fashion; Homespun; Men's Dress, Confederate Civilian; Men's Dress, Union Civilian; Mourning Clothes; Shortages, Clothing; Textiles; Undergarments; Uniforms, Confederate; Uniforms, Union; Women's Dress, Confederate; Women's Dress, Union; *Housing and Community*: Slave Life

FURTHER READING

Anonymous, *Manners and Rules of Good Society, or, Solecisms to Be Avoided*. London: Frederick Warne & Company, 1887.

Douglass, Frederick. "Narrative of the Life of Frederick Douglass, an American Slave." In Henry Louis Gates, Jr., ed. *The Classic Slave Narratives*. New York: Signet Classics, 2002, pp. 323–436.

Wilcox, R. Turner. *Five Centuries of American Costume*. New York: Charles Scribner's Sons, 1963.

Worrell, Estelle Ansley. *Early American Costume*. Harrisburg, PA: Stackpole Books, 1975.

DRESS, SLAVES

Slave clothing was utilitarian, shaped by the availability of materials and to a lesser extent by African heritage, mostly in headdress and accessories. Slaves came from many different cultures in mainly West Africa, only to be united under slavery in the United States. By the Civil War, many enslaved African American had been born in the United States and had no direct contact with or knowledge of Africa. Because the slaveholding states covered a large geographic area, there was no one definitive slave dress. The climate was varied, from the eastern seaboard states to the Southwest. The way enslaved people were treated and clothed also varied by the slaveholders themselves. In general, however, slave clothing was plain, utilitarian, and lacking in individuality.

Most of what is known about slave clothing comes from slave narratives, many of which were recorded as a Works Progress Administration (WPA) project in the 1930s, and from descriptions by eyewitnesses to slave ship voyages and slave auctions. Little slave clothing has been preserved. Although slave clothing was often described in advertisements for runaways, there are few photographs.

Cloth and wool might be grown on plantations and spun, woven, and sewn on site, or it could be purchased commercially. Slaveholders had to clothe their slaves, if only to

Photograph of an enslaved family in a cotton field near Savannah, ca. 1860. Slave clothing was utilitarian and was generally made of rough material or was handed down from slaveholders. (Bettmann/Corbis)

protect their property. Sometimes masters or mistresses would give clothing to the slaves, but most often they left clothing manufacture to the enslaved people themselves; clothes were homespun, and often inadequate for the weather and living conditions. The fabric used by enslaved people was mostly white or black, but might be dyed blue from indigo or brown using bark, leaves, and berries. Calico was considered dressy. Some homespun was checked or striped. Young girls (age 14 and over) wore blue, white, and black. Children mostly wore brown.

Fabrics were rough and uncomfortable. Patterns were generic and unfitted, cut without regard to gender or size, and not made to fit any particular person. Clothes were boxy and meant to be quickly sewn. "Tow," a rough fabric from flax, was used for work clothes. Booker T. Washington (1856–1915) compared the ordeal of wearing flax to having being pricked by pins all over his body. Hemp also made rough clothing. Burlap bags and grocery sacks were often turned into clothing simply by cutting out holes for arms and head.

There was a hierarchy among enslaved people in the clothing they wore. House slaves, especially those who would interact with visitors to the plantation household, wore livery or suits, and often would receive hand-me-downs from their masters. Drivers' "uniforms" might consist of tall hats, brass buttons, and boots. Maids had starched white aprons. Slaveholders strictly controlled—designed, chose, and regulated—the clothing worn by their house slaves. Enslaved people with a skill such as blacksmithing might dress in a manner similar to their white counterparts. Slave dress also varied by geographic region.

Although there was diversity among house or urban slaves' clothing, field or "crop negroes" mostly wore white or blue garments made of osnaburg, a coarse linen. Women wore fitted tops, called waistcoats, with sleeves and a full long skirt. Men and women would have fitted woolen jackets for winter. Men wore coarse linen breeches. A woven wool called "plains" or "Negro cloth" was used for winter jackets. Women wore quilted or woolen undergarments to keep warm in winter. These pantalets were worn under skirts that they tied above the knees. Underwear and outerwear was worn in winter only. Some enslaved people reported never having underwear. Clothing was distributed seasonally or annually, and was rarely adequate.

Both boys and girls wore identical long shirts, called a shirt if boys wore it and a dress if a girl wore it. Boys were dressed in long pants when grown, which could mean anywhere between ages 10 to 15, or even as late as age 21. They would be given pants if going off the plantation. Children in rural settings often went naked, and some had no shoes.

Enslaved people in urban areas could hire themselves out to earn money and buy clothing. Plantation slaves might be able to work at night by selling eggs, weaving baskets, or hunting to earn money to purchase clothing, but most was homemade. In addition, slaves sometimes got hand-me-downs from their masters and wore these nicer clothes to church. To save wear, they would carry their shoes until close to the church before putting them on. They might wear berries or chestnuts as necklaces, both for decoration and for health, and for special events such as church, marriages, or funerals.

If enslaved people had socks or stockings, they were hand knit. However, they often wore sacks wrapped around their ankles and feet to keep warm and protect their feet from hard shoes. Booker T. Washington wore awkward and uncomfortable shoes made of wood. Some plantations had shoemakers, but more often itinerant cobblers would make shoes. Enslaved people often worked barefoot, even in winter and snow. Some slaves expressed a preference for being barefoot in the summers. Most who had shoes described them as heavy brogans (pronounced bro-*gans)*, a thick heavy ankle high shoe. The soles were wood or leather attached to leather uppers with pegs, with brass studs at the toes. The brass tacks might poke through at ankles and toes and become painful to wear, but many slaves were required to wear them anyway. They were heavy, stiff, inflexible, and uncomfortable. These shoes were not distinguished by left or right, often did not have holes for laces, and might only be in small medium or large. One narrative described how enslaved people had their feet measured for shoes in the fall. If the shoes arrived and did not fit, they had to wear them anyway or go barefoot. One slave commented that brogans never wore out, people just outgrew them. For church, a slave might try to improve the look of the shoes by "polishing" them with soot and egg white. Variations of brogans were called red russets, red rippers, and red russells. They were stiff, made from untanned cowhide with the hair on the outside. If the shoes were too large, they might be stuffed with paper. The paper stuffing led to the nickname of "program shoes" for those stuffed with theater programs.

Enslaved people wore several types of hats. Men and women would wear straw or cloth brimmed bonnets, sometimes tied on with ribbons, for work in the field. Women's hats might be dressed up with ruffles and then called poke bonnets. Hats were mostly homemade and woven with straw, although they were sometimes given by the master or mistress. Sunhats with capes covering ears and necks could be hot in the summer, but many slaves were required to keep them tied under their chins. Handkerchiefs tied around the head as well as more elaborately wrapped turbans were also used a head covering for slave women.

Jane Brodsky Fitzpatrick

See also: *Clothing, Fashion, and Appearance*: Homespun; Shortages, Clothing; *Family Life and Gender Roles*: Slave Families

FURTHER READING

Foster, Helen Bradley. *"New Raiments of Self": African American Clothing in the Antebellum South.* New York: Berg, 1997.

Library of Congress. *Born in Slavery: Slave Narratives from the Federal Writers' Project, 1936–1938.* http://memory.loc.gov/ammem/snhtml/snhome.html. Accessed July 31, 2014.

Washington, Booker T. *Up from Slavery: An Autobiography.* New York: Dodd Mead, 1965.

WNET. *"The Slave Experience: Men Women and Gender, in Slavery and the Making of America."* 2009. http://www.pbs.org/wnet/slavery/experience/gender/feature.html. Accessed July 31, 2014.

FASHION

Fashion in the Civil War varied by social and economic status, but was essentially the same across the country, north and south, west and east. Conformity, not individuality, was valued. Those who could not afford or obtain finer fabrics or hoops would approximate and adapt the fashionable look according to their means. Magazines such as *Godey's Lady's Book* offered pictures of and recommendations on the latest fashions, including patterns and instructions. By the end of the war, even as the South suffered shortages of materials, women continued to dress fashionably, although possibly wearing hand-me-downs and clothes refashioned from existing garments.

Women's dresses were floor-length throughout the war years. The ideal feminine shape was one with a narrow waist emphasized by wide shoulders and large skirts. If working in fields or in factories, women might forego hoops and corsets, but for any social events, corsets were considered essential for proper appearance. Hoops were used as crinolines, lighter in weight than layers of many petticoats needed to support and ensure the fullness of a large skirt. Between the beginning and the end of the war, dress profiles evolved from skirts that were huge and circular at the bottom to those that were elliptical and had a flat front profile.

Bodices or waists, today called blouses, were tightly fitted and in colors contrasting with the skirt. The fashionable bright red Garibaldi shirt (patterned on the shirt worn by the Italian independence fighter Giuseppe Garibaldi), with baggy sleeves, was a precursor to the modern blouse, and was worn by men and women of all ages. Braid trim, emulating military uniforms, was also popular in women's and children's clothing. During the war, homespun fabric became a source of patriotic pride among Southern women, who suffered shortages more than their counterparts in the North where textile mills were located. High-cut necklines were standard for daytime, while evening dresses were low cut for young women.

February 1865 fashion plate from *Godey's Lady's Book*, showing five women wearing fashionable gowns and child holding cat. Even during wartime, fashion magazines included pictures of the latest styles. Women's fashions emphasized narrow waists with wide shoulders and large skirts. (Library of Congress)

"Berthas" were ruffles or other decorations added to low-cut bodices for modesty. Because skirts were long, shoes were rarely seen.

Civil War era people wore several types of jackets. A short fitted jacket covering the bodice was called a "paletot." The French military inspired Zouave, or bolero jacket, ending at the waist with an open curved front, was popular as well. There were some Northern regiments that wore a Zouave uniform consisting of baggy pantaloons, embroidered jackets, and gold-tasseled fezzes. Various styles of tightly fitted jackets of varying lengths were also worn.

Cloaks were the most prevalent outerwear for women and children. They were commonly made from wool or velvet, and were very long, to cover the skirt. They sometimes had hoods and slits rather than sleeves. Capes were wraps that fastened at the neck to provide warmth. A coat with sleeves, known sometimes as a "pardessus," was adopted in the early 1860s. Although similar to today's overcoat, it might also have been just a cloak with sleeves. Women often wore bonnets with brims that shielded their faces, and long ribbons for decoration.

Sleeves evolved from full bell shape to bishop sleeves that were gathered at top and bottom, better suited to daily tasks. Although daytime dresses had high-cut necks, evening wear had low-cut necklines and wide off-the-shoulder sleeves for girls as well as for women. Brooches were the most common jewelry accessory, and almost all women had one. Jewelry made of human hair, particularly from loved ones, was also popular at the time.

Men, too, commonly wore jackets and vests. For men of all classes, vests were always part of their dress, whether under a work apron or a jacket, and came in many colors and fabrics. It would be highly unusual for a man to wear a shirt and no vest. The frock coat, almost knee length, was part of a vested suit, and usually black. In the East, the outfit would be completed by a top hat. In the West, the looser shorter sack jacket was the fashion for daywear, topped by a low crown hat. The sack style became popular as a more practical and less expensive jacket for working classes. Less fitted at the waist, it was more easily ready-made and ultimately mass produced. The sack jacket was paired with matching pants and vest, while the frock or waistcoat could have pants and a vest of different fabric and color, and was more formal. A tie and detachable collar would be added for Sunday dress. Men almost always wore hats or caps. For more formal occasions men would also wear gloves, in part to avoid bare hands touching a woman's skin, for instance, at a dance. Canes and umbrellas were the accessory of choice for gentlemen, used mostly for decoration. Soft leather boots were the norm for all except working-class men and slaves, who wore crude thick brogans.

North and South, all infants wore long gowns or dresses, not differentiated by gender until age two or later. Nightgowns were not very different from the day dresses. Poorer families might simply dress infants in an older child's shirt or a cloth diaper, financially unable to dress babies in the idyllic fashion of the time. Toddlers were also dressed undifferentiated by gender, both in hair and in clothing style. For infant gowns as well as for older children's clothes, the style was wide off the shoulder with short puffed sleeves. As they got older, girls were dressed in small versions of women's styles, even with small hoops for skirts while in fashion. Girls' dresses would be shorter than women's, allowing pantalettes and boots to show. Girls' dresses were not as low cut as an adult's.

After infancy, boys were dressed in short pants, not graduating to long pants until adulthood, although there was no specific agreed-upon age for this transition. Knickerbockers, short loose pants ending at or just below the knee, were worn with loose shirts and a short bolero-style jacket until the boy was old enough for long pants, usually between the ages of 10 and 12. At that point, boys' dress was not much different from adult men's. An exception might be a younger boy from a poorer family who would need long pants if he had to work to support his family. Long pants were fitted, rather than blousy style like the short drawers. Ankle high laced or buttoned boots were the shoe fashion of the time.

Jane Brodsky Fitzpatrick

See also: *Clothing, Fashion, and Appearance*: Children's Dress, Confederate; Children's Dress, Union; Clothing, Status and Position; Clothing, Style and Function; Dress, Slaves; *Godey's Lady's Book*; Homespun; Hoop Skirts; Men's Dress, Confederate Civilian; Men's Dress, Union Civilian; Mourning Clothes; Shortages, Clothing; Undergarments; Women's Dress, Confederate; Women's Dress, Union

FURTHER READING

Library of Congress American Memory Project, Civil War. http://www.loc.gov/pictures/collection/civwar/. Accessed July 31, 2014.
Stamper, Anita A., and Jill Condra. *Clothing Through American History: The Civil War Through the Gilded Age, 1861–1899*. Santa Barbara, CA: Greenwood, 2011.

GODEY'S LADY'S BOOK

In 1830, Louis Antoine Godey, an American editor, began publishing a magazine designated for contemporary women called *Godey's Lady's Book*. The *Lady's Book* was one of the first publications directed entirely at women and it included poetry, essays, book reviews, advice, and other articles pertaining to fashion and tastes of the time. Although Godey's main goal in publishing his *Lady's Book* was to make a profit, he also expressed a desire to disseminate higher manners and morals to a wider public, and he largely succeeded. By the eve of the Civil War, Godey could boast of over 150,000 subscribers. Largely due to the fact that the publication was aimed at women, *Godey's* was also one of the first periodicals to employ women in high positions within the staff. Most importantly, Godey employed Sarah Hale, who was likely the most influential editor of the *Lady's Book* and one of the most important American women of her time.

Issues of *Godey's Lady's Book* often contained articles that pertained to or drew directly from contemporary French trends. This direction was part of the general attitude of the time. In the Enlightenment tradition that prevailed, men and women were supposed to be cosmopolitan; they were to concern themselves with a wide spectrum of world issues. American citizens focused on everything from fashion to literature in various countries, but they mostly concentrated on information coming out of European nations like France and England. In the first years of Godey's publication, the publisher emphasized these trends and the magazine quickly became known for its concentration on fashion.

The publication changed significantly when Sarah Josepha Buell Hale (1788–1879) became editor in 1837 and used her position to promote many of her ideals. Born in a small town in New Hampshire in 1788, Hale was a lifelong patriot and dedicated to education. Her parents believed in equal education for both men and women and ensured that she received the equivalent of a college education. She married lawyer David Hale in 1813 and they parented five children together. However, in 1822, David died suddenly and Hale turned to her literary skills to support her family. By 1825, Hale was publishing short stories, poems, and articles in various magazines. In addition, she produced a successful novel, titled *Northwood: Life North and South* or alternatively called *Northwood: A Tale of New England*. The success of these publications gained Hale enough prestige that she caught the attention of Reverend John Blake who requested that she immediately begin editing his *Ladies' Magazine*.

During her time with the *Ladies' Magazine*, Hale promoted education and the moral uplift of her readers. She included articles on plants and animals, literature, and poetry. Hale even produced many poems herself. In 1830, she published several poems in a collection, titled *Poems for Our Children*. The work included the popular poem "Mary's Lamb," more commonly known as "Mary Had a Little Lamb." She also produced several other works for children during this time.

In the late 1830s, Godey announced his intent to merge his periodical with Hale's in an effort to have her work for him. The *Lady's Book* was already well known for its exquisite and pronounced emphasis on fashion by the time Hale took over, but she insisted that the periodical should dedicate at least half its content to literary materials. Edgar Allen Poe and Harriet Beecher Stowe were just two of the numerous authors Hale featured in *Godey's* during her tenure as editor.

However, Hale's emphasis on literature was not the only thing she brought to the *Lady's Book*. Hale also used the periodical to covertly promote her strong sense of patriotism and nationalism. Outside of the magazine, Hale was instrumental in making George Washington's home, Mount Vernon, into a historically preserved site, and she was a strong advocate for the Bunker Hill Monument that immortalized the influential American Revolution battle.

The strength of Hale's devotion, however, worried Godey. Women from both the North and South subscribed to the *Lady's Book*, and Godey insisted that his periodical would not publish any articles that might offend any of his readers. In the rising tensions before and during the Civil War, Godey was determined that his periodical would "be insulated from reporting of the conflict and not a source for reporting on it." Hale overtly abided by Godey's policy, but in maintaining control over the selection of which poems, articles, and works of fiction to print, she was able to transmit some of her views to *Godey's* extensive readership. As tension mounted toward war, Hale increasingly stressed the need for unification in the domestic sphere. She did so by advocating for a new national holiday: Thanksgiving. Hale emphasized that Thanksgiving would allow Americans an opportunity to annually celebrate the creation of the United States, implicitly stressing the importance of continued unification of the country.

Hale also veiled many of her opinions about the Civil War in a domestic context. She published stories supposedly aimed at children that often held lessons for the mothers. In this way, she stressed connections between her readers; mothers were mothers, whether they were from the North or South. Hale also emphasized a unified womanhood of which all of *Godey's* female readership could identify. She stressed that all women understood certain aspects of life, including the need to care for and protect one's family. Hale accomplished her task with articles about infant nutrition, exercise for children, and jobs and property rights for women.

Hale retired from editing in 1877 at age 88. That year, Godey sold his *Lady's Book* to another local publisher. He died one year later.

Kelli Nelson

See also: *Arts*: Art; Literature, Northern; Literature, Southern; Poetry; *Clothing, Fashion, and Appearance*: Fashion; *Family Life and Gender Roles*: Cult of Domesticity; Motherhood; Womanhood, Northern; Womanhood, Southern

FURTHER READING

Finley, Ruth. *The Lady of Godey's*. Philadelphia: J.B. Lippincott Co., 1931.

Howe, David Walker. *What Hath God Wrought: The Transformation of America, 1815–1848*. New York: Oxford University Press, 2007.

Parker, Gail Underwood. *More Than Petticoats: Remarkable New Hampshire Women*. Guilford, CT: Globe Pequot, 2009.

Sherrer, Grace Bussing. "French Culture as Presented to Middle-Class America by *Godey's Lady's Book* 1830–1840." *American Literature* 3:3 (November 1931): 277–286.

Sommers, Joseph Michael. "*Godey's Lady's Book*: Sarah Hale and the Construction of Sentimental Nationalism." *College Literature* 37:3 (Summer 2010): 43–61.

HOMESPUN

The Civil War took place in the midst of rising industrialization throughout the United States that increasingly widened the divide between the North and the South. At this time, homespun—clothing, sheets, tablecloths, napkins, quilts, and other textiles made or spun at home—became idealized. As men and women confronted the rapid changes brought on by industrialization, the thought of homespun reminded American citizens of a mythologized past of simpler times of independence. Homespun represented the ability for American households to maintain life without having to depend on anyone or anything else. Homespun also reinforced the idea of separate spheres for men and women in the nineteenth century; the men labored outside while women worked within the home to support their families. During the war, Northern blockades of Southern trade and the South's already diminished capacity for wide-scale manufacturing forced Southerners to rely on homespun materials. As they did so, Southerners couched their ideas in the same mythology that citizens had about homespun before the war and this image of the Southern woman laboring to outfit her Confederate soldier became an important part of Confederate nationalism.

In the nineteenth century, homespun began to represent many things and became an important part of American identity. American citizens saw the activity as patriotic because they understood it as a connection to their colonial past. In their eyes, homespun was part of a mythologized traditional America where citizens worked hard and toiled on their own land, out from under the rules of an oppressive government. This type of independence has long been part of Americans' national identity. Owning land, producing one's own food, and making one's own clothing were all part of a subsistence ideal that thwarted corruption and promoted virtue.

Many believed that industrialization made citizens lazy or nonproductive. Homespun was the opposite of this idea, especially for women, who traditionally did most of the sewing, dyeing, and spinning within the household. Homespun activities allowed women a greater opportunity to contribute to the family production and subsistence.

However, this idea was more complex in the South. In elite Southern homes, enslaved women often performed any of the homespun activities that might be necessary. The white women of large plantation houses were seen as above this type of work. However, homespun activities were not always necessary in these homes, and most homespun was used to outfit the enslaved people. One mark of the upper class in the industrial age was their ability to purchase garments and materials outside of the home. They could go out to purchase dresses, tablecloths, and other fineries from stores or markets. If it was necessary to sew clothes within the larger homes of the South, then the women were at least able to purchase finer cloth. Lower class women, on the other hand, still had to sew and dye their own garments. Even in families that owned one or a few slaves, the women of this class often had to perform many of the same activities that might have been designated as "slaves' work" in elite homes.

Once the war began, however, much of this home manufacture changed. The availability of manufactured goods decreased dramatically as Northern blockades cut off trade lines to the South. This blockade was vastly important because

Southern manufacturing remained significantly behind that of the rest of the country in 1861. The Southern economy heavily relied on trade both in and out of the area because Southerners were not producing finished products within the region. Therefore, during the Civil War both white and black women in all households had to turn toward spinning and producing fabric at home.

As shortages became increasingly drastic, Confederate leaders called on households to do their duty in supporting the army by constructing cloth and garments at home. Newspaper writers worked to promote the idea of homespun. They couched their articles in an atmosphere of loyalty to the Confederacy in general, and the idea of homemade cloth became an integral part of Confederate nationalism. Southern men and women scoffed at the idea of wearing any garment produced in the North. It was their patriotic duty to produce and support the Confederacy with homespun materials.

White women who early joined in the work of homespun even began to ridicule others who refused to do so, and resistance was not uncommon. Some elite women resisted because they saw homespun as a mark of the lower classes. Many white men did not want their wives participating in the activity either, again because of the pre-war stereotypes that black women were supposedly the ones who should be performing such tasks. However, as the war continued, many of these women did not have a choice. The amount of work necessary to clothe themselves, their families, and even their slaves was more than enslaved women alone could handle. Therefore, the only way to maintain their households was to make the garments themselves.

In addition, other obstacles remained despite propagandists' attempts to reorient the image of homespun into an appealing idea. Due to the fact that homespun had generally been unnecessary in the antebellum era, many women lacked the skills to produce cloth at home and few existed who had the knowledge or time to instruct other women. Spinning and weaving cloth took a significant amount of time and skill that few had the need or opportunity to master. In addition, homespun activities required many materials that were often hard to find in the Civil War South, especially wheels and looms. All cotton cards, used for combing the cotton fibers before spinning, were manufactured outside of the South prior to the war. As women used the cards, the instruments wore down and Southerners had no way of replenishing their supplies.

Despite the obstacles, Southern women persisted in creating their own garments as well as materials for Confederate soldiers throughout the war. After the war, ideas of homespun materials supporting the Confederacy became one of the most common images of Confederate loyalty during the conflict. In the postwar era, Confederate nationalists probably exaggerated the prevalence and scope of such wartime activities.

Kelli Nelson

See also: Clothing, Fashion, and Appearance: Children's Dress, Confederate; Children's Dress, Union; Dress, Slaves; Men's Dress, Confederate Civilian; Men's Dress, Union Civilian; Shortages, Clothing; Women's Dress, Confederate; Women's Dress, Union

FURTHER READING

Faust, Drew Gilpin. *Mothers of Invention: Women of the Slaveholding South in the American Civil War*. New York: Vintage Books, 1996.

Massey, Mary Elizabeth. *Ersatz in the Confederacy: Shortages and Substitutes on the Southern Homefront*. Columbia: University of South Carolina Press, 1952; 1993.

Ulrich, Laurel Thatcher. *The Age of Homespun: Objects and Stories in the Creation of an American Myth*. New York: Alfred A. Knopf, 2001.

HOOP SKIRTS

Although many young people today are perhaps less familiar with *Gone with the Wind* than those of prior generations, the image of Vivian Leigh as Scarlet O'Hara, wrapped in curtains made into a hoop-skirted dress, pervaded American culture as a Civil War staple for decades. Hoop skirts, with their wide diameters and circular frames, preceded the war and disappeared shortly thereafter, but continue as a key visual element of how people imagine the war era.

Skirts—the lower half of a woman's dress independent of the bodice, as blouses were uncommon until the 1860s—had grown during the first half of the nineteenth century to some rather impressive widths. American fashion was based on European trends, and French design in particular had gone from a lithe Greek-inspired silhouette of the early century to, by the 1830s, a remarkably wide skirt. The skirts, composed of several yards of fabric, draped across fabric petticoats underneath, themselves made larger with copious ruffles. These petticoats got rather heavy as they increased in size to add to skirt diameter, and women found physical movement became rather difficult. Whalebones were sometimes added to petticoats to improve their strength, but they sometimes collapsed or became misshapen with the weight of the skirts or the wearer performing simple actions like sitting down or going through a doorway.

By the 1840s, designers engaged in some elaborate construction to move beyond the petticoat-bulked skirt to a more engineered undergarment. The hooped petticoat that resulted was an improvement over simple fabric petticoats, but was still rather cumbersome—it consisted of rings made of various materials, bound with string but which did not stay in place particularly well. In the 1850s, the cage crinoline was born—a sequence of hoops, widening as they descended to the ground, held in place with a series of tapes that connected each hoop vertically from eyelets at the waist. This crinoline improved upon the hooped petticoat and earlier piles of petticoats by adding width and lift without weight. By the late 1850s, cage crinoline hoops were made of spring steel, a type of metal that can be bent, squished, and otherwise manipulated but which will bounce back into its proper form. Thus doorways and chairs were not nearly as challenging as they had been, though the metal frames and enormous amounts of fabric still took up a significant space; skirts could span several feet in diameter. Omnibuses in New York and elsewhere charged women who wore them more money to ride, as they took up more space than those without hoop skirts.

Women of all classes wore cage crinolines and hoop skirts, though enslaved women only rarely had access to them. Although most people in the nineteenth century lacked the sheer quantity of clothing held by many Americans today, women generally had at least a few day dresses made of cotton calico or silk featuring a buttoned front bodice, short or long sleeves, and limited ornamentation. They also usually had one "Sunday" or nicer dress. In addition to day dresses, women who could afford them had morning and afternoon dresses made of cotton or silk; wrappers which were cotton dresses that closed at the front, seen only by family, and worn over other dresses if one thought one might get dirty; walking dresses, whose skirts could be pulled above the ankle and fixed there using ribbons, thus facilitating movement; visiting dresses akin to day dresses but with a more jacket-like bodice; riding dresses which were usually hoopless for safety reasons; and evening dresses that could be off-the-shoulder ball gowns often in elaborate brocades, taffetas, and lace, with low-cut décolletage.

Many women in the war era also had mourning dresses if they had lost a spouse and could afford such dresses. Mourning dress included black versions of their regular wear, donned for an average of two and a half years. In addition to the greater range of fabric and dresses purchased by wealthier ladies, elite women wore cage crinolines made of finer materials than those that sold for less.

Although hoop skirts became the norm on the home front, elsewhere they were quite risky. Union Civil War nurses found their hoop skirts prohibited by Dorothea Dix, Superintendent of Women Nurses, because the hoop's unwieldy breadth interfered with hospital function. Steel hoops could potentially snag patients in critical states, knock things over, and inhibit nurses from performing their jobs. Some nurses maintained some breadth of skirt by wearing simple petticoats underneath. Nurses' dresses, as befit their work, were usually of simple cotton, dark in color. Cotton washed easily, and dark dyes hid the dirt and gore women met every day at soldiers' bedsides.

Hoop skirts arguably both heightened awareness of women's sexuality and insisted upon their untouchability. Always paired with a corset, the hoop skirt drew attention to narrow waists and wide hips, symbols of both beauty and fertility in Western culture at the time. Evening gowns only reinforced the focus with their eye-catching necklines. At the same time, the size of the skirts themselves served to quite literally keep suitors at a distance from those who wore them; by the trend's end, women were more easily approached at the front and side than they had been for some years.

As the war wound down in the mid-1860s, so did the hoop skirt fashion that had begun decades before. The hoops largely disappeared, save for the back—by the end of the decade, the wide, round hoopskirt became the bustle, a horizontal projection perpendicular to the woman's backside. Bustles were constructed in such a way that the skirt and engineered undergarment could easily collapse when a woman sat, no small matter as bustles grew in size, and then bounce back into shape. Corsets fit tightly and skirt fronts flattened. As the century ended, so did the bustle and the long tradition of lower-form body elaboration.

Jennifer Cote

See also: *Clothing, Fashion, and Appearance*: Clothing, Status and Position; Clothing, Style and Function; Fashion; Mourning Clothes; Women's Dress, Confederate; Women's Dress, Union; *Family and Gender Roles*: Widows, Confederate; Widows, Union; Womanhood, Northern; Womanhood, Southern; Young Women; *Science and Technology*: Nursing

FURTHER READING

Laver, James, Amy de la Haye, and Andrew Tucker. *Costume and Fashion: A Concise History*. 5th ed. London: Thames and Hudson, 2012.

Muckenhoupt, Margaret. *Dorothea Dix: Advocate for Mental Health Care*. New York: Oxford University Press, 2004.

Stamper, Anita, and Jill Condra. *Clothing Through American History: The Civil War Through the Gilded Age, 1861–1899*. New York: Greenwood, 2010.

JEWELRY

Wearing jewelry was popular during the nineteenth century. The discovery of ruins at Pompeii and Herculaneum, two Roman cities destroyed by Mount Vesuvius's eruption in 79 CE, at the end of the eighteenth century heightened women's obsession with wearing gems. In addition, Brazil's mining trade's production of a supply of diamonds and other rare gems to American consumers, and the mass production in the textile industry created an affordable and accessible market for less expensive pieces. As a result, jewelry in all forms and fashions attracted women concerned with aesthetics and self-expression through style. However, the indulgence of purchasing and wearing fine jewelry brought with it questions concerning whether a luxurious appetite aligned with moral uprightness. For nineteenth-century Americans acquiring jewelry was an enticing endeavor, one fraught with class, moral, monetary, and decorum issues.

During the late eighteenth century, the ruins at Pompeii and Herculaneum influenced the Western obsession with exoticism; this exotic style took the form of simplicity in jewelry and often depicted scenes of Greco-Roman goddesses to represent American attention to Roman and Greek artifacts. Also among the prized pieces were precious gems and stones, which proliferated as a result of Brazil's growing mining industry. The high demand for precious stones, especially diamonds, led to high prices for genuine pieces; however, since most moderate-income Americans could not afford the real thing, manufacturers began producing imitations, which became exceedingly popular for women caring less about authentic stones and more about displaying fashionable jewelry. The third growing trend during the nineteenth century was the return of the cameo—an oval-shaped carved piece, depicting a profile, typically of women, engraved into various kinds of shells, mother-of-pearl, coral, or agate. As the cameo made its way back into style, it became the popular centerpiece in every kind of jewelry piece imaginable, including brooches, earrings, necklaces, belts, and rings for both women and men.

Despite the rising obsession with jewelry in the second half of the nineteenth century, the shift in taste for expensive and exotic jewelry seemed to run counterculture to traditional American values concerning faith and leading a simple life. Jewelry, like all fashion pieces, was a way to express individuality, class, and taste; this hierarchy of taste challenged American sensibilities regarding human nature and morality. This moral conundrum, however, did not deter Americans from their attraction to consuming jewelry, nor their need to wear it.

Taking advantage of this trend in the consumption of precious metals and stones, jewelers brought forth a proliferation of jewelry stores in America. As access to the prized pieces increased, purchasing jewelry as a gift alleviated cultural tensions related to the appropriateness of a gift, especially with the varying costs and wide availability of products. Jewelry became the chosen gift for any occasion, especially Christmas. Advertisements, which included mail-order catalogues by companies like Sears by the end of the century, spoke to every occasion, encouraging men to bedazzle their loved ones with jewelry for religious holidays, birthdays, anniversaries, and engagements. Unfortunately for men, it was not appropriate for a gentleman to sport gems and precious metals—it was seen as indulgent, effeminate, vulgar, and thus disdainful. Therefore, the commodification of jewelry was twofold: men purchased the items, and women displayed them.

During the Civil War, some women were able to afford jewelry plated with low-carat gems, allowing them the ability to express themselves through fashion and style. However, unlike many other fashion industries, which were concerned primarily with the low cost of production and establishing prices that accommodated the rising American income, jewelry makers had to take into high consideration the aesthetic whims of consumers. These concerns resulted in a creative model for gems and precious metals that could not be standardized.

The shift in America's ready-to-wear industry brought with it affordable garments, accessories, shoes, and jewelry, which made it possible for people from all classes to follow the fashion of the day. By the end of the Civil War, Newark became a center for the jewelry industry and produced an endless array of pieces at affordable prices; New Jersey thus became the American capital for fine jewelry. With the high production of affordable jewelry and clothing came the blurring of class boundaries, and the middle class sought to emulate the wealthier classes and establish their aspirations for economic and social status elevation, which pushed dress toward a luxury-based, high-fashion style.

The jewelry industry of the nineteenth century relied upon the aesthetic sensibilities of consumers. Though technological advances afforded women of all classes the ability to express their personal sense of taste and luxury, the constant ebb and flow fashion sensibilities and the impossibility of determining which new style would become en vogue made it difficult to determine what the population would desire and demand. For American jewelry makers in the nineteenth century, the supply was entirely determined by the demand, and though that demand was unwieldy and mysterious, it was met largely as a result of the revolution within the industry.

April Anderson

See also: *Clothing, Fashion, and Appearance*: Fashion; Women's Dress, Confederate; Women's Dress, Union

FURTHER READING

Carnevali, Francesca. "Fashioning Luxury for Factory Girls: American Jewelry, 1860–1914." *Business History Review* 85:2 (2011): 295–317.

Gordon, Eleanor. "Everywoman's Jewelry: Early Plastics and Equality in Fashion." *Journal of Popular Culture* 3:4 (1980): 629.

Jones, Geoffrey. "Globalization and Beauty: A Historical and Firm Perspective." *EurAmerica* 41 (2011): 887–918.

Joselit, Jenna Weissman. *A Perfect Fit: Clothes, Character, and the Promise of America.* New York: Henry Holt and Company, 2001.

Kim, Duol. "The Next Best Thing to Getting Married: Partnerships Among the Jewelry Manufacturers in the Providence/Attleboro Area During the Nineteenth Century." *Enterprise & Society* 8 (2007): 106.

Scranton, Philip. "The Horrors of Competition: Innovation and Paradox in Rhode Island's Jewelry Industry, 1860–1914." *Rhode Island History* 55:2 (1997): 46.

Tandberg, Gerilyn. "Decoration and Decorum: Accessories of Nineteenth-Century Louisiana Women." *The Southern Quarterly* 27:1 (1988): 8.

Vickers, Anita. *The New Nation: American Popular Culture Through History.* Westport, CT: Greenwood Press, 2002.

White, Carolyn L. "What the Warners Wore: An Archaeological Investigation of Visual Appearance." *Northeast Historical Archaeology* 33 (2004): 39.

MEN'S DRESS, CONFEDERATE CIVILIAN

Confederate civilian menswear in the Civil War era usually consisted of a coat, waistcoat, shirt, cravat, trousers, and hat. Within this basic set of garments, there were a number of possible variations.

The most popular suit coat for civilian wear was the sack coat, a loose-fitting jacket similar in style to today's suits. Wool was worn year-round, and cotton or linen suits were used only in summer. Frock coats, which were considered more formal than sack coats, were also worn. They were longer than sack coats, reaching almost to the knee. Frock coats were typically made of wool, and were often worn by older men. Suits were sometimes matched, but were often of different fabrics. Matched three-piece suits were called "ditto suits." Coat linings were usually of glazed cotton, or sometimes wool for a warmer garment, and the interiors of pockets were often made from scraps of cotton.

Under the suit jacket, men wore waistcoats (vests), which usually had a collar and were single-breasted. They were often colorful and decorative, and were long enough to cover the waistband of the pants. A pocket watch was often worn with the waistcoat, with the chain draped across the waistcoat to the watch pocket.

Shirts were usually white, although checks, stripes, and colors were often used for work shirts. Shirts typically had turned-down collars and were worn with cravats (also called ties). In the 1860s, cravats were narrow, and they were typically worn once around the neck and tied in a flat bow or a knot; sometimes they were wrapped twice around, but this style began to go out of fashion in the 1860s. Work shirts often featured a standing collar band only; these were worn without cravats.

Trousers of the 1860s were loose-fitting and featured buttoned fly fronts, with no pleats or creases. They were made in a variety of different fabrics, ranging from fine wool to inexpensive cotton jean. They were typically dark-colored. Trousers did not have belt loops in this period; instead, "braces," or suspenders, were worn to support the pants. Some working men wore overalls over their trousers, with colored work shirts.

The typical man wore his hair relatively short, parted on the side. About half of the men seen in photographs were clean-shaven, and about half had facial hair (usually beards). Mustaches were also worn alone, but were less common.

A large variety of hats appear in period photographs. Top hats were most popular; soft felt hats, bowler hats, and others were also frequently worn. Hats were made in a variety of materials, including silk (used for top hats), felt, and straw. Farmers and railroad workers often wore cloth caps with bills.

Etiquette books of the period emphasized the importance of inconspicuousness and simplicity in dress. Evening dress for men consisted of black trousers, a black coat, a black or white cravat, and a black or white waistcoat. Removable, highly starched collars were worn with dress shirts. Evening shirts featured starched, tucked fronts. White gloves were worn with evening dress, and light-colored suits were considered inappropriate for evening.

For outerwear, men had several options. One popular choice was the "Inverness" cape, which featured a shorter layer to cover the arms, over a longer, knee-length layer. Other coat types included a frock overcoat, a loose-fitting paletot, and a "Chesterfield," which was the overcoat version of a sack coat. Raincoats made of India-rubber or oilcloth were also available.

Men wore long drawers with a buttoned fly. The drawers featured a cuff at the ankle that was fastened with buttons or with a drawstring.

Clothing worn by enslaved men in the South differed widely. Some wore cast-off clothing, including coats, vests, and other articles of clothing, which was given to them by slaveholders; this practice appears to have been used especially for more favored slaves. House slaves were typically dressed in better-quality, more fashionable garments than were field hands. Clothing designed for slave use, used particularly for field hands, was simply designed and very durable. Slave clothing was made of a variety of different fabrics. It is believed that homespun was the most frequently used fabric. Homespun could be produced on the plantation or purchased from merchants. Other commonly used fabrics included jean, which was a durable twill-weave fabric, and osnaburg, a coarse cotton fabric, although a variety of other fabrics were also used. Some merchants of the period offered fabrics and shoes specifically designed for slave use; these were usually advertised as being very durable. Most enslaved men probably wore hats; like the hats worn by other men of the period, these varied widely in style.

Sewing machines were in widespread use during the 1860s and were frequently used for sewing menswear. These sewing machines, however, were only capable of straight stitching, so buttonholes and other specialty stitches were always sewn by hand. A surprising variety of button types were used for Southern men's clothing, including porcelain buttons printed with various designs, decorative shell and mother-of-pearl buttons, cloth-covered metal buttons, metal buttons, and horn or bone buttons. Cloth-covered buttons were used most frequently on coats. Bone buttons were used on a variety of garments, particularly on drawers. Metal buttons were sometimes used on coats and trousers, and occasionally on undergarments of lower quality.

Charity S. Everett

See also: *Clothing, Fashion, and Appearance*: Clothing, Status and Position; Clothing, Style and Dress, Slaves Function; Fashion; Homespun; Men's Dress, Union Civilian; Uniforms, Confederate; Uniforms, Union; *Family Life and Gender Roles*: Young Men; *Housing and Community*: Slave Life; *Recreation and Social Customs*: Dances and Balls; Leisure Time

FURTHER READING

Abraham, Donna J. *The Way They Were: Dressed in 1860–1865*. Gettysburg, PA: Abraham's Lady, LLC, 2008.

Hartley, Cecil B. *The Gentlemen's Book of Etiquette and Manual of Politeness*. Philadelphia: G.G. Evans, 1860. https://archive.org/details/gentlemensbookof00hart.

Hunt-Hurst, Patricia. "Round Homespun Coat & Pantaloons of the Same: Slave Clothing as Reflected in Fugitive Slave Advertisements in Antebellum Georgia." *The Georgia Historical Quarterly* 83 (1999): 727–740.

Putman, Tyler Rudd. "Every Man Turned Out in the Best He Had": Clothing and Buttons in the Historical and Archaeological Records of Johnson's Island Prisoner-of-War Depot, 1862–1865." *Northeast Historical Archaeology* 40 (January 2011): 86–103.

Severa, Joan. *Dressed for the Photographer: Ordinary Americans and Fashion, 1840–1900*. Kent, OH: Kent State University Press, 1995.

Shep, R. L., and W. S. Salisbury. *Civil War Gentlemen: 1860s Apparel Arts and Uniforms*. Mendocino, CA: R.L. Shep, 1994.

MEN'S DRESS, UNION CIVILIAN

Civilian dress varied based on an individual's position in society, his region, age, and occupation. In some cases, even men connected to the U.S. military wore civilian dress to protect selves them from enemy fire.

During the Civil War, businessmen and politicians wore Victorian-style clothing. Men often wore knee-length frock coats with two external pockets. The coats were

Photograph of George Opdyke, mayor of New York City during the Civil War (1862–1863). Wartime businessmen and politicians wore Victorian-style clothing which often included a knee-length frock coat in black, brown, gray, dark gray, or forest green, trousers made of black super-fine wool broadcloth, bleached white cotton shirts with fold over collars, and satin or silk neck cloths. Men also wore top hats or stovepipe hats for style and warmth. (Library of Congress)

lined with cheap cotton, wool, or silk. Mid-thigh–length sack coats were worn for less formal occasions and greatcoats in the standard caped style as well as oilcloth raincoats were used for cold or wet conditions. Shawls were universal to all classes of men, and capes just served as formal shawls for men of means. Most coats came in limited colors—black, brown, gray, dark gray, and forest green. Pocket watches served as a common accessory. Chains of gold, gold substitute, silver, or nickel silver attached to the vest with an "S" hook or "T" bar, and many men completed and complimented their outfits with a handsome walking stick or cane. Canes were usually lacquered wooden shafts with brass tips and occasionally had ornamental handles. For example, South Carolina representative Preston Brooks used a cane made of gutta-percha with a solid gold top to beat nearly to death a defenseless senator Charles Sumner in the Senate chamber on May 22, 1856.

Black super-fine wool broadcloth was most often used for men's trousers, and late in the war some civilian trousers had stripes running down the outside seam. Bleached white cotton shirts, some pleated, with fold over collars, were worn with satin or silk neck cloths, cravats, and mufflers in various colors. The double Windsor knot that men use to tie their neckties made its appearance in the 1860s. Top hats made of wool or beaver pelt or stovepipe hats, made famous by President Abraham Lincoln, were worn for style and warmth. By 1860 middle-class men began to wear a melon-shaped hardhat called a derby, and workingmen wore a slouch hat with a broad brim to shade the face or wore straw hats also with wide brims. Clergy wore a hat with a broad brim and a four-inch crown encircled by a ribbon often the same color as the hat. A European style or immigrant hat was also popular among laborers. The hat had a short bill connected to a three-inch band with a floppy top that laid flat.

Civilian dress shoes were made of leather with elastic sides and a tab in the back allowing for more ease in pulling the shoes on the feet. Shoes for both right and left feet were the same.

African Americans, both enslaved and free, often wore clothing made of burlap or, in the case of slaves freed as a result of Union Army occupation, wore threadbare pants and jackets being thrown away by the soldiers. Shoes, if enslaved people had them, were ill fitting and, consequently, painful. A photograph taken at Gettysburg in the autumn of 1863 shows free blacks each wearing a white shirt, light colored vest, coarse looking pants, and slouch hats.

Civilian attire was also found on men attached in civilian capacities to the military. For example, the Construction Corps of the United States Military Railroad wore civilian attire. One of the first civilians called to Washington to contribute his technical skills to managing the railroads for the army, Herman Haupt refused to wear a uniform. Instead, he wore a loose-fitting woolen waistcoat typical for working men of the period. His trousers, also made of wool, were a solid color—black, gray, or brown—with a button fly instead of a front flap, which was popular in men's clothing in the 1850s. His civilian laborers wore "Shoddy" trousers made of reprocessed wool produced during the war or Jean cloth, which was a mixture of coarse cotton or linen warp and wool weft or "fill." Civilian men also wore canvas or denim pants. Light colored cottons and linens were worn in hot weather. Haupt wore a loose pullover cotton shirt with a single button front opening with a narrow facing and a narrow band collar and cuffs. Men of the Construction Corps who worked for Haupt, as well as farmers and laborers of the day, wore shirts of coarse linen. Because at the time men's shirts were considered underwear, both Haupt and his workforce wore vests. Two popular styles of vest were the English workingman's vest, which buttoned to the breast, and the shawl collar vest, which buttoned just above the belly button. Checked vests were popular in greens, blues, and reds.

Several styles of boots were worn by working men. Riding boots were either turndowns or Wellingtons, which had a front that came up over the knee and a back lower in the bend of the knee. Heavy leather workboots made in two pieces, which covered the ankles and laced up, were popular. Brogans were common with their prominent feature of square chisel toes and smallish heels. Common material for workers shoes was waxed calfskin that presented a rough outer surface and a smooth inner one.

Clergy attached to the military also wore civilian attire, to protect them from being mistaken by the enemy as part of the military. The idea was that although groups of civilians found themselves in combat areas, their dress would prevent the enemy from shooting them, but it might not prevent capture. General Order No. 102 issued on November 25, 1861, laid out the dress of Union chaplains. They were ordered to wear plain black frock coats, black pants, and black felt hats.

Thomas Army

See also: Clothing, Fashion, and Appearance: Clothing, Status and Position; Clothing, Style and Function; Textiles; Uniforms, Union; *Religion and Belief*: Clergy

FURTHER READING

"Battle of Gettysburg: Chaplain Horatio S. Howell, 90th Pennsylvania, U.S.A." *The American Civil War and the Battle of Gettysburg*. www.brotherswar.com/Gettysburg-1v. htm. Accessed March 4, 2013.

Creighton, Margaret S. *The Colors of Courage: Gettysburg's Forgotten History*. New York: Basic Books, 2005.

"Quartermaster Shop: Civilian Cloths." www.quartermastershop.com. Accessed February 28, 2013.

"Stone Sentinels: Father William Corby." www.gettysburg.stonesentinels.com/individuals/Corby.php. Accessed February 28, 2013.

Wilcox, R. Turner. *Five Centuries of American Costume*. New York: Charles Scribner's Sons, 1963.

MOURNING CLOTHES

During the nineteenth century, when upper- and middle-class women mourned the loss of a loved one they demonstrated their grief by wearing clothing intended to reflect their emotional pain. Through mourning dress, women publicly demonstrated that they grieved for and honored their dead. According to the social rules governing mourning dress, women wore different types and colors of clothing, for varying lengths of time, according to their relationship to the deceased. Upper-class women followed strict rules of formal mourning and policed other women to ensure that all upper-class ladies mourned properly. The rules of mourning required women to reflect an appropriate amount of grief in their physical appearance, but mourning dress offered important emotional and social benefits as well. As the death toll of the Civil War rose, women struggled to maintain appropriate mourning dress even when the war made it difficult to acquire proper mourning clothes.

Although men's grief at the loss of a loved one was as powerful as that of women, Victorian society regarded women as the emotional center of the household. After the death of a loved one, men returned to public life as quickly as possible, leaving the public display of mourning to women. For a man, fashionable mourning demanded little more than a strip of crape (a dull, crinkly black fabric associated with funerals and mourning) wrapped around his hatband. Societal expectations for mourning were also relaxed for children, who typically wore white or grey with black trimming when dressed in mourning. Meanwhile, women expressed their family's grief through their clothing, mourning the dead through a long process that made their private sorrow publicly visible. When a woman dressed in mourning, associates and even strangers understood her emotional state at a glance. As a result, mourners expected strangers to respond with an appropriate level of pity, sympathy, and respect.

Photograph of an unidentified woman, possibly Mrs. James Shields, holding a young boy and wearing mourning dress and a brooch that has an image of a Confederate soldier. Nineteenth-century etiquette dictated that a woman wear mourning dress for determined amounts of time based on her relationship to the deceased. Mourning dress signaled the woman's situation to the community as a whole and often allowed her to act in ways not permitted to married women. (Library of Congress)

The stages of mourning dress aimed to reflect the natural reduction of sorrow that mourners felt as time passed, but women faced harsh criticism if they appeared to mourn too little. During the period immediately following a death, called full or deep mourning, mourners preferred dull, lusterless fabrics like black crape. Women avoided social outings during deepest mourning, although the rules of mourning allowed them to attend church and conduct business. As time passed, mourners moved into second or half mourning and gradually replaced flat black wardrobes with shiny black silk, subdued dresses in gray or lavender, and simple prints. Mourning clothing followed the cut of popular styles, but ornaments and embellishments were limited during the first stages of mourning and were slowly reintroduced over time. Women wore the clothing of deep mourning upon the death of a close relative, including husbands, children, parents, grandparents, or siblings. When uncles, aunts, cousins, and close friends died, women wore the grays and lavenders of half mourning from the beginning of the mourning period.

Women mourned for different lengths of time depending on their relationship to the deceased. Widows mourned the longest, remaining in deep mourning for at least a year before transitioning to half mourning. When widows appeared in public, the "widow's weeds" they wore included a long, crape weeping veil that hid their tears from public view. The length of this veil shortened as time passed and the widow transitioned from deep to half mourning. Most widows mourned for two years, although some women, including Queen Victoria and Mary Todd Lincoln, never ceased mourning their husbands and wore black for the rest of their lives. Mourning lasted a year for parents, six months for siblings or children, and three months for aunts, uncles, nieces, and nephews. If a woman received an inheritance, she mourned the deceased for at least six months. The long periods of mourning meant that women with extended family networks might wear mourning for years, never completing the mourning process for one relative before another died.

For women during the 1860s, mourning dress comforted the bereaved, assured the community that women respected their family relationships, and smoothed a widow's entrance into public spaces as she took over her husband's business affairs after his death. For mourners facing overwhelming sadness, the stages of mourning suggested that the grief they felt immediately after a death would lessen with time. The black wardrobe of deep mourning identified grief-stricken women, thereby protecting them from callous treatment by insensitive strangers. Meanwhile, mourning clothes demonstrated that women's internal emotions corresponded to the expectations of upper-class society. New widows often needed to make business arrangements. At a time when respectable women remained at home while men conducted the family's business and women rarely went out without a male escort, a widow's mourning clothes silently explained her presence in public places like courthouses and banks, ensuring her admission without calling her respectability into question.

Mourning dress offered women emotional, social, and practical benefits and they struggled to dress in mourning even when the Civil War made it difficult to do so. The war disrupted Northern supply lines less than Southern supply lines, making it easier for middle-class Northern women to follow mourning conventions throughout the war. As the death toll of the Civil War mounted, many Southern women found it difficult to acquire the materials necessary for proper mourning dress. If women could not buy or borrow mourning clothes or cloth to make their own, they dyed their existing clothing. Even when women were unable to alter their clothing to match their grief, they still considered themselves in deep mourning. Casualties among Southern troops were so widespread that few families escaped the loss of a loved one during the Civil War. Despite rising prices and clothing shortages, Southern women dressed in full mourning for their dead whenever possible. When Northern troops took Richmond in 1865, Northern observers commented that almost all the women in the city were dressed in mourning.

Jama McMurtery Grove

See also: *Family Life and Gender Roles*: Widows, Confederate; Widows, Union; *Religion and Belief*: Burial; Death; Eulogies; Mourning

FURTHER READING

Brett, Mary. *Fashionable Mourning Jewelry, Clothing & Customs*. Atglen, PA: Schiffer Publishing, 2006.

Faust, Drew Gilpin. *This Republic of Suffering: Death and the American Civil War*. New York: Alfred A. Knopf, 2008.

Halttunen, Karen. *Confidence Men and Painted Women: A Study of Middle-Class Culture in America, 1830–1870*. New Haven, CT: Yale University Press, 1982.

Hillerman, Barbara Dodd. "Chrysalis of Gloom: Nineteenth Century American Mourning Costume." In Martha V. Pike and Janice Gray Armstrong, eds. *A Time to Mourn: Expressions of Grief in Nineteenth Century America*. Stony Brook, NY: Museums at Stony Brook, 1980, pp. 91–106.

Wood, Kirsten E. *Masterful Women: Slaveholding Widows from the American Revolution Through the Civil War*. Chapel Hill: University of North Carolina Press, 2004.

PERSONAL HYGIENE

By the middle of the nineteenth century the link between cleanliness and health was understood. Individuals began paying closer attention to cleanliness and grooming to maintain a healthy life. Even with these advances, scientists' connection of germs to disease was not discovered until late in the nineteenth century. Cleanliness as a cause of the spread of disease was not widely acknowledged, and disease spread in hospitals due to mishandling of human waste, as well as from the reuse of surgical knives, sponges, and dishes. In addition, fresh air was often considered unhealthful, so rooms were rarely ventilated.

People might bathe only on Sundays, and many bathed only once every two to three weeks or less. Bathing and fresh air were often seen as risky, not healthy.

Before indoor plumbing, filling and heating water in a bucket was labor intensive, especially in cold weather. Soap was not generally used as baths were mostly for a quick rinse that only sometimes included a sponge wipe. By the early 1860s there was a movement to promote public baths in cities not only for cleanliness, but also for moral and hygienic purity.

Competing religious and social movements sought to influence hygienic behavior. Sylvester Graham (1795–1851) led a reform movement that encouraged bathing three times a week, eating whole grains, and becoming vegetarian. He began lecturing in 1830 and based his scientific theories of healthy hygiene on physiology. Graham's philosophy for healthy clean living was based on the belief that temperance should be practiced for food as well as alcohol, reforming the typical mid-nineteenth century meal that generally included a lot of meat, rich starches, and wine.

The "Physical culture" movement took Grahamism further, recommending water cures (hot and cold) and establishing hydropathist institutes. Seventh-Day Adventist Ellen Gould Harmon White (1827–1915) believed in hygienic living, wholesome eating, and refraining from tobacco, alcohol, and caffeine. Drugs and other medicines were discouraged in favor of natural cures. The human body, considered a temple, was to be taken care of through religion.

Skin care was based on the ideal of pure natural white skin, but was not always healthy. Arsenic, used as a base for treating acne, was also used as face cream. Women used powders that often contained deadly mercury and lead. Rather than use commercial products, some women used creams and ointments made from recipes handed down through generations. Eventually peddlers, then manufacturers, began to make and sell soap and lotions. Makeup had been condemned earlier in the century when physical beauty was linked to moral purity, but by the 1860s the use of makeup, including lipstick, rouge, and mascara, became acceptable. Its use increased among middle-class and wealthy women.

Hair grooming also displayed individuals' sense of personal hygiene. Men's hair was groomed with Macassar oil, which was so greasy that antimacassar was created to protect furniture from oily stains. Women used powders and dyes on their hair. Lye soap was harsh, so they often used herbal treatments as conditioner. Many people had problems with lice and had to use fine-toothed combs to remove lice.

Fashion was also linked to health. Women wanted small waists and laced their corsets so tightly that headaches and fainting became common. Uterine and spinal ailments may also have resulted from tight lacing. Tight clothing was considered harmful to women's reproductive and mental health. Long skirts were deemed unhygienic as they would pick up dirt and germs from streets and sidewalks. Tight corsets were also blamed for poor posture, and tight shoes made walking difficult.

To be fashionable, affluent women wore flimsy silk shoes rather than waterproof boots, and delicate shawls over short sleeves rather than warm weatherproof cloaks of flannel and wool, which were not considered ladylike, until late in the war.

The National Dress Reform Association (NDRA) was formed to address the relationship of health to fashion. The NDRA favored shorter skirts worn over pantaloons or bloomers rather than full-length skirts. The basic premise was to prevent disease through a healthy lifestyle. However, there were some religious groups, such as the Seventh-Day Adventists, that opposed the masculine appearance of women in pants. Because some in the women's rights movement had advocated bloomers and pantaloons, politics also had an impact on this mode of dressing.

Women's gym wear was loose to allow athletic movement, but was acceptable only when worn in the company of other women. Dr. Dio Lewis excoriated women for wearing corsets that inhibited proper breathing, and shoes too small to walk in. Water cure patients who dressed in loose-fitting clothing, the American Costume, during treatment renounced the outfits when finished with treatment.

Advances in personal hygiene also included tooth care. Dentistry in mid-nineteenth-century America was underdeveloped. Toothbrushes, handmade of wood with boar bristles, were rare and were not mass-produced until late in the century. Toothpowder, available commercially, or homemade, was used to clean teeth. Diet was not conducive to healthy teeth.

Military recruits were required to have enough opposing upper and lower front teeth to bite off the end of the powder cartridges to load into rifles. Although the Confederate Army established a dental corps, the Union did not. Military dentists cleaned teeth, filled cavities, and often worked on jaw injuries. Although different metals were used for filling cavities, gold was the most common as it lasted a long time without deleterious effect. Tin was sometimes used as a cheaper substitute during the war.

It was difficult for Civil War soldiers to keep up with personal hygiene on the battlefields and in camps, so disease spread easily. A majority of deaths among soldiers in the Civil War resulted from diseases such as diarrhea, dysentery, and typhoid fever. The lack of clean water was one obstacle to cleanliness. In addition, general knowledge of and attitudes toward hygiene were also limited by the lack of widespread indoor plumbing in both urban and rural communities. Soldiers from rural communities were not used to latrines, and often did not use them in the camps, creating unsanitary conditions. In addition, those who did not understand that hospital water closets were only for human waste often plugged them up with other things. In some camps, poorly placed latrines contaminated water supplies leading to the spread of disease.

In 1861, the United States Sanitary Commission (USSC), an umbrella organization for the numerous volunteer organizations run by women in the North, was established. After surveying and discovering unsanitary camp conditions, the members of the USSC raised money from private donations and distributed supplies to the soldiers. They also provided nurses to Union hospitals. Their efforts greatly reduced the numbers of deaths from disease.

Hygiene in the Civil War years was poor, but developing. It was not until late in the nineteenth century that healthy lifestyle reform movements began to grow.

Jane Brodsky Fitzpatrick

See also: Clothing, Fashion, and Appearance: Clothing, Status and Position; Clothing, Style and Function; Fashion; Undergarments; *Economy and Work*: Rural Life, Northern; Rural Life, Southern; Urban Life, Northern; Urban Life, Southern; *Family Life and Gender Roles*: United States Sanitary Commission (USSC); *Politics and Warfare*: Camp Life; *Science and Technology*: Disease; Hospitals; Sanitation

FURTHER READING

Banner, Lois W. *American Beauty*. Chicago: University of Chicago Press, 1983.
Fischer, Gayle V. *Pantaloons and Power: A Nineteenth-Century Dress Reform in the United States*. Kent, OH: Kent State University Press, 2001.

SEWING SOCIETIES

At the beginning of the Civil War, both Union and Confederate women formed sewing societies to provide uniforms, underclothing, blankets, socks, tents, haversacks, regimental flags, and other necessities for soldiers in the field. Part of a massive voluntary effort by women on the home front, sewing societies often evolved into more general soldiers' aid societies, and people made little distinction between the two. Through sewing societies, women of all ages contributed to the war effort, gained a sense of civic usefulness, exchanged news and information about the war, and socialized. After the war, women transformed many of these societies into memorial organizations and relief associations dedicated to the needs of veterans and former slaves.

When the war began, many women expressed a strong desire to support their male relatives and other enlistees from their communities. Most mid-nineteenth-century women sewed or knit on a daily basis, so they immediately considered how they might use needle and thread to provide for the soldiers. Although countless women pursued this work individually in their homes, many also chose to sew with others in organized groups. Throughout the North, sewing circles and other female voluntary associations had become widespread during the antebellum period, and wartime sewing societies often grew out of these organizations. Female associations had been much less prevalent in the South before the war, given the more rural nature of the region and the greater emphasis on the patriarchal family within society. Still, within urban areas of the South, by 1861 considerable numbers of women belonged to female voluntary organizations.

North and South, many women had their hands full providing food and clothing for their own families, before helping to clothe and equip the armies. Most sewing societies, therefore, were founded by middle- and upper-class women who had the time and resources to spare. Some of the larger sewing societies provided income for less-privileged women and specifically sought to employ the wives of soldiers. Slaveholding women enlisted their enslaved women to assist with the work. In both sections of the country, organizers of sewing societies used their local newspapers to solicit new members and donations of materials.

Most sewing societies had a fairly narrow focus when first created. Organizers sought to outfit specific military units that included local men. Newspaper announcements about the formation of sewing societies made note of the military companies to be supplied. Societies created by free black women in the North, however, often had a broader outlook than did associations organized by white women. African American women's groups initially focused on providing clothing and other items for the divided nation's ex-slaves who had sought refuge behind Union lines. These organizations eventually also supplied black soldiers once they were permitted to join the Union Army in 1863.

Sewing societies ranged from informal groups to highly structured organizations. Some met in private homes, while others gathered at local churches. A print published in Baltimore in 1863, for example, showed three Confederate women spinning, weaving, and sewing in a household setting. The more complex sewing societies developed as women sought to meet the vast need of supplying the men in the field. In September 1861, for example, several female leaders in Memphis, Tennessee, promoted "systematic and united action and effort" through a centralized "Military Aid Society" focused on sewing; the organizers appealed to women to form branches in each ward of the city. In order to purchase needed supplies, some sewing societies took on additional responsibilities by organizing fund-raisers, including fairs, dramatic tableaux, and concerts. In the North, some local associations were formally connected to the United States Sanitary Commission and other national relief organizations.

The more formal sewing societies provided women with experience at large-scale organizing and fund-raising, but they were not for everyone; some women rejected sewing societies as too hierarchical and cliquish. In addition, as the war dragged on, some societies died out as women became exhausted by the demands of the

1861 engraving by Winslow Homer showing female members of a Civil War Sewing Circle making havelocks for the Union soldiers. Women in the North and South formed sewing societies to help provide uniforms, undergarments, blankets, hats, socks, tents, haversacks, regimental flags, and other necessary items to their soldiers. Sewing societies allowed women of all ages to contribute to the war effort as they socialized and traded news about the war and their loved ones. (Bettmann/Corbis)

war or, especially within the Confederacy, because they could not obtain essential raw materials.

Many women and men defined wartime sewing as evidence of female patriotism. Associating sewing with civic duty promoted the idea that women could be contributors to the public good, beyond their roles as mothers and wives.

Northern pictorial envelopes contained scenes of individual women sewing for the soldiers. One showed a woman sewing while sitting under an American flag, with the caption, "Our Hearts are with our Brothers in the Field." In diaries and letters, women referred to their sewing efforts as their way to further the cause from the home front. Appeals by the organizers of sewing societies encouraged women to join so that they could do their part to bring about victory. Within the Confederacy, where industrial production was far behind that in the North, many women recognized the importance of home production to the war effort. Even as women on both sides expressed their civic pride at contributing to a national cause, some women still wanted to personalize their work and sent along notes of encouragement with the items they sewed.

Sewing societies did not directly challenge accepted gender roles. Sewing was a feminine domestic task, and the goal of the societies was to provide for men in the field. After the war, women's memorial associations and relief organizations similarly fulfilled a traditional supportive role, but, like sewing societies, also gave women opportunities for leadership and civic responsibility.

Antoinette G. van Zelm

See also: Family Life and Gender Roles: Aid Societies; United States Sanitary Commission (USSC); *Recreation and Social Customs*: Fairs and Bazaars; Sanitary Fairs

FURTHER READING

Faust, Drew Gilpin. *Mothers of Invention: Women of the Slaveholding South in the American Civil War.* New York: Vintage Books, 1996.

Janney, Caroline E. *Burying the Dead But Not the Past: Ladies' Memorial Associations and the Lost Cause.* Chapel Hill: University of North Carolina Press, 2008.

Library of Congress. "Our Hearts Are with Our Brothers in the Field. [Pictorial envelope]." Civil War Treasures from the New-York Historical Society, 2013. http://memory.loc.gov/cgi-bin/query/r?ammem/cwnyhs:@field(DOCID+@lit(aj88007)). Accessed April 10, 2013.

Silber, Nina. *Daughters of the Union: Northern Women Fight the Civil War.* Cambridge, MA: Harvard University Press, 2005.

SHORTAGES, CLOTHING

The Confederate States experienced severe clothing shortages by the end of the Civil War as a result of several combined factors. One of those factors was the South's limited production of finished cloth compared to that of the North and Europe, creating a dependence on imported textiles. These imports became limited with the implementation of the Union blockade. Without new imported textiles Southern women responded by weaving their own cloth, called homespun, and remaking old garments. Shortages worsened as more fabric was needed for the war effort, and cotton crops were destroyed by warfare. By the end of the Civil War in 1865, several relief efforts were starting to focus on relieving the clothing shortages that had developed throughout the South.

One of the South's largest cash crops was cotton. A labor-intensive crop, cotton could be easily ruined by changes in weather or pests such as armyworms. However, after the invention of the cotton gin, it became easier to harvest and possible to turn a greater profit. Southern farmers primarily sold their cotton to European textile manufactures or textile manufacturers in the Northern states; very little remained in the South for manufacturing. Exporting the cotton thus allowed Southern farmers to immediately profit from their crop and import finished textiles of varying grades from abroad.

Before the Civil War the cotton that remained in the South was manufactured primarily in Georgia and Alabama. The region was not entirely bereft of textile manufacturers, but the mills built prior to 1830 tended to be temporary structures. They were meant to serve the local clientele for a few years, potentially while there was a cotton surplus on the market, and then to have key pieces of the manufacturing moved. By the 1840s more permanent mills developed, often associated with a key family or town figure. Although many of these mills also disbanded within a few years, others lasted until the start of the Civil War and were able to produce cloth for the Confederacy. However, because the limited number of mills were concentrated in one geographic region they could not develop production levels to meet the South's growing needs. Recognizing these issues early during the war, many plantations and smaller farms began producing homespun cloth but with limited success due to a lack of experience and tools.

The production levels in Southern mills could not be brought up to the needed levels, so some decided to continue the importation of finished textiles. Blockade running was a dangerous but lucrative means of alleviating shortages for the wealthy, who could pay the fees set by those risking the consequences of smuggling items through the Union blockade. Materials brought in by blockade runners were often imported from Europe and met the same high standards as antebellum clothing, but only the wealthy members of society who lived near major harbors had the ability to purchase these materials. For those members of society with fewer financial means and who did not live along the Atlantic coast but near Union lines, a similar option was also available. Men and women could cross Union lines to acquire much-needed supplies, including new fabric for clothes. Crossing Union lines had dangers of its own, and many were not willing to risk them unless the need was dire or they could profit financially. By the end of the Civil War men or women who wore new clothes in the latest fashions were believed to have crossed Union lines. Many are believed to have acted as spies for either the Union or the Confederacy.

The majority of people, however, did not have access to the textiles being produced in the South and could not afford materials which had been brought through Union lines. Their one clear option was altering old garments in an attempt to make them both last longer and imitate the latest fashions. Another option was to construct garments out of materials that had previously never been considered for the task. Although new dresses for special occasions were quickly abandoned because it was prohibitive to purchase material for a full dress, certain occasions such as weddings required the bride to be dressed in something special. One popular method of extending a garment's life, called turning, was often used to make a new bridal dress. Using this method the wearer would wait until the garment became worn and faded, perhaps even singed from cooking, then take the garment apart and turn it inside out reconstructing it so that the bright, unworn interior became the exterior. Another option was to create the dress out of fabric that was on hand but was not traditionally dress material. Mary Boykin Chesnut (1823–1886), the wife of Confederate general James Chesnut, recorded in her diary constructing a wedding dress out of curtain muslin for the daughter of Governor Aiken. She also gave several accounts of Confederate brides wearing turned dresses. For more routine wear women patched garments and updated them with new decorative details to extend their use. When a garment became too worn for someone of the same size to continue wearing, it might be resized for a younger family member or, if no repairs could be made, it could be made into bandages for the soldiers. In the rare cases that a family had excess clothing, it could be sold to acquire other much-needed resources.

The needs of the military complicated the clothing shortages. The Confederacy made use of manufactured textiles produced in the South to create uniforms for the troops, but it also required linen for bandages. By the end of the war, the Confederacy's soldiers required more uniforms than could be made with cloth manufactured in Southern mills. As a result civilian families were forced not only to clothe themselves but also to outfit male relatives in the military. To complicate matters as the war traveled further south and east, cotton crops were destroyed, eliminating the raw materials that the South needed to produce the vast quantities of cloth that they required.

Siobhan Fitzpatrick

See also: *Clothing, Fashion, and Appearance*: Children's Dress, Confederate; Clothing, Status and Position; Dress, Slaves; Fashion; Homespun; Men's Dress, Confederate Civilian; Sewing Societies; Textiles; Women's Dress, Confederate

FURTHER READING

Chesnut, Mary Boykin. *Mary Chesnut's Civil War*. Edited by C. Vann Woodward. New Haven, CT: Yale University Press, 1981.

Faust, Drew Gilpin. *Mothers of Invention: Women of the Slaveholding South in the American Civil War*. Chapel Hill: University of North Carolina Press, 1996.

Massey, Mary Elizabeth. *Ersatz in the Confederacy: Shortages and Substitutes on the Southern Homefront*. Columbia: University of South Carolina Press, 1952; 1993.

Rable, George C. *Civil Wars: Women and the Crisis of Southern Nationalism*. Urbana: University of Illinois Press, 1991.

Turner, Julie. "Textile Industry in LaGrange, Georgia." Historic American Engineering Record (HAER No. GA-98). Washington, DC: U.S. Department of the Interior, National Park Service, 1998.

Volo, Dorothy Denneen, and Jame M. Volo. *Daily Life in Civil War America*. Santa Barbara, CA: ABC-CLIO, 2009.

TEXTILES

At the beginning of the Civil War, textile manufacturing in the United States held the dominant role in generating industrial production and wealth. Goods manufactured in mills built along the Quinebaug-Shetucket and Blackstone River valleys in eastern Connecticut and western Rhode Island in the early nineteenth century had slowly replaced homespun goods. As demand for textiles expanded in the decades to follow, U.S. Census figures captured the unprecedented expansion in textile manufacturing. For example, in Massachusetts alone $17.4 million was invested in the industry by 1840, and by 1860 that number rose to $33 million.

Textiles in 1860 fell into four categories or classes: cotton; woolens, silk, and flax; hemp; and mixed fabrics such as *mouselline de laine*. Cotton generated the greatest capital investment in the economy, and produced the largest profits. The first cotton factory in the United States was built in Beverly, Massachusetts, in 1787 and contained a spinning jenny with a carding machine constructed by Joshua Lindly of Providence, Rhode Island. Eleven years later, Samuel Slater arrived in Providence and, using what he remembered of Richard Arkwright's English design, built the first water-frame machinery in the United States, and opened a new cotton mill in Pawtucket, Rhode Island.

In 1800, 14 mills operated fewer than 200 spindles and by 1804 the number of mills in Rhode Island, Massachusetts, and Connecticut doubled. By 1820, there was approximately one loom for every 160 spindles, and an estimated 167,000 spindles in Rhode Island, Massachusetts, Connecticut, and New Hampshire.

The Southern states also enjoyed unprecedented economic development in the same four decades earning the sobriquet "The Cotton South," and "King Cotton." As the North and West demanded raw cotton from the South, the South demanded finished textile products from the North and West. This symbiotic relationship, however, led to different economic and labor patterns within the various sections of the country. Whereas the North expanded industrial technology, manufacturing practices, and a free labor force, the South expanded its agricultural property, plantation culture, and enslaved labor force.

Despite these distinct patterns of economic formation there was some overlap. The South enjoyed modest success in the textile industry building mills in Virginia, North Carolina, South Carolina, and Georgia. At first, poor whites outnumbered enslaved blacks working in these Southern mills, but as transportation costs increased and competition with the North intensified, Southern mill owners found it practical to pay slaveholders anywhere between $110 and $160 per year for the use of their slaves in the mills. Furthermore, after 1840, as manufacturing technology improved and Northern mills started producing vast quantities of cloth,

Southern textile manufacturing began to decline. At the same time the North and Great Britain's demand for raw cotton increased, making the South's economic priority the growing and selling of cotton. By 1860 the combined capital investment for cotton goods manufactured in the entire South was only $9.5 million, in New England it was $66 million, and in the Middle States it was $17 million.

Next to cotton manufacturing, woolen and worsted goods were produced on an extensive scale. As the region did with cotton, New England in general and Massachusetts in particular made the finest products in the United States. Pennsylvania, Ohio, Kentucky, and Virginia also had some woolen mills scattered throughout their borders, but for the most part these states only made yarns consumed for domestic use. These products from these mills contrasted sharply with woolen goods made in Massachusetts's establishments.

The Bay State Mills in Lawrence, Massachusetts, manufactured a variety of fabrics. With 2,200 employees, 1,200 of them women, and working with carding machines, looms, dye works, and printing shops for flannels and carpets, the factory made thousands of yards of plain flannels, twilled flannels, cassimeres, satinettes, broadcloths, beaver-cloths, felted carpets, felted linings, all wool long shawls, and all wool square shawls. The mill dyed the flannels in a number of colors, and a fringing machine made the fringes on each shawl.

By 1860 the woolen industry expanded further than did the manufacture of cotton, and a number of small mills producing linseys and flannels appeared in the western states. These businesses provided basic cloth for western farmers and consequently felt no compunction to politically support the Northeast's demand for high protective tariffs directed at British woolen goods. The Walker Tariff of 1846 and the even lower Tariff of 1857 invoked the ire of large woolen manufacturing companies. In New England, New York, and Pennsylvania where the combined total of the annual woolen product value was $34 million, British competition in woolen goods was viewed as threatening, and these states demanded greater protectionism. As large water-powered mills continued to drive new textile machinery, New England entrepreneurs invested huge amounts of capital into new technologies and products. The tariff was a contentious issue as the war approached.

Before the war, silk fabric in the United States was not made in significant quantities. Virginia, Ohio, Kentucky, and Tennessee cultivated silk, and some businesses could produce as much as 3,000 pounds of the thread from the cocoons. The largest mills were located in Connecticut and New Jersey, and these factories produced sewing silks, floss silks, ribbons, and silks for fringes and gimps.

Hemp used in the production of ropes, cables, sailcloth, and some carpeting was grown in Missouri and Virginia and some hemp was imported. Flax grown in

Pennsylvania and Ohio was used in the manufacturing of linens, and the seed was used for oil making. Finally, manufactured mixed fabrics such as *mouselline de laine*, which was made mostly of wool, were made in New England in very small supply.

Just before the war, some Southerners promoted manufacturing as a way to increase economic independence. Southern nationalist Edmund Ruffin, for example, believed an independent manufacturing base was essential to support a potential independent Confederacy. Abundant raw materials and waterpower provided fine conditions for an emerging textile industry. Some in the planter class, however, felt threatened by attempts to introduce industrialization into the region, and small farmers could not generate enough capital to start a business. Moreover, because Southern agriculture flooded the English market with raw cotton and enjoyed a reciprocal free trade arrangement with Great Britain, some worried that a strong manufacturing sector of the economy might hurt the South's own cotton trade. A higher tariff to protect the South's nascent manufacturing industry from English textiles would elicit a sharp response from Britain. From 1851 to 1855 Southern nationalists met at an annual convention to discuss the establishment of a manufacturing base so they could break the strangle hold they felt Northern manufactures had on them. Nothing came of these meetings before the shots were fired at Fort Sumter.

Thomas Army

See also: *Economy and Work*: Factory Owners; Factory Workers, Northern; Factory Workers, Southern; Slavery; *Family Life and Gender Roles*: Immigrants; Young Men; Young Women; *Housing and Community*: Factory Towns; *Science and Technology*: Factories

FURTHER READING

Clark, Victor S. *History of Manufactures in the United States, Vol. 1, 1607–1860*. Reprint ed. New York: Peter Smith, 1949 (1929).

Department of State, *Statistics of the United States of America as Collected and Returned by the Marshals of the Several Judicial Districts Under the 13th Section of the Act for Taking the Sixth Census Corrected at the Department of State June 1, 1840*. Vol. 4. Washington, DC: Blair and Rives, 1841.

Secretary of the Interior. *Manufactures of the United States in 1860; Compiled from the Original Returns of the Eighth Census*. Prepared in American Industry and Manufactures in the 19th Century. Vol. 6. Elmsford, NY: Maxwell Reprint Company, 1970.

Wallis, George, and Joseph Whitworth. *The American System of Manufactures: The Report of the Committee on the Machinery of the United States 1855 and the Special Reports of George Wallis and Joseph Whitworth*. Edited by Nathan Rosenberg. Edinburgh, Scotland: Edinburgh University Press, 1969.

UNDERGARMENTS

Undergarments worn during the Civil War were designed with the practical purpose of providing warmth and cover-up for men. However, women's undergarments were designed to shape the body.

Men's undershirts were called simply "shirts," while "blouse" or "top-shirt" described what are now known as shirts. Undershirts were long pullovers, sometimes fastened at the neck with buttons or lace. In addition to shirts, men wore knee or ankle-length drawers under their pants, usually made of wool, but also made with muslin (cotton) or jersey. The drawers had an open fly front that buttoned at the top and adjusted at the back with a buckle or lacing. Laces at the ankle or knee would keep the drawers from riding up. Often, men wore long shirttails instead of drawers and the army-issued drawers were sometimes the first they ever wore. The final article of underwear was a pair of socks, almost always made of wool and often handmade. If socks were not entirely handmade, then female pieceworkers added toes and heels by hand to tubes manufactured in mills. Women and girls wore stockings rather than socks, which came up above the knee and were fastened by garters.

Underwear was often in short supply during the war for soldiers, especially for prisoners of war. Although the Union Army purchased almost 11 million sets of drawers for Northern soldiers, these were only made in three sizes, which did not fit well and could be uncomfortable. In addition, army-issued underwear often shrank when laundered. Many factories produced drawers for the army, sometimes using knit fabric or merino wool. As a result of the shortage of drawers, soldiers who raided homes and supply depots often took undergarments as part of their spoils of war.

To supplement the soldiers' army-issued undergarments, women in both the North and South sewed drawers and shirts for Civil War soldiers. Canton flannel, cotton with a fleecy lining, was often used for these undergarments. Women would often tear their own clothing so that they could reuse it to make shirts and drawers for the men in the field. There was a shortage of undergarments in hospitals, and a plea was sent to women to volunteer to sew more using a specified pattern.

Rather than launder their undergarments, many soldiers relied on new supplies to be sent from home. Hygiene was difficult at best, and soldiers might not change underwear more than once a week, some even went as long as six weeks without a clean set of drawers. Although flannel underwear was hot to wear in summer, it protected men from the chafing of their woolen military pants.

Women's underwear was more elaborate than was men's since its purpose was to shape women's waists and bosoms. During the course of the Civil War, the profile of women's dress changed from a completely round shape to a flat front with a train. Petticoats were responsible for maintaining the correct shape of a garment. Metal hoops, made of flexible steel, were like cages that kept skirts full. By the Civil War, corsets had become short garments closed by front clips rather than the back-laced garments of the 1850s. Corsets were sometimes worn over crinolines (hooped petticoats) and petticoats to create as small a waist as possible. Although usually white, corsets were occasionally off-white, red, or black. By the end of the Civil War, busks (long steel rods inserted into the front of a corset to keep the corset rigid) replaced rear laces for putting on and removing the corset. Petticoats began to show when skirts were hiked up in the back and became colorful with the advent of new aniline dyes.

Women also wore chemises, large garments tightened at the neck with drawstrings that had large sleeves that would be pressed into pleats. Chemises could be worn over or tucked into drawers. Chemises and drawers were worn against the skin, and the corset was worn on top of the chemise to shape the body for the dress. Often hand sewn, chemises would be made of fine linen and could be elaborately decorated. Patterns were published in *Godey's Lady's Book*. Knickers, or drawers, consisted of separate sections that laced together only at the back of the waist, but were otherwise open from waist to the leg edge. The open crotch made trips to the outhouse easier. They were secured at the waist by overlapping and crossing ties and were voluminous. By the 1860s, there were several patents for various bust-enhancing garments.

During the Civil War, women's undergarments also became difficult to procure. Many women stopped wearing hoops and wore fewer petticoats under their clothing.

Jane Brodsky Fitzpatrick

See also: *Clothing, Fashion, and Appearance*: Clothing, Style and Function; Fashion; *Godey's Ladies Book*; Homespun; Hoop Skirts; Personal Hygiene; Sewing Societies; Shortages, Clothing; Uniforms, Confederate; Uniforms, Union; Women's Dress, Confederate; Women's Dress, Union; *Science and Technology*: Factories

FURTHER READING

Ewing, Elizabeth. *Underwear: A History*. New York: Theatre Arts Books, 1972.
Stamper, Anita A., and Jill Condra. *Clothing Through American History: The Civil War Through the Gilded Age, 1861–1899*. Santa Barbara, CA: ABC-CLIO, 2011.

UNIFORMS, CONFEDERATE

Confederate soldiers went to war more hastily than did their Union counterparts. When they left for war, Southern soldiers needed uniforms to distinguish themselves from civilians and from the enemy forces. Uniforms also helped to encourage group solidarity. Initially the government provided cash payments to soldiers who outfitted themselves. As a result, most Confederate soldiers left for war in 1861 with locally made uniforms. Consequently, there was very little uniformity in their dress.

In response to the difficulties of identifying Confederate soldiers by their dress, by 1862 the Confederate Congress mandated that soldiers wear regulated uniforms provided by the government instead of those made locally. These regulation uniforms would include a gray frock coat, a shirt, dark blue trousers, shoes, and a cap. Although the Confederate government stated its intention to provide to soldiers specific uniforms that conformed to military regulation, in reality the government had little ability to provide adequate supplies to its troops. Although the Confederacy had vast amounts of raw materials at its disposal, it did not have the manufacturing capacity to turn these raw materials into finished products. It took the Confederacy until 1863 to establish an internal manufacturing base to provide soldiers with the proper equipment to fight the war. Once the manufacturing capabilities had been established and factories in North Carolina, Tennessee, and Virginia were producing Confederate uniforms, these products were not necessarily of good quality.

The inferior quality of the uniforms issued by the Confederate government caused the soldiers to look elsewhere for their clothing so that they could avoid marching into battle dressed in rags. They once again turned to their families to provide them with the supplies that they needed to defend the Confederacy. The women on the home front continued to produce shirts, coats, pants, socks, undergarments, and other necessary items for the soldiers. These homespun clothes were usually more comfortable and more durable than the uniforms provided by the Confederate government. The homespun clothing was distinguishable from the uniforms issued by the Confederate government due to the distinct color of "Butternut"; the use of this dye for clothing was a direct result of the effectiveness of the Union Naval blockade of the South as the war progressed. The dye became the symbol of the homespun clothing movement that kept the Confederate soldiers, and the civilians on the home front, clothed as the war progressed.

In addition to the problems encountered in manufacturing sturdy Confederate uniforms, the lack of early regulations prescribing the proper uniform to be worn by Confederate soldiers continued to make things difficult for Confederate soldiers and commanders. Confederate citizens stressed issues of state's rights even in relation to providing proper uniforms for their soldiers. The decentralized nature of the Confederate economy and its manufacturing lent itself to problems of hoarding on the part of the individual states. States within the Confederacy hoarded reserves of supplies, including uniforms, that surpassed their own needs, insisting that they might need these supplies in the future for their own soldiers. Because the Confederate government had been established with the principles of state's rights at its core, the central government could not argue against the problem of hoarding. Individual states in the Confederacy also further infringed upon the central government's ability to outfit its soldiers by buying up the uniforms produced by local factories and outfitting the units themselves. Although the purchase of uniforms by communities to outfit their soldiers seems like a positive thing for the Confederacy, it did not prove so. After purchasing these uniforms, states would subsequently request the money allocated for the uniforms from the Confederate government.

Although the Confederacy did not start the war with the best systems in place or much uniformity, by 1863 much had been standardized in the way of uniforms for its soldiers. By that point, the war had become one between the Union blue and Confederate gray. However, just as the Confederacy had finally achieved some standardization with respect to its military uniforms, the Union blockade caused Confederates to look elsewhere for resources to make those uniforms. As a result, a lack of uniformity returned to the Confederate ranks.

Sean M. Walsh

See also: *Clothing, Fashion, and Appearance*: Homespun; Textiles; Uniforms, Union; *Family Life and Gender Roles*: Womanhood, Southern; Young Women; *Science and Technology*: Factories

FURTHER READING

Arliskas, Thomas M. *Cadet Gray and Butternut Brown: Notes on Confederate Uniforms.* Gettysburg, PA: Thomas Publications, 2006.

Barton, Michael, and Larry M. Logue, eds. *The Civil War Soldier: A Historical Reader.* New York: New York University Press, 2002.

Haythornthwaite, Philip J. *Uniforms of the American Civil War.* Poole, UK: Blandford Press, 1975.

Uniform and Dress of the Army of the Confederate States. Adjutant and Inspector General's Office. Richmond, VA: Chas. H. Wynne, 1861.

Uniform and Dress of the Navy of the Confederate States. Washington, DC: Government Printing Office, 1898.

Waugh, Joan. "Military Uniforms of the Civil War." In Joan Waugh and Gary B. Nash, eds. *Encyclopedia of American History: Civil War and Reconstruction, 1856 to 1869.* Revised ed. Vol. V. New York: Facts on File, Inc., 2010. *American History Online.* Facts On File, Inc. http://www.fofweb.com/activelink2.asp?ItemID=WE52&iPin=EAHV296&SingleRecord=True. Accessed October 7, 2013.

UNIFORMS, UNION

During the American Civil War, military uniforms provided physical protection for the soldier and ideological cohesion within the unit. Uniforms promoted a sense of identity, loyalty, and pride. The Union Army was better equipped and more uniformly clad than its Southern counterpart as the North maintained manufacturing bases and international trade throughout the war. Naval blockades and poor distribution networks handicapped the Confederate Army's ability to obtain coherent uniforms. Blue was associated with Union Army uniforms, while gray was associated with Confederate Army uniforms.

Military uniforms were designed to allow the distinction between civilians and the military as well as to distinguish one army from another. They also helped promote a group identity among the soldiers. Military uniforms at the time of the American Civil War were meant to meet those established criteria, but these goals were not always accomplished in the best manner possible for the soldiers.

When the war began in 1861 the Union Army needed to outfit its new recruits similarly so they would be easily identified as soldiers of the Union military. Army

Wartime image of uniforms worn by Union soldiers. Uniforms helped foster cohesion among soldiers as it distinguished one army from another. Most Union soldiers wore blue uniforms. (National Archives)

regulations laid out what every soldier was to be issued, including the standard infantry uniform of a blue frock coat, "sack" coat, shirt, wool socks, and light blue trousers. In addition, soldiers were issued a high black hat with a wide brim, called a "Hardee hat," although most preferred a smaller forage cap for marching. Furthermore, each soldier was issued brogans. The Office of the Quartermaster was responsible for outfitting the soldiers with their uniforms. Along with their uniforms, Union soldiers were also issued necessary items that included canteens, blankets, tents, haversacks, and muskets. As the war progressed the War Department provided manufacturers with measurements, or sizes, for different items of clothing for the soldiers.

Early in the war, communities provided their soldiers with uniforms. As a result, there was little uniformity in Union military uniforms. This provisioning by the town was usually done out of patriotic fever, but also gave each unit a style of its own. Local outfitting made things cheaper for the War Department, which subsequently did not have to provide these soldiers with uniforms. However locally supplied uniforms rarely met the regulations laid out by the War Department. Even though homemade uniforms were usually of higher quality than the uniforms supplied by the War Department, the look and style of these uniforms did not meet military regulations.

The uniforms of the 114th Pennsylvania and 164th New York Zouaves illuminate the wide variety of locally supplied uniforms. Zouaves typically wore exotic and colorful uniforms that looked nothing like the army-issued items. The *New York Times* noted the non-uniform nature of the Union uniform situation in 1861. To add further dissemblance, in the hotter months and while in the field, soldiers quickly took to lightening their load. Soldiers often stripped down their uniforms to what they truly needed, leaving behind coats and other winter items.

In the early days of the war, the War Department was able to get uniforms to the soldiers, although the distribution system lacked a cohesive method of dispersal. In an attempt to correct the mistakes caused by this disarray, soldiers would trade among themselves for uniforms that fit them better or for other specific items that they needed. Shortages in the uniforms themselves, in addition to their poor quality and their inadequate distribution, can be explained by the surrounding circumstances.

The problems with the actual clothing provided to soldiers of the Union Army often made a soldier's life much more difficult. Even the shoes provided by the military could make life painful. In most cases, soldiers preferred to march barefoot than to subject their feet to the inadequate shoes provided by the War Department. Disgusted by their government-issued shoes, Union soldiers often joked "Trust in God; but keep your shoes easy."

By 1863, the War Department had mostly gotten control over the outfitting of the soldiers. From that point on, the soldiers fighting to preserve the Union had uniformity in their attire and were issued the proper equipment to go into battle.

Sean M. Walsh

See also: *Clothing, Fashion, and Appearance*: Uniforms, Confederate

FURTHER READING

Barton, Michael, and Larry M. Logue, eds. *The Civil War Soldier: A Historical Reader.* New York: New York University Press, 2002.

Bates, Christopher. "Industrial Development During the Civil War." In Joan Waugh and Gary B. Nash, eds. *Encyclopedia of American History: Civil War and Reconstruction, 1856 to 1869.* Revised ed. Vol. V. New York: Facts on File, Inc., 2010. *American History Online.* Facts on File, Inc. http://www.fofweb.com/activelink2.asp?ItemID=WE52&iPin=EAHV153&SingleRecord=True. Accessed October 7, 2013.

Haythornthwaite, Philip J. *Uniforms of the American Civil War.* Poole, UK: Blandford Press, 1975.

Illustrated Catalogue of Arms and Military Goods, Containing Regulations for the Uniform of the Army, Navy, Marine and Revenue Corps of the United States. New York: Schuyler, Hartley, and Graham, 1864.

Smith, Robin. *American Civil War: Union Army.* London: Brassey's, 2003.

U.S. Army. *Regulations for the Uniform and Dress of the Army of the United States, June 1851.* Philadelphia: William A. Horstmann and Sons, 1851.

U.S. Government Printing Office. *Regulations for the Uniform and Dress of the Navy of the United States.* New York: Tomes, Melvain & Company, 1864.

U.S. War Department. *Revised Regulations for the Army of the United States, 1861, with a Full Index, by the Authority of the War Department.* Philadelphia: George W. Childs, 1862.

Waugh, Joan. "Military Uniforms of the Civil War." In Joan Waugh and Gary B. Nash, eds. *Encyclopedia of American History: Civil War and Reconstruction, 1856 to 1869.* Revised ed. Vol. V. New York: Facts on File, Inc., 2010. *American History Online.* Facts On File, Inc. http://www.fofweb.com/activelink2.asp?ItemID=WE52&iPin=EAHV296&SingleRecord=True. Accessed October 7, 2013.

WOMEN'S DRESS, CONFEDERATE

Women's clothing in the South marked vast extremes of wealth and poverty, freedom and servitude. Upper-class women, the wives and daughters of planters and merchants, were some of the most fashionable women in the United States before the Civil War. Enslaved African American women wore what planters provided to them, what they could barter for with itinerant merchants, or what they could weave and sew on their own. Rural and working-class women often manufactured their own clothing from cotton and linen they wove at home and colored with plants and other natural dyes. Because of wartime shortages women's dress in the South, especially among the upper class, diverged sharply from that in the North. Women north and south, however, used clothing to project their identity and individuality according to their own needs and the standards of their communities.

Women's clothing in the nineteenth century was elaborate, heavy, and restrictive. Layered undergarments and hoops or crinolines beneath dresses and gowns shaped the silhouette, emphasizing a narrow waist by widening the shoulders and hips. Hoops created a dome around the legs several feet in diameter, while tightly strung corsets artificially—and often painfully—narrowed the waist and enforced rigid posture. Clothing revealed little more than the face, neck, and hands during the day; evening gowns sometimes featured lower necklines that revealed the shoulders. In addition to the ways it shaped the body and created an ideal

Wartime photograph of a Confederate woman, her soldier husband, and their baby. Nineteenth-century Southern women wore fashions that were generally elaborate, heavy, and restrictive and emphasized small waists by widening the shoulders and hips. When material became scarce during the Civil War, many Southern women took pride in wearing dresses made of homespun cotton. (Library of Congress)

of feminine beauty, clothing provided a screen for the modesty of middle- and upper-class Southern women, who were expected to project an air of refined, unaffected propriety at nearly all times.

Less privileged women owned fewer articles of clothing than their elite counterparts. The ready availability of cotton, flax, jute, and hemp in the South, however, ensured that rich and poor alike were often dressed in the same fabrics. Light, relatively durable, and inexpensive cotton was the most widespread. "Lowell cloth" manufactured in New England textile mills was popular, although poorer women and bondservants were often garbed in homespun cotton fabric. Linen, most often made from flax, was ideal for working clothes, aprons, and other items that needed to be durable. Farms across the South maintained flax patches for this ready supply of raw material. Although commercial dyes were available in the 1850s, women favored natural dyes made from plants for clothing, which was soaked in a mordant after dying to set the color. Stripes, checks, ribbons, buttons, and small floral prints embellished the quietly harmonious color palettes produced by these natural dyes. Wool was also popular during colder months. Silks, available from Northern and European suppliers through local factors or occasionally sold by itinerant vendors in the countryside, were relatively rare among all but the most privileged. In all aspects of dress, Southern women both subscribed to the aesthetic and moral requirements of their communities and expressed their own individuality as their means allowed.

Enslaved African American women expressed many of the same ideals through their clothing, both voluntarily and involuntarily. Slave codes and plantation practice determined how bondservants should look; servility and inferiority was the rule. Despite their sense of patriarchal benevolence, planters distributed cheap, coarse, drab, and often poorly constructed clothing to field laborers, designed to last only until the next clothing allotment later the same year or as much as three years later. When available, shoes for enslaved laborers were of the lowest quality, often manufactured by leather workers on the plantation. Domestic servants, who represented the planter in public and in the home, were given finer clothing in keeping with their status. Rather than expressing the individuality of the wearer, however, these uniforms marked bondservants as well-maintained property of the wealthy planter whose household they served.

Clothing was an integral part of slavery. Certain articles of clothing and particular fabrics were associated with enslaved African Americans in the South. White women facing shortages during the war often complained of wearing homespun "Negro cloth," for example—a coarse burlap made of flax, hemp, or jute. Other items, like headwraps and large pockets on the dress, differentiated enslaved women from the ruling class even further. Despite these limits and expectations, African American women strove to express their individuality through dress. West

African clothing traditions varied widely, but the loose, colorful fabrics characteristic of African dress persisted among the enslaved communities in the American South. This was especially true of women's headwraps, which differed remarkably from the bonnets and other headgear favored by white Southerners. Jewelry and other adornments, like Chinaberry beads strung around the neck or coins around the ankle, allowed African American women to express both their individuality and their spirituality. Some women traded the produce of their garden patches with itinerant merchants for finer fabrics and accessories, while others, particularly men and women working in towns and cities, saved money for more fashionable items as well. Women in enslaved communities were especially well dressed on Sundays and other holidays, often in spite of the limitations placed on their appearance and self-expression by the institution of slavery. They made their own hoops for skirts; fabricated their own buttons, embellishments, and jewelry; and created their own distinctive headwear.

The Civil War challenged the vestimentary status quo throughout the South. Facing shortages, absences, and other challenges, women abandoned many aspects of the feminine ideal. Younger women often cut their hair short in an effort to spare impractical grooming and express solidarity with soldiers. Some women argued, with reformers in the North, that petticoats were impractical for women maintaining farm and household on their own. Shortages, meanwhile, limited the options available to Southern women. As clothes broke down, women repurposed household items like curtains and tablecloths to repair them and make new items. In addition to their association with bondservants and poorer women, homespun fabrics were often uncomfortable and difficult to produce as war ravaged the fields. The prevalence of hoop skirts subsided in the South as existing crinolines broke down. War in the South blurred the lines between home and battlefield, men and women.

Christopher B. Crenshaw

See also: *Clothing, Fashion, and Appearance*: Children's Dress, Confederate; Clothing, Status and Position; Clothing, Style and Function; Dress, Slaves; Fashion; *Godey's Ladies Book*; Homespun; Hoop Skirts; Jewelry; Mourning Clothes; Personal Hygiene; Sewing Societies; Shortages, Clothing; Textiles; Undergarments; Women's Dress, Union; *Family Life and Gender Roles*: Young Women; *Recreation and Social Customs*: Etiquette, Advice Manuals

FURTHER READING

Faust, Drew Gilpin. *Mothers of Invention: Women of the Slaveholding South in the American Civil War*. Chapel Hill: University of North Carolina Press, 1996.

Foster, Helen Bradley. *"New Raiments of Self": African American Clothing in the Antebellum South.* New York: Berg, 1997.

Perrot, Philippe. *Fashioning the Bourgeoisie: A History of Clothing in the Nineteenth Century.* Princeton, NJ: Princeton University Press, 1994.

Volo, Dorothy Denneen, and James M. Volo. *Daily life in Civil War America.* Westport, CT: Greenwood Press, 1998.

WOMEN'S DRESS, UNION

Clothing marked a Northern woman's class, status, employment, and beliefs before, during, and after the Civil War. Cumbersome, restrictive, and costly, women's cloth-

ing in the 1860s was perhaps more elaborate than at any other point in the century. On a daily basis, women of the upper- and middle-classes wore garments weighing as much as 25 pounds; wide hoops, restrictive corsets, and layers of undergarments shaped and often damaged their bodies, while etiquette and fashion for these most fortunate women required frequent changes throughout the day as well. Although working-class women were not held to the same elaborate standards of refined fashion, propriety called on women of all classes to project an idealized version of feminine respectability through their attire. Some women rebelled against the demanding fashion of the era, however, arguing that women's clothing damaged their health and symbolized political and

Photograph of Kate Chase (later Sprague), the daughter of widowed United States secretary of the treasury Salmon P. Chase and his hostess during his time in Washington, D.C. Even during the war wealthy women tried to keep up with fashions, wearing wide hoops, restrictive corsets, and layers of undergarments. (Library of Congress)

economic oppression. Their efforts made little impact during the 1860s. Northern women throughout the war years enjoyed continued access to the latest fashions.

Ready-made clothing was relatively rare in Northern cities and towns in the 1860s. Department stores in several major cities provided women with ready-to-wear dresses, undergarments, and accessories, but the majority of garments were still custom-made. Fashion plates in magazines like *Godey's Lady's Book* introduced new looks inspired by the design houses of Paris and New York, but women negotiated the dictates of fashion within local contexts, adapting sleeve and skirt lengths, headwear, and outerwear to their own needs and to the expectations of their communities. Women of all classes often made or adjusted their own clothes from manufactured or repurposed fabric. Those of the lower middle class or working class often purchased items from secondhand clothing vendors before adjusting them to their own fit and needs. High fashion was available to only the most privileged.

Clothing in the 1860s was made of linen, cotton, wool, or silk—all available in numerous weights and styles. Coarse and durable linen produced from plant fibers was considered ideal for laborers or rural women, while silk was often prohibitively expensive and kept for only the most special occasions. Although abolitionist women sometimes boycotted cotton, its ready availability, comfort, and affordability contributed to the widespread popularity of cotton clothing, especially during warmer months. Dots, checks, stripes, calicoes, and small floral patterns embellished the somewhat limited range of colors available from natural dyes. Because many fabrics and dyes could not withstand frequent laundering, garments were often disassembled and cleaned according to contact with the body. Some components that made direct contact with the body, like collars, were designed to be removed frequently for cleaning and replaced without disassembling the entire garment. Frequent clothing changes among the more privileged removed some of the burden of laundering but clothes in general, especially the outermost layers of the elaborate costumes fashionable during the period, were laundered less often than they are today.

Despite these differences in regional and class context, manufacture, and material, fashion enforced an ideal female silhouette that emphasized a slender waist by accentuating the hips and shoulders. Shaping the body into this ideal silhouette began with extensive undergarments. Stockings gartered above the knee covered the legs, first, beneath a pair of "drawers" or pantaloons that fell slightly below the knee. Women donned a chemise or vest and petticoats over the pantaloons before entering a corset stiffened with whalebone, metal, or wood strips. When laced tightly, corsets constricted the waist and enforced a rigid, upright posture. After donning a corset cover to protect the dress bodice from the corset's rigid stiffening strips, women in the 1860s fastened a wide set of hoops or cage crinoline at the waist. Fashion was not static during the war. Hoop skirts reached a maximum circular width in the early 1860s; by 1865, the most fashionable silhouette was flatter on the front and flared in the back. Outer garments went on last, over the hoops and corset cover.

Dresses, jackets, blouses, and accessories reinforced the idealized hourglass silhouette. Bodices were wide at the top and gathered in at the waist. Sleeves were often very wide, attached to the bodice at an angle to create a wider appearance at the shoulders. Women wore undersleeves beneath the widest sleeve cuts to conceal the skin of the forearm. Skirts extended over the tips of the shoes but rarely touched the ground. Young women often wore vests or jackets with blouses. Zouave jackets modeled on the French military uniform popular among soldiers in the early years of the war were popular among women throughout the war; Garibaldi shirts with wide sleeves and prominent trim, based on those worn by the "redshirt" Italian freedom fighters in 1860, were popular as well. Various fichus (elaborate shoulder coverings), sashes, headwear, and jewelry rounded out the wardrobe of Northern women according to their means.

Clothing's purpose was both aesthetic and symbolic. Etiquette manuals offered fashion advice for morning, noon, and night. Lighter clothing at night and in the morning gave way to increasingly heavy and elaborate day dresses and gowns as the day progressed into evening. At all times, however, women's dress was required to project an unaffected air of feminine propriety. Multiple layers of clothing screened the body from scrutiny, often exposing only the hands and (ideally) unadorned face, while wide hoops created a protective perimeter around women in public. Relatively inconspicuous accessories, minimal jewelry, harmonious colors, and sparse trim projected self-control and respectability. Garments restricted movement, forced an upright—often painful—posture, and created the illusion that women glided rather than walked.

Not all women agreed with moralists and fashion editors. Reformers like Elizabeth Cady Stanton argued that women's dress was impractical, dangerous, and symbolic of their oppression. While "bloomers"—popularized by Stanton's friend Amelia Bloomer in 1851—enjoyed a brief vogue in the early 1850s, dress reform was largely abandoned 10 years later. Hoops widened, skirts lengthened, and etiquette manuals continued to advise women on respectable dress. Women's dress in the North continued to evolve and reflect the society it served during the Civil War.

Christopher B. Crenshaw

See also: *Clothing, Fashion, and Appearance*: Children's Dress, Union; Clothing, Status and Position; Clothing, Style and Function; Dress, Slaves; Fashion;

Godey's Ladies Book; Homespun; Hoop Skirts; Jewelry; Mourning Clothes; Personal Hygiene; Sewing Societies; Shortages, Clothing; Textiles; Undergarments; Women's Dress, Confederate; *Economy and Work*: Slavery; *Family Life and Gender Roles*: Young Women; *Recreation and Social Customs*: Etiquette, Advice Manuals

FURTHER READING

Cunningham, Patricia A. *Reforming Women's Fashion, 1850–1920: Politics, Health, and Art*. Kent, OH: Kent State University Press, 2003.

Halttunen, Karen. *Confidence Men and Painted Women: A Study of Middle-Class Culture in America, 1830–1870*. New Haven, CT: Yale University Press, 1982.

Perrot, Philippe. *Fashioning the Bourgeoisie: A History of Clothing in the Nineteenth Century*. Princeton, NJ: Princeton University Press, 1994.

Volo, Dorothy Denneen, and James M. Volo. *Daily Life in Civil War America*. Westport, CT: Greenwood Press, 1998.

ECONOMY
AND WORK

INTRODUCTION

When the Civil War began, the slaveholding South was predominantly rural and agricultural, while the Northern states contained many farms but were becoming more urban. There, the nation's cities became the focal point of the region's economy and home to the large populations. The rural areas contained farms that held livestock and grew cotton, tobacco, sugar, rice, wheat, and other products. In the rural slaveholding states, plantations dotted the countryside but small farms also existed.

Although large slaveholders were the minority of the population, they had a large share of the political and cultural power. Plantations varied in size, but all used enslaved African Americans as workers. The enslaved people were forced to work from sunup to sundown doing whatever the master requested; however they still found ways to create a community. Because family members might be sold away from the plantation, those on each plantation created their own families, caring for each other when they needed it.

Farms and plantations faced many problems during the Civil War. Impressment by the governments often forced landowners to give up valuable food and supplies. In addition, foraging by soldiers stripped farms and plantations of their bounties.

Urban life differed significantly from rural life in both pace and focus. During the war, cities grew in size as civilians flocked to urban areas to find safety and jobs. Women worked in government positions that had been vacated by the men who enlisted. In the Confederacy, young women in Richmond signed Treasury bills. Women in the United States filled similar government posts during the war. In addition, cities saw an influx of prostitutes who found work in these growing urban areas with their concentrated populations. Artisans provided needed services for local populations.

The necessities of war promoted the growth of factories. Thousands of people, enslaved and free, young and old, black and white, worked in factories. The Springfield Armory in Massachusetts produced many of the firearms used by Union soldiers. The South's largest factory, the Tredegar Iron Works in Richmond, produced weapons as well as iron and steel. During the war, women worked in munitions factories, textile factories, and other factories. Although often doing the same jobs as their male counterparts, they were paid a lower wage.

Military encampments had their own economies as well. In addition to the soldiers who made up the army, military encampments often had camp followers. These included male sutlers who sold their wares to the soldiers and women who served as laundresses and cooks, prostitutes, and slaves. In addition, family members often followed men to the battlefields.

AGRICULTURE

Farming still dominated American life on the eve of the Civil War, even though it no longer had the supremacy it had at the start of the century. The ideal of the self-sufficient farm was rapidly fading as improvements in transportation and communication changed the nature of agriculture. Northern farms tended to adopt change more rapidly than their Southern counterparts, and the outcome of the war was influenced by the consequences of decisions made by farmers.

The U.S. Census collected information on agriculture in 1860, providing a window into the condition of farming before the Civil War. That year the nation had over two million farms that encompassed 407 million acres with the average farm size equaling 194 acres (for comparison, in 2012 the United States had over two million farms spread across 914 million acres with average farm size equaling 434 acres). These farms produced enough wheat for every person in America to have 5.5 bushels of the grain (about 330 pounds). Although every state grew wheat, free states grew more of it than slave states, and Border South states grew the most out of the slave states. Northern farms grew the most oats and Irish potatoes, while Southern farms dominated in cotton and sweet potatoes.

Land was cheap, but farm labor was not. Throughout the nation smaller farms relied upon the work of individual families in both North and South, but the two sections pursued different solutions when it came to large-scale farming. Slave labor was the preferred solution in the South, even though a majority of Southern farmers had no enslaved workers. The plantations of the minority that did use enslaved labor produced much of the region's wealth through cash crops like cotton, tobacco, sugar cane, and rice. "King Cotton" was especially valuable, feeding the industrial textile mills in Britain and New England.

Slave labor, plantation agriculture, and cash crops had long dominated the South, but the North began the nineteenth century as a land of mostly self-sufficient farms. This self-sufficient focus changed as canals and railroads brought farmers

1862 photograph of enslaved African Americans preparing cotton for the cotton gin on Port Royal Island, South Carolina. Enslaved labor was seen by wealthy white planters as vital in the production of the South's cotton crop. (Library of Congress)

closer to city markets where crops could be sold to the growing urban population. The most prosperous farms hired field hands to help with farming, bringing wage work to agriculture.

As Northern farms became more dependent on the market and on wage labor, many farmers sought to improve agriculture. New technologies like improved steel plows, mechanical seeders, and threshers advanced Northern crop production, and discussions of the best farming techniques filled Northern periodicals. Consequently, farm reformers had an easier time in the North than in the South, where Southern farm reformers were often ignored.

By the start of the war, two divergent systems of agriculture divided into two different nations. The pressures of war tended to expose the weaknesses in the Confederacy's slave system as they confirmed the strengths of the Union's free labor system. Even though the war put many Northern farmers into uniforms, the North's substantially larger population prevented the loss of too much farm labor. Additionally, as laborers became rare, farms increased their use of farming technology to further boost productivity. The Union also benefitted from a more complete railroad network than that in the South and from most Northern farms being spared the ravages of actual fighting.

On the opposite side, Confederate agriculture collapsed during the war from troubles in labor, supplies, transportation, and destruction by Union armies. The Confederacy extracted a greater percentage of its farmers to serve in the army, and consequently farming became the responsibility of the women and enslaved people left behind. When the Confederacy instituted a draft in 1862, planters with 20 slaves or more were exempted, even though larger plantations were best able to absorb the labor loss. With the white power structure strained in fighting the Union, enslaved people began to take advantage of the lessened supervision and productivity fell. Additionally, as Union armies pushed further southward, many enslaved African Americans managed to escape to freedom. The Confederacy's slave labor system slowly unraveled.

Lack of supplies and transportation failures compounded the Southern labor crisis. The Union instituted a naval blockade of the Confederacy, preventing ships from carrying anything but smaller items like weapons that could be smuggled through. Border slave states that remained in the Union worked against the Confederacy as their rich supplies of livestock and grain fell into Union hands. Although most Southerners preferred pork, the region was not self-sufficient in hogs and the Confederacy had to look to Texas beef for meat. This supply was cut off once the Union captured Vicksburg and the Mississippi River in 1863. The meat that remained faced spoilage as a salt shortage crimped preservation efforts. The fractured Confederate rail system strained to get food and supplies to soldiers and cities even before Union raiders began their systematic destruction of the railroads.

Finally, Southern farms faced direct attack in the final year of the war. Union cavalry devastated Virginia's rich Shenandoah Valley by burning crops and destroying farm buildings. The Confederate capital of Richmond, already hungry due to poor railroad shipments, edged closer to starvation. The Deep South was also devastated by General William T. Sherman's marches through Georgia and the Carolinas. The Union Army lived off the rich supplies they found in the plantation belt and destroyed most of the excess. In attacking farms, Union strategists hoped to sink a nation that prided itself on its agricultural prowess.

For farmers returning from fighting in the war, agriculture was never the same. Northern farming accelerated into larger and more mechanized forms. Southern farmers returned to ruined fields and destroyed buildings. The biggest question, about the nature of the postwar labor force, remained unanswered. The eventual answer was a virtual slavery for black and white in the form of sharecropping, which lasted for nearly a century.

Jonathan David Hepworth

See also: Arts: Newspapers, Northern; Newspapers, Southern; *Economy and Work*: Impressment; Landowners; Plantations; Rural Life, Northern; Rural Life, Southern; Slaveholders; Slavery; *Food and Drink*: Food, Shortages; Foraging; Salt; Substitutes, Food and Drink; Tobacco; *Housing and Community*: Slave Life; *Politics and Warfare*: Blockades; *Religion and Belief*: Religious Social Services, Home Front; *Science and Technology*: Inventions

FURTHER READING

Brady, Lisa M. *War upon the Land: Military Strategy and the Transformation of Southern Landscapes During the American Civil War.* Athens: University of Georgia Press, 2012.

Danbom, David B. *Born in the Country: A History of Rural America.* 2nd ed. Baltimore: Johns Hopkins University Press, 2006.

Danhof, Clarence H. *Change in Agriculture: The Northern United States, 1820–1870.* Cambridge, MA: Harvard University Press, 1969.

Otto, John Solomon. *Southern Agriculture During the Civil War Era, 1860–1880.* Westport, CT: Greenwood Press, 1994.

United States Census Bureau. *Census of Population and Housing, 1860.* http://www.census.gov/prod/www/decennial.html. Accessed July 31, 2014.

United States Department of Agriculture. *Census of Agriculture.* http://www.agcensus.usda.gov/Publications/Historical_Publications/index.php. Accessed July 31, 2014.

ARTISANS

Artisans in different fields played an important role in nineteenth-century America. The manufacture and repair of many sorts of everyday items made of metal, wood, or leather depended on skilled artisans. Woodworkers often specialized in one field, such as carpentry, shipbuilding, cabinet making, or carriage building. For example, barrels were an important form of storage and shipping containers, and coopers needed different skills for making barrels for wet or dry contents. Coopers specialized in wet casks or dry casks, each kind of work requiring different skills. The use of horses required saddlers and harness makers. Clothing trades employed tailors, hat makers, and boot and shoemakers. As a national average in 1860, wages for blacksmiths, leather workers, printers, and similar artisans ran about $30 per month, or from $5 to $10 per month more than that of unskilled laborers. Carpenters earned around $45 per month. Skilled ironworkers might earn as much as $6 a day.

Industrialization and technology brought great changes to the lives of artisans. Most workers were learning their trades in lower-paid, entry-level positions, rather than in the old formal apprenticeship system when they had been bound to a master. Steam travel lowered shipping costs, enabling production to concentrate in large centers at the expense of small-scale manufacturers. Machines began to displace many craftsmen, and others needed training for only a limited range of tasks. Nationwide, wages for artisans were stagnant or falling during the antebellum era. The outbreak of war disrupted business in 1861, driving thousands of firms into bankruptcy. In the industrial North, the shoe, furniture, textile, and iron industries suffered. Unemployment drove many artisans to enlist before war-related business began stoking the economy.

Many Southern artisans were enslaved African Americans. As a result, wages and job opportunities for newcomers to the South were limited, and European immigrants found better potential in the free states. Generally, artisans worked in cities and towns, which were much more numerous in the North than in the agrarian South. Partly because the North attracted so many more immigrant artisans than the South, the Confederate war effort suffered from a shortage of skilled craftsmen.

Recognizing the need for artisans to ply their trades to produce war materials, conscription laws exempted workers in several fields. Confederate laws exempted shoemakers, tanners, blacksmiths, wagon makers, artisans in government employment, and workers in wool, cotton, and paper mills.

Wartime inflation pressured artisans and their families. A blacksmith or carpenter serving as an enlisted man felt an income cut of one half or more upon entering the military. Enlisted personnel received small raises during the war, but pay remained far from adequate to comfortably provide for an artisan's family. In the North wages rose during the war, but pay increases averaging about 50 percent fell far short of enabling families to cope with the 80 percent rise in the cost of living by 1865. Inflation was far higher in the Confederacy, and its impact on craftsmen and their families was severe. By 1865, a barrel of flour cost $425 in Richmond, more than even highly paid artisans earned in a month.

The 1860s artisan might work as much as 10 or 11 hours a day, in a six-day work week. Strikes were sometimes successful in obtaining increased pay to cope with inflation, but labor unions were still in their infancy. Particularly in the North, workers might belong to local labor organizations called trades' assemblies. Confederate authorities ended several strikes, including one at the Tredegar Iron Works, by threatening to fire the workers involved. Loss of employment would end the workers' draft exemptions and subject them to conscription.

The Confederate capital of Richmond became the South's primary center for manufacturing military equipment. In particular, Southern war production depended on the Tredegar Iron Works. Richmond printers turned out government forms and currency. The influx of craftsmen and skilled workers to the city contributed to Richmond's wartime overcrowding and food shortages. Several times, when Union armies or raiders threatened the city, draft-exempt war workers were banded together into armed companies and temporarily sent to the front lines. War production was slowed in such times, and the inevitable casualties cost the South irreplaceable trained workers and further hampered production.

Artisans and their training were necessary to the armies and navies. Union Army regulations in 1861 stated that carpenters, joiners, carriage-makers, blacksmiths, saddlers, and harness makers could be enlisted as artisan troops called "artificers." Most artificers served in the cavalry, artillery, or as the engineers rather than in the infantry. Artificers received extra pay for their skills. In 1861, the Union Army paid artificers such as a cavalry "farrier and blacksmith" and an "artificer of artillery" $15 a month, which was $1 higher than a corporal's pay. Master blacksmiths, carriage-makers, and armorers in the Ordnance Department received $34 monthly.

Enlisted men with antebellum experience as carpenters or blacksmiths might be transferred from their regiments and assigned to special duty in their fields. Confederates detailed as blacksmiths or mechanics received an extra 40 cents per day while on special duty. Because of a shortage of trained shipbuilders, soldiers trained as carpenters were sometimes temporarily transferred to work in shipyards for the Confederate Navy.

Navy pay was generally higher than that of army pay. Several types of artisans were necessary to running a ship. Enlisted men with these specialized skills received naval "ratings" or ranks that entitled them to better pay. Naval ratings for artisans included carpenter, cooper, sail maker, painter, and armorer. Their monthly pay in the Union Navy in 1864 ranged from $22 up to $30 for a carpenter's mate. With room and board included, pay for these ratings compared favorably with civilian wages.

David A. Norris

See also: *Economy and Work*: Slave Life; Slavery; Tredegar Iron Works; Urban Life, Northern; Urban Life, Southern; *Family Life and Gender Roles*: Immigrants; Young Men; *Food and Drink*: Food, Shortages; *Housing and Community*: Refugees; *Science and Technology*: Factories; Inventions

FURTHER READING

Barnes, Diane. *Artisan Workers in the Upper South: Petersburg, Virginia, 1820–1865*. Baton Rouge: Louisiana State University Press, 2008.

Commons, John R., David J. Saposs, Helen L. Sumner, E. B. Mittelman, H. E. Hoagland, John B. Andrews, and Selig Perlman. *History of Labor in the United States*. 4 vols. New York: The MacMillan Company, 1926.

Coulter, E. Merton. *The Confederate States of America*. Baton Rouge: Louisiana State University Press, 1950.

Ringle, Dennis J. *Life in Mr. Lincoln's Navy*. Annapolis, MD: Naval Institute Press, 1998.

U.S. Department of Commerce. *Historical Statistics of the United States, Colonial Times to 1970*. Washington, DC: Government Printing Office, 1970.

CAMP FOLLOWERS

The term "camp followers" refers to individuals, generally women, who traveled with armies in war time and lived in the military camp environment. Although camp followers could travel with an army for any length of time—short or long—the tradition of camp following general refers to those women who maintained long-term living arrangements alongside military camps. In general, camp followers accompanied military encampments because of their attachment to a particular serviceman or servicemen. For example, a wife might decide to become a camp follower to remain close to her husband during the war. While her husband did his military service and fought in battles, a camp follower wife would provide other support such as laundering clothes, mending, cooking, and other services. Although some women elected to follow their husbands out of a desire to remain close to them, camp following was, for many, a necessity. Women who traveled with their spouses and the army could not only remain close to their loved ones, but also hoped for more regular access to food and other supplies that may have been difficult to acquire at home. For many women, the choice was to try to eke out a living alone on the home front, or to seek out protection, shelter, food, and funds by traveling with the army itself.

The tradition of women as camp followers emerged long before the American Civil War. During the American Revolution in the eighteenth century, for example, female camp followers were a common sight. Not only did camp followers take on domestic duties for their fighting husbands, such as cooking and mending and cleaning clothes, but camp followers also often provided these services—sometimes for a fee—to other men in the military detachment who lacked family members to provide such support in the field. Margaret Corbin, for example, was one American Revolution camp follower whose services extended beyond domestic support: when her husband was wounded in battle, she famously took his place at the cannon to help the army keep the battle going. The legend of

Molly Pitcher, who carried water to wounded troops, is yet another example of a famous camp follower from the American Revolution.

Women were present as camp followers from the earliest days of the Civil War and traveled with both Union and Confederate troops, with many women taking up this option either temporarily or permanently. Camp following could be a respectable option for married women following their spouses, but not all camp followers were there for their husbands. Camp followers during the Civil War also included unattached women who took on roles cooking, washing clothes, or serving as prostitutes to the troops.

In the early nineteenth century, a new term for camp followers emerged out of a French tradition. "Vivandieres," or "daughters of the regiment," a French variation on the camp follower idea, originally referred to women who traveled with militaries to provide medical care and to sell food and other supplies that soldiers might want or need. In the American Civil War, many Union and Confederate armies adopted the term to refer to women who traveled with their units to provide similar support, often referring to the wives of officers or young women who were selected as the "daughter of the regiment."

Whether known as vivandieres or not, camp followers took on a number of tasks associated with military field support, from selling food, alcohol, and supplies, to providing domestic support or establishing field hospitals as needed in the aftermath of battles. Although camp followers did not provide formal fighting support, some carried weapons in case they needed to defend themselves from the enemy, as Annie Etheridge (Third and Fifth Michigan) and Marie Tepe (114th Pennsylvania Volunteers, also known as the Collis' Zuaves) did during their years as vivandieres.

Etheridge and Tepe earned formal recognition for their support of the military during the war. During her years serving with Michigan regiments, Annie Etheridge (1840–1913) provided support during at least five major battles, including First and Second Bull Run and Gettysburg. Etheridge gained particular attention for her services as a medic, bringing medical supplies and relief to wounded men. In serving so close to the front lines, camp followers like Etheridge faced many of the same risks as soldiers: Etheridge came close to becoming a prisoner of war and was wounded slightly at the Battle of Chancellorsville in 1863. Likewise, Marie Tepe (1834–1901), or "French Mary," was wounded in the ankle at the Battle of Fredericksburg in 1862. Tepe and Etheridge became the only two women awarded the Kearny Cross for their bravery.

Southern women also served as camp followers, receiving local recognition of their own for the support they provided their troops. Lucy Ann Cox (ca. 1820–1891) followed her husband with the 13th Virginia regiment, traveling as far north as Maryland providing aid to the troops until the Confederate surrender at

Appomattox. As a testament to her services, a monument was erected in her honor in Fredericksburg, Virginia, in 1894. While with the Confederate troops, she provided a range of support services, including nursing wounded soldiers.

Because camp followers served no official military role, there are no records of exactly how many women pursued this lifestyle during the Civil War. Camp followers seem to have been particularly common in the early days of the war, when many believed the war would be a short affair that would end quickly. By the last year of the war, some commanders were increasingly limiting women's ability to serve in this role. In 1864, for example, General Ulysses S. Grant decided that women should no longer be present at any military camps under his command. For many women with Union troops, this order meant that they would need to find new ways to provide services. Although many camp followers returned home, other women found new roles serving in hospitals and other places during the final months of the war.

Tanya L. Roth

See also: *Economy and Work*: Prostitutes; Sutlers; *Politics and Warfare*: Camp Life; Female Combatants; *Science and Technology*: Nursing

FURTHER READING

Hall, Richard. *Patriots in Disguise: Women Warriors of the Civil War*. New York: Paragon House, 1993.

Hughes, Susan Lyons. "The Daughter of the Regiment: A Brief History of Vivandieres and Cantinieres in the American Civil War." 2000. http://ehistory.osu.edu/uscw/features/articles/0005/vivandieres.cfm. Accessed July 31, 2014.

Massey, Mary Elizabeth. *Women in the Civil War*. Lincoln: University of Nebraska Press, 1994. (Originally published as *Bonnet Brigades*. New York: A. A. Knopf, 1966.)

Mayer, Holly A. *Belonging to the Army: Camp Followers and Community During the American Revolution*. Columbia: University of South Carolina Press, 1999.

National Park Service. "Annie Etheridge." 2012. http://www.nps.gov/resources/person.htm?id=162. Accessed July 31, 2014.

CATTLE INDUSTRY

Prior to the Civil War, cattle production in the United States was typically localized to subsistence farming. In some cases, cattle were raised in the Midwest where corn was prevalent and were subsequently driven by foot to eastern markets or shipped on barges on the Ohio or Mississippi Rivers for slaughter and distribution. Moreover, before the Civil War, pork was the primary protein consumed in

1864 image of cattle marching with the army. During the Civil War cattle became an important source of food for both Northern and Southern armies. They could be herded with marching armies, thus providing a non-salted source of meat. (Library of Congress)

the United States, not beef. Cattle were too expensive because they required large amounts of grain or vast tracts of land to support. Without the aid of refrigeration, spoilage of fresh beef was also a concern. Thus, most cattle were harvested in the fall and winter months. Lastly, Native Americans—primarily the Cherokee, Creek, and Choctaw—living on the plains of the Oklahoma Territory owned the largest herds of cattle. The outbreak of war in April 1861, however, fundamentally changed the cattle industry and its related industries.

With the mobilization of thousands of men in wartime, cattle played a critical part of both Northern and Southern wartime logistical efforts. With the larger carcass weights, cattle provided a perfect solution to feed large armies and offered an alternative to salted meats. Several sources were used to supply the large armies with fresh beef. Both the Confederate and Union Subsistence Bureaus allotted one pound of salted or fresh beef to each soldier. The Army of the Potomac was supplied with cattle that were mostly sourced from the plains of Illinois and Chicago's two stockyards—Lake Shore and Cottage Grove. These animals arrived in lots of 500 head and were shipped by railroad to the front lines. Typically, cattle followed behind either Confederate or Union forces and were driven by civilian contractors or commissary soldiers with droving experience. Commissary officers, those in charge of procuring food for soldiers, also paid private citizens to pasture animals. When supply lines were disrupted, quartermasters secured cattle from other sources. Union and Confederate quartermasters purchased cattle from local farmers, forcefully requisitioned cattle from farmers, or in rare cases, were given livestock by patriotic citizens. By the end of 1863, Confederate reliance on cattle gradually declined because Union forces occupied important agricultural centers of the Confederacy, especially in Tennessee. To make up for these procurement deficiencies, Confederate forces raided the herds of the Five Civilized Tribes in the Southwestern theatre of the war. Confederate forces also conducted cattle raids on plentiful Union herds. The most successful raid was conducted in September 1864 during the Siege of Petersburg when Confederate general Wade Hampton's forces rustled 2,000 head of Union cattle. The importance of cattle to the Union war effort cannot be understated. During General William T. Sherman's march through Georgia in November and December 1864, 3,400 head of cattle were herded behind the army. Near the end of the war in March 1865, nearly 5,000 head of cattle accompanied the Army of the Potomac.

The Civil War also realigned the cattle and meatpacking industry. Whereas meatpacking was centralized near the Ohio Valley before the Civil War, the disruption caused by war and the Union blockade of the Mississippi River and subsequent closure of Southern markets shifted cattle production to Chicago, Illinois. The Windy City played a critical role in supplying beef cattle to Union armies because it possessed the infrastructure necessary to produce and distribute beef cattle. Chicago was the most significant railroad hub tying Midwest growers to eastern markets, so cattle were shipped by rail from Chicago or slaughtered at Chicago's meatpacking plants and then distributed. Ultimately, the Civil War cemented Chicago's place in the cattle and meatpacking industry. The Union Stockyard and Transit Company, planned near the end of the Civil War and completed in the winter of 1865, became the largest feed operation, railroad hub, and meatpacking operation in the country and remained so until 1920.

The Civil War also stimulated important technological changes in the meatpacking industry. Whereas prior to the war beef was processed during the cooler months of the year, the call for American beef during the Civil War led to the precursor of the refrigerated boxcar. Beef was loaded into an insulated boxcar and then crushed ice or blocks of ice were packed on top of the car. This practice, often referred to as "top-loading," ensured that fresh beef did not spoil. Because of this innovation, cattle were produced year-round.

The Civil War spurred important changes in government land and agricultural policy in the North, thereby setting the stage for the advancement of the cattle industry. The defection of many Southern Democrats to the Confederacy in 1861 allowed a Republican-controlled Congress to pass two important acts in 1862: the Homestead Act and the Morrill Land Grant Act. The Homestead Act granted settlers 160 acres of land for $1.25 an acre, which opened the American West to cattle ranching after the war. The Morrill Act granted qualified states 30,000 acres of federal land to be sold or used to establish colleges that emphasized agricultural and mechanical studies. Following the war, these state schools provided an important training ground for generations of veterinarians and meat scientists to improve the cattle industry.

The sustained and aggressive growth of the cattle industry from 1865 to 1900 in the United States would not have been possible without the Civil War. The opening of the American West also allowed the expansion of the railroads and provided the impetus for a boom market. Southern cattle herds—totaling about five million head in Texas alone—that were largely displaced because of the Civil War were rounded up and driven or shipped by rail to burgeoning cattle towns of Abilene, Texas, and Wichita and Dodge City, Kansas. As a result, the cattle industry and its related industries became integral to the cultural, environmental, and economic development of the Midwest and the Great Plains.

Matthew C. Sherman

See also: *Economy and Work*: Agriculture; Rural Life, Northern; Rural Life, Southern; Urban Life, Northern; *Food and Drink*: Food, Northern; Food, Shortages; Food, Upper Classes; Salt; *Science and Technology*: Railroads

FURTHER READING

Olson, K. C. "Development of the National Cattle Trade." *Rangelands* 23 (October 2011): 3–6.

Skaggs, Jimmy K. *Prime Cut: Livestock Raising and Meatpacking in the United States, 1607–1983*. College Station: Texas A&M University Press, 1986.

Taylor, Lynette S. *"The Supply for Tomorrow Must Not Fail."* Kent, OH: Kent State University Press, 2004.

Wade, Louise Carroll. *Chicago's Pride: The Stockyards, Packingtown, and Environs in the Nineteenth Century*. Urbana: University of Illinois Press, 1987.

FACTORY OWNERS

Factory owners in the North and South became important tools in the Union and Confederate war efforts. As a result of the need for large amounts of goods to supply the soldiers, both governments signed contracts with factory owners to produce the necessary items.

To operate at maximum efficiency, the armies of the Union and Confederacy needed guns, ammunition, gunpowder, cannon, uniforms, knapsacks, tents, blankets, wagons, telegraph wire, ironclads, steam engines, rail lines, food for men and animals, cooking implements, and myriad other items critical to military operations. Except for food and a few other goods, all of these products could be produced most efficiently and in the greatest quantity in a factory. Throughout the Civil War, factory owners were constantly being pushed and pulled. On the one hand, the government wanted goods made as quickly as possible, but on the other hand it wanted these goods to be as high a quality as possible. Factory owners had to hire more workers to produce more goods, but they also needed to find ways of doing so efficiently to offset the costs of hiring more workers. At the same time, they were interested in making a profit for themselves, but they had to deal with workers who demanded more money for their necessary labor.

There were many more factories in the North than in the South because during the antebellum period America's industrial growth was almost entirely located in the Northeast. The North and South had an important economic relationship whereby Southerners grew cotton and sent it to textile mills up North and in England. As a result, Southern factories were rarely needed. A few large factories existed in the South, mostly in Richmond, Virginia. The most famous Southern factory was the Tredegar Iron Works, which had produced cannons for the U.S. Navy before the war. However, the majority of factories in the region were textile mills that hired poor white workers to produce cloth. North and South, factory owners relied upon working-class men and women to produce their goods at the lowest cost possible.

It was this type of drive toward more production that pushed artisans to begin expanding their operations in the 1820s and 1840s along the waterways of the Northeast, which provided power for the factory machines. Most owners started their businesses sometime in the prewar period, which meant that the majority of factories were expanded rather than created during the war. The Springfield Armory, for example, employed 200 people in 1860 and expanded to 2,600 by the end of the war. However, most factories were very small compared to those built in the 1880s and 1890s. In Cincinnati in 1870, the average factory employed 14 people or less. As a result, most factory owners worked very closely with their employees.

These owners were part of a new class of capitalists who believed in classical liberalism, an ideology developed in the mid-1700s and early 1800s that stressed the need for society to allow greater individual freedom. Philosophers like Adam Smith and John Locke believed that the freest, most prosperous countries were those where individuals had economic freedom and were subject to as little governmental control as possible. Many future factory owners adopted this ideology for themselves and began investing money in small manufacturing concerns in the decades before the war. Those who were successful might choose to take some of the profit and invest it back into their business to hire more workers or move into a larger building so that they could earn even more money. How to capitalize on the factory and determine a course of action to increase income was the most important issue a factory owner faced before, during, and after the war.

Throughout the war, factory owners had to work with their employees to figure out how to increase their profits, even though workers and owners sometimes fought over issues of pay and working conditions. To increase profits, owners tried to increase production efficiency; they wanted to get more work from laborers and to waste fewer resources in the production of an item. An example of production efficiency included designing a product that could be made from the scraps of leather left in a hide after cutting out large pieces used in shoemaking.

Owners also made their workers more efficient during the war by redesigning products to work with interchangeable parts. Before industrialization, every single part was made exactly for one specific machine: a trigger for one gun would not fit on another gun. The desire for wartime efficiency and profit moved owners toward interchangeable parts.

Factory owners also pushed their workers to reduce the number of "steps" each worker performed. Prior to the 1820s, most products were made from start to finish by one or two people. Factory owners discovered that breaking down the process into smaller steps and having workers specialize in a certain portion of production allowed items to be produced more quickly. These steps made items cheaper and more plentiful than before, and they also required less skill from workers. Consequently factory owners began paying workers lower wages, which sometimes led to conflicts between workers and owners. Though the first labor organizations were just being created before the war, there were several labor strikes during the Civil War that owners had to deal with quickly so as not to lose a government contract.

Adam Carson

See also: *Clothing, Fashion, and Appearance*: Textiles; *Economy and Work*: Artisans; Factory Workers, Northern; Factory Workers, Southern; Munitions Factories; Springfield Armory; Tredegar Iron Works; Urban Life, Northern; Urban Life, Southern; *Family Life and Gender Roles*: Immigrants; Young Men; Young Women; *Housing and Community*: Factory Towns; *Science and Technology*: Factories; Inventions; Weapons

FURTHER READING

Eaton, Clement. *A History of the Old South: The Emergence of a Reluctant Nation.* 3rd ed. Prospect Heights, IL: Waveland Press, Inc., 1989.

Gallman, J. Matthew. *Northerners at War: Reflections on the Civil War Home Front.* Kent, OH: Kent State University Press, 2010.

Paludan, Phillip Shaw. *"A People's Contest:" The Union and Civil War, 1861–1865.* New York: Harper & Row, 1988.

FACTORY WORKERS, NORTHERN

Factories and factory work had existed in the United States for nearly 40 years before the beginning of the Civil War. As a result, even though the conflict has been referred to as the first "industrial" war, the Civil War did not fundamentally change the way Americans understood manufacturing. Furthermore, the war did not dramatically increase the amount of the population working in factories; most Northerners still lived and worked on farms before, during, and after the war. In fact, the percentage of agricultural workers in America only fell 3 percent between 1850 and 1880. Although many people moved from rural areas to factories looking for work, most workers had lived in and grown up in cities and, often, whole families worked together in the same factory. However, the number of women working in factories increased during the war.

Traditionally, physical labor or working in public was considered a man's job, and women were supposed to work in the house or to do those types of jobs for others that were considered traditionally feminine like cooking, taking care of children, or cleaning. These jobs typically mirrored the skill sets women would have learned growing up, while men's work mirrored masculine skill sets. Consequently, women who worked in Northern factories often did jobs that reflected feminine skills. For example, if the factory made soldiers' cartridge pouches, male workers would cut out the leather pieces and women would sew them together.

When women entered into the factory, it often created problems for workers of both sexes. The public worried that these women would fall prey to male vices or that they would engage in illicit behavior with male factory workers. As a result, many Northern factories were sex-segregated—men worked in one area and women worked in another. This segregation, however, did not stop women from being exposed to harassment from male workers during the day. Threatened by the presence of women in their workplace, some men actively worked to make the factory unpleasant for women.

In addition, in such a male-dominated space, cussing, drinking, and telling crude jokes were normal parts of everyday work life; this type of behavior helped bind men together. Some women working in factories engaged in questionable behavior with their male coworkers and were not necessarily the delicate creatures depicted in popular publications. These realities further fueled the public debates over the dangers that such working conditions held for women. Men and women's experiences in Northern Civil War factories were important because they caused many Americans to question the meanings of masculinity and femininity, especially in regards to the work that each sex supposedly performed.

Despite workplace separation, many male and female workers came together to try and improve their positions. Even before factories were created, workers had begun organizing to use their collective strength to bargain for better pay and/or working conditions. This trend continued during the Civil War as workers continued to lose control of the pace at which they were required to work and the environment in which they were required to work.

Most Northern factory workers could be divided up into two groups: those who worked in small shops of fewer than 20 people and those who worked in larger factories of 50 or more. The majority of workers worked in smaller shops and had a great deal of interaction with their bosses, which allowed these workers to have a greater say in how and when they worked and how much they would get paid for doing so. Those workers in larger factories had less leverage over their employer and, more often, had to grudgingly accept their employer's rules. However, because the larger businesses were more profitable, those workers were usually paid more. Many factory workers had to choose between working in a small or a large shop, which was an important decision because factory conditions were usually unpleasant. The size of the factory where people worked, however, was not the only thing that determined their wages.

Factory workers could also be divided between skilled and unskilled labor. Those who were skilled usually possessed some kind of specialized training, which, in the past, would have allowed them to be referred to as an artisan. Though industrialization eroded the status of artisans, it also opened up opportunities for workers to become specialized in working with machines, such as steam engines or boilers. Specialized workers were paid more than unskilled laborers who were usually tasked with performing the same types of repetitive jobs that any able-bodied person could do. During and after the Civil War, the distance between skilled and unskilled labor increased, as did their pay gap, which caused both groups to see less common ground between them as workers.

Women participated in strikes, but less so than did men because women had even less job security than unskilled men. One reason for this precarious job security was that women were often understood to be seasonal workers whose jobs were not essential to their family's incomes. Either way, the Civil War was not a revolutionary step toward industrialization, but it challenged gender roles in some ways and provided a push toward workers deciding to act collectively. The nation's first labor union, the National Labor Union, formed one year after the end of the war.

Adam Carson

See also: Economy and Work: Factory Owners; Factory Workers, Southern; Urban Life, Northern; Urban Life, Southern; *Family Life and Gender Roles*: Cult of Domesticity; Immigrants; *Housing and Community*: Factory Towns; *Science and Technology*: Factories; Time

FURTHER READING

Frisch, Michael H. *Town into City: Springfield, MA, and the Meaning of Community, 1840–1880*. Cambridge, MA: Harvard University Press, 1972.

Giesberg, Judith. *Army at Home: Women and the Civil War on the Northern Homefront*. Chapel Hill: University of North Carolina Press, 2009.

Paludan, Phillip Shaw. *"A People's Contest:" The Union and Civil War, 1861–1865*. New York: Harper & Row, 1988.

Ransom, Roger L. *Conflict and Compromise: The Political Economy of Slavery, Emancipation, and the American Civil War*. New York: Cambridge University Press, 1989.

FACTORY WORKERS, SOUTHERN

The slave states nurtured a small but burgeoning industrial movement in the antebellum years, marked by experimentation in the use of enslaved and free labor. Skilled and unskilled white and black workers labored in the South's largest industries: tobacco and textiles. Others operated in iron bloomeries and foundries, mines, flour mills, machine shops, sawmills, tanneries, paper mills, oil mills, and harness shops, many of which could be found in rural areas like the Shenandoah Valley or major cities like Richmond or Nashville. The 1860 federal census counted just over 200 woolen mills and 157 cotton mills. The future Confederate States also boasted over 200 iron forges. Southern industries claimed 110,721 hands of both sexes employed in manufacturing or 11 percent of the national total. Industrialists initially leaned toward the use of enslaved labor in a variety of factories and, on the eve of the Civil War, hired enslaved laborers predominated in some locations. However, as enslaved labor proved more expensive than free white labor, many factory owners, particularly in textiles, turned to the use of white women and their children as the chief operators at looms and machines, while white men occupied the most skilled positions and supervisory roles.

War transformed the Southern labor force. As skilled white men departed the factories for the military, the number of industries necessary to support the war effort expanded and those industries came under increasing sway of Confederate political power. For instance, new clothing manufactories sprang up near textile mills in the North Carolina piedmont. These factories employed white women, while in Richmond, new state-run salt works hired hundreds of enslaved African Americans. Manchester Mill, a privately owned textile producing factory in the same city, hired 122 enslaved workers in 1863, its first enslaved hires since the 1840s. Tredegar Iron Works also turned to enslaved hires to keep its factory in operation. New gunpowder factories and arsenals appeared everywhere from Richmond to Texas, particularly in Augusta, Georgia, under the aegis of the Confederate Ordnance Department headed by General Gabriel Rains. The Ordnance Department's Nitre and Mining Bureau created facilities for the extraction and refinement of copper, lead, and nitre. Employees at both old and new factories not only operated machinery but also hauled wood, made boxes, and transported finished goods.

Textile production became a central node of Confederate industry as states and the central government required a continual supply of material for uniforms, tents, and other equipment. Clothing manufactories, particularly, absorbed labor from the countryside, employing poor women as seamstresses. Though not at work in a factory setting, thousands of Confederate women sewed at rural homesteads, thus playing a key role in the manufacturing system while maintaining a marginal economic existence. Skilled pattern cutters cut out pattern pieces, and seamstresses, often the wives and widows of soldiers, received bundles of pattern pieces with buttons and thread, sewed them together as finished garments—pants, drawers, shirts, jackets, caps, and overcoats—then returned them to the manufactory for inspection and payment. These seamstresses tended to finish one or two pieces a day and received $1 to $4 per finished garment. Women used the much-needed money to support their families.

In factories producing cloth, iron, weapons, and gunpowder, free and enslaved laborers tended to work 12 hours a day. Wages or payments to owners never kept up with inflation. In August 1864, one male mill operative in North Carolina earned $152 a month, while four months later, a female employee was paid with wood, syrup, flour, peas and salt. Barter became a common form of payment. Thomas Holt, owner of Granite Mills in North Carolina, complained to the state quartermaster about the constant demands of his operatives.

Southern industrialists had long praised their own enterprise for offering economic and educational opportunities for the South's socially marginal people. Although mill owners, especially in more rural areas, continued to regard their efforts as partial obligation to poor people, some outside observers thought otherwise—one federal officer noted the women at Saluda factory in South Carolina were dirty and ignorant.

Distance from the front lines did not mean a respite from danger for industrial laborers. In crowded working and living spaces, communicable diseases ravaged populations. One such epidemic affected hundreds of women and children in the factories along the Savannah River in Georgia. Even in smaller places like Buffalo Forge near Lexington, Virginia, both enslaved laborers and white workers suffered fatal bouts of diphtheria that temporarily halted the operation. Nearly every gunpowder factory complex suffered major explosions that killed workers. Explosions killed 32 women in Richmond, Virginia, 15 in Jackson, Mississippi, and 4 in Raleigh, North Carolina. Some workers even experienced forced migration as federal armies roamed the South, as when General William T. Sherman transported 16 rail cars full of Roswell, Georgia's textile workers to Union lines.

Industrial laborers in the Confederacy became pawns in political and economic negotiations as the central government extended authority over Southern manufactories, most notably with the Conscription Act of 1862. The Conscription Act enrolled all eligible men for military service and subsequently "detailed" them back to the factories they worked in. Thus, the Confederate government leveraged its power over factory labor to enforce price and production controls on recalcitrant factory owners. Some owners attempted to avoid these constraints by hiring an all-enslaved workforce, or one composed entirely of foreign nationals. Other factories ceased operation, while most continued under straitened circumstances.

Thousands worked in factories or in support of the manufacturing system in the Confederacy. Whether enslaved or free, male or female, they all suffered the misfortunes of wartime politics and deprivation.

Christopher A. Graham

See also: *Economy and Work*: Factory Owners; Factory Workers, Northern; Slavery; Tredegar Iron Works Urban Life, Southern; *Family and Gender Roles*: Womanhood, Southern; *Religion and Belief*: Religious Social Services, Home Front; *Science and Technology*: Disease

FURTHER READING

DeCredico, Mary A. *Patriotism for Profit: Georgia's Urban Entrepreneurs and the Confederate War Effort.* Chapel Hill: The University of North Carolina Press, 1990.

Delfino, Susanna, and Michele Gillespie, eds. *Neither Lady Nor Slave: Working Women of the Old South.* Chapel Hill: The University of North Carolina Press, 2002.

Delfino, Susanna, Michele Gillespie, and Louis M. Kyriakoudes, eds. *Southern Society and Its Transformations, 1790–1860.* Columbia: University of Missouri Press, 2011.

Dew, Charles B. *Ironmaker to the Confederacy: Joseph R. Anderson and the Tredegar Iron Works.* New Haven, CT: Yale University Press, 1966.

Rable, George C. *Civil Wars: Women and the Crisis of Southern Nationalism.* Urbana: University of Illinois Press, 1989.

Takagi, Midori. *"Rearing Wolves to Our Own Destruction": Slavery in Richmond, Virginia, 1782–1865.* Charlottesville: University Press of Virginia, 1999.

Wilson, Harold S. *Confederate Industry: Manufacturers and Quartermasters in the Civil War.* Jackson: University Press of Mississippi, 2002.

GOVERNMENT GIRLS

The Civil War was not the first time women had held jobs with the federal government; for example, Clara Barton (1821–1912), who would later go on to gain fame as a nurse and founder of the Red Cross, began her career in the 1850s as a clerk in the United States Patents Office. However, the war marked the largest number of women on the federal payrolls than ever before, gaining them the nickname "government girls," a term that stuck for women in both the Union and the Confederacy. Because the armed forces needed so many men to fight the war itself, government departments in both the Union and Confederacy found themselves short-staffed and turned to women as a new major source of applicants. Moreover, with fathers, spouses, brothers, and sons away at the war, paid work for the government became an important way for women to earn money that could help their families survive during the war years.

The idea of women working for money was not unknown during the middle of the nineteenth century, but the Civil War created opportunities that many women might otherwise not have had. Although many women participated in wage labor during the first half of the nineteenth century, the growth of the Cult of Domesticity in the decades leading up to the Civil War dictated that a white woman's primary role should be as wife and mother. Before the war, a young woman might work briefly in the years before she married, but her family expected she would give up the job in favor of a family. Only lower-class, poor, or immigrant women were expected to work for any significant period in their lives. In the antebellum South the wealthiest women would not have been expected to work, but during the war many of these women would seek government employment to help them in times of extreme hardship.

Hundreds of white women in both the Union and Confederacy sought government work to support their families during the Civil War. North and South, women secured civilian posts in a number of departments, but with most concentrated in the Treasury Department in both the Union and the Confederacy. Many worked as well in the War Department, the Post Office, and the Quartermaster General.

No matter what the department, however, jobs for women were generally clerical positions, or clerkships that involved work that might later be classified as secretarial, such as processing and creating correspondence, filing and organizing documents, or, in the Treasury Department, signing and preparing banknotes. In the Confederacy, several thousand additional women sewed for the Clothing Bureau, making money based on the number of pieces of clothing they completed for soldiers.

Not everyone welcomed "government girls," however. Although government officials who granted jobs to women saw their work as both temporary and necessary to support the war effort, others accused "government girls" of being immoral individuals who were not content with their proper places at home. Some critics also believed that the presence of women in the workplace would only distract the male workers who remained and would make them unable to complete their own work. Southern diarist Mary Chesnut, an elite slave owner who did not work during the war, believed it was simply inappropriate for women to engage in paid work rather than remaining in the prescribed domestic sphere of the home.

In both the Union and the Confederacy, personal recommendations could be an important way to secure a government job. In the Confederacy in particular, women petitioned for government jobs on the basis of personal need and sacrifice, as well as with strong recommendations from individuals well connected to the government offices. In the Union, many well-connected young women also gained government jobs thanks to personal influence. General George Meade's sister Margaret began working in federal government in 1863 and remained in the position until she was dismissed as unsuitable in 1867, even obtaining another job afterward with the Quartermaster Depot.

Payment for women's government work varied. Although women in the Treasury Department in the federal government made a standard annual wage of $720 by the latter part of the Civil War, there was no standard uniform rate of pay across government jobs. Women in departments such as the Post Office, for example, routinely made less money than men working the same jobs. In contrast, in the Confederacy female clerks earned $65 a month by 1863, while the lowest-ranking men in the Confederate Army earned only $11 a month. By the end of the war, women working for the Confederate government saw salaries as high as $3,000 a month, but by this time Confederate currency was worth so little that it was actually the equivalent of perhaps $150 in gold. For many women, however, the money earned in a government job in the Union or Confederacy was far greater than what they could expect in jobs in their hometowns. However, costs of living also tended to be much higher in areas where most "government girls" held jobs during the war.

With the end of the war and the fall of the Confederacy in 1865, Southern "government girls" found themselves without jobs, while positions still remained for women in the federal government as the Union transitioned into Reconstruction. Additionally, increased applications for veterans' pensions meant that plenty of work remained in places like the Pensions Office. Other women found new opportunities in the Freedman's Bureau during Reconstruction. Within a decade after the end of the Civil War, women had secured what seemed to be a permanent role in government employment. Although not all women remained in their jobs in the years after the war, at least five women who began their government work during the Civil War continued in their employment for two decades or more.

Tanya L. Roth

See also: *Economy and Work*: Treasury Girls; Urban Life, Northern; Urban Life, Southern; *Family Life and Gender Roles*: Cult of Domesticity; Womanhood, Northern; Womanhood, Southern; Young Women

FURTHER READING

Clinton, Catherine. *The Other Civil War: American Women in the Nineteenth Century.* New York: Hill and Wang, 1984.

Faust, Drew Gilpin. *Mothers of Invention: Women of the Slaveholding South in the American Civil War.* Chapel Hill: The University of North Carolina Press, 1996.

Harper, Ida Husted. "The Life and Work of Clara Barton." *The North American Review* 195 (1912): 678, 701–712.

Kessler-Harris, Alice. *Out to Work: A History of Wage-Earning Women in the United States (20th Anniversary Edition).* New York: Oxford University Press, 2003.

Massey, Mary Elizabeth. *Women in the Civil War.* Lincoln: University of Nebraska Press, 1994. (Reprint of *Bonnet Brigades*. New York: A. A. Knopf, 1966.)

IMPRESSMENT

Impressment, the seizure or compulsory purchase of private property for military use, was widely used by the Confederate government during the Civil War.

American forces used impressment during the Revolutionary War and the War of 1812. By a long-accepted legal principle, governments were obligated to pay a reasonable price for property taken for military use. The rules governing impressment were laid out in the last clause of the Fifth Amendment to the U.S. Constitution, which declares that private property cannot "be taken for public use without just compensation." A similar proviso appeared in the Confederacy's Constitution. During the Civil War, the Union's resources and transportation networks made the practice of impressment rare for the Union. However, it was still employed at times.

Without clear standards, impressment by the Confederate Army as well as by the Confederate and state governments began in 1861. Army units too far from commissary and quartermaster depots to resupply themselves took food, forage, horses, or other necessities from the countryside. In response to complaints about abusive seizures of private property, the Confederate Congress passed the Act to Regulate Impressments on March 26, 1863. On April 30, Congress extended provisions of the act to authorize impressments by the navy.

Under the act, impressments were to be made only by duly authorized military officers. Army officers convicted of taking impressed property for personal profit could be demoted. When the army took private property, officers issued certificates that the owners could present to the government for payment.

Officers were to resort to impressment only when owners refused to sell their products to the government. Only surplus products could be impressed, and a farm family was allowed to retain a sufficient quantity for their own use. The law set out prices for impressed supplies and also determined the rates for government use of civilian wagons, teams, and drivers. Appointed commissioners helped set prices, which were frequently updated and widely printed in newspapers. There was an appeal process if sellers disagreed with payment rates. Despite the commissioners' input and complaints from the public, sellers suffered financially because official impressment price figures were nearly always well below market value.

The military also seized wagons and draft animals. Farmers often found that replacing an impressed horse or mule was difficult if not practically impossible, even with fair compensation. People in Richmond, Virginia, suffered from aggravated food shortages partly as a result of impressment. Farmers avoided taking their produce to sell in the city because they feared that while en route army officers would seize their goods, as well as their irreplaceable wagons and teams.

The Confederate government, as well as state governments, also impressed slaves so that they could use their labor. Their most common work was on fortifications, but many enslaved African Americans were impressed to do work in hospitals or as teamsters. Monthly rates were paid to owners, while enslaved people were fed and boarded at government expense. However, many slaveholders strongly objected to impressment, especially at harvest time. Some slaveholders charged that the government failed to provide proper food and medical care. Another objection was that enslaved people building fortifications near Union forces would be tempted to run away into the enemy lines. Free blacks were also forced to work on military construction projects.

Soon after the passing of the Impressment Act, the Confederate Congress passed a "tax in kind" on April 26, 1863. By setting a 10 percent tax, sometimes called a tithe, on all agricultural products and livestock, the government hoped to obtain enough food for the army to reduce the necessity of impressment. In practice impressment was still seen as necessary by the army, and combined with the unpopular tithe, it caused great disaffection in the South.

Impressments often happened without warning. An officer with a party of soldiers would appear, and announce that they were seizing livestock or part of the year's harvest. Enslaved or free blacks might be taken from farms, or plucked from the streets in towns, and forcibly taken to work on fortifications. Wagon and horseback errands might be interrupted by soldiers, who would confiscate horses and vehicles, leaving citizens to walk home.

In letters to newspapers and officials, citizens complained of numerous impressment abuses by high-handed army officers. Some soldiers took property without proper authorization, and criminals posed as impressment officers. Because of the South's overburdened rail system, impressment fell disproportionately upon farms near the main armies. In hard-pressed areas, civilians lost so much property that they felt little difference between a Confederate impressment party and a Union raiding party. State authorities often clashed with the national government over the issue. North Carolina governor Zebulon Vance wrote Secretary of War James Seddon in late 1863, complaining of rampant abuses by Confederate cavalrymen impressing horses and feed in his state.

Although primarily used in the agricultural sector, impressment was felt throughout the Confederate economy. Saltpeter, shoes, and cloth were also forcibly sold to the government. The Confederate Navy impressed rails from little-used railroad lines and sidings, and used the rails to make armor plating for ironclad gunboats.

Cotton was impressed to sell in Europe to raise money for supplies to be run through the blockade. In August 1863 Secretary of War Seddon ordered authorities in Wilmington, Charleston, and Mobile to impress half the space on outgoing blockade runners to carry government-owned cotton. Ship owners were offered set rates for the cargo space; they had to accept or face seizure of their vessels.

The Confederacy's national policy of impressment was always at odds with concerns for states' rights. By late in the war the scarcity of goods, hoarding, and stiff public opposition reduced the use of impressment, and the army often had to buy supplies on the open market.

David A. Norris

See also: *Economy and Work*: Agriculture; Plantations; Rural Life, Northern; Rural Life, Southern; Urban Life, Northern; Urban Life, Southern; *Food and Drink*: Food, Shortages; Food Riots; Foraging; Substitutes, Food and Drink; *Politics and Warfare*: Morale; *Science and Technology*: Railroads; Transportation

FURTHER READING

Blair, William A. *Virginia's Private War: Feeding Body and Soul in the Confederacy, 1861–1865*. New York: Oxford University Press, 1998.

Goff, Richard. *Confederate Supply*. Durham, NC: Duke University Press, 1969.

Grimsley, Mark. *The Hard Hand of War: Union Military Policy Toward Southern Civilians, 1861–1865*. New York: Cambridge University Press, 1995.

Martinez, Jaime Amanda. *Confederate Slave Impressment in the Upper South*. Chapel Hill: University of North Carolina Press, 2013.

Todd, Richard Cecil. *Confederate Finance*. Athens: University of Georgia Press, 1954.

LANDOWNERS

Landowners played important roles in the Civil War, including as soldiers, commanders, and providers of supplies. As a result, the use and capture of private land and property became a strategic tool in the Civil War, one used by both sides to strike at landowners. The movement toward governing land rights in the United States occurred during the nineteenth century as an effort to fashion policies that would stimulate economic growth. Even with these regulations on how land should be used, landowners became instrumental in using the land to define separate spheres of class culture and power that reflected their interests and opinions about the situation up to and throughout the Civil War.

Before the Civil War, the differences between North and South were reflected in the ways elite plantation owners and slaveholders wielded influence over Southern society. However, as the economy shifted toward other ventures for economic stability and gain, large landowners no longer dictated Southern values and virtues. As a whole, large landholders supported secession and the Civil War, especially because they presented an opportunity to reinvigorate the old view of the slaveholding plantation aristocracy and build Southern nationalism to help maintain their interests. Seeing a threat to their economic and property holding interests in the divide over slavery, Southern landowners propagated the old image of antebellum Southern plantation society to paint an image of a unique Southern lifestyle that was under attack from the North. By supporting the break with the Union, these landowners sought to regain their position of power. Through promoting an idealized image of their culture, elite slaveholders rallied other white citizens to the Confederate cause. Those who left for the battlefield left their wives in charge of the plantations and farms.

In the North, among those who owned land were small family farmers. The Union lured many of these farmers into battle with offers of a regular salary and potential for more earnings through bounties. When they left for the battlefield, these men left behind their wives to take care of their land. Thus, many Northern women became the head of their households. These farmlands were important to the war effort as they supplied Union soldiers with food, a boon to the farming industry and farm owners.

The Union also utilized government legislation about Southern land as a way to support its war efforts. On March 12, 1863, Congress passed an act allowing Union forces to confiscate private land and property during war campaigns. This tactic hurt the production of Confederate resources and also allowed Union forces to take those resources as well as to find housing for Union troops. The effects of these land confiscations on the owners of the land were significant. Southern landowners lost their land until they renounced their Confederate ties and swore a loyalty oath to the Union. Only when one's loyalty to the Union was proven would the land be returned to its Southern owner. After they recovered their land, often years later, many Southern landowners discovered their farms and plantations in disarray or destroyed.

Once seized, these properties were given to lessees to work. They cultivated the land, but often neglected the regular maintenance and upkeep required of the large agricultural and plantation properties that had been seized. In many cases, the occupants of the land focused on cultivating the immediate rations and resources for sale to the Union Army, rather than properly tilling and cultivating the land with long-term farming and use in mind; sometimes it was left uncultivated for months at a time. Being dispossessed of their land—even if temporarily—led many Southern property owners to bear the burden of returning their former property back to its previous state after it had been destroyed by indiscriminate cultivation and subpar maintenance.

Battles fought across the South also wreaked havoc on property holdings and severely changed the landscape. During the war, soldiers plundered farmlands to feed themselves and their horses. In addition, Southern agricultural fields were transformed into trenches and tunnels and contained housing wreckage and corpses of fallen soldiers. Such damage and destruction intensified during the Union's "hard war" campaigns in 1864. For example, during William Tecumseh Sherman's march through Georgia and the Carolinas innumerable amounts of provisions, barns, mills, and farming implements were taken or destroyed. It would take Southern landowners many years to repair the costly damage that the war inflicted upon their land.

Alexander Lalama

See also: *Clothing, Fashion, and Appearance*: Shortages, Clothing; *Economy and Work*: Impressment; Plantations; Rural Life, Northern; Rural Life, Southern;

Slaveholders; Slavery; *Family and Gender Roles*: Womanhood, Northern; Womanhood, Southern; *Food and Drink*: Food, Shortages; Foraging; Gardens; Substitutes, Food and Drink; *Housing and Community*: Destruction of Homes and Personal Property

FURTHER READING

Brady, Lisa M. *War upon the Land: Military Strategy and the Transformation of Southern Landscapes During the American Civil War*. Athens: University of Georgia Press, 2012.

Clark, Thomas D., and Albert D. Kirwan. *The South Since Appomattox: A Century of Regional Change*. New York: Oxford University Press, 1967.

Ely, James W. *The Guardian of Every Other Right: A Constitutional History of Property Rights*. New York: Oxford University Press, 1992.

Giesberg, Judith A. *Army at Home: Women and the Civil War on the Northern Home Front*. Chapel Hill: University of North Carolina Press, 2009.

Nelson, Megan Kate. "The Environment." Pp. 64–75 in Maggi M. Morehouse and Zoe Trodd, eds. *Civil War America: A Social and Cultural History*. New York: Routledge, 2013.

Randall, James G. "Captured and Abandoned Property During the Civil War." *The American Historical Review* 19:1 (October 1913): 65–79.

Volo, Dorothy D, and James M. Volo. *Daily Life in Civil War America*. Westport, CT: Greenwood Press, 1998.

MUNITIONS FACTORIES

Industrial productivity increased during the Civil War, both in the Union and in the Confederacy, especially regarding the manufacture of munitions. To supply Union forces, Northern factory workers produced approximately one billion cartridges and percussion caps during the period. Although Southern manufacturing never reached the capacity of its Northern opposition, Confederates seized factories in the South upon secession and developed additional munitions sites, which allowed them to contend during the war. Laborers in the munitions factories—North and South—consisted of men, women, boys, and girls, both free and enslaved. Although the experiences of soldiers have largely overshadowed those of munitions workers, these factory workers contributed to and sacrificed for their respected causes in equal magnitude.

During the antebellum period, manufacturing in the North prospered, and by the beginning of the Civil War the North controlled 92 percent of the nation's manufacturing output. The North contained approximately 110,000 factories compared to 18,000 in the South, which gave the Union a significant advantage in producing the munitions required for war. The majority of factories were located within the metropolitan areas of New England, the Mid-Atlantic, and the Midwest. Factory owners and other leading industrial capitalists benefited the most during the war, due to the procurement of government contracts to produce munitions. Northern factory owners earned substantial profits, largely, at the expense of their workers, who received poor wages for long hours in dangerous conditions.

Many munitions workers had immigrated to the United States from Europe during the first half of the nineteenth century. The bustling urban areas of the North offered the immigrants an opportunity for employment, which only increased with the addition of numerous munitions contracts. Some munitions factories hired entire families to produce cartridges, percussion caps, fuses, and primers. However, fulfilling the enlistment quotas of the Union Army and Navy required the service of Northern men and boys. As a result of the absence of men on the home front, women and girls constituted the majority of munitions workers in the North.

Cover illustration from *Harper's Weekly* July 20, 1861, issue showing women filling cartridges at the United States Arsenal at Watertown, Massachusetts. During the Civil War, Northern factory workers produced approximately one billion cartridges and percussion caps for Union soldiers; although not in as large numbers as their Northern counterparts, Southern workers supplied the Confederate troops with similar supplies. Men, women, and children, both enslaved and free, worked in munitions factories during the war. (Library of Congress)

As their fathers, husbands, sons, and brothers enlisted to fight in the war, many women entered the munitions factories to serve as their households' primary source of income. Although they commonly received less compensation than their male counterparts, most female munitions workers earned enough to provide for their families. By entering the munitions factories each day, the war became a part of the daily lives of women, during which they contributed to the war effort in equal significance. Some women even asserted that men relied on their work to win the war.

However, the contributions and sacrifices of women did not occur without societal concern. Many civilians—North and South—called for the preservation of the traditional gender roles of women: keeping them in the home. Even the military's hiring of women to work in the munitions factories developed from the social norm that women should remain obedient. Thus, when some women viewed their contributions as grounds for obtaining equal rights to men in the workplace, controversy developed. The resistance women received from military leaders and factory owners led many to join labor organizations during the final stages of the war and after the war to advocate for equality in the workplace. Several decades would pass before much would be accomplished.

Over 30 explosions in Northern munitions factories occurred, taking the lives of hundreds of civilian workers. On September 17, 1862, the same day as the Battle of Antietam, a series of explosions set fire to the Allegheny Arsenal near Pittsburgh, Pennsylvania. The catastrophe claimed the lives of 78 workers and seriously injured several others. Almost two years later, on June 18, 1864, the inadvertent ignition of several artillery pieces at the Washington Arsenal led to the death of 21 women and girls. Because the accident occurred in the capital, the Lincoln administration provided money for the funerals and Congress apportioned funds for the orphans of the deceased workers and the surviving victims who sustained critical injuries. Of all the explosions that transpired, the victims and families associated with the Washington Arsenal were the only individuals to receive retribution from the government.

From the beginning of the colonial period, the South had developed an agrarian-based economy. As a result, only a limited number of factories were constructed in the region. Therefore, to supply their army and navy with munitions, the Confederate government relied on smuggling, trade with European nations, the confiscation of arsenals, and the development of new munitions factories. Confederate quartermaster general Abraham Myers ordered the formation of several factories in Charlotte, North Carolina, and Atlanta, Georgia, which transformed the prewar towns into bustling cities. Atlanta's population alone doubled during the war, due in large part to the addition of numerous munitions workers.

As they did in the North, women and girls worked throughout the South in munitions factories. In addition to entering the munitions factories for economic reasons, many women possessed patriotic fervor and desired to assist in the success of their cause. On March 13, 1863, many dedicated Southern women perished along with a 15-year-old boy in the explosion of the Confederate States Laboratory on Brown's Island in the Confederate capital. Approximately 45 munitions workers died in the explosion, which devastated the citizens of Richmond, Virginia.

Unlike in the North, numerous Southern munitions factories employed enslaved African Americans. Enslaved workers were leased at half of the daily wages paid to white workers. Factory owners commonly expected enslaved workers to produce twice as much as their white counterparts, despite the hazardous conditions and limited rations. Ultimately, the contributions of enslaved people in Confederate munitions factories helped incite the passage of the Confiscations Acts and the Emancipation Proclamation, both of which targeted slave labor as a vital cog in the Confederate war effort. In addition, due to the shortage of white males in the South, free blacks entered the workplace. For many of the freemen, the opportunity to work in the munitions factories provided higher salaries and improved standards of living.

Carl C. Creason

See also: *Economy and Work*: Factory Owners; Factory Workers, Northern; Factory Workers, Southern; Slavery; Tredegar Iron Works; Urban Life, Northern; Urban Life, Southern; *Family and Gender Roles*: Free Blacks; Immigrants; *Housing and Community*: Refugees

FURTHER READING

Bergin, Brian. *The Washington Arsenal Explosion: Civil War Disaster in the Capital.* Edited by Erin Bergin Voorheis. Charleston, SC: History Press, 2012.

Burton, David L. "Friday the 13th: Richmond's Greatest Home Front Disaster." *Civil War Times Illustrated* 21:6 (October 1982): 36–41.

Giesberg, Judith Ann. *Army at Home: Women and the Civil War on the Northern Home Front.* Chapel Hill: The University of North Carolina Press, 2009.

Jordan, Ervin L., Jr. *Black Confederates and Afro-Yankees in Civil War Virginia.* Charlottesville: University Press of Virginia, 1995.

Nelson, Scott Reynolds, and Carol Sheriff. *A People at War: Civilians and Soldiers in America's Civil War.* New York: Oxford University Press, 2007.

Wudarczyk, James. *Pittsburgh's Forgotten Allegheny Arsenal.* Apollo, PA: Closson Press, 1999.

PLANTATIONS

Although the institution of slavery was certainly not an American invention by any stretch of the imagination, the American plantation system presented a new facet to the age-old practice of human bondage that came directly from the United

States. Most historians generally define a plantation as a large estate in the Southern region of the country, where whites held large numbers of African Americans in bondage. These masters used enslaved people to harvest cash crops such as tobacco and cotton to increase their personal wealth. The most defining aspect of the plantation came in the form of the unique social hierarchy it unintentionally instituted on the property. Although all whites were placed on a level above that of any black, various levels of social status even existed among those in bondage. The type of work that each individual engaged in often defined the social status of that enslaved person.

The standard division of labor on an antebellum plantation usually lay between house work and a field work. Gender created no further distinctions, as enslaved women were often used in the fields to pick cotton or harvest crops and enslaved men were tasked as stewards and butlers in the master's household. Field slaves performed extremely backbreaking work for long hours each day, and were viewed as residents of the slave working class. The tasks they were forced to execute included planting and harvesting crops, maintaining buildings around the property, and tending to the master's animals. Enslaved people working

Nineteenth-century image by Currier and Ives of a cotton plantation along the Mississippi River. Southern plantations relied on the labor of enslaved African Americans to harvest crops and take care of the house and its white inhabitants. Plantations were designed to display the wealth of their owners. (Library of Congress)

the fields found themselves at a clear disadvantage, as slaveholders had a certain fondness for physically punishing those that were kept out of sight from outsiders. Overworked and underfed, these bondsmen and women experienced a shorter life expectancy than did house servants.

Some enslaved people viewed those fortunate enough to work in the estate's main house as being among the highest rungs of the slave social order. These enslaved workers tended to be better cared for by the masters and were much more likely to be viewed favorably by their owners. Performing childrearing duties, as well as cooking and cleaning for their white families, their daily interactions created a sense of familiarity between the house slaves and masters. However, the close interactions between the white slaveholding family and their enslaved house servants could also be dangerous for young enslaved women, who often had to deal with the unwanted attention of their master and other men in the house.

Interactions between enslaved blacks and elite whites created interesting dynamics on Southern plantations. Constant contact between the two races sometimes led to affection between individuals. White mistresses might teach their house slaves to write or read to pass the time, an offense that was illegal in many Southern states during this time period. In addition, being reared by a black mammy figure manifested a sense of kinship in the minds of many white children. These privileged children formed strong bonds with their mammy, and often played with the enslaved black children around the plantation. Although most whites seemed to have no problem with these activities, their attitudes appeared to have changed once their children began to reach the age of puberty. By the time the children had grown into young teenagers, their respective families had schooled them in the ways of race relations in the South during the antebellum period. White children were instructed in the ways of being masters and ruling over the supposed sub-human enslaved blacks. Transversely, blacks tried to stress to their offspring the importance of survival and remaining quiet in an effort not to draw attention to one's self. Those who successfully managed to do so might be able to escape harsh punishments and separation from their families.

The most peculiar characters on a plantation appeared to be the overseers and drivers. Overseers were white men, often of lower social standing than the plantation owner, who in a middle management capacity were hired to maintain control of the enslaved workers in the physical absence of the master. Drivers performed many of the same duties as an overseer, but on a much smaller level. They went into the fields with the enslaved workers, encouraging—usually by yelling—them to work harder and faster. These men also acted as security guards, making certain that slaves did not attempt escape during the work day.

In addition, some trusted enslaved black men served as drivers on their plantations. Although such an appointment was to be seen as a privilege and a sign of trust, it did not always appear so to the men raised to that position. Black drivers seemed to lose their standing in the enslaved community as they rose among the ranks of the plantation hierarchy. Once given a sense of power by the white master, fellow enslaved workers viewed the black driver as a traitor or a spy for the whites, who could not be trusted not to snitch on those who crossed him.

Even white men did not fare well in the overseer and driver roles. They did not fit in with the enslaved people or with the slaveholding family who employed them. Frustrations from both sides seemed to boil over in the laps of these men. Masters urged the overseer to push the enslaved laborers harder and produce more output, while enslaved people had better access to them than the masters and could exact their revenge if they so wished. Either way, the men who performed these jobs were placed in an impossible situation of which they certainly were not going to come out of unscathed. Overseers and drivers did not last very long in their positions and moved to another plantation quite frequently.

Although masters, overseers, and drivers were very liberal in their senses of crime and punishment, enslaved people also administered their own version of plantation justice. Despite strong familial ties in the enslaved community, criminals among them were not given a free pass to do as they pleased, especially when it came to crimes against their fellow slaves. Thievery became one of the most common offenses committed and also one of the most intensely punished. Flogging and whipping served as standard forms of punishment, but they were not the only ones. Some masters cut off fingers and hands to prevent stealing, while others chained slaves to walls or caused permanent injuries to legs to dissuade blacks from running away.

The uniqueness of the American plantation system allowed the enslaved the ability to create a life and a community for themselves. In spite of the harsh conditions that they faced, the enslaved people and their families were able to survive and thrive. To this day, many customs of the black community can be traced to their origins in antebellum slavery from the plantations in the South.

Amy Kirchenbauer

See also: *Economy and Work*: Rural Life, Southern; Slavery; *Family Life and Gender Roles*: Manhood, Southern; Womanhood, Southern; *Housing and Community*: Slave Life; Slave Quarters

FURTHER READING

Berlin, Ira. *Many Thousand Gone: The First Two Centuries of Slavery in North America.* Cambridge, MA: The Belknap Press of Harvard University, 1998.

Blassingame, John W. *The Slave Community: Plantation Life in the Antebellum South.* New York: Oxford University Press, 1972.

Fox-Genovese, Elizabeth. *Within the Plantation Household: Black and White Women of the Old South*. Chapel Hill: University of North Carolina Press, 1988.

Genovese, Eugene D. *Roll, Jordan, Roll: The World the Slaves Made*. New York: Vintage Books, 1972.

POVERTY

In the wake of the Industrial Revolution, America's quest to establish economic independence led to a heavy reliance on manufacturing and production. In the Southern states, advancements in science and technology increased agricultural output and dependence on enslaved labor; in the North, factories sprouted and cities began to swell. The economy boomed until a combination of domestic and international factors triggered a panic in 1857. As domestic economic conditions worsened, a gulf grew between the rich and the poor and poverty became a pervasive social issue. During the decade before the Civil War, the U.S. pauper rate increased over 70 percent.

Urbanization radically altered life in the Northern states. In early America, towns had functioned as tight-knit communities, and citizens had connected regularly through social and religious events. Trades had been taught by apprenticeship, with master craftsmen personally instructing and watching over their underlings. When families fell on hard times, neighbors banded together and supported one another. However, these dynamics disappeared as factories began to dominate the landscape. Immigrants and native-born citizens flocked to the cities where jobs were plentiful. Paternalistic connections gave way to impersonal leadership as overseers were tasked with watching over large numbers of employees instead of shaping and guiding the output of a few.

Long factory days necessitated nearby housing, so existing dwellings were subdivided and transformed to accommodate the masses. Backhouses and basements were also used, as formerly grand, single-family homes became perilously packed tenant houses. It was common for a family of 10 or more people to share one dark, poorly ventilated bedroom. Barrack-like tenement buildings were soon erected, but even these were not enough to alleviate crowded conditions. Ethnic groups clustered together, and cultural differences were accentuated as proximity reinforced cultural and religious traits and traditions. Undesirable behaviors also grew as desperation permeated the living conditions; crime and alcohol abuse surfaced as common outlets for frustration. In addition, close living quarters and poor sanitation allowed diseases to spread among inhabitants so mortality rates were high.

As the number of people seeking employment began to outweigh the number of jobs available, begging for assistance became commonplace. One economic upside of the Civil War was the fact that many unemployed Northerners were able to find jobs as soldiers. However, Union expenditures related to feeding, clothing, arming, and transporting soldiers led the government to increase taxes and move away from currency backed by gold and silver. These actions led to price inflation and created further frustrations for the poor. The institutional structure of urban life had removed most communal connections between neighbors; as a result, private assistance became uncommon and public solutions became necessary.

Upper elements of Northern society started to scorn the less fortunate and question their moral fiber; as a result, "indoor" options like poorhouses and asylums began to take precedence over "outdoor" handouts of money and food. Putting the indigent into homes allowed authorities to control and shape resident behavior; strict rules were created in an attempt to uplift and enforce moral standards. Many were forced to perform labor as quid pro quo for their room and board. Impoverished children were removed from their families and placed into orphanages or foster care in an attempt to better their lives. Young boys were often "placed out," sent to live with new families on farms in the new frontier.

In 1862, the Homestead Act offered free land to citizens over the age of 21; consequently many families decided to move west and create new lives for themselves. The territories presented opportunities and obstacles, but homesteading was a popular solution for those looking to make a fresh start. Hard work turned dry plains into productive farmland and rural regions swelled. Transportation and communication continued to improve, making remote areas more connected to the rest of the country.

Northern and Southern poverty problems were distinct, but the regions had shared characteristics. The separation between successful Northern industrialists and factory workers was similar to the division between wealthy plantation owners and enslaved laborers in Southern society. Plantation owners lived luxurious lives, while enslaved workers toiled in the fields. African American workers were seen as possessions, not people, who lacked personal rights as well as opportunities for advancement. However, because they were considered valuable, their basic needs were met. Enslaved people were not treated well, but they were generally provided with the minimum food and shelter required to make them productive.

Subsistence farming was dramatically different from plantation life. Small farms often produced only enough food for the family's survival. Sometimes, even basic nutrition proved impossible and poor farming families became "clay eaters," swallowing clumps of earth to fill the emptiness of their stomachs. In such precarious settings, education was neglected and children frequently grew up ignorant and hungry. Some subsistence farmers managed to generate small surpluses, but weak Southern transportation systems made it difficult for them to move crops to market.

Both large and small farms were impacted by the war, because most Civil War battles were fought on Southern lands. Food shortages arose because many plantations were devoted to the production of cotton, not grain. In addition, Northern blockades impeded the flow of goods into the South, and the scarcity of railway routes made it difficult to move soldiers and supplies. Furthermore, hungry soldiers from both sides regularly pillaged crops and stole livestock from Southern farms. General William Tecumseh Sherman and other Northern commanders burned and leveled Southern cities and farms as they marched across the land, leaving a wake of destruction behind them.

After Lincoln's Emancipation Proclamation took effect on January 1, 1863, Southern battlefield losses also led to the loss of enslaved laborers. Without these essential workers, many plantation operations were crippled. Freedpeople faced formidable challenges; they had no education, no money, and very few skills. Black Codes clarified the freedmen's lowly social status and made unemployment illegal; these discriminatory laws forced many blacks to return to low-wage fieldwork. Racial tensions and economic challenges abounded during Reconstruction.

After the war, surviving soldiers returned home and cities became flooded with desperate workers. Unemployment increased and streets were filled with out-of-work beggars. States soon enacted provisions against vagrants and vagabonds, but conditions continued to worsen. Wartime inflation had left prices astronomically high. An initial postwar boom was followed by an economic slide, culminating in another economic panic in 1873.

Amy Orr

See also: *Clothing, Fashion, and Appearance*: Shortages, Clothing; *Economy and Work*: Factory Workers, Northern; Factory Workers, Southern; Impressment; Rural Life, Northern; Rural Life, Southern; Slavery; Urban Life, Northern; Urban Life, Southern; *Family Life and Gender Roles*: Aid Societies; Immigrants; *Food and Drink*: Food, Shortages; Foraging; Hunting; Substitutes, Food and Drink; *Housing and Community*: Slave Life; *Science and Technology*: Education, Northern; Education, Southern

FURTHER READING

Brace, Charles Loring. *The Dangerous Classes of New York and Twenty Years' Work Among Them*. New York: Wynkoop & Hallenbeck, 1872.

Kiesling, L. Lynne, and Robert A. Margo. "Explaining the Rise in Antebellum Pauperism, 1850–1860: New Evidence." *The Quarterly Review of Economics and Finance* 37:2 (Summer 1997): 405–417.

Ransom, Roger L. *Conflict and Compromise: The Political Economy of Slavery, Emancipation, and the American Civil War.* New York: Cambridge University Press, 1989.

Riis, Jacob A. *How the Other Half Lives: Studies Among the Poor.* London: Sampson Low, Marston, Searle, & Rivington, 1891.

Smith, Billy G. *Down and Out in Early America.* University Park: Pennsylvania State University Press, 2004.

Wright, Gavin. *Slavery and American Economic Development.* Baton Rouge: Louisiana State University Press, 2006.

PROSTITUTES

Prostitution, or the practice of getting paid for sex or sexual acts, was not a new occurrence during the American Civil War. In the mid-nineteenth century, prostitution referred primarily to the practice of male clients paying women for sex. Women engaged in prostitution for a number of reasons. Some scholars point to the connection between poverty and prostitution, emphasizing that many women participated in prostitution primarily for economic reasons. Some of the most impoverished women who turned to prostitution did so because they felt they had no choice. However, prostitution also paid much better than other wage work such as factory jobs. For some women, then, participating in prostitution over a long term could become a way to improve their lives in terms of acquiring goods, property, and personal connections. Some scholars also suggest that still other women became prostitutes because they enjoyed not only their ability to earn good money, but also because they enjoyed sex.

In the decades leading up to the Civil War, the visibility of prostitution appeared to increase. Potential clients could purchase publications that gave them the locations of brothels and similar places to find prostitutes in a number of cities, including New Orleans. By 1858, prostitution was seen as such a clear social issue that Doctor William Sanger compiled the first study on prostitutes to understand more about women engaged in the practice. When Sanger completed his study, he calculated that there were more than 6,000 prostitutes in New York City alone, about one prostitute for every 117 people living in the city. Before the war, Nashville had just over 200 prostitutes, but almost 1,500 prostitutes by 1863, partially because of the large numbers of soldiers who came to the city. Washington, D.C., saw as many as 5,000 prostitutes during the war, compared to the 500 in the area during the antebellum period.

During the Civil War, prostitutes were found in cities, near military camps, and in locations throughout the Union and Confederacy. Some women worked in brothels, houses where multiple women worked as prostitutes; other women worked independently as streetwalkers. However, not all women who engaged in prostitution were professionals or engaged in prostitution for extended periods of time; rather, women could also engage in prostitution temporarily. For some women left without male support on the home front, prostitution became a wartime solution that allowed them to pay bills, care for other family members, or keep a roof over their heads. Other women became camp followers trailing along with military troops who could provide a steady customer base.

Along with the increased presence of prostitutes during the Civil War, sexually transmitted diseases (STDs)—known also as venereal diseases—were something that concerned military officials. Although both the Confederate and Union armies developed treatments for the most common STDs of the mid-nineteenth century, the medical field was not yet advanced enough to understand the science behind what caused and spread gonorrhea or syphilis. Doctors knew that the diseases happened because of sexual contact, but they had not yet learned how to best treat these diseases. Moreover, although most soldiers would have known about condoms, which had been in use for at least 200 years before the Civil War, condoms were viewed primarily as a birth control method. Military leaders worried about prostitutes because healthy soldiers who developed STDs could soon become useless on the battlefield. Although both sides had ways to treat syphilis and gonorrhea, soldiers who developed these diseases could find themselves spending more time in a hospital than on the battlefield. By the end of the war, scholars estimate that three out of every five soldiers had died from disease, although not all of these deaths were from STDs.

To try to reduce venereal disease, military leaders imposed restrictions on prostitutes and on brothels more specifically. In some places, these restrictions included rounding up prostitutes and imprisoning them under vagrancy laws designed to prevent people from loitering or sleeping outside. In other locations, prostitution became more strictly controlled. Nashville, for example, created legal restrictions on prostitution that had not previously existed. Although military officials initially tried to remove prostitutes from the city entirely, they were unsuccessful. Beginning in 1863, prostitutes had to be licensed and were subject to weekly health examinations to make sure they did not have any diseases. In case any prostitute was discovered to have venereal disease, the new rules also called for the creation of a hospital to care for ill prostitutes—paid for by a weekly tax on each licensed prostitute. Unlicensed prostitutes caught trying to engage clients would be jailed. By 1864, Memphis had instituted similar regulations on prostitutes.

One Union general's method of trying to control prostitution by putting all prostitutes in one region of Washington, D.C., backfired. Popular myth also links the origin of the nickname of "hookers," often used to refer to prostitutes, to Civil War general Joseph Hooker. Although some scholars have traced the term "hooker" to the pre–Civil War era, during the war Hooker developed a reputation connected with prostitutes when he tried to help control what he saw as a prostitution problem. Hooker relocated many prostitutes into a specific area of town, which became known as "Hooker's Division" and was noted frequently in papers as a place where men could find prostitutes.

In general, women who worked as prostitutes were seen as disreputable. Union general Benjamin Butler used this idea to try to control Confederate women when he occupied New Orleans beginning in 1862 and he disliked how enemy women treated Union soldiers. Butler's General Order No. 28 specified that women who acted disrespectfully toward Union troops would be treated as prostitutes and fined and jailed. However, Union troops themselves declined to enforce this measure and the outrage from New Orleans people led to its repeal not long after.

Tanya L. Roth

See also: *Economy and Work*: Camp Followers; Poverty; *Family Life and Gender Roles*: Young Men; Young Women; *Politics and Warfare*: Camp Life; *Science and Technology*: Disease

FURTHER READING

Clinton, Catherine. *The Other Civil War: American Women in the Nineteenth Century.* New York: Hill and Wang, 1984.

Clinton, Catherine. " 'Public Women' and Sexual Politics During the American Civil War." In Catherine Clinton and Nina Silber, eds. *Battle Scars: Gender and Sexuality in the American Civil War.* New York: Oxford University Press, 2006, pp. 61–77.

Faust, Drew Gilpin. *Mothers of Invention: Women of the Slaveholding South in the American Civil War.* Chapel Hill: University of North Carolina Press, 1996.

Lowry, Thomas P. *The Story the Soldiers Wouldn't Tell: Sex in the Civil War.* Mechanicsville, PA: Stackpole Books, 1994.

Massey, Mary Elizabeth. *Women in the Civil War.* Lincoln: University of Nebraska Press, 1994. (Originally published as *Bonnet Brigades.* New York: A. A. Knopf, 1966.)

Sanger, William W. *The History of Prostitution: Its Extent, Causes, and Effects Throughout the World.* New York: The Medical Publishing Company, 1910.

Schogol, Jeff. Rumor Doctor Blog Archive. "Do 'Hookers' Owe Their Moniker to a Civil War General?" April 28, 2011. *Stars and Stripes.* http://www.stripes.com/blogs/the-rumor-doctor/the-rumor-doctor-1.104348/do-hookers-owe-their-moniker-to-a-civil-war-general-1.142179. Accessed July 31, 2014.

Stansell, Christine. *City of Women: Sex and Class in New York, 1789–1860.* Urbana: University of Illinois Press, 1987.

RURAL LIFE, NORTHERN

During the Civil War, the North was home to approximately 21 million people. Of these, about 16.5 million lived outside of significant urban centers. Despite the dramatic increase in population that Northern cities experienced throughout the first half of the nineteenth century, rural dwellers outnumbered America's urban population until the 1920s. Thus, a good deal of Northern territory was considered rural. Everyday life for these Northerners varied, and depended on numerous geographical, economic, and social factors.

Outside of cities, Northerners lived in towns, in villages, and on farms. The chief economic occupation of such places was agriculture. Rural families often gathered in villages and small towns to bring their goods to market, to conduct other business, to purchase items they could not produce themselves, to worship, and for social reasons. Towns and villages ranged in size depending on their location and economic importance. Farming families sometimes formed "rural neighborhoods" to ease the burden of isolation and to create a sense of community. Typically towns found in rural areas served as a hub for surrounding farms and smaller villages, and contained the homes of inhabitants along with general stores, inns, taverns, and churches. More prosperous towns in close proximity to major transit routes such as rivers and railroads boasted banks and telegraph offices.

In addition to surpassing the South in manufacturing, the North was able to feed its population during the war and, with the exception of cash crops like cotton and tobacco, outpaced the South in agricultural output in nearly every category. The goods of Northern farmers were not only purchased by the government for the war effort, but were also exported to nations such as England, providing the United States with valuable political leverage against potential Southern allies. The success of Northern farmers could largely be attributed to the Industrial Revolution, felt in the countryside as well as in cities, in which the 50 years prior to the Civil War witnessed tremendous growth and advancement in agricultural technology. Along with increases in the use of horsepower, a greater understanding of fields vital to agriculture such as fertilization and crop breeding encouraged farmers to specialize in growing staples such as wheat or corn. Additionally, improvements in existing equipment such as the steel plow and mechanical binders as well as the invention of new labor-saving devices such as grain drills and reapers greatly increased the productive capabilities of farmers, who took advantage of these developments whenever they were able to do so.

Throughout the Civil War era, the typical Northern farm was approximately 60 acres in size and family owned; farms further west tended to be larger and more isolated than the farms of the East. Unlike the vast plantations of the South, such farmsteads formed the heart of the Union's agricultural might. Although there existed numerous economic and regional differences between Northern farms, most consisted of a home along with other structures for the storage of animals, crops, and equipment. Successful farms boasted two-story houses that usually included a spare, ground-level bedroom that was often rented out to travelers for extra income.

Labor on family farms was largely segregated by gender, and children played an important role in a farm family's economic success. They began helping out with chores around the age of 5 and were expected to keep pace with adults by 13. From sunup to sundown, boys worked with their fathers in the field and tended to the livestock while girls helped their mothers maintain the home, minded their younger siblings, and tended to the poultry. Because children were an important source of labor on the farm, rural families were often large. When needed, farmers could also take on hired help for varied amounts of time, from a week or two at a time to the whole season.

Food shortages did not plague the North during wartime as they did the South, and the typical rural Northern family fared significantly better than its Confederate counterpart. Additionally, many families kept gardens and orchards for personal use, and were able to supplement their diets with an array of fresh fruits and vege-tables along with those they pickled or canned. The most prevalent meat consumed was pork, which was preserved in the form of ham and bacon. Raising hogs also produced quantities of lard, valued for its versatility in cooking and preservation. Other typical meats included beef, chicken from hens that no longer produced eggs, and a variety of wild game and waterfowl including duck, pheasant, turkey, rabbit, and deer. Those rural dwellers that lived near lakes and rivers and along the coast, also consumed fish and seafood, including bass, catfish, pike, crabs and lobster. Oysters were eaten fresh, pickled, or smoked.

Homemade baked goods were widely consumed by rural families, and included bread, biscuits, cakes, and pies. Common sweeteners included honey, sugar, and maple syrup. Fruits and vegetables were consumed fresh on a seasonal basis and preserved and pickled in the form of jellies, sauces, and catsups to last throughout the year. Numerous varieties of vegetables, notably peas, corn, potatoes, beets, cabbages, and turnips, could be dried or stored in root cellars to consume in winter months. Candy was a popular treat that could be purchased in town general stores. Along with water, coffee, and tea, rural families enjoyed many homemade soft drinks and alcoholic beverages. Some of the more popular drinks included lemon-ade, hard apple cider, and whisky.

Social life for rural Northerners varied. Families often had close relationships with their neighbors and depended on each other for company and occasional help on the farm. Most attended religious services on Sundays at the closest church of their choosing. Traveling to the nearest village or town also offered a chance to visit friends, shop, and enjoy entertainment. Though options for entertainment were more limited in the rural areas than in cities, rural dwellers enjoyed a variety of minstrel shows, fairs, festivals, traveling circuses, and sporting events.

Although the Northern countryside was not nearly as devastated as its Southern counterpart, rural families felt the impact of the war in many ways. Young men from rural areas, many of whom had never traveled far from their homes, comprised a substantial portion of the U.S. Army's recruits. Thus, a significant percentage of men, constituting a large part of the rural labor force, volunteered or were drafted into the military. Those who remained on the farm, mainly women, children, and the elderly, carried on as best they could. The death of a husband or son devastated many rural families, and towns and villages in which large numbers of men enlisted together were grief stricken when many of them did not return. Following the war, men suffering from debilitating physical and psychological wounds returned to their families and tried to reintegrate into society, often with difficulty.

It is commonly accepted that Northern victory in the Civil War was the result of its superiority in manufacturing, concentrated in its numerous large cities. However, more than half the population of the Union states consisted of rural dwellers who provided great quantities of manpower and foodstuffs necessary to win the war. Life for these people represented what life was like for the majority of Americans at the time. In the next 50 years, their lives would significantly change as urbanization continued its upward trend.

Justin Riskus

See also: *Economy and Work*: Agriculture; Landowners; Rural Life, Southern; Urban Life, Northern; *Family Life and Gender Roles*: Household Entertainment; Manhood, Northern; Womanhood, Northern; *Food and Drink*: Food, Northern; Food, Shortages; Food, Upper Classes; *Housing and Community*: Architecture, Northern; *Recreation and Social Customs*: Hospitality

FURTHER READING

Finkelman, Paul. *Encyclopedia of the United States in the Nineteenth Century*. New York: Charles Scribner's Sons, 2001.

Marten, James. *Civil War America: Voices from the Home Front*. Santa Barbara, CA: ABC-CLIO, 2003.

Miller, Randall M., and James M. Volo. *The Greenwood Encyclopedia of Daily Life in America*. Vol. 2. Westport, CT: Greenwood, 2009.

Rose, Anne C. *Victorian America and the Civil War*. New York: Cambridge University Press, 1994.

Varhola, Michael J. *Everyday Life During the Civil War*. Cincinnati, OH: Writer's Digest Books, 1999.

RURAL LIFE, SOUTHERN

During the Civil War era, the majority of Americans lived in rural areas. Rural life was most common in the Southern slaveholding states. Of the nine million inhabitants of the Confederacy, only 10 percent lived in urban areas. The remainder of the population lived on farms and plantations, as well as in villages and small towns. Rural life across the South varied and was largely dependent on one's economic status.

Small farmers, or yeomen, who lived at or slightly above subsistence levels, populated the rural South. They earned their living growing and raising an array of agricultural products, which included cash crops like cotton and tobacco as well as produce and livestock. Corn, which could serve as food for humans or animals or be turned into whiskey, was a staple as were hogs, whose meat was easily preserved and whose lard was highly valued. Men and boys also went hunting and fishing to supplement the family diet.

A typical yeoman farm consisted of about 60 acres with a simple one-story house and a barn, along with other assorted small buildings. More prosperous farms boasted two-story homes that included a bedroom on the ground floor, often rented out to travelers for the night. Families worked hard, starting their chores at dawn and working until sunset, depending on the season. After feeding the livestock, tending to crops occupied most of the day, especially labor-intensive ones such as cotton or tobacco. A man's domain was outdoors caring for animals, chopping wood, and farming, among other things. The women of the family spent most of their days within the home preparing meals, childrearing, and mending clothes. However, in poorer families, women also helped with the crops and other chores. Rural families spent a large part of the day together and were often close knit.

Rural life could be lonely, as the distance between farms was often significant. Attending church services on Sunday in the nearest town or village brought neighbors together at least once a week, as did the fairs and festivals held throughout the year. On occasion a traveling circus or other variety show held in the nearest town provided an opportunity for families to travel. Neighbors generally got along, and depended on each other for help throughout the year. Calling on neighbors to visit and socialize was common. Education was sparse compared to today's standards, and most rural children attended one-room schoolhouses or were taught at home.

The majority of small farms in the South did not completely depend upon enslaved labor. Those who could afford it often bought one or two slaves to help on the farm, but few owned more than five. Small farmers highly valued their status as free men and thus supported plantation owners and their use of enslaved labor. Though he might be poor, a yeoman farmer understood that enslaved people would always be below him in status in Southern society. This attitude partly explains the great number of Southerners who fought against the Union but held no slaves.

In addition to the small farms throughout the South there were plantations, typically isolated and ranging in size from approximately 500 to 1,000 acres or more. Plantations were large agricultural ventures typically owned by a single family. In Southern society, the owner of a plantation was called a "planter" rather than a farmer. It was on such plantations that more than half of all the enslaved people in the Confederacy worked. During the Civil War era, a midlevel planter had between 15 and 45 enslaved people, while larger plantations generally had 50 or more enslaved African Americans. It was not uncommon for the wealthiest planters in the South to own over 100 enslaved people. Each plantation usually specialized in producing one cash crop, such as rice, cotton, or tobacco, and each was largely self-sustaining.

The planter and his family lived in the main house, and the opulence of the home often reflected the wealth and social status of its owner. A plantation also had many other buildings. The overseer who ran the plantation and the enslaved people who worked it lived in smaller houses and huts. Thus, a plantation was essentially a small village, complete with its own stables, storage buildings, mills, and workshops.

For the planter and his family, the quality of life on the plantation was substantially higher than the average person's life throughout the South. The "plantation aristocracy," as they were often called, enjoyed fine food, luxuries imported from Europe, and vacation homes. Their children benefited from private tutors and sometimes attended college. Socially, planters competed with each other by hosting elaborate balls and dinners demonstrating their wealth. Other leisure pursuits in the country included hunting and horse racing. Those planters who had the desire, financial means, and the time to pursue positions of power came to dominate Southern politics.

Life for enslaved African Americans on a plantation presented a stark contrast. In general, the character of the plantation owner and overseer largely dictated the quality of life for the enslaved people. Working daily from sun up to sun down, and by moonlight during the harvest season, they lived a meager existence. Enslaved laborers had little free time. They lived in crude shacks with dirt floors. Unlike the elaborate meals enjoyed by their owners, enslaved people ate simple fare, making do with what was provided. Any meat given to enslaved people for their meals was usually the undesirable parts of the animal, namely offal. When permitted, enslaved people could hunt and fish to supplement their diets. Those who were chosen for domestic duties, often based on the lightness of their skin, sometimes lived slightly better than their field hand counterparts. Due to the intentional separation of nuclear families and the harshness of enslaved life, enslaved persons formed tight bonds with each other.

The impact of the Civil War was greatly felt on the farms and plantations of the rural South. Most yeomen farmers left to serve in the Confederate Army; many were killed or maimed throughout the course of the war. Their absence was sorely felt at home, where women had to manage the farm and make do as best they could. Widespread shortages of staples like flour, salt, and sugar made life difficult. Invading armies and hungry soldiers from both sides often ravaged farms near theaters of war.

Planters and their overseers were exempt from military service, provided they owned 20 slaves or more. Considered the backbone of the Confederate economy, plantations were awarded special treatment in most cases. As the war dragged on and the Union blockade proved effective, the Confederate government put increasing pressure on planters to grow food instead of cash crops like cotton and tobacco so that they could feed the military and civilian populations. Plantations near the fighting, prone to pillaging from Union armies, fared the worst. For example, Union general William Tecumseh Sherman's "March to the Sea" in 1864, which targeted wealthy plantations and the politically influential Southern elite who owned them, inflicted more than $100 million in damage upon the economy and infrastructure of the South.

Although rural life in the South had some similarities to rural life in the North, Southern farmers felt the effects of the Civil War much greater than did their Northern counterparts. The absence of men produced great strains across rural areas, as too did the foraging and pillaging of both armies. It would be many years before the rural South recovered from the destruction wreaked by the Civil War.

Justin Riskus

See also: *Economy and Work*: Agriculture; Impressment; Landowners; Plantations; Rural Life, Northern; Slaveholders; Slavery; Urban Life, Southern; *Family Life and Gender Roles*: Household Entertainment; Slave Families; *Food and Drink*: Food, African Americans; Food, Shortages; Food, Southern; Food, Upper Classes; Foraging; Gardens; Hunting; Moonshine; Salt; Spirits; Substitutes, Food and Drink; Tea; Tobacco; *Housing and Community*: Architecture, Southern; Destruction of Homes and Personal Property; Plantation Houses; Slave Life; Slave Quarters; *Recreation and Social Customs*: Fairs and Bazaars; Fishing; Holidays; Hospitality; Leisure Time; Sport Hunting; *Religion and Belief*: Religious Revivals; Religious Social Services, Home Front; *Science and Technology*: Education, Southern

FURTHER READING

Felton, Rebecca. *Country Life in Georgia in the Days of My Youth*. Atlanta, GA: Index Printing Company, 1919.

Kagan, Neil. *Eyewitness to the Civil War: The Complete History from Secession to Reconstruction*. Washington, DC: National Geographic, 2006.

McCurry, Stephanie. *Masters of Small Worlds: Yeoman Households, Gender Relations, and the Political Culture of the Antebellum South Carolina Low Country*. New York: Oxford University Press, 1995.

Miller, Randall M., and James M. Volo. *The Greenwood Encyclopedia of Daily Life in America*. Vol. 2. Westport, CT: Greenwood, 2009.

Rose, Anne C. *Victorian America and the Civil War*. New York: Cambridge University Press, 1994.

SLAVEHOLDERS

Slaveholders shaped the course of secession and Civil War. Although not the majority of Southern whites, slaveholders held an inordinate amount of power in the slaveholding states.

On the eve of the Civil War, almost four million Americans lived in bondage. Enslaved African Americans comprised nearly half the population of Alabama, Florida, Georgia, and Louisiana, and more than half the population of Mississippi and South Carolina was enslaved. In many cases, slaveholders turned to the Bible and the Constitution to defend the South's "peculiar institution." As the nineteenth century wore on, slavery threatened to tear the nation apart.

Slave states in the South and West feared that with a Republican president the federal government would end slavery. For slaveholders, many who were born into families that had owned enslaved people for generations and who had blood ties to their "property," the demise of slavery was unthinkable. From Florida to the western states and territories, whites and Indians profited immensely from enslaved labor, which likely made it easier for slaveholders to overlook the harsh realities of the institution. In 1860, the monetary value of the nation's enslaved was approximately $3 billion, and was second only to the value of its farmland—more than $6 billion.

In addition to propping up the Southern economy, slavery was intricately connected to the social fabric of the slaveholding states. Slaveholders viewed the antislavery movement not only as an attack upon the economic foundations of the Old South, but also as a threat to their very way of life and their sense of self. Whether they were slaveholders or non-slaveholders, white Southerners' sense of self was grounded in a collection of hierarchical differences. Even though the majority of the people living in the South were not slaveholders, Southerners viewed themselves and those around them in terms of whiteness and blackness, masculinity and femininity, independence and dependence, strength and weakness.

Southern slaveholders required obedience without question, from enslaved people and wives alike. In Southern society a woman's submission to white male authority was considered implicit, just as a slave's submission to his or her master was thought to be a part of the natural order. The plantation mistress was locked in a constant struggle to instill order in her children and in her enslaved house servants, whom she frequently accused of laziness and disobedience. From the perspective of the slave plantation mistress, evil was everywhere, and her role was to serve as a moral compass.

Slaveholders used violence to ensure discipline, leading enslaved men, women, and children to resist in nonviolent and violent ways. To maintain order and prevent enslaved people from running away—or sometimes simply for profit—slaveholders routinely sold husbands, wives, mothers, fathers, and children away from each other to slaveholders on other plantations, in different states, or even in a different country.

Just as slaveholders were willing to use violence to maintain the system of slavery, they were equally willing to secede from the Union to defend the institution. Men's willingness to kill for the sake of keeping their property was perhaps the most important cause of the Civil War. Had the value of the nation's enslaved people not been so great, the argument over the demise of slavery would not have been as volatile.

Although it is commonly believed that only a small proportion of Southerners owned slaves, and fewer still owned large numbers of slaves, recent studies have shown that the data used to determine the number of enslaved people each slaveholder owned is complex, and there were more large slaveholders than was previously understood. For instance, Levin R. Marshall owned more than 1,000 slaves, but they lived in six different counties in Mississippi and Louisiana. Therefore, unless census records for particular counties and states are pieced together and viewed as a whole, they do not offer a complete picture of the number of slaves Marshall and other large slaveholders actually owned. Interpreting census data in a piecemeal fashion also obscures the family relations of slaveholders and fails to reveal the connections between large slaveholding families. At least 339 elite slaveholders owned more than 250 enslaved people each during the 1850s. One of the wealthiest of these planter-aristocrats, South Carolinian Nathaniel Heyward, owned between 1,829 and 2,340 slaves at the time of his death in 1851. Francis Surget of Mississippi owned approximately 1,300 slaves in 1850; however, if the number of enslaved people owned by Surget's entire extended family is taken into consideration, the Surget family owned a total of 5,287 slaves.

Slaveholders were not willing to sacrifice enslaved property, valued at more than $3 billion, without a fight. As a result, Southerners continued to turn not only to the Bible and the Constitution to defend slavery, but also to history. All of the great civilizations of the world, they argued, had practiced slavery. They also noted that slavery had played a vital role in the Northern economy until relatively recently, and that the belief in white supremacy and its corollary, black inferiority, thrived not only in the South but also in the North. One of the defining characteristics of the South, however, was that it continued to function as a slave society long after the practice died a slow death in the North. Enslaved labor was the driving force behind the Southern economy, social structure, and culture. As a result, the Civil War disrupted, and ultimately destroyed, slavery and much of the Southern economy.

Peggy Macdonald

See also: *Arts*: Slave Narratives; *Economy and Work*: Landowners; Plantations; Rural Life, Southern; Slavery; Urban Life, Southern; *Family Life and Gender Roles*: Manhood, Southern; Patriarchy; Slave Families; Womanhood, Southern; *Housing and Community*: Plantation Houses; Slave Life; *Politics and Warfare*: Abolitionists; Morale; Secession; Surrender, Confederate; *Religion and Belief*: Lost Cause

FURTHER READING

Clinton, Catherine. *The Plantation Mistress: Woman's World in the Old South*. New York: Pantheon Books, 1982.

Faust, Drew Gilpin. *Mothers of Invention: Women of the Slaveholding South in the Civil War*. Chapel Hill: University of North Carolina Press, 1996.

Fox-Genovese, Elizabeth, and Eugene D. Genovese. *The Mind of the Master Class: History and Faith in the Southern Slaveholder's Worldview*. New York: Cambridge University Press, 2005.

Glymph, Thavolia. *Out of the House of Bondage: The Transformation of the Plantation Household*. New York: Cambridge University Press, 2008.

Huston, James L. *Calculating the Value of the Union: Slavery, Property Rights, and the Economic Origins of the Civil War*. Chapel Hill: University of North Carolina Press, 2003.

Scarborough, William Kauffman. *Masters of the Big House: Elite Slaveholders of the Mid-Nineteenth-Century South*. Baton Rouge: Louisiana State University Press, 2003.

SLAVERY

Slavery, a system whereby one human being owned another, was practiced in America beginning in the early 1600s. When the American Revolution began in 1775, every colony had enslaved people. However, over the next generation, Northern and Southern states diverged on the issue. All states north of the Mason-Dixon Line passed legislation to outlaw the practice, yet the institution of slavery remained critical in the South where enslaved people made up most of the labor force. Abolitionists and growing numbers of their political supporters denounced the institution as sinful, economically backward, and anti-republican, while proslavery ideologues passionately defended it as a "positive good" that benefited both the enslaved and slave owners alike. In the antebellum decades, the issue of slavery polarized the North and the South. Eventually, feeling that the institution of slavery was threatened, 11 Southern states broke away to form their own nation, and civil war ensued. When the conflict began, ending slavery was not a primary war aim of the Union, yet by its end, emancipation had become a priority.

Early in the war, President Abraham Lincoln's administration adopted a vacillating policy with regards to enslaved African Americans and the institution of

Photograph of enslaved African Americans on the J.J. Smith plantation in Beaufort, South Carolina, in 1862. Enslaved labor formed the backbone of the antebellum Southern economy. (Library of Congress)

slavery. Enslaved people, however, did not wait for the U.S. government to adopt a course of action regarding emancipation. Rather, once war commenced, large numbers of enslaved people fled their bondage and sought refuge behind the lines of the Union Army, who they hoped represented a liberating force. In the spring of 1861, General Benjamin Butler, whose command at Fortress Monroe in Virginia had become a magnet to self-emancipating slaves, declared that since enslaved workers had been used in erecting Confederate defenses and other war-related activities, these refugees should not be returned to their masters, but rather declared "contraband of war" and put to work for the Union Army. However, other federal officers expressed the conviction that all refugees from slavery should be returned to their masters.

Not until Congress passed the First Confiscation Act in August of 1861 was anything resembling a uniform policy by the U.S. government applied to fugitives from slavery. The act declared that any property used in aiding the insurrection could lawfully be seized whenever found. In the case of enslaved people, they were to be freed. However, as the Union Army pressed southward and enslaved African Americans flocked to their lines, there were still no clear guidelines for their treatment. In December 1862, General Rufus Saxton sought to clarify this confusion by issuing an order that former slaves be allotted small plots of abandoned land to raise crops for themselves and cotton for the Union Army. Still, through the final months of the war, there were questions over which of the Treasury or War Departments were to administer the aid to former slaves and the contraband camps. As federal policy lagged, private philanthropists in the North organized to supplement it. These relief associations solicited funds, provided food and clothing, and sent agents into the South to administer to the needs of the quickly growing freedpeople population behind Union lines. One of the most pressing needs of the former slaves was education and to that end, philanthropic organizations sponsored scores of teachers who organized schools and oversaw the education of thousands of freedmen.

None of these initial measures represented a commitment on behalf of the U.S. government to emancipation. Lincoln, in particular, had to tread a fine line between competing political factions who disagreed on the legality and propriety of emancipation as a war aim. He nullified emancipatory proclamations by generals John C. Fremont and David Hunter in the first 13 months of the war. At the same time, the president proposed plans of compensated emancipation to the Border States who remained in the Union and the District of Columbia. In all cases, Lincoln initially hoped to couple emancipation with emigration of the freed slaves, and to that end he actively pursued different colonization schemes through mid-1862.

In June 1862, however, a clearer policy with regards to slavery began to take shape. On June 19, Lincoln signed a bill abolishing slavery in the territories. In

July, the Second Confiscation Act became law, freeing all enslaved people who took refuge in Union-controlled territory. Then, after weeks of discussions with his closest advisors and what he interpreted as a decisive Union victory at the battle of Antietam, Lincoln issued a preliminary emancipation proclamation. In it, though continuing to hold out the possibility of compensated emancipation followed by colonization, Lincoln declared that on January 1, 1863, all slaves then held in rebellious states would be "then, thenceforward, and forever free."

Though Lincoln cited justice and humanitarianism as partial motivations for his final proclamation, it was clear that his primary justification was military necessity and his actions were taken under his authority as commander in chief of the armed forces. The proclamation drew widely mixed reactions in the North. Radicals criticized the proclamation for technically not freeing a single enslaved person and for not affecting the nearly 800,000 enslaved African Americans then held in the Border States. However, from other perspectives it was a resounding success. Militarily, it allowed for the enlistment of African American troops, over 180,000 of whom served through the end of the war. Moreover, it created great confusion in the South and, by encouraging slaves to escape their bonds, deprived the South of much of its wartime laboring force. To slow the wholesale exodus of their slaves, the patrol laws in the Confederate States were strengthened and owners often removed their enslaved people to a distant location when Union forces drew near.

By the final months of the war, a majority of Northerners had concluded that the abolition of slavery was a necessary and proper war aim, not only to justify the conflict's bloody toll, but also to cripple the stubborn Confederate will to fight. Lincoln's re-election in 1864, seen by many as a mandate for freedom, set the stage for the passage through Congress of a Thirteenth Amendment outlawing slavery to the U.S. Constitution. When Georgia became the 27th state to ratify the proposed amendment in December 1865, it became law.

J. Brent Morris

See also: *Arts*: Douglass, Frederick (1818–1895); Slave Narratives; *Uncle Tom's Cabin* (1852)*; Economy and Work*: Plantations; Rural Life, Southern; Slaveholders; *Family Life and Gender Roles*: Free Blacks; Slave Families; *Politics and Warfare*: Abolitionists; Contrabands; Emancipation; 54th Massachusetts Infantry; Freedmen's Bureau

FURTHER READING

Johnson, Walter. *River of Dark Dreams: Slavery and Empire in the Cotton Kingdom*. Cambridge, MA: Harvard University Press, 2013.

Johnson, Walter. *Soul by Soul: Life Inside the Antebellum Slave Market*. Cambridge, MA: Harvard University Press, 2000.

Kolchin, Peter. *American Slavery, 1617–1877*. New York: Hill and Wang, 1993.

Manning, Chandra. *What This Cruel War Was Over: Soldiers, Slavery, and the Civil War*. New York: Alfred A. Knopf, 2007.

Schwalm, Leslie A. *A Hard Fight for We: Women's Transition from Slavery to Freedom in South Carolina*. Urbana: University of Illinois Press, 1997.

SPRINGFIELD ARMORY

The Springfield Armory proved to be of vital importance for the Union in the Civil War. Armory workers produced approximately 805,538 rifles during the war at a cost of just $12 per rifle. The Springfield Model 1861 was the most widely used firearm by the Union Army and those who carried it into battle regarded it as an accurate and reliable weapon. The armory also had a dramatic impact on the town of Springfield and the economic development of the region. The factory employed approximately 2,600 workers during the Civil War, an impressive number given that the town of Springfield only numbered around 20,000 people. Furthermore, the armory subcontracted with several firms in the area, providing even more munitions and ordnance to the Union Army and driving the economy of the town. A history of the factory sheds light on the thousands of individuals who worked producing armaments for the Union Army.

The Springfield Armory was first established during the Revolutionary War after being recommended by Henry Knox and scouted by George Washington. The site was approved because of its connections to three rivers and four major roads as well as its secure position on a high bluff and away from ocean-going vessels. An arsenal was established to store muskets and cannons for use, though contemporary historians are unsure as to whether arms were manufactured at the armory at that time. After the war ended, the army decided to maintain the armory at the site. In 1794, when Washington was president, he proposed a bill that created four public manufacturers of arms, to eliminate the waste in dealing with private manufacturers. The Springfield Armory was chosen as the first new public manufacturer of arms in the country.

Prior to the Civil War, the Springfield Armory was a leader not only in the production of munitions but also in industrial practices. Superintendents quickly developed a division of labor among the workforce, eventually creating 64 specializations. The armory also developed the technology to create interchangeable parts. Previously, musket manufacturing required each part to be specially and uniquely fitted to each other part, making the production of goods slow and repair difficult. While working at the Springfield Armory, Thomas Blanchard developed a lathe that could produce gunstocks, an irregular shape that previously had to be carved by hand. Administration of the armory was complicated, as it was controlled by the War Department in Washington but it relied on local administrators and labor.

When the Civil War began, the armory was far from efficient. Slightly fewer than 200 men worked there. The armory was soon swamped with requests for arms. The Union's loss of Harper's Ferry to the Confederacy resulted in the loss of a key manufacturing base. At face value, the Springfield Armory faced tremendous challenges during the war: shortages of skilled workers and critical resources, such as iron, made it difficult to manufacture and deliver the necessary arms. The armory's leadership responded by developing more interchangeable parts and by creating more specialized steps in the musket's construction. When the war began, the plant was producing 800 rifles a month, a figure that quadrupled to 3,200 by the end of 1861. By 1864, the plant was sending out nearly 26,000 rifles each month.

Previously, the armory's relations with the town of Springfield were strained. The fact that the armory was controlled from Washington meant that decisions about hiring or wages were made without the community's consent. During the war, however, the people of Springfield generally put aside their feelings; townspeople volunteered to ward off Confederate saboteurs and put out fires.

The armory's operations drastically affected the growth of the town. During the Civil War, Springfield was one of the few communities in Massachusetts that experienced economic growth. By virtue of the armory's size and its fluctuating labor force, other companies tended to gravitate around it. As a result, Hampden County and Springfield became the center of arms manufacturing in Massachusetts. The armory also provided lucrative subcontracts to companies to produce machinery. This boom is reflected in the growth of industrial production from 1855 to 1865, where it grew from $2.5 million to $7 million. This growth happened at a time when most other cities in the state experienced sluggish growth, if any growth at all.

In addition, the population of Springfield grew immensely during the Civil War. As people flocked to the urban center to find work, the town grew in size by 45 percent between 1860 and 1865. Even the numbers of young men, who were heavily recruited into the Union armies, saw an increase of around 2,000 into the city; most of these men came to Springfield seeking work. This population growth led to a housing crisis in the city. Apartments that had earlier cost $50 each month soon cost double or even triple that rate. Developers were too slow to respond, in part because housing construction was not a particularly lucrative field for investment. Eventually, the reluctance to invest in land faded, and a massive real estate boom swept Springfield.

Many of the town's citizens worried that the end of the war would bring an end to the vibrancy of Springfield. However, although after the war 2,000 positions at the armory were eliminated, a core of 500 workers stayed on to continue producing Springfield Repeating Rifles. These rifles would remain in use by the U.S. Army until the Spanish-American War.

Zeb Larson

See also: *Economy and Work*: Tredegar Iron Works; Urban Life, Northern; *Housing and Community*: Refugees; *Science and Technology*: Factories; Firearms; Minié Ball; Weapons

FURTHER READING

Cooper, Carolyn C. "'A Whole Battalion of Stackers': Thomas Blanchard's Production Line and Hand Labor at Springfield Armory." *IA: The Journal of the Society for Industrial Archeology* 14:1 (1988): 36–58.

Frisch, Michael H. *Town into City; Springfield, Massachusetts, and the Meaning of Community, 1840–1880.* Cambridge, MA: Harvard University Press, 1972.

Raber, Michael S. "Conservative Innovators, Military Small Arms, and Industrial History at Springfield Armory, 1794–1918." *IA: The Journal of the Society for Industrial Archeology* 14:1 (1988): 1–22.

SUTLERS

Vast armies of the Civil War quickly became accustomed to marching at the expressed wishes of their commanders. However, as Napoleon noted, armies march not only on the orders of their generals, but also on those of their stomachs. So too did combatants of the Civil War overcome hardships through simple items of basic necessity. In an era when the War Department did not always supply goods of everyday use to troops in the field, soldiers frequently looked elsewhere for luxury goods and products of comfort. An industrious cadre of entrepreneurial individuals known as sutlers quickly filled this void for soldiers.

Such a vendor was a civilian who was officially licensed to conduct business transactions with military personnel at a camp, outpost, or hospital. Most often, sutlers sold small and common goods such as matches, needles, thread, buttons, toothbrushes, combs, gloves, writing utensils, and even souvenirs to mail home. In certain instances sutlers were suspected of inflating prices and taking advantage of military men by peddling shoddy goods. War correspondent Edwin Forbes commented on the temptations sutlers faced in setting prices above an item's worth so they could make higher profits. Known as "carpetbaggers" and "Shylocks" by

Photograph of a sutler's tent in Brandy Station, Virginia, 1864. Sutlers provided soldiers with opportunities to purchase luxury items as well as small and common goods such as matches, needles, thread, buttons, toothbrushes, combs, gloves, writing utensils, and souvenirs to mail home. In addition, some sutlers sometimes sold food, including fruits, lobster, milk, coffee, liquor, and tobacco. (Library of Congress)

some, these hucksters could face persecution in more ways than one. Many sutleries were eventually burglarized out of spite. The troops had little remorse for the plight of the robbed seller. But problems did not end there. Regimental commanders of state militia units were frequently permitted to choose their own sutlers for regiments. Such arrangements commonly led to corrupt bargains between officers and vendors, causing additional inflation at the sales counter.

These schemes were chronicled in a December 1861 report conducted by the United States Sanitary Commission (USSC) that was sent to Secretary of War Edwin Stanton. In this exposé, gouged prices were declared one of the "evils" that sutlers perpetrated upon sometimes unsuspecting servicemen. Of the some 200 units the USCC inspected throughout 1861, over 90 percent had a sutler, and the colonel of the regiment had appointed half of those sutlers. Many of the rest were political appointees from the War Department. At the same time, newspapers complained that rotgut "Whiskey and stale pies" sold by sutlers resulted in "disordered bowels and fevers." Soldiers, as well, highlighted the stomach problems often caused by "sutler pies." In addition, columnists argued that 50 percent of camp illnesses were due to soldiers' patronage of sutlers. Some even claimed that soldiers would prefer to have the sutlers driven from their regiments, but others disagreed and pointed to the need for such salesmen.

Despite the challenges of overcharged costs, high interest rates on store credit, and use of scrip, soldiers flocked to these vendors out of necessity, desire, and personal boredom. Sutlers reaped the financial benefits of these military contract monopolies, as did their suppliers and manufacturers in the burgeoning Northern industrial centers. Some politicians claimed that total sutler gross earnings surpassed $10 million per year. Although many Americans emerged from the Civil War ravaged and destitute, most sutlers walked away with tidy sums of cash in their pockets and banks. In the ensuing years, many of them trekked westward with the rest of the nation, establishing similar general stores and commissaries at military posts and in mining towns.

In the meantime, Confederates were left awestruck and embittered by the extravagance displayed in the inventories of Union sutlers. These plentiful stores further denoted the disparity between Union and Confederate supply lines. One hungry Southern foot soldier marveled at the discovered stockpile of a sutler. It contained items he had not seen in a long time, including fruits, lobsters, milk, coffee, liquor, and tobacco. For war-weary Confederates, stumbling across an abandoned sutler's wagon or tent was equivalent to discovering buried treasure.

Indeed, sutlers offered a vast array of unique and convenient products that served as pleasant distractions even if they were overpriced. Union soldier John Billings wrote that most of the stocked goods "answered the demands of the stomach" but featured other valuable wares as well. Many of these items were not products out of the ordinary. However, soldier life was not an ordinary one—and even simple trinkets could alter one's disposition. Pocket mirrors were sold to teenage recruits who someday dreamed of using them to shave. Patriotic stationary and the words written on them allowed soldiers to keep high the spirits of forlorn loved ones on the home front. Candy such as peppermint sticks and sugar wafers satisfied the youngster's sweet tooth. Coffee quickly became the preferred beverage of the soldier—making it the staple refreshment it is today. Some sutlers even had within their tents photography studios, offering military families stirring and enduring images of sons, brothers, and fathers in service. For these reasons and more, sutlers were an important feature of daily army life.

War forces those involved to adapt. As artist Edwin Forbes claimed, sutlers were not necessarily the crooks some made them out to be. In most instances, he argued, these sellers offered "honest goods" as a "necessary evil" to weary and homesick soldiers who very much welcomed them.

Jared Frederick

See also: Economy and Work: Camp Followers; *Politics and Warfare*: Camp Life

FURTHER READING

Billings, John Davis. *Hardtack and Coffee, Or, The Unwritten Story of Army Life*. Alexandria, VA: Time-Life, 1982.

Delo, David Michael. *Peddlers and Post Traders: The Army Sutler on the Frontier*. Salt Lake City: University of Utah Press, 1992.

Forbes, Edwin. *Thirty Years After: An Artist's Memoir of the Civil War*. Baton Rouge: Louisiana State University Press, 1993.

Garrison, Webb B., and Cheryl D. Garrison. *The Encyclopedia of Civil War Usage: An Illustrated Compendium of the Everyday Language of Soldiers and Civilians*. Nashville, TN: Cumberland House, 2001.

"Serious Complaints About Army Sutlers." *Philadelphia Press*, December 4, 1861.

Varhola, Michael O. *Everyday Life During the Civil War*. Cincinnati, OH: Writer's Digest, 1999.

TREASURY GIRLS

In 1862, both the Union and the Confederacy hired women to fill jobs left vacant when young male clerks joined the army. In the Confederacy, the Treasury Department was the earliest and largest employer of women. Female treasury clerks, popularly called "treasury girls," earned high wages for signing and cutting Confederate currency. Although not difficult, treasury clerkships required excellent penmanship, a quality usually acquired by educated, upper-class women. Many of the women who became treasury girls had never previously performed any work outside of the home. As husbands, brothers, and fathers left for the front, upper-class women who had relied on male protectors for income found themselves driven to work for pay. Compared to male clerks, female treasury clerks worked fewer hours for less money, but by accepting these wartime positions, the treasury girls stepped outside their traditional gender roles. As the Confederacy dissolved, so too did the female clerks' positions as wage earners.

Although some upper-class women hated the idea of accepting a governmental position, for women pressed into the workforce by the circumstances of war, a position with the Treasury Department was highly desirable. Secretary of the Treasury Christopher G. Memminger (1803–1888) regularly received 100 applications for each open position. Several applicants suggested that, since the Confederacy had called away the men who had previously supported them, governmental officials now owed them a position that would allow them to support themselves. Women stressed their lack of male support, financial need, educational background, family connections, and any previous experience managing financial affairs. Applicants recruited ministers, politicians, military leaders, and even Confederate First Lady Varina Davis to act as references.

Potential treasury employees fought hard for positions because the work they sought was among the highest-paid employment in the Confederacy. Treasury girls earned one-half of the salary paid to male clerks, but even with this gender gap, they made $65 a month in 1862. At the time, Confederate privates earned only $11 a month, female workers at the Georgia Soldiers Clothing Bureau earned between $24 and $48 a month, and female arsenal workers earned around $30 a month. Treasury girls worked from 9:00 A.M. until 3:00 P.M. for five days a week, which meant that they worked less than male clerks in comparable positions. In an unsuccessful effort to keep up with rising prices, the government regularly increased wages; by 1864, Treasury Girls earned $3,000 a year. Inflated prices outran the Treasury girls' wages despite the raises they received, but throughout the war, these women remained among the highest-paid workers in the Confederacy.

The actual work was not physically difficult, but it was repetitive and required careful attention to detail. Treasury clerks worked as either note clippers or signers. Note clippers trimmed the Confederate bills, while signers carefully signed each trimmed note. Supervisors expected workers to complete over 3,000 bills a day without error. Treasury girls needed excellent penmanship and applicants were evaluated based on their handwriting. Workers were docked 10 cents for every damaged bill, imperfect signature, or blotted spot of ink.

The application and employment process favored upper-class women over poorer women. Upper-class women could use impressive family connections during the application process, and the fine penmanship that the Treasury Department demanded was more common among women who had benefited from an expensive education. To some observers, including poorer women performing harder work for lower wages, the treasury clerks looked like nothing more than the privileged friends of well-placed politicians. To upper-class women determined to remain inside the protective walls of their homes despite the war, the treasury clerks seemed to have abandoned the upper-class rules of proper female behavior.

Accounts from treasury girls give weight to these accusations, indicating that women worked to maintain their lifestyles rather than to avoid starvation and often enjoyed the freedom and independence that came with their new jobs. The Treasury Department was located in Richmond until April 1864, when Memminger relocated the Treasury. The department that housed the Treasury Girls moved to Columbia, South Carolina, and hired new clerks in Columbia to replace women who had remained behind in Richmond.

Young Confederate widow Malvina Waring was hired on in Columbia. While working as a treasury girl, Waring lived in her parents' home, took German language lessons, read Victor Hugo's *Les Miserables*, and used her earnings to buy clothes. The Treasury Department evacuated from Columbia back to Richmond just before Union general William Tecumseh Sherman's troops took the city on February 17, 1865. When Waring fled the city with other Treasury employees, she had six gold watches hidden in her clothes. On the way to Richmond, Waring worried about her family and her home, but she also happily explained that she and other treasury girls were addicted to their new life of dances, parties, and handsome military officers. Another treasury girl, Adelaine Stuart, also loved her new life as a wage earner, even going so far as to express gratitude for the loss of property that forced her into the workplace.

The female clerks lost their positions with the collapse of the Confederacy in 1865. On March 1, 1865, Waring arrived in Richmond along with several other treasury girls. The Treasury Department housed the women in the Ballard House hotel, where they enjoyed a stream of visitors, but the Confederate capital was flooded with people fleeing the Union Army. Food was increasingly scarce and expensive. By March 7, the treasury girls in the Ballard House were hungry. Waring, the remaining treasury girls, and their friends evacuated Richmond just before General Ulysses S. Grant's forces took the city on April 2, 1865. Seven days later, Confederate general Robert E. Lee surrendered to Union general Ulysses S. Grant at Appomattox Courthouse. After the war, men reclaimed jobs that had temporarily opened to women during the war, including clerkships like those held by the Treasury Girls.

Jama McMurtery Grove

See also: *Economy and Work*: Government Girls; *Family Life and Gender Roles*: Young Women

FURTHER READING

Faust, Drew Gilpin. *Mothers of Invention: Women of the Slaveholding South in the American Civil War*. Chapel Hill: University of North Carolina Press, 1996.

Kaufman, Janet E. "Working Women of the South: 'Treasury Girls.'" *Civil War Times Illustrated* 25 (1986): 32–38.

Waring, Malvina S. "A Confederate Girl's Diary." In United Daughters of the Confederacy, ed. *South Carolina Women in the Confederacy*. Columbia, SC: State Co., 1903, pp. 272–288. http://archive.org/details/southcarolinawom00unit.

TREDEGAR IRON WORKS

The Tredegar Iron Works represented a major effort by antebellum Southerners to develop their region's indigenous iron and steel industry. The South had a fraction of the nation's industrial capacity; the slave plantation system had discouraged investment in industrialization and mechanization. However, the railroad-building boom in Virginia in the 1830s provided a major incentive for investors, government officials, and local businessmen to invest in foundry and mills in the state capital of Richmond. Erected in 1836, the Tredegar Iron Works took its name after the Tredegar, a Welsh town in Great Britain famous for its iron production. Beset by years of difficulties due to the financial crisis of 1837, the owners in 1841 asked Joseph Reid Anderson, a Virginian and ex-army officer, to assume leadership of the company. Under his direction, the Iron Works expanded.

What began as a single foundry and rolling mill grew into a major industrial complex. The manufacturing center eventually contained over a dozen separate facilities including a machine shop, a rolling mill, a blacksmith shop, a small brass foundry, a spike factory, a cooper stop, a pattern storage attic, a gun mill, a locomotive shop, a boiler shop, and a carpenter shop. On the eve of the Civil War the Tredegar was one of the nation's largest iron and steel production centers. At peak

April 1865 photograph of the Tredegar Iron Works in Richmond, Virginia. Built in 1836, the Tredegar Iron Works was one of the nation's largest producers of iron and steel and was comprised of over one dozen separate facilities. It produced most of the ordnance for the Confederacy during the war. (Library of Congress)

production, the facility consumed 12,000 long tons of pig iron and over 16,000 tons of coal in a year. It was powered by water from the canal drawn from the James River.

Virginia seceded from the Union in April 1861 with the largest population among the seceded states. It also boasted the prestige of the contributions to the founding of the Republic by its native sons like George Washington and Thomas Jefferson. Virginia also had the Tredegar Iron Works, the only facility in the South capable of manufacturing heavy ordnance Josiah Gorgas, chief of the Ordnance Bureau for the Confederacy, expanded the new nation's armaments industry by establishing armories and foundries throughout the South, but none could match Tredegar in terms of size, production capacity, and strategic importance. Without the Tredegar Iron Works and its labor force, the South would have lacked any modern weapons. For four years the workers at Tredegar produced the instruments of war that kept the Confederate armies supplied and equipped for battle. From its shops came heavy naval guns, artillery pieces, ammunition, spikes for railroad and ship construction, and armor plates for the world's first ironclad, the CSS *Virginia* (ex-USS *Merrimac*).

Although children could be found in many factories throughout nineteenth-century America, Tredegar relied primarily on adult workers. As the factory expanded its workforce to meet the wartime rush of orders from the Ordnance Bureau, however, boys were hired as apprentices. Approximately 50 boys were apprenticed in the various departments during the first year of the war. By the end of 1861, nearly 1,000 men and boys labored at the complex; enslaved workers amounted to 10 percent of the work force.

At the time of Virginia's secession, Northern and foreign-born workers made up the bulk of the white labor force, which included both skilled and unskilled laborers. The steelworkers were a hodgepodge of various nationalities: Canadians, Irish, Welsh, German, and English. Suspicion clung to these non-Southerners; three men were discharged in July for suspected disloyalty to the South. Those who stayed, however, did not do so without pushing for better pay. In September 1861, the Irish workers went on strike demanding better wages, which Anderson granted them. A skilled white laborer in the South in 1861 made up to $3 a day; by early 1864, the daily rate had risen to $4.50. However generous these numbers seemed compared to the prewar salaries, the salaries earned by the white laborers could not keep up with the ruinous inflation that plagued the Confederacy.

At the beginning of the war, enslaved workers were found in only two sections of Iron Works, the rolling mill and the blacksmith shop. About 80 enslaved blacks worked on the site, and Anderson owned 28 of them. During the war approximately 45 additional slaves were added to the black labor force at the Iron Works.

In addition, under the supervision of a white foreman, a group of African American boys built kegs in the cooper shop. The company paid rent to the owners of the slaves. However, the enslaved workers received overtime pay, which they could keep for themselves. As the industrial workers of a largely agrarian Southern nation, African American factory workers, like the free whites who labored beside them at Tredegar, were a minority. By November 1864, the number of free white laborers had dropped from an 1861 peak of between 400 and 500 to 100. The enslaved population, however, increased significantly, as the factory became increasingly reliant on skilled slave labor. The expansion of the enslaved labor force meant that blacks could now be found in departments that had previously been limited to white men.

The enslaved workers slept near the facility in a tenement. The company fed and clothed them and provided a hospital on the grounds for medical care. Anderson was not known as a disciplinarian. The desperate need of the Confederate war industry for skilled black laborers in its few factories and foundries gave the enslaved people increased leverage at places like the Tredegar Iron Works. Even so, enslaved workers sought to escape from the company. For example, in April 1863, five slaves made an unsuccessful bid to flee from Tredegar's coal mines.

Despite the shortages of food, labor, and raw materials, and the increasing inability of the Richmond government to pay its bills, Tredegar continued to produce arms into 1865. The Ordnance Bureau owed almost $900,000 to the Tredegar Iron Works at war's end. On April 2, 1865, the Confederates abandoned Richmond to the Union's Army of the Potomac. Fire and looting gutted large parts of the Confederate capital. Although the explosion of the arsenal building damaged the Iron Works, Anderson and his men, armed with muskets, fended off the mob and saved the works from complete destruction.

The Tredegar Iron Works survived into the Reconstruction era. The need to build new railroads and repair damaged ones in the defeated South created an enormous demand for the iron and steel it produced. Anderson continued to employ African Americans, now free under the Thirteenth Amendment, at Tredegar. In 1870, African Americans made up about 300 of the 650 workers. In Richmond, as in other parts of the postwar South, the destruction of slavery improved the bargaining position of free white laborers, who now could no longer be threatened with the possibility of losing their jobs to slave labor.

Long Bao Bui

See also: *Economy and Work*: Factory Owners; Factory Workers, Southern; Munitions Factories; Slavery; Urban Life, Southern; *Family Life and Gender Roles*: Immigrants; Slave Families; *Science and Technology*: Factories; Firearms; Weapons

FURTHER READING

Dew, Charles B. *Ironmaker to the Confederacy: Joseph R. Anderson and the Tredegar Iron Works*. New Haven, CT: Yale University Press, 1966.

McPherson, James M. *Battle Cry of Freedom: The Civil War Era*. New York: Oxford University Press, 1988.

Varhola, Michael O. *Life in Civil War America*. Cincinnati, OH: Family Free Books, 1999.

URBAN LIFE, NORTHERN

The Civil War touched every aspect of urban life in the North. Hundreds of thousands of Northern city-dwellers lined up at recruiting tents during the war years. Factories churned out war materiel, warships and freighters steamed or sailed in and out of Northern ports, political battles over conscription and labor demands raged in the streets, and families simultaneously mourned the dead and supported the living as they awaited their return from distant battlefields. Even as Northerners directed a vast and expanding industrial infrastructure to the war effort, however, they drew on earlier preindustrial rituals and traditions to face the conflict's many challenges. This process of accommodation and change characterized Northern city life both before and after the war, but it came into sharp focus during the war years in the streets, factories, and homes of Northern cities.

Northern cities on the eve of the Civil War were engaged in a long-term process of industrialization that began in the late eighteenth century and continued long after the war. This process was unbalanced throughout the North. Cities like New York and Philadelphia were already teeming with an urban working class and facing the challenges of a rapidly changing economic, cultural, and environmental order. Smaller cities, especially emerging communities in the West, entered the war on a more preindustrial footing but experienced rapid growth and development during the war years.

Industrialization brought significant changes to Northern city life. Municipal governments struggled to keep up with the challenges of frenzied growth. They enacted building restrictions, expanded police and firefighting services, and attempted to enforce strict sanitation guidelines. Some cities, like Milwaukee and Buffalo, were only beginning to enact these types of measures in the early 1850s. Factories created a large and mostly impoverished working class, meanwhile, which strained the cultural fabric of the community. A growing population of workers—many foreign-born—organized, went on strike, and caroused late into the night in districts like the Five Points in New York. Even as the majority of these workers enlisted throughout the war, those who remained or returned from service were a continuous, vocal presence in the cities. At the same time, industrialization created new fortunes and expanded old ones. Northern cities were thus marked by extremes of poverty and wealth, squalor and luxury.

Industrialism facilitated the growth of new forms of recreation. These changes were most apparent at night. As laborers left their homes in increasing numbers to work in factories, the patterns of everyday life shifted to accommodate their new schedules. Thus, even as advances in lighting technology allowed factories to add night shifts and improved night-time traffic flows, the same gas lamps also enabled the swelling ranks of single men in the cities to spend their surplus income in saloons, theaters, dance halls, and bordellos. Opportunities for more wholesome forms of recreation were abundant as well, day and night. Shakespeare was a perennial favorite in Northern theaters, and governments and voluntary associations funded new libraries and promoted the development of parks and other spaces for outdoor recreation. Construction on New York's Central Park, for example, began in 1857 and continued throughout the war. Despite these changes, older traditions and celebrations continued to provide an outlet for Northern urbanites. As they had in the eighteenth century, parades, toasts, parties, lectures, and banquets still filled Northern social and ritual calendars.

Political changes further transformed Northern city life in the years before the Civil War. City politics took on a life of its own as democratization and the second party system created local "rings" and "machines" that dominated local politics. Antebellum city government shifted essential services like firefighting from voluntary associations to professional, government-funded workforces, as an emerging free-market sensibility led cities to withdraw from market regulation and charities. These political transformations complicated already contentious issues of race and gender.

The abolition of slavery in the North created large free African American communities that mingled with the white immigrant working class in multiethnic communities like the Five Points, for example, while an emerging African American middle class formed alliances with the forces of radical abolitionism that set the political tone across the nation from the 1830s. Women, too, began to take on more visible political roles. Industrialization led women into the workforce in growing numbers. No longer dependent on male heads of household, they staked out new positions of power and influence. Elite Northerners responded to the new power and visibility of working-class women and African Americans with dual impulses of revulsion and reform, even as they embraced their counterparts in the middle class.

The war brought these trends and continuities into sharp focus. The industrial working class was impacted dramatically. Although high demand and steady government contracts reduced unemployment, for example, high inflation simultaneously reduced the real wages of the workers pulled into service. Workers responded with strikes throughout the war. The military presence in Northern cities magnified these labor conflicts. Soldiers enlisted at the numerous recruiting tents and barracks during the war, but military demands were often unpopular.

In one of the most remarkable incidents of wartime tension, race and labor frictions came together in the 1863 New York City Draft Riots. Infuriated by conscription and the ability of wealthier men to send substitutes into service, working-class New Yorkers—mostly Irish immigrants—torched buildings and clashed with police and the military before turning their rage on African Americans, who they viewed as competitors in the labor market. At least 120 civilians were dead after four days of riots; thousands more were wounded. Similar riots, though less deadly, were frequent occurrences in Northern cities throughout the war.

Ultimately, it was in their response to the everyday challenges of wartime that Northerners most clearly demonstrated the patterns of change and tradition that characterized Northern urban life. Factories supplied medical equipment alongside war materiel, while new building technologies allowed Northerners to build hospitals alongside barracks. An older tradition of voluntarism and community service, however, met these innovations and gave Northern urbanites the emotional tools to grieve and cope, the drive to staff the hospitals and enlist in the army, and the public rituals to commemorate and understand the war.

Christopher B. Crenshaw

See also: *Economy and Work*: Factory Owners; Factory Workers, Northern; Munitions Factories; Poverty; Prostitutes; Urban Life, Southern; *Family Life and Gender Roles*: Aid Societies; Free Blacks; Immigrants; *Politics and Warfare*: Draft Riots and Resistance; *Recreation and Social Customs*: Leisure Time; *Religion and Belief*: Rituals; *Science and Technology*: Factories; Sanitation; Transportation

FURTHER READING

Baldwin, Peter C. *In the Watches of the Night: Life in the Nocturnal City, 1820–1930.* Chicago: University of Chicago Press, 2012.

Bridges, Amy. *A City in the Republic: Antebellum New York and the Origins of Machine Politics*. New York: Cambridge University Press, 1984.

Gallman, J. Matthew. *Mastering Wartime: A Social History of Philadelphia During the Civil War*. New York: Cambridge University Press, 1990.

Harris, Leslie M. *In the Shadow of Slavery: African Americans in New York City, 1626–1863*. Chicago: University of Chicago Press, 2003.

McKay, Ernest A. *The Civil War and New York City*. Syracuse, NY: Syracuse University Press, 1990.

Stansell, Christine. *City of Women: Sex and Class in New York, 1789–1860*. New York: Knopf, 1986.

Wilentz, Sean. *Chants Democratic: New York City and the Rise of the American Working Class, 1788–1850*. New York: Oxford University Press, 1984.

URBAN LIFE, SOUTHERN

In comparison to many regions in the North, the South was largely rural and agricultural on the eve of the Civil War. Despite this reality, the South witnessed significant growth of its cities just prior to, and especially during, the war. In 1860, the largest Southern cities included New Orleans, Louisiana; Charleston, South Carolina; Richmond, Virginia; Mobile, Alabama; Memphis, Tennessee; Savannah, Georgia; Petersburg, Virginia; Nashville, Tennessee; Norfolk, Virginia, and Alexandria, Virginia. The population of each of these cities was less than a tenth of what it was in the largest of the Northern cities, namely New York and Philadelphia.

Although Southern cities had never rivaled those in the North with regards to population size, manufacturing, and other things, Confederate cities experienced monumental, and largely involuntary, population growth during the war as refugees poured in from the Southern countryside. Richmond, the capital of the Confederacy, for example, swelled to six times its 1860 size during the Civil War. In addition to refugees, Confederate soldiers, bureaucrats, laborers, spies, journeymen, gamblers, prostitutes, and speculators flooded that capital. African Americans comprised anywhere from one quarter to two-thirds of the overall population of Southern cities at this time. Perhaps more importantly, the Civil War more directly impacted—and forever altered—Southern urban centers in ways it never did within the Union. As the Union Army encroached farther and farther into Confederate territory, a number of Southern cities came under assault and eventually under Union control. Thus, while the Civil War brought a few triumphs to Southern cities between 1861 and 1865—including major strides in industrial and public works development—it also brought heartbreaking defeats and setbacks. These included physical destruction as well as social, economic, and political unrest.

Amid the chaos of the Civil War, Southern urban areas experienced significant development in their industrial and public sectors. Before the war, the South lagged far behind the North relative to industrial investment and output. In 1860, the future 11 states of the Confederacy accounted for a mere 16 percent of the

U.S. capital invested in manufacturing. During the war years, Confederate cities, then facing difficult new challenges, began to throw off their former backward and antimodern images. In fact, some of them matured into veritable industrial boom towns. As the Confederacy lost access to Northern markets, secessionists insisted that it was essential that the South produce its own supplies and goods for both its military and its civilian populations. As such, leaders promoted investment in industrial development and predicted that the South would ascend to international industrial prominence after the conclusion of the conflict. Although the former may have been a reality during the Civil War, the latter was not achieved.

Nonetheless, evidence of Southern urban industrial accomplishments during the conflict was impressive, by any standards. For example, Augusta, Georgia, boasted the largest and most productive gunpowder works—North or South—during the Civil War. Petersburg, Virginia, and Columbia, South Carolina, both manufactured 20,000 pounds of powder a month, quantities that rivaled the outputs of any major Northern city. Charlotte, North Carolina, staffed the Marine Engineering Works, famous for constructing the Confederate Navy literally from the bottom up. Selma, Alabama, built a cannon foundry, home to Brooke Company guns and other war materiel. Richmond, and particularly the Tredegar Iron Works, supplied the Confederate government with iron cladding and heavy ordnance for naval vessels as well as with bullets and buttons. Josiah Gorgas, Confederate Ordnance Bureau chief, declared in 1864 that the Confederacy was self-sufficient relative to the production of war materiel. Furthermore, significant industrially related public works projects were launched in such Southern cities as Atlanta, New Orleans, and Memphis. These included the enactment of a series of programs that provided for extended street and sewerage systems, new reservoirs, and better public health.

White Southern women and African American bondspeople were crucial participants in the South's quest for industrial self-sufficiency and independence from the Union. Although many white women and enslaved people remained on their respective plantations and farms for the duration of the Civil War, many others—black and white—migrated to the cities to contribute to the war effort or simply to work to support their families. For example, white women filled key positions in government, including at the Treasury Department, the Quartermaster Department, the Ordnance Department, and the Confederate commissary. Other women worked in factories, where they, for example, manufactured uniforms and weaponry or signed currency. Enslaved men, especially those with industrial skills, enjoyed a taste of freedom for the first time. Such bondsmen discovered that their labor was in particularly high demand and that they could typically command high wages. African American women found employment in lower-level government positions and as laundresses, seamstresses, and cooks.

Although the Civil War brought modernity, progress, and even initial financial success to the urban South, it also brought deprivation, disorder, and destruction. For many Southern cities and their denizens, the clouds of war cast a long and ominous shadow. With each passing Confederate defeat on the battlefield, urban dwellers grew poorer and the number of homeless civilians increased. Particularly contributing to poverty were the effects of shortages, profiteering, and inflation. Throughout the conflict—and especially in those areas of the South where the two armies were warring against one another for control over some of the finest Confederate farmland—many consumer items, food and fuel in particular, grew alarmingly scarce. Southern merchants, many of whom were located in the region's urban areas, often took advantage of such consumer scarcities via profiteering. This specifically meant that Southern business owners engaged in such behaviors as unpatriotic and unethical price gouging and price fixing. However, inflation—brought on by a combination of scarce goods and virtually worthless Confederate money that was not backed by gold—was perhaps the most serious of these predicaments. In Richmond, prices were nearly 700 percent higher in 1863 than they had been at the start of the conflict. Ultimately by the latter half of the war, urban residents often resorted to a barter economy simply because merchants were unwilling to accept Confederate currency.

Accompanying the financial woes of Southern cities during the Civil War were breakdowns in law and order, class conflicts, bread riots, overcrowding, epidemics, and the Confederates' own scorched earth policy that destroyed sections of Richmond, Virginia, Columbia, South Carolina, and Montgomery, Alabama, among others. Local police forces in Southern urban areas were modestly sized at the beginning of the war, and then they struggled to contain civilian unrest and crime. However, as the war dragged on and the South's prospects grew increasingly bleak, police forces grew increasingly ineffective and, in some cases, were disbanded entirely.

After the Civil War ended in 1865, many Southern cities spent years rebuilding the progress that they had achieved just before and during the war.

Katherine E. Rohrer

See also: *Economy and Work*: Government Girls; Treasury Girls; Tredegar Iron Works Urban Life, Northern; *Food and Drink*: Food, Shortages; Food Riots; *Housing and Community*: Refugees; Sieges

FURTHER READING

DeCredico, Mary, and Jaime Amanda Martinez. "Richmond During the Civil War." In Brendan Wolfe, ed. *Encyclopedia Virginia*. Virginia Foundation for the Humanities.

http://www.EncyclopediaVirginia.org/Richmond_During_the_Civil_War. Accessed July 31, 2014.

Doyle, Don H. *New Men, New Cities, New South: Atlanta, Nashville, Charleston, Mobile, 1860–1910*. Chapel Hill: University of North Carolina Press, 1990.

Goldfield, David R. *Cotton Fields and Skyscrapers: Southern City and Region, 1607–1980*. Baton Rouge: Louisiana State University Press, 1982.

Morgan, Chad. *Planters' Progress: Modernizing Confederate Georgia*. Gainesville: University Press of Florida, 2005.

Thomas, Emory M. *The Confederate State of Richmond: A Biography of the Capital*. Baton Rouge: Louisiana State University Press, 1998.

Towers, Frank. *The Urban South and the Coming of the Civil War*. Charlottesville: University of Virginia Press, 2004.

WARTIME RECONSTRUCTION

The U.S. government's policies for wartime reconstruction, as well as the ways that reconstruction was actually experienced, emerged out of the evolving contests and collaborations between President Abraham Lincoln, Congress, the Union military, Southern unionists, defeated Confederates, and black freedmen. In 1861, at its most basic level, reconstruction policy implied merely the restoration of the seceded states to the Union under legitimate state governments, composed of loyal Southern whites. After January 1, 1863, emancipation portended the adjustment of reconstruction policy. Although conservative forces continued to pull back against revolutionary change, the real experience of black freedom was itself momentous. Throughout the process, individuals influenced the course of reconstruction.

Reconstruction began shortly after the first wave of secession in the Deep South when Lincoln declared in his inaugural address that he intended to restore the renegade Southern states to the Union. Lincoln's early approach to reconstruction varied from state to state as the Union Army conquered territory, but at its base was the goal of supporting a nucleus of loyal white Southerners in each state who could then rally support for restoration.

At the same time, Congress and Southern unionists sought to direct this process. In July 1861, Congress recognized the "Restored Government of Virginia" under Francis Pierpont after a convention of unionists had chosen him and other leaders to collaborate in the separation of West Virginia from the rest of the state. Once this was accomplished in June 1863, Lincoln continued to support Pierpont as governor of Virginia. Elections were held in the occupied eastern parts of the state and a new state constitution was written.

Similar processes occurred in other Union occupied states. In March 1862, after the Union occupation of Nashville, Lincoln appointed Andrew Johnson as military governor of Tennessee. The following month, Lincoln sent Edward Stanley to form a Union government in occupied portions of North Carolina. Shortly after the capture of New Orleans, military and civilian officials became entangled in a messy attempt to hold elections and organize a loyal government for Louisiana. Lincoln's appointment of Andrew Jackson Hamilton, a loyal Texan, as military governor of his home state while still in exile revealed the tenuous nature of these incipient governments. Nevertheless, wartime reconstruction in the South was a serious matter for Southern whites, who found professing their Union loyalty easier than agreeing on self-government. After Lincoln announced his intention to issue an emancipation proclamation, Stanley resigned his North Carolina post and partisanship intensified in Tennessee and Louisiana between conservative unionists opposed to emancipation and those who accepted it.

It was likely in response to such contention, not only among Southern unionists, but also in the halls of Congress, that Lincoln outlined his official policy for reconstruction on December 8, 1863. The Proclamation of Amnesty and Reconstruction pardoned anyone who would swear an oath of future loyalty to the United States and an adherence to the Emancipation Proclamation, excluding certain classes of Confederate leaders. After one-tenth of the number of voters who cast ballots in the 1860 election took the oath, a new state government could be formed. Lincoln's views suggested continued faith in the future self-government of loyal Southern whites and did not yet look toward a greater overhaul of Southern society beyond the abolition of slavery. Congress continued to assert its own desire to control reconstruction policy by passing the Wade-Davis Bill in July 1864, which would have required more stringent tests of loyalty and guarantees of legal equality for freedmen than Lincoln planned. Lincoln pocket vetoed the bill and suggested that the Southern states could voluntarily choose Congress's policy. Also in 1864, Arkansas, Louisiana, and Tennessee joined Pierpont's Virginia government in meeting the requirements set by Lincoln for writing new constitutions and holding elections. Although Congress refused to recognize any of these state governments as legitimate and none were restored to the Union prior to the end of the war, Lincoln's policies affected the experiences, options, and choices of Southerners, both black and white.

Black freedmen influenced wartime reconstruction by asserting their own expectations for the new social order. Whether liberated by their own efforts or by the Emancipation Proclamation and the arrival of the Union Army, African Americans experienced freedom by leaving plantations and enlisting as soldiers. In late 1861, after the capture of the South Carolina Sea Islands, African Americans organized their own agricultural communities on the abandoned lands. White missionaries came from the North to educate these families and to aid in their transition to free labor. However, disputes between freedmen, missionaries, land speculators, and army officers attracted criticism. Efforts by freedmen to restructure their lives were far more successful on David Bend plantation, south of Vicksburg, Mississippi. There, in 1862, the former slaves of Jefferson and Joseph Davis set up their own self-reliant community with its own system of government and agriculture. The community would provide notable black leaders in the postwar period.

In other occupied areas, the Union military guaranteed emancipation, but also forced blacks to enter into annual contracts with white plantation owners. Lincoln and Republican congressmen were very conscious of the ambiguous status of the freedmen. Lincoln worked energetically to push the thirteenth amendment abolishing slavery through Congress. When Congress then passed the Freedmen's Bureau Bill in March 1865 to distribute food and supplies to freedmen and to provide abandoned lands preparatory to actual purchase, Lincoln signed it into law. Finally, just days before being assassinated, Lincoln expressed a preference for limited black suffrage in Louisiana, though he did not indicate that he would require it. When the war came to a close, radical Republicans were still demanding a more extensive reconstruction policy, including guarantees of political and civil equality for freedmen. Some expected further punishment of rebel leaders, though others concurred in Lincoln's outline for reunion. A final settlement of these issues would not be reached until long after Union victory and Confederate defeat.

Brian K. Fennessy

See also: *Economy and Work*: Slavery; *Politics and Warfare*: Emancipation; 54th Massachusetts Infantry

FURTHER READING

Currie, James T. *Enclave: Vicksburg and Her Plantations, 1863–1870*. Jackson: University Press of Mississippi, 1980.

Foner, Eric. *Reconstruction : America's Unfinished Revolution, 1863–1877*. New York: Harper & Row, 1988.

Harris, William C. *With Charity for All : Lincoln and the Restoration of the Union*. Lexington: University Press of Kentucky, 1997.

Rose, Willie Lee. *Rehearsal for Reconstruction: The Port Royal Experiment*. Indianapolis: Bobbs-Merrill Company, 1964.

FAMILY LIFE AND GENDER ROLES

INTRODUCTION

Gender and family life shaped many interactions in nineteenth-century America. Family roles, which were often determined by gender, helped families survive shortages during the war. In addition, gender often determined one's place in society and the particular roles that one was expected to fulfill. Throughout their childhood and adolescence, youngsters were taught society's ideas of gender roles. Girls were dressed similarly to their mothers and boys to their fathers. In addition, although early in life mothers cared for all children, boys were expected to follow their fathers' examples and girls their mothers' examples as to the roles in the family and larger community. Young women and men were expected to behave in socially acceptable ways that fit with their sex.

Family life was circumscribed by particular roles. The nineteenth century saw the growth of ideals of the "cult of true womanhood" and the "cult of domesticity." True women were expected to be pious, pure, domestic, and submissive. Their lives revolved around the domestic sphere, although that sphere could be expanded into public life as long as women's domestic roles were stressed. Womanhood required an adherence to societal rules about women's proper place in society. Gendered roles persisted in courtship rituals and marriages. Although poorer women were expected to perform more physical tasks than wealthy women, all women had prescribed roles within the family.

Women's roles as mothers led the expectation that they become the caregivers of the family. Childbirth was a domain largely restricted to women, although during the nineteenth century, male doctors were increasingly replacing midwives. During the war, women used ideas about domesticity to venture into the public sphere. They became wartime nurses and spent time visiting wounded soldiers at the hospitals.

During the Civil War, commanders used ideas about gender to attack the enemy. For example, in New Orleans Union general Benjamin Butler issued what would become known as the "Woman Order," which threatened Confederate women who did not treat Union soldiers with respect. According to the order, those women who refused to politely deal with Union men would be treated as prostitutes. The use of gender to punish women resulted in an outcry from men and women around the Confederacy.

The war created many widows, North and South. Widows, too, had prescribed roles in society. They were expected to dress a particular way while in mourning so that they could be identified as widows. In addition, they gained some freedom as widows. Although many widows found themselves under the care of fathers and brothers, others used their status to take on more public roles in society. Widowhood allowed women the freedom to run a family business and take care of a household. Divorce, however, did not always give newly single women the same freedoms as widowhood.

Men's roles were also determined by societal expectations. Ideals about manhood differed in the North and the South. Southern men used ideas about patriarchy and slavery to maintain their honor. Their concern with outside validation required that they be seen as the heads of their households in both words and actions.

African American families also struggled in the Civil War era. In the South, enslaved people formed fictive kinship networks on their plantations because family members were often sold away from each other. In enslaved communities as well as in free ones, men and women still fulfilled specific gender roles. Women served as caregivers for children and sick members of the community. Men served as the authority figures in the slave quarters or free families.

AID SOCIETIES

Citizens made significant home front contributions during the Civil War, especially through the various aid societies that helped to support soldiers and former slaves as government officials struggled to create an efficient wartime system. Women played an important role by collecting and making food, clothing, and bedding, and by providing medical supplies for their male relatives and community members who did not receive adequate provisions through military channels. Antislavery groups and abolitionists actively did the same for the African Americans displaced by a war they hoped would lead to the end of slavery.

Citizens created aid societies based on the models provided by antebellum voluntary associations and benevolent societies. Groups chose organizational leaders, including a president, vice president, secretary, and treasurer. They held weekly or monthly meetings to make or gather donated supplies and to plan fund-raising efforts. Civil War aid societies were sometimes related to prewar organizations, others formed within church congregations, but many were created specifically as Soldiers Aid Societies or Freedmen's Aid Societies after the conflict began.

The people who supported and participated in aid societies were a diverse group. Some were affluent members of the community, others were clergyman or educators, but many were average citizens, young and old, who hoped to make a contribution to the war effort. Due to both Christian duty and notions of female patriotic sacrifice, women made up the majority of members in the thousands of aid societies that supplied millions of dollars worth of goods to both the Union and Confederate armies and to Southern freedmen.

After the April 12, 1861, firing on Fort Sumter, civilians in the North and South began organizing almost as quickly as men responded to state and federal military calls. Men and women created aid societies to provide the supplies needed by their family members and neighbors who joined inadequately supplied regiments. At first, many of the aid societies were local community groups, which often focused on providing for their own men, but regional and national organizations emerged to meet the unprecedented challenges created by war. These larger groups often sent the goods to military hospitals.

In addition to collecting donated food and materials to make hospital necessities, members sought financial contributions. Women held local fund-raising bazaars and dinners, and later in the war organized special events such as the large sanitary fairs held in over two dozen Northern cities. In the South, Ladies Gunboat Societies formed in several cities to help purchase war materiel for the Confederacy. Some societies focused on the families left behind, such as the New York Ladies' Educational Union for the Protection and Education of the Homeless or Destitute Children of Deceased or Disabled Soldiers. Although their actions related to children, clothing, and food remained within the more socially acceptable female realm, the businesslike work of fund-raising demonstrated that women could do more than they had done previously. In addition, because the assistance was needed, social restrictions became less binding as some women expanded their contributions to serve in structured, organized, wartime work that provided administrative experiences few had access to before the national conflict.

The United States Sanitary Commission was the largest and most organized Civil War civilian aid association. Although led by prominent Northern men, the national organization depended on the donations provided by local soldiers' aid societies operated by women. Through a vast network of mostly female volunteers, the Sanitary Commission collected donated money and supplies, organized fund-raisers and lectures, created hospitals for returning soldiers, and sent nurses to military hospitals. This work required extensive recordkeeping, correspondence, financial management, and coordination between thousands of individuals and groups who were donating countless hours to the home front war effort.

One of the ways that Civil War aid societies differed from antebellum benevolent associations was that many of the women who participated in the work to help soldiers also had the responsibility of maintaining the family households, farms, and sometimes businesses while their male relatives served in the war. They made and gathered items similar to those that they handled in antebellum benevolent work, such as clothing and food. However, during the national conflict they focused more on collecting items that fulfilled the needs of sick and wounded soldiers. Probably the most different aspect of the volunteer work performed by the aid societies was that the community members contributed and participated while fearing for the health and safety of their loved ones. No longer simply an act of uplifting benevolent Christian charity, the realities of wartime aid cast a more serious and tragic mood on the citizens' actions.

By early 1862, Northern abolitionists and some relief societies began to focus on the appalling conditions faced by African American refugees, or contrabands, who sought protection near Union lines after running away from enslavement. White citizens and free blacks formed freedmen's aid societies to provide clothing, food, and medical care to former slaves who lived in camps. Societies sprung up throughout the Union states, and even in a few Southern ones. They varied in the size of their membership and contributions.

Members of regional and state organizations, such as the New England Freedmen's Aid Society, understood both the immediate and long-term needs of those who had been enslaved. They collected donations and supplies for the relief of destitute freedmen and established the foundation for black education in the South when they sent teachers to establish schools. Assistance came from hundreds of auxiliary societies and from agents who collected donations in the states and abroad. Some of the freedmen's aid societies received government aid to transport goods. This aid especially helped groups that collected agricultural implements and household goods, including sewing machines, for the former slaves who sought to establish their own homes and farms.

Women had an important role in the freedmen's associations. Female sewing societies provided much of the clothing distributed to freedpeople, and a number of female teachers went south during the war. The Contraband Relief Association was organized by free black women in Washington, D.C. By mid-1863 they also provided assistance to black Union soldiers and their families. The women changed their organization's name to the Freedmen and Soldier's Relief Association in 1864 to better describe their work and to dissociate the group from the term "contraband." Southern blacks also created aid societies; for example, the Educational Association of Colored People of Savannah and the Negro Ladies Patriotic

Association helped make and collect clothing for the indigent in Charleston, South Carolina.

Citizens had a significant impact on the war. Women, black and white and from all geographic regions, played an unprecedented role in the effort. The millions of dollars in goods and services contributed by aid societies during the Civil War helped to fill the void in soldier and freedmen's care that both the Union and Confederate governments struggled with throughout the national crisis.

Kelly Selby

See also: *Clothing, Fashion, and Appearance*: Sewing Societies; *Family Life and Gender Roles*: United States Sanitary Commission (USSC); Womanhood, Northern; Womanhood, Southern; Young Women; *Politics and Warfare*: Freedmen's Bureau; Morale; *Recreation and Social Customs*: Fairs and Bazaars; Sanitary Fairs

FURTHER READING

Cox, Karen L. *Dixie's Daughters: The United Daughters of the Confederacy and the Preservation of Confederate Culture*. Gainesville: University Press of Florida, 2003.

Faust, Drew Gilpin. *Mothers of Invention: Women of the Slaveholding South in the Civil War*. Chapel Hill: University of North Carolina Press, 1996.

Giesberg, Judith. *Army at Home: Women and the Civil War on the Northern Homefront*. Chapel Hill: University of North Carolina Press, 2009.

Silber, Nina. *Daughters of the Union: Northern Women Fight the Civil War*. Cambridge, MA: Harvard University Press, 2005.

CHILDBIRTH

Between 1820 and 1850 America's population growth exploded, with the *Southern Quarterly* suggesting that white populations grew by 65 percent and black and enslaved populations grew by 61.5 percent. Most data from the time, in regards to populations, is deeply segregated by race. These population growth percentages contrast the rates of infant mortality, which reveal that 146 in 1,000 white births resulted in infant death, whereas 183 in 1,000 black/enslaved births resulted in infant deaths. When examining these numbers, it is clear that during the period leading up to and after the Civil War, childbirth remained a status and reminder of impending death and insurmountable pain, reiterating a passage from Genesis: "In sorrow thou shalt bring forth children."

Throughout the nineteenth century the period in which a pregnant mother labored with child was referred to as confinement. This term, summoning images of imprisonment or restraint, expresses the privacy and isolation placed upon women while in the final throes of their pregnancies. Moreover, during the Civil War, a woman in labor, while enduring labor pains, often became the guinea pig on which new medical technologies were practiced: forceps, the intercession of male doctors, and anesthesia.

Despite its more common practice today, women in the North and South did not begin birthing children in hospitals until late in the nineteenth century. In 1850, nearly 95 percent of childbirths were conducted within the home, as it represented a more stable, comfortable, and oftentimes, more hygienic location. Confinement for most women became the site of a deeply female space. In fact, the home as locale for the birth enabled the female community to assist the new mother and child. For laboring mothers, the home fortified the relationship between mother (soon to be grandmother) and daughter. Additionally, this intimate, white female space provided the erasure of racial walls. In the South, enslaved women were often invited into the white birthing room, especially if the enslaved woman was a black midwife, or granny midwife. On plantations, granny midwives were granted more freedom than other enslaved black women, and often given free reign of the plantation, with supplies and a horse and buggy. The prestige allotted to these enslaved women, though, was limited to their utility for white births.

However, pregnant enslaved women were not afforded the same comforts as their white counterparts, and, assuredly, there was limited white female kinship in the black birthing room. For example, one doctor recommended that new mothers rest, without strenuous movement or activity for seven to ten days; enslaved women, on the other hand, rarely experienced this grace period and were, more often than not, expected to be back in the fields or to resume their duties as soon as a few days postpartum. As a result, black mothers formed a system of necessitated female kinship. Given that the slave trade often divided families and bloodlines, enslaved women turned to one another for fictive bonds. Consequently, the black birth room became a space for these fictive bonds to materialize and create a community of black motherhood.

By the middle and end of the nineteenth century, these networks of female spaces began to disappear. The new medical technologies were most trusted and secured in the hands of male doctors, which triggered the slow demise of midwifery. With the popularization of forceps in England in the eighteenth century, male doctors began to practice this new medicine on birthing mothers. However, the rise of the mass reproduction of forceps doubled with the lack of standardization of forceps technique created more of a problem than a solution. The lack of medical standardization resulted in countless prolapsed uteri and significantly multiplied the number of infant deaths and internal or permanent damage to the mother. Male doctors who were off-put by the new technology often relied on infant craniotomies, which placed the infant's health in danger by infection and resulting sepsis. Ironically, the invention of the forceps was meant to waylay surmounting difficulties with childbirth. However, it was too often the exception rather than the rule.

In many ways, the use of these technologies doubled the pain that women experienced during childbirth. Expectant mothers during the Civil War were intimately familiar with female relatives or friends who had died during childbearing, either out of medical malpractice or due to the excruciating pain. Moreover, by 1880, there were nearly 13 maternal deaths per 1,000 live births, which would shrink by more than half only 50 years later.

The rise of anesthetics during this time was intended to alleviate the pain of contractions and hopefully quell the high rate of maternal deaths. The most readily available anesthetics were chloroform or nitrous oxide (laughing gas). Many laboring mothers received these sedatives with open arms. However, due to the lack of standardized medicine, the medical community expressed mixed feelings about the use of these drugs during childbirth. For example, many hesitant medical professions warned that anesthesia would leave the mother physically or mentally damaged and lead to the possibility of leaving the child similarly incapacitated. In many cases, doctors noticed that the use of anesthesia, while easing the mind of the expectant mother, extended the duration of the labor. Without standard measurements to gauge the amount of anesthesia each mother should receive, the cure-all representative of anesthesia often resulted in labor complications and overdoses that placed both the lives of mothers and children at risk.

Throughout the nineteenth century, the flourishing medical technologies attempted to alleviate the complications arising from childbirth, as a means of solidifying white birth rates, and those for enslaved people, the working population, especially in light of the Civil War. American birth rates varied from North and South, but by the end of the nineteenth century, white women in the North averaged 3.56 children, while white women in the South averaged nearly 6. It appears that despite the turmoil, risks, and difficulties associated with pregnancy during and following the Civil War, medical technologies and medical intercessions began to stabilize alongside the population.

Jeremy Chow

See also: *Economy and Work*: Rural Life, Northern; Rural Life, Southern; Urban Life, Northern; Urban Life, Southern; *Family Life and Gender Roles*: Death, Civilian; Free Blacks; Midwifery; Motherhood; Slave Families; Womanhood, Northern; Womanhood, Southern; Young Women; *Religion and Belief*: Death; *Science and Technology*: Disease; Hospitals; Medicine, Practice of; Nursing; Sanitation

FURTHER READING

Jenkins Schwartz, Marie. *Birthing a Slave: Motherhood and Medicine in the Antebellum South*. Cambridge, MA: Harvard University Press, 2006.

Kelly, Kate. *Old World and New: Early Medical Care, 1700–1840*. New York: Facts on File, 2010.

Kennedy, V. Lynn. *Born Southern: Childbirth, Motherhood, and Social Networks in the Old South*. Baltimore: Johns Hopkins University Press, 2010.

Lee, Anne S., and Everett S. Lee. "The Health of Slaves and the Health of Freedmen: A Savannah Study." *Phylon* 38:2 (1977): 170–180.

Lewis, Catherine M., and J. Richard Lewis. *Women and Slavery: A Documentary History*. Fayetteville: The University of Arkansas Press, 2011.

Marland, Hilary, and Anne Marie Rafferty. *Midwives, Society, and Childbirth: Debates and Controversies in the Modern Period*. New York: Routledge, 1997.

McMillen, Sally G. *Motherhood in the Old South: Pregnancy, Childbirth, and Infant Rearing*. Baton Rouge: Louisiana State University Press, 1990.

Stephan, Scott. *Redeeming the Southern Family: Evangelical Women and Domestic Devotion in the Antebellum South*. Athens: University of Georgia Press, 2008.

Walzer Leavitt, Judith. *Brought to Bed: Childrearing in America, 1750–1950*. New York: Oxford University Press, 1986.

Wolf, Jacqueline H. *Deliver Me from Pain: Anesthesia and Birth in America*. Baltimore: Johns Hopkins University Press, 2009.

CHILDHOOD AND ADOLESCENCE, NORTHERN

Although the American Civil War was fought by armies of men and debated among politicians, children in both the North and South played active parts in the decades leading up to the attack on Fort Sumter, throughout the duration of the war, and in the immediate postwar years. As a sizeable minority of the population, children were both eyewitnesses to, and participants in, the nation's most destructive and transformative conflict.

During the nineteenth century the young population of the North was significantly different from what it is today. Despite a half-century of urbanization and industrialization, three-quarters of Northern children still lived in rural communities. The population of the Northern states was skewed heavily toward children—over 40 percent of the population was under the age of 16. Over 98 percent of Northern children were white, and over 94 of them were native born.

In the decades leading up to the Civil War, the concepts of childrearing and of childhood itself were undergoing fundamental changes. Antebellum Americans no longer considered children to be small adults, but they were for the first time recognizing childhood as a distinct phase in human development. This change occurred simultaneously with rising urbanization and increased immigration, both considered by middle-class reformers as a corrupting influence. Consequently, Americans at mid-century displayed an almost obsessive preoccupation with the prospect of moral corruption and their children's development. Whereas colonial parents had sought to prepare their children for vocations through apprenticeships, antebellum Americans sought to shelter their children from worldly corruption. Young children, from birth to age five or six, were to be kept at home under the nurturing and moral authority of their mother. Parenting experts warned mothers against providing intellectual stimulation at too early an age, urging them instead to focus on developing children's morality. Children were not to be left to frivolities and gaiety; childhood was the time for planting the seeds of good character.

Wartime photograph of a "powder monkey" on the deck of the USS *New Hampshire*. The Union Army employed boys to keep gun crews supplied with gunpowder and shot. Although notions of childhood were shifting toward protecting children, boys still took on military and industrial roles during the Civil War. (Library of Congress)

Unlike children in the Southern states, Northern children were largely sent to school. Since the 1840s, publicly funded education had been a priority for Northerners. In contrast to school-aged children in the South, at the time of the 1860 census, 73 percent of Northern children between the ages of 5 and 15 were in school. It was while at school, under the guardianship of their teachers, that adolescents were to develop the proper social networks that would enable them to enter the competitive world of politics and work without losing their morality. Literacy acquisition was vital, as the ability to read and write was considered inextricably bound together with notions of civic consciousness and republican virtues.

Approximately 20 percent of the men who served in the Union Army were married with children at the time of their enlistment. Family men with young children often wrote about them as being their motivation for enlisting in the Union Army. By fighting to preserve the United States, they were ensuring that their children would grow up in a representative democracy. However, concern for their children could also provide the impetus for soldiers' desertion. Union soldiers invaded the Confederacy, and as such they were often pulled quite far away from home. Soldier fathers could go months or even years without seeing their children, and often wrote in their diaries that they feared their young children wouldn't recognize them when they returned home. The fear of being perceived as a stranger by their own child caused a great deal of anxiety that Union soldiers with families recorded in their writings and diaries.

Children in their adolescent years could provide a valuable source of information and vital boost to morale. Fathers wrote letters to their teenage children filled with parental advice and domestic expectations. Because these fathers weren't around to supervise their domestic education, they often implored their children to study diligently and assist their mothers with household chores. For Northern children, the Civil War represented an unpleasant distraction. Their fathers and older brothers were off in the military, but unlike Southern children who were directly exposed to the horrors of combat, Northerners were largely sheltered from the brutalities of war.

The Civil War produced hundreds of thousands of fatherless orphans, North and South. These families were deprived of their legal guardian as well as primary breadwinner. As such, reformers in the North wrote about the needs of the state to take care of the orphans of war. It was for this reason that widows were paid a pension of $2 per month for each of their children until 16 years of age. But despite this, most of the care of orphans was organized locally at the state level. Asylums and orphanages were created to provide parentless children with shelter and education. This was done to both honor the sacrifice of Union soldiers and to ensure the children did not succumb to poverty and immorality.

John Patrick Riley

See also: *Clothing, Fashion, and Appearance*: Children's Dress, Union; *Economy and Work*: Rural Life, Northern; Urban Life, Northern; *Family Life and Gender Roles*: Childhood and Adolescence, Southern; Cult of Domesticity; Immigrants; Manhood, Northern; Motherhood; Widows, Union; Womanhood, Northern; *Science and Technology*: Education, Northern

FURTHER READING

Finkelstein, Barbara. "Casting Networks of Good Influence: The Reconstruction of Childhood in the United States, 1790–1870." In Joseph M. Hawes and N. Ray Hiner, eds. *American Childhood: A Research Guide and Historical Handbook*. Westport, CT: Greenwood Press, 1985, pp. 111–152.

Foroughi, Andrea R. *"Go if You Think It Your Duty": A Minnesota Couple's Civil War Letters.* St. Paul: Minnesota Historical Society Press, 2008.

Marten, James, ed. *Children and Youth During the Civil War Era.* New York: New York University Press, 2012.

Marten, James. *The Children's Civil War.* Chapel Hill: University of North Carolina Press, 1998.

Mitchell, Reid. *The Vacant Chair: The Northern Soldier Leaves Home.* New York: Oxford University Press, 1993.

Ruggles, Steven, J. Trent Alexander, Katie Genadek, Ronald Goeken, Matthew B. Schroeder, and Matthew Sobek. *Integrated Public Use Microdata Series: Version 5.0* [Machine-readable database]. Minneapolis: University of Minnesota, 2010.

Werner, Emmy E. *Reluctant Witnesses: Children's Voices from the Civil War.* Boulder, CO: Westview Press, 1998.

CHILDHOOD AND ADOLESCENCE, SOUTHERN

Although the American Civil War was fought by armies of men and debated among politicians, children in both the North and South played active parts in the decades leading up to the attack on Fort Sumter, throughout the duration of the war, and in the immediate postwar years. As a sizeable minority of the population, children were both eyewitnesses to, and participants in, the nation's most destructive and transformative conflict.

Life for children in the South shared similarities with that of their Northern counterparts, but was also distinguished by uniquely Southern developments. Children under the age of 16 composed over 45 percent of the population. Additionally, there were few cities in the South compared with the burgeoning urbanization of the North. Over 92 percent of Southern children resided in rural communities, and many of those lived on farms.

Unlike in the North, where middle-class reformers had made considerable effort in the decades leading up to the Civil War to push publicly funded education, the schooling priorities of Southern families were different. At the time of the 1860 census, only 44 percent of white children aged 5 to 15 were reported as currently attending school. Instruction was focused more at home than in school settings, with literacy being imparted largely from the parents. Once children entered their teens, education tended to differ based upon social standing and gender. The children of wealthy planters, particularly the sons, were sent to preparatory schools in urban settings, often located in the North and Europe. Poorer families kept their children close to home, because children were economic assets necessary to running a farm.

In many ways childrearing in the South during the antebellum years represented a break from the previous decades. Parents were less likely to employ corporal punishments as a means to enforce discipline as they had been earlier; however spanking was still widespread and accepted. The use of moral suasion and guilt were considered the best means of correcting behavior. Women, even elite planter wives, nursed their children as much as possible. However, nursing could be physically taxing, especially on new mothers. As such, enslaved wet nurses were used to ensure that the child received enough nutrition.

Children in the South were intricately and inextricably interwoven with the institution of slavery. Especially in the wake of *Uncle Tom's Cabin*, Southern writers were increasingly on the defensive over slavery's impact on the nation's most sacred of institutions: the family. Tapping into the rhetoric of portraying slavery as a positive good, Southern literature and advice manuals touted the benefits of raising children in the midst of chattel slavery. In particular, children raised by slaveholders were said to have learned valuable life lessons such as how to govern with respect and self-control. These children possessed, so it was argued, the appropriate perspective for understanding and thriving in a hierarchical society such as the South. Young children quickly learned the privileges of growing up white in a slave society. Although young black and white children might play together, planter parents took steps to ensure that their children never were too friendly or familiar with enslaved children. White children were taught to always be aware of the racial hierarchies that existed in the house and in society, so as to prepare them for eventual mastery.

When war broke out, family men found themselves motivated to enlist. One of the principal reasons for volunteering was the belief that by securing independence for the Confederacy they were ensuring that their children would grow up in a world of white privilege amid black chattel slavery. By fighting for the rebellion these men were not only fulfilling their duty to the state, but were also fulfilling their patriarchal duty to their wives and children.

Just under half of the men who served in the Confederate armed services were married. Like their Northern counterparts, rebel fathers worried about their children at home. As Union armies occupied Confederate territory, children could find themselves behind enemy lines and cut off from their fathers. Rapid inflation and supply shortages caused considerable difficulties for soldiers attempting to provide for their wives and children. Temporary desertion was common, especially around planting and harvest or when the army was close to home. Confederate soldiers would sometimes abscond without permission to see their children and ensure they had sufficient food and money, often at great risk to themselves.

Southern states established few homes for orphans in the postwar generation. These states were economically devastated and lacked the resources to care for the thousands of fatherless children that the war produced. Instead, Southern groups such as the United Daughters of the Confederacy sought to preserve the memory of Southern veterans. They sponsored scholarships for orphans, sought to abolish Lincoln's birthday holiday, and engaged in vigorous textbook campaigns to ensure that the legacy of the Confederacy would survive in the hearts and minds of children in the postwar years.

John Patrick Riley

See also: *Arts: Uncle Tom's Cabin* (1852); *Clothing, Fashion, and Appearance*: Children's Dress, Confederate; *Economy and Work*: Rural Life, Southern; Slaveholders; Slavery; Urban Life, Southern; *Family Life and Gender Roles*: Childhood and Adolescence, Northern; Cult of Domesticity; Manhood, Southern; Motherhood; Widows, Confederate; Womanhood, Southern; *Science and Technology*: Education, Southern

FURTHER READING

Censer, Jane Turner. *North Carolina Planters and Their Children: 1800–1860*. Baton Rouge: Louisiana State University Press, 1984.

Finkelstein, Barbara. "Casting Networks of Good Influence: The Reconstruction of Childhood in the United States, 1790–1870." In Joseph M. Hawes and N. Ray Hiner, eds. *American Childhood: A Research Guide and Historical Handbook*. Westport, CT: Greenwood Press, 1985, pp. 111–152.

Marten, James, ed. *Children and Youth During the Civil War Era*. New York: New York University Press, 2012.

Marten, James. *The Children's Civil War*. Chapel Hill: University of North Carolina Press, 1998.

Rozier, John, ed. *The Granite Farm Letters: The Civil War Correspondence of Edgeworth and Sallie Bird*. Athens: University of Georgia Press, 1988.

Ruggles, Steven, J. Trent Alexander, Katie Genadek, Ronald Goeken, Matthew B. Schroeder, and Matthew Sobek. *Integrated Public Use Microdata Series: Version 5.0* [Machine-readable database]. Minneapolis: University of Minnesota, 2010.

Werner, Emmy E. *Reluctant Witnesses: Children's Voices from the Civil War*. Boulder, CO: Westview Press, 1998.

COURTSHIP AND MARRIAGE

As the American Civil War unfolded and subsequently altered the political, social, and economic landscape of the United States, so too did the war modify the social rules and regulations that defined courtship rituals and the institution of marriage for single American women.

Before the Civil War, most single women received romantic appeals for affection from male suitors that sought a marital union. Depending on one's social status, class, or regional affiliation, these overtures varied greatly from woman to woman. Those born into elite, well-connected Southern families usually experienced a rather elaborate courtship that lasted over a period of months, while the male suitor romantically pursued his love interest through gallant, heroic acts. Attending balls, dances, and horse races afforded eligible young women the opportunity to meet and mingle with available bachelors. These festivities were unavailable to women of modest means. As for women below elite class, yeoman farmers and poor Southerners pursued their potential partners in a more casual fashion. Little free time and limited monetary resources prevented such grand gestures and the majority of Southern women met their future husbands at church or through family members.

Enslaved women too, engaged in various courtship rituals with their potential suitors. For black women, meeting a potential mate proved easier than for their white counterparts as they interacted with enslaved men frequently, either in the fields or at church on Sundays. Among enslaved people, the courtship ritual was anywhere from casual to very romantic. Some black men sought out conjurers that placed spells on a woman so as to make her fall in love with him. However, elaborate and defined courtship rituals were rare because enslaved people were kept extremely busy on plantations.

Although couples in the North participated in a form of courtship, their ritual was less dramatic. Single women met their partners through family members and friends or through their church.

The Civil War challenged traditional courtship practices, but did not discourage eligible singles from pursuing relationships. Rather, courting practices adapted to circumvent the inconveniences brought upon by the war. Couples resorted to writing letters, visiting military camps, and utilizing furloughs. Ultimately, the conflict relaxed these guidelines, and the paucity of suitors forced eligible women to modify their criteria as they sought out a husband. Prior to the Civil War, most women dared not venture outside of their economic or social station to find a mate, but as the war raged on many women accepted proposals from younger and less affluent prospects.

Even if American women preferred not to marry, society expected them to do so. Northern and Southern parents allowed their children the freedom to choose their respective partners and rarely did their opinion prevent a couple from marrying. For all women, marriage presented a new, and, in many cases, harsh reality marked by hard work, sacrifice, and little authority.

Particularly for Northern middle class and elite Southern women, marriage instantly curtailed any autonomy a woman had experienced during her single years. In the North, middle-class women grew up in a Victorian household that often promoted female education and allowed them the ability to work or volunteer outside the home. Upon marriage, however, a new wife was expected to embrace domestic responsibilities so that she might provide a haven for her hard-working husband as well as moral instruction for her children. Ultimately, the home provided the Northern wife with a sense of accomplishment and a large degree of authority over her family's moral and religious instruction. As the conflict ignited, their influence—along with the importance of home life—slowly dissipated as their husbands and sons enlisted in the war effort. As this exodus occurred, women struggled to reconcile their sense of loss with the need to support the war effort. Eventually, though, women accepted that the war superseded their domestic authority and sought ways to contribute their personal time, particularly working as nurses and wage earners as well as engaging in partisan politics.

Marriage also abruptly ended the carefree childhood days and offered up new and unknown challenges to Southern women. Just as Northern women presided over the domestic sphere, Southern women served as mistresses of their own households, regardless of their wealth or lack thereof. In contrast to the Northern women who enjoyed a degree of authority in their homes, Southern women's husbands maintained much control over the households. Still, Southern women were often left in charge of the kitchen and domestic affairs of the home.

In some cases, fortunate women enjoyed cordial relations with their husbands and were included in family affairs, such as managing the family farm or business. Many endured tumultuous marriages, however, that consisted of abuse, infidelity, and indifference. It was not unusual for husbands to squander away family wealth or have sex with some of the family's enslaved women.

As sons and husbands left for the Civil War, Southern women took on responsibility as managers of the family farm or plantation, often with little guidance or direction from their husbands. Although Southern wives had at one time only presided over the household management, during the war they had to take on financial and agricultural responsibilities. Sources show that husbands often offered advice and support through letters about managing slaves, finances, and the homestead. Although some women rose to the occasion and excelled in their new role, many wives expressed anxiety about their husband's absence.

Most Civil War battles occurred in the South, so white Southern wives witnessed the trauma firsthand. In most cases, Southern wives encouraged and supported their husbands' involvement in the effort and even openly criticized those men who did not defend the cause. Letters by Union soldiers to their wives provided descriptions of these fierce female Southerners and even lamented that their own wives lacked such resolve.

The enslaved wife's experience contrasted dramatically from that of the white woman. Even though their marriages went unrecognized, enslaved couples engaged in ceremonial rituals to formalize their union. Slave marriages, however, remained fragile and longevity was never certain as a slaveholder had the authority to sell either spouse at any point. Additionally, enslaved communities made it easy to dissolve their marriages. During the Civil War, many enslaved men escaped to enlist in the Union Army to fight for freedom. After emancipation, former slaves took great measures to find loved ones that had been sold away, but more often than not, a reunion between husband and wife proved unlikely.

Amber Surmiller

See also: Economy and Work: Plantations; Rural Life, Northern; Rural Life, Southern; Slavery; Urban Life, Northern; Urban Life, Southern; *Family Life and Gender Roles*: Childbirth; Cult of Domesticity; Divorce; Honor; Slave Families; Womanhood, Northern; Womanhood, Southern; Young Women; *Science and Technology*: Nursing

FURTHER READING

Hunter, Tera. *To 'Joy My Freedom: Southern Black Women's Lives and Labors After the Civil War*. Cambridge, MA: Harvard University Press, 1997.

Jabour, Anya. *Scarlett's Sisters: Young Women in the Old South*. Chapel Hill: University of North Carolina Press, 2007.

McMillen, Sally G. *Southern Women: Black and White in the Old South*. Baton Rouge: Louisiana State University Press, 1990.

Mintz, Steven. *Domestic Revolutions: A Social History of the American Family*. New York: The Free Press, 1998.

Ott, Victoria E. *Confederate Daughters: Coming of Age During the Civil War*. Carbondale: Southern Illinois University Press, 2008.

Silber, Nina. *Daughters of the Union: Northern Women Fight the Civil War*. Cambridge, MA: Harvard University Press, 2005.

CULT OF DOMESTICITY

The Cult of Domesticity, also referred to as the Cult of True Womanhood, was a nineteenth-century concept that dictated appropriate behavior for women in the United States during the period. The idea was first coined by historian Barbara Welter in a 1966 article entitled "The Cult of True Womanhood: 1820–1860" and emphasized women's weaker physical and intellectual capacities in comparison to men.

The Cult of Domesticity was based on the Doctrine of Separate Spheres that maintained women should exist solely in a private sphere encompassed by the home while men should exist primarily in a public sphere of work and commerce.

This separation was thought to have biological justifications because women were viewed as intellectually and physically inferior to men. Scientists and social critics believed that women were lesser than men because they typically had smaller bodies, including smaller brain sizes, and because they menstruated.

Because women were restricted to the private sphere throughout the 1800s, they often developed close relationships with other women and were generally unaccustomed to interacting with men outside of their families until marriage. Although these limitations fostered very strong friendships among young women and promoted close connections between mothers and daughters, the resulting unfamiliarity with men sometimes posed problems in developing healthy marital relationships.

Popular literature of the mid-nineteenth century commonly celebrated these close female relationships. Perhaps the most prominent work of the period that was largely based on women existing together within their private sphere is Louisa May Alcott's *Little Women* (1868). Throughout this novel, the women of the March family are seen working together to maintain their Massachusetts home while their patriarch is away fighting in the Civil War.

To successfully fulfill the roles prescribed by the Cult of Domesticity, women had to adhere to the four core principles of piety, purity, submissiveness, and domesticity. First, women were expected to be devout Christians. Through paying close attention to religious instruction and devoting significant amounts of time to church activities, women were thought to grow and fortify themselves as exemplars of their faith. Also, because church life was a structured and sheltered part of society, volunteering for church activities was seen as an extension of women's roles in the home. Church activities also stressed the important role women played in ensuring their children matured into informed and obedient Christians.

A second core principle of the Cult of Domesticity focused on purity. Throughout the antebellum era, women were seen as innocent and fragile creatures. This innocence, however, was the most important piece of a woman's value and was closely linked to her marriageability. A woman was supposed to abstain from all sexual thoughts and actions until she was married. This act of saving herself sexually for her husband was thought to be the greatest gift she could offer her groom. Men, on the other hand, were seen as sexual aggressors. Consequently a young woman had to be vigilant to keep sexually charged men from taking her virginity, placing all of the responsibility for sexual abstinence on her.

This charge to remain sexually abstinent until marriage sometimes conflicted with the third principle of the Cult of Domesticity, submissiveness. Founded on the belief that men were superior spiritual and moral beings, women were supposed to remain submissive recipients of male instruction and desire. Wives were expected to obey their husbands' commands in all areas of life and refrain from offering advice unless asked. Submissiveness was also thought to uphold the natural order of society that elevated men to heads of households because they were believed to be stronger and more capable human beings. Issues sometimes arose, though, when unmarried women felt pressured into sexual activities by fiancés and other men; they were expected to remain virgins until marriage but they were also taught to obey male commands.

The final core principle women were expected to adhere to was domesticity. This aspect of the Cult of Domesticity stressed that women should only be concerned with issues in their homes. Ultimately, women could aspire to no higher calling than that of wife and mother. In some ways, women were seen as taking refuge in their homes because they were delicate and in need of male protection. In other ways, however, women were held responsible for the condition of their homes and the care of their families. A wife was supposed to make her home a warm and inviting place for her husband so that he could escape the dirty and stressful world of business and hard labor. Wives were also expected to serve as full-time nurses and educators, caring for their children when they became sick and instilling in them good moral beliefs at all times. Additionally, wives and mothers were responsible for tidying, sewing, and cooking, among other tasks.

Although these tenets bound women to the home, they also gave women some power within their households. The same ideals that emphasized women's piety and purity allowed these women to be the moral compasses and educators of their families. Women in the nineteenth century also controlled the activities in their homes. In wealthy homes, white women managed the household slaves or servants. Although men were considered the heads of the household, women controlled what happened inside their homes.

Throughout the nineteenth century, all American women were expected to focus on piety, purity, submissiveness, and domesticity to become proper women. Although these ideas informed women's views of themselves in all regions of the country, few women were actually able to meet the rigid standards embodied in the Cult of Domesticity. Women from poorer families in all regions of the country and non-white women were rarely able to conform to these guidelines. Often, working-class whites and black women did not have the option to remain sequestered in their homes because their labor outside of the private sphere was necessary to support their families. Additionally, a lack of men at home and a higher demand for battlefield nurses during the Civil War served to undermine the Cult of Domesticity in many ways, bringing women outside of their domestic spheres to contribute to the war effort.

Lance E. Poston

See also: *Arts*: Diary Writing; Letter Writing; Literature, Northern; Literature, Southern; *Family Life and Gender Roles*: Childhood and Adolescence, Northern;

Childhood and Adolescence, Southern; Motherhood; Patriarchy; Womanhood, Northern; Womanhood, Southern; Young Women; *Religion and Belief*: Reformers; *Science and Technology*: Education, Northern; Education, Southern

FURTHER READING

Cott, Nancy. *The Bonds of Womanhood: "Woman's Sphere" in New England, 1785–1835.* New Haven, CT: Yale University Press, 1977.
Jabour, Anya. *Scarlett's Sisters: Young Women in the Old South.* Chapel Hill: University of North Carolina Press, 2007.
Welter, Barbara. "The Cult of True Womanhood: 1820–1860." *American Quarterly* 18 (1966): 151–174.

DEATH, CIVILIAN

It is not surprising that civilians died as a result of the Civil War, especially considering how often the battlefield intruded on the home front during its duration. Towns and homesteads became theatres of war as battling armies ranged across the country, exhausting all necessities and leaving disease and death in their wake. Inevitably, the war resulted in the deaths of untold numbers, probably tens of thousands, of noncombatant men, women, and children. Nevertheless, with the exception of a few high-profile examples, like young Jennie Wade (1843–1863)—killed by a stray bullet at the Battle of Gettysburg—civilian deaths have drawn little historical attention. For civilians as well as for soldiers, however, death defined the Civil War experience.

Since the end of the war, government officials and historians have made a tremendous effort to calculate the number of soldier deaths. To this day, however, no one has yet undertaken a systematic attempt to count civilian deaths or even suggested a method by which a count might be made. Part of the difficulty is determining which civilian deaths qualify. There is no consensus among scholars on whether only deaths directly caused by military action should be counted or whether war-related deaths from social disruption, hardship, and disease should be included as well. These problems are further complicated by the lack of any consistent death records for civilians, particularly Southerners.

In the face of these difficulties, historians can offer only best-guess estimates of the number of civilian deaths during the Civil War. Renowned historian James McPherson believes the war probably resulted in 50,000 civilian deaths and many scholars agree this is a realistic number. For example, J. David Hacker, the

A family of Civil War refugees from northern Missouri. During the Civil War, many civilian families were forced to leave their war-torn homes to become refugees. While they hoped to make a living further away from the center of the battle, many died on the road. (Library of Congress)

historian responsible for calculating the most comprehensive total of Civil War soldier deaths, endorses McPherson's number while admitting it is impossible to be more precise.

It is undeniably certain, however, that American civilians died in tremendous numbers from a variety of causes, all related to the prosecution of the Civil War. Commitment to the war effort strained resources on both sides—no one had adequately prepared for a war of this scale. The provisioning of armies left civilians with little food, clothing, or medical supplies to spare. Even in cities like Richmond, civilians starved to death. Out of desperation, many people became refugees, hoping to make a living further from the front lines. Some died along the road. It was sickness, however, that brought about the most civilian deaths. In fact, wartime conditions created an environment in which disease reached epidemic proportions. Contagion spread from unsanitary military prisons, camps, and make-shift hospitals, reaching as far as the White House itself. In 1862, President Abraham Lincoln's (1809–1865) son William (1850–1862) died from typhoid, a disease he contracted after drinking water contaminated by a nearby army encampment.

Civilians also encountered death as a direct result of military action. Both Northerners and Southerners denounced the deliberate targeting of civilians, except in the case of military necessity, but civilian deaths marred the duration of the entire Civil War. In the first days of the war, for example, riots in St. Louis and Baltimore resulted in the deaths of dozens of civilians and at the first Battle of Bull Run, stray cannon fire killed an elderly woman named Judith Henry (1776–1861) as she lay in her own bed. Later, civilians in Vicksburg, Mississippi, endured a month-long bombardment that resulted in a few deaths while in Lawrence, Kansas, guerrillas murdered more than one hundred civilians. Enemy armies, however, were not the only source of mortal danger faced by civilians. War work also proved lethal for nurses, who risked additional exposure to diseases, and munitions workers, who sometimes died in accidental explosions.

Whatever the case, women and African Americans undoubtedly experienced the highest fatality rates. Often left to fend for themselves on the home front, women of all backgrounds and classes struggled to make do and disproportionately suffered illness and starvation. Others, like Wade and Henry, fell in the crossfire. African American civilians also endured catastrophic mortality rates. Enslaved and newly freed African Americans were especially vulnerable to sickness, violence, and death. Among those with little to live on, they were the last to be provided for. The Union Army established "contraband camps" to offer former slaves food and shelter, but the camps became breeding grounds for disease. Those who could not escape slavery faced the additional threat of death from racial violence. Because manpower shortages made managing enslaved people increasingly difficult, even rumors of slave revolt elicited murderous responses in the Confederacy. In 1861, for example, the threat of a slave uprising led to the execution of 31 enslaved people in Adams County, Mississippi. Free blacks in the North also experienced racial violence. During the 1863 Draft Riot in New York City, mobs killed 11 African American men because the federal government did not consider them citizens and so they were not eligible for the draft.

The war exacted a terrible toll on the civilian populations of both sides. Unfortunately, it is impossible to be more specific about the nature of civilian death during the Civil War. Even if an exact number of fatalities could be determined, it would not necessarily communicate the impact of those deaths. The terrible extent of death during the Civil War defined that era. It not only hindered the efforts of both sides to reconcile for decades after the war, but it also forced Americans to reevaluate their cultural understanding of death. Civil War deaths—both military and civilian—transformed America.

Amy L. Fluker

See also: *Economy and Work*: Impressment; Slavery; *Family Life and Gender Roles*: Childbirth; Free Blacks; *Food and Drink*: Food, Shortages; Food Riots; *Housing and Community*: Cemeteries; Refugees; *Politics and Warfare*: Blockades; Bombardments; Draft Riots and Resistance; Guerrilla Warfare; *Religion and Belief*: Burial; Death; Eulogies; Mourning; *Science and Technology*: Disease; Hospitals; Medicine, Practice of; Nursing; Sanitation

FURTHER READING

Faust, Drew Gilpin. *This Republic of Suffering: Death and the American Civil War*. New York: Vintage Books, 2008.

Hacker, J. David. "A Census-Based Count of the Civil War Dead." *Civil War History* 57:4 (2011): 306–347.

McPherson, James. *Battle Cry of Freedom: The Civil War Era*. New York: Oxford University Press, 1988.

DIVORCE

The half-century preceding the American Civil War saw a number of changes to divorce laws. Requirements for separation were made less restrictive, and individual men and women sought to escape from bad spouses through the courts. Depending upon the circumstances of the case, couples could be awarded a partial separation or a full divorce.

Divorce in the mid-nineteenth century took one of two forms. Depending upon the circumstances of the case, a couple could either be awarded a divorce *a mensa et thoro* or *a vinculo matrimonii*. The former, from Latin literally meaning "from table and bed," was a formal separation. Legally, the two individuals were still married, and neither of them could remarry so long as the separation continued. The husband was to provide alimony for the care of his wife, but she was not required to reside with him. This form was the most common form of divorce in the antebellum years, and was used largely by women to escape from undesirable unions. Very early in the nineteenth century, courts began to grant divorces *a mensa et thoro* for women whose husbands were physically abusive.

As the century progressed, new provisions were added, increasing women's rights to seek redress from husbands who were neglectful or intemperate. These separations could be for short periods of time or last indefinitely, depending upon the request of the complainant and the discretion of the presiding judge.

The second form of divorce, *a vinculo matrimonii*, Latin for "from the bounds of marriage," was a full divorce, legally severing any ties between the couple. In most states, this form of divorce was only available in cases of adultery. There were often restrictions placed upon divorced couples. In New York, for example, the complainant of a successful divorce suit was free to remarry, as if his or her spouse had died. In the eyes of the law, this person was a widow or widower. The adulterer was forbidden to remarry until his or her former spouse was actually dead. To attempt to remarry while the former spouse was still living was akin to bigamy in the eyes of the law.

Divorce proceedings in the nineteenth century were often rigidly formulaic. Mutually amicable or no-fault divorces were illegal; there had to be a victim and a villain. Often, the complainant was the victim, seeking redress against the defendant for his or her mistreatment. Concurrently, there had to be a claim of fault. A person could not escape a marriage simply because he or she was unhappy or wanted better. The defendant had to be accused of a specific act, such as cruelty or abandonment. As such, couples who wished mutually to separate had to find a way to do so that met these requirements. Often, the defendant would simply fail to appear. Most divorce cases during the antebellum period were uncontested. When the defendant failed to appear, the court took the charges "as confessed." The defendant's failure to appear was akin to an admission of guilt, and the complainant's suit was granted.

The most common grounds for divorce in the nineteenth century were abandonment. Husbands who wished to rid themselves of an undesirable wife or children would simply vanish. The rapid growth of cities provided anonymity, and the migration of people westward afforded another avenue of escape. Court testimonies are full of depositions from wives who claimed their spouse set out in search of a new career or better opportunities, with promises of sending for them someday. But as the months and years went by with little or no word, these women found themselves forgotten and often without money. As such, they were able to turn to the courts for redress.

Divorces were handled according to the laws of the individual states. South Carolina, for example, did not permit divorce until after the Civil War. However, this state was the exception. States granting divorces typically began doing so in the legislature. Immediately after the American Revolution, it was illegal for most couples to divorce, so state legislatures would pass resolutions granting exceptions to a specific individual on a non-precedential basis. As the population of the states rapidly increased, this method became cumbersome. As a result, divorce laws were codified to permit the judiciary to take over. A few states, such as Maryland, Ohio, and Virginia, kept legislative divorce as late as the 1840s. Depending upon how the state's judicial system was structured, divorces would be heard either by the Chancery Court, the Supreme or Superior Court, or the local circuit courts.

With the onset of the Civil War, there was a flurry of marriages among soldier-aged Americans. A combination of the uncertainties of war and the fears of spinsterhood drove young people to the altar and county courthouses. During the war itself, there were relatively few divorces filed. Antebellum divorce had been a tool mainly for women to escape from undesirable husbands. The war provided its own form of reprieve for these women. Few couples felt the need to bother getting divorced when they could enjoy all the benefits of a separation without the social stigma and legal costs. Husbands were away and wives enjoyed a form of autonomy over the household as well as greater control of the family finances.

John Patrick Riley

See also: *Family Life and Gender Roles*: Courtship and Marriage; Manhood, Northern; Manhood, Southern; Patriarchy; Womanhood, Northern; Womanhood, Southern

FURTHER READING

Bardaglio, Peter. *Reconstructing the Household: Families, Sex, & the Law in the Nineteenth Century South*. Chapel Hill: University of North Carolina Press, 1995.

Basch, Norma. *Framing American Divorce: From the Revolutionary Generation to the Victorians*. Berkeley: University of California Press, 1999.

Lamphier, Peg A. *Kate Chase and William Sprague: Politics and Gender in a Civil War Marriage*. Lincoln: University of Nebraska Press, 2003.

Silkenat, David. *Moments of Despair: Suicide, Divorce, & Debt in Civil War Era North Carolina*. Chapel Hill: University of North Carolina Press, 2011.

Sokoloff, Alice. *Kate Chase for the Defense*. New York: Dodd, Mead, 1971.

Stowell, Daniel W., ed. *In Tender Consideration: Women, Families, and the Law in Abraham Lincoln's Illinois*. Urbana: University of Chicago Press, 2002.

FREE BLACKS

By the outbreak of the Civil War, a significant population of free African Americans resided in the United States. Perhaps having been born into freedom or having gained it through a variety of methods, members of this group found themselves occupying a unique and often vulnerable position in American society. Although technically free, most found their lives and actions severely limited by the circumstances and characteristics of nineteenth-century America.

The number of free African Americans in the United States stood at nearly one-half million by 1861. By that time, group's overall population growth had slowed substantially from its pace earlier in the nineteenth century. Between 1820 and 1830, for example, the population expanded from 233,504 to 319,599 for an increase of some 36.9 percent. Yet for the 10-year span between 1840 and 1850, the total number increased from 434,449 to only 488,070. This change marked an increase of only 12.3 percent. Further, free African Americans' percentage of the total African American population in the United States fell from 13.2 percent in 1820 to 11 percent in 1860.

A primary reason behind the slowed population growth was increased tension within the nation during this period. During the 1840s and 1850s, a decrease in the freeing of enslaved people corresponded with the noticeable growth of slavery as a highly contested topic in the United States. Southern slaveholders, upset and anxious over the development of a vocal and significant abolitionist movement and feeling that the institution of slavery was under attack, became more defensive and protective of slavery. In this almost paranoid and protective setting, the freeing of enslaved people became more controversial and less common than it had been earlier.

African Americans who had already obtained their freedom oftentimes found themselves only slightly less confined than those who remained in bondage. Throughout the antebellum period, free African Americans encountered limited rights, discrimination, and lack of opportunity. One scholar of the period has referred to antebellum and Civil War era free African Americans as "slaves without masters."

The rights of most free African Americans were severely curtailed. Typically, free African Americans were allowed to own property, make their own money, enter into binding contracts, and in some instances exercise the right to vote. In rare instances, free blacks even owned their own slaves. Black slaveholding, however, was unusual, as most struggled to prosper in a society that increasingly limited their opportunities and rights as the Civil War approached.

Antebellum voting rights demonstrate the increasing discrimination free African Americans faced. Before 1820, Tennessee, North Carolina, Maryland, New York, Pennsylvania, New Jersey, and the five New England states allowed free African Americans the vote. However, during the 1820s and 1830s, as more whites gained the vote because of property requirement removals, Tennessee, North Carolina, Maryland, New York, Pennsylvania, New Jersey, and Connecticut removed or severely restricted free African Americans' voting rights. All new states that entered the Union following 1820 to the time of the Civil War also prohibited African Americans from voting.

Free African Americans also experienced restrictions of other rights. Some, if they had been previously enslaved, were forbidden to live in the state of their enslavement after having been freed. Most were denied the right to serve on any jury of an accused white person. Numerous "Black Codes" or antebellum laws aimed at controlling behavior, defined many aspects of life for free African Americans. Various laws and ordinances across the South, for example, forbade free African Americans from owning firearms, assembling for meetings at certain times, working with enslaved African Americans, and traveling without paperwork proving one's freedom. If found in violation of such regulations, free African Americans regularly faced the same penalties as enslaved African Americans. In some cases, such as in Virginia in 1860, courts ruled that free African Americans could be sold into slavery if convicted of a felony. Simply put, these codes were intended to keep free African Americans as near a state of bondage as possible.

The emergence of Black Codes was particularly evident in urban areas with larger concentrations of free African Americans. After obtaining their freedom many formerly enslaved individuals moved to towns and cities in hopes of finding work and association with other people like themselves. Subsequently, the most visible communities of free African Americans existed in cities. These communities created much anxiety among white slaveholders who often viewed free African Americans as fomenters of rebellion among the enslaved members of their race. Many slaveholders argued that even without direct agitation the population's very existence as a free group promoted ideas of emancipation and thus rebellion among those who remained in bondage. Subsequently, free African Americans in towns oftentimes found themselves living under the control of strict laws aimed at limiting their freedom.

Even free African Americans serving in the U.S. military during the Civil War faced discrimination based on their race. White officers commanded African American regiments. Also, early on African American soldiers received significantly less pay than did white soldiers. This latter injustice resulted in an equitable pay movement within the Union Army led by free African Americans from the Northern states. By employing publicity and writing campaigns that many had learned previously in the abolitionist movement, the movement succeeded in bringing about popular condemnation of the practice. More equitable pay scales soon followed.

The wartime military also served as a place of cultural exchange between Northern free blacks, more experienced with freedom and recently freed Southern blacks. This difference in experience did, at times, lead to tension. Free African Americans from the North tended to have higher literacy rates and levels of education than their Southern counterparts. These individuals often considered themselves superior to former slaves that also filled out the ranks. Such attitudes quickly became problematic as they embraced a perceived duty to uplift and civilize former slaves. Even in the area of religion and religious practice, free Northern African Americans sometimes concerned themselves with transforming the views and practices of the previously enslaved. The institution of slavery, they argued, had tainted the religion of the formerly enslaved.

Regardless of such tensions, free African Americans fought valiantly and contributed to the Union victory and the ultimate demise of slavery. They did so at great risk to themselves, while living in a society that did not treat them as equal citizens.

Jonathan Foster

See also: Arts: Douglass, Frederick (1818–1895); Slave Narratives; *Economy and Work*: Slavery; Urban Life, Northern; Urban Life, Southern; *Family Life and Gender Roles*: Slave Families; *Politics and Warfare*: Emancipation; 54th Massachusetts Infantry; Freedmen's Bureau

FURTHER READING

Berlin, Ira. *Slaves Without Masters: The Free Negro in the Antebellum South*. New York: Pantheon Books, 1974.

Bodenhorn, Howard. "A Troublesome Caste: Height and Nutrition of Antebellum Virginia's Rural Free Blacks." *The Journal of Economic History* 59 (December 1999): 972–996.

Degler, Carl. *Neither Black Nor White: Slavery and Race Relations in Brazil and the United States*. Madison: University of Wisconsin Press, 1971.

Pressly, Thomas J. "The Known World of Free Black Slaveholders: A Research Note on the Scholarship of Carter G. Woodson." *The Journal of African American History* 91 (Winter 2006): 81–87.

Schweninger, Loren. "Prosperous Blacks in the South, 1790–1880." *The American Historical Review* 95 (February 1990): 31–56.

Stampp, Kenneth. *The Peculiar Institution: Slavery in the Ante-Bellum South*. New York: Vintage Books Edition, 1984.

Sydnor, Charles S. "The Free Negro in Mississippi Before the Civil War." *The American Historical Review* 32 (July 1927): 769–788.

Wade, Richard C. *Slavery in the Cities: The South 1820–1860*. New York: Oxford University Press, 1964.

Wilson, Keith. *Campfires of Freedom: The Camp Life of Black Soldiers During the Civil War*. Kent, OH: Kent State University Press, 2002.

HONOR

The concept of honor guided social relations in the antebellum South and colored all aspects of society. Depending on outward estimations of personal worth, white Southerners used concepts of honor and shame to understand their world and their place in it. In addition, they responded to Northern critiques of Southern life and institutions as an affront to Southern honor.

Divergent notions of honor between North and South, as much as the split between Northern and Southern Christianities and the division of political parties into Northern and Southern wings, explain the rapidity with which the Union dissolved in 1861. For example, the caning of Massachusetts senator Charles Sumner by South Carolina representative Preston Brooks in May 1856 all but proved to Northerners that the Southern ethos had descended into barbarism. In fact, the Southern ethos had remained remarkably static from colonial times through the Civil War. It was the residents of the Northern states, on the other hand, with their

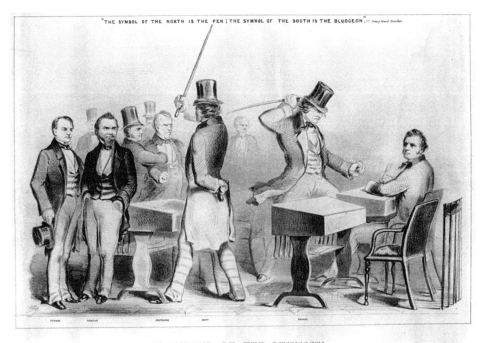

Image entitled "Arguments of the Chivalry," showing South Carolina representative Preston Brooks caning Massachusetts senator Charles Sumner. The assault took place on the Senate floor in May 1856 and demonstrated Brooks' dedication to honor and his willingness to fight for it. Honor, a system based on outward recognition, guided the South's attitudes toward abolitionists, Abraham Lincoln, and the Union. (Library of Congress)

growing emphasis on reform and the development of a more civic consciousness that had changed. In short, the honor that informed Southern identity on the eve of the Civil War had once existed in colonial New England as well, but whereas the Northern states had repudiated that ethic, the slave states continued to embrace it.

Brooks attacked the seated Sumner with a gold-ornamented cane, citing Sumner's "Crimes against Kansas" speech as libelous to both his state and his relative. The caning, which ultimately cast Sumner as a martyr in the free states and Brooks as a hero in the slave states, provides a window into the differing notions of honor between North and South. Sumner, in accordance with Northern notions of reform and equality before the law, argued for the immediate admittance of Kansas as a free state and condemned the "slave power," utilizing sexual imagery. Brooks was infuriated and considered challenging Sumner to a duel in retribution for Sumner's attack on his kinsman's and South Carolina's honor. After consulting with a fellow South Carolinian, he determined that Sumner's choice of language proved that he was no gentleman and that as such, beating Sumner with his cane in public view would restore honor to Brooks and his kinsman.

The essence of Southern notions of honor resided in public evaluation of the individual and possessed three basic components. First, honor was the essence of self-worth. Second, one had to establish his honor publicly. Finally, the public had to validate that claim. In the Old South, honor and reputation were synonymous. Dueling had its origins within the ethic of honor whereupon a perceived insult that threatened one's honor necessitated a public forum in which one could restore his honor. Brooks felt himself publicly shamed in the course of Sumner's speech and responded within the terms of honor; Brooks caned Sumner to restore the balance.

Honor in the Old South belonged almost exclusively to the upper classes, but lower-class whites could also achieve honor. Among poor Southern whites, contests of honor might take the form of public brawls, eye-gougings, and blood feuds between kinship networks. Among the planters however, such honor contests followed strict rules of procedure and rarely, if ever, bled beyond class lines. Southern paternalism in which, to the outsider, women were venerated and protected, actually constrained women within strict guidelines of proper feminine behavior. Breaches of womanly etiquette might threaten a planter husband's honor and result in some sort of violent public rebuke.

By contrast, as antebellum reforms swept through the Northern states, notions of honor there aligned with respectability, freedom from vice, and a sense of collective, rather than individual, sense of duty. Dueling in the South continued for some time after the 1803 duel between Alexander Hamilton and Aaron Burr at Weehawken, New Jersey. In the Northern states, however, pressure by the church and by evangelical activists like the Reverend Lyman Beecher ultimately eradicated dueling. Further, activities like gambling and drinking associated in the

South with manliness were largely pushed underground in the North and became associated with a weak individual constitution. Northerners tended to trust governmental institutions to a greater degree than did Southerners and put their faith in them as arbiters of justice whereas in the South, communal notions of public retribution held sway well up to the Civil War and beyond. As a result, Northerners enlisted in the Union Army largely out of a sense of duty, whether in 1861 to preserve the Union or later to emancipate the slaves. To shirk that duty was akin to silent complicity with immorality. Northerners also tended to see themselves as Americans first, and citizens of their state second. As such they possessed a deep-seated commitment to their vision of what the United States stood for, unlike their Southern brethren who tended to see things more parochially, aligning themselves more closely to their kinship groups and their states.

The ideals of honor help explain disunion. Southern notions of honor did not accord with Northern ideals, and Northerners increasingly interpreted Southern actions and claims to constitutional and scriptural respectability as intransigent. The ramifications of Northern abolitionism and notions of equality could not coexist side by side with a system structured upon slavery and white supremacy. Slavery and privilege were attendant features of the Southern social order and loosening them even slightly threatened that order. The prospect of lost honor led to Southern secession.

Mark A. Panuthos

See also: *Arts*: Literature, Northern; Literature, Southern; *Economy and Work*: Rural Life, Southern; Urban Life, Southern; *Family Life and Gender Roles*: Childhood and Adolescence, Southern; Manhood, Southern; Patriarchy; Womanhood, Southern; Woman Order (General Order 28); *Housing and Community*: Nationalism, Confederate; *Politics and Warfare;* Secession; *Recreation and Social Customs*: Gambling

FURTHER READING

Hoffer, Williamjames Hull. *The Caning of Charles Sumner: Honor, Idealism, and the Origins of the Civil War*. Baltimore: Johns Hopkins University Press, 2010.

Volo, Dorothy Denneen, and James M. *Daily Life in Civil War America*. Westport, CT: Greenwood Press, 1998

Wiley, Bell Irvin. *The Life of Billy Yank: The Common Soldier of the Union*. Baton Rouge: Louisiana State University Press, 1952.

Wyatt-Brown, Bertram. *Honor and Violence in the Old South*. New York: Oxford University Press, 1986.

Wyatt-Brown, Bertram. *The Shaping of Southern Culture: Honor, Grace, and War, 1760s to 1890*. Chapel Hill: University of North Carolina Press, 2000.

Wyatt-Brown, Bertram. *Southern Honor: Ethics and Behavior in the Old South*. New York: Oxford University Press, 1982.

HOSPITALS, VISITORS TO

Hospital visitors during the Civil War were volunteers, men and women with no official responsibilities or schedule of duties as part of the military hospital system. These persons might visit on their own initiative or as representatives of an organized group. In either case, hospital visitors provided useful and often necessary services to the hospitalized soldiers.

Because hospitals were not a common part of life before the Civil War, sick and wounded soldiers were often frightened at the prospect of being sent to one. Further, the hospitals, especially early in the war or after a large battle, were poorly organized, overcrowded, and undersupplied. Nurses were not professionally trained but instead learned their duties on the job. Because they were mainly soldiers detailed (assigned) from the ranks, these nurses were not always willing, able, or adept at their tasks. There was a good deal of turnover when the prospect of military action caused these men to be recalled to their regiments as soldiers. Nurses usually had plenty to do to care for the basic needs of the soldiers and could rarely provide special attention to those who needed it.

In addition, wartime hospital diets were not necessarily well suited to the needs of sick and convalescing patients. Although doctors recognized the need for a variety of special diets for the patients, including milk, eggs, chicken, fruit, and vegetables, these were not items that were available through the military commissary department. Depending on the location of the hospital, appropriate foods

1862 image of wounded soldiers, nurses, and visitors in a ward at the Philadelphia Citizens Volunteer Hospital during the Civil War. Many civilians in the North and South volunteered their time to help their nation's wounded by visiting hospitals throughout the war. These volunteers often brought food and supplies to wounded soldiers, spent time talking and reading to the men, and wrote letters for those who were unable to do so themselves. (Library of Congress)

might be difficult to find and purchase in the surrounding countryside, especially if the area had seen battles or troop movements. In some cases, breaks in transportation could also lead to severe shortages in the area as well as in the hospitals.

Hospital visitors did not replace nurses or supplies provided by the military, but rather supplemented the official hospital care as individual patients needed help. Although a hospital visitor might come on his or her own or under the auspices of a local, state, or national organization, he or she would do the same basic types of things.

One of the major functions of hospital visitors was to provide supplies that the soldiers could not get otherwise. These might include items of clothing such as shirts, drawers (underwear), and socks, or basic hygiene items like handkerchiefs, toothbrushes, soap, towels, or combs. Visitors also sometimes arrived with food that would promote the health of the patient or provide variety to a boring hospital diet, including canned and fresh fruit, jelly, wine, brandy, pickles, cheese, dried fruit, lemonade, ice cream, cookies, and candy. At times visitors tried to find or prepared particular foods, such as rice pudding, that a soldier craved. On special occasions local visitors supplied the hospitals with complete dinners. Visitors brought stationery, stamps, envelopes, and pencils to the patients and sometimes wrote letters to loved ones for those who were too disabled to write for themselves. Hospital visitors also distributed books and magazines to help convalescents pass the time.

Visitors might bring these supplies from home or be delegated to personally deliver items gathered or purchased by a local relief organization. In Washington, D.C., visitors might be able to meet a particular need from the United States Christian Commission storehouse where the commission stockpiled supplies for distribution.

Visiting involved giving attention, whether for minutes or hours, to individual soldiers. Many patients were homesick, and female visitors provided comfort simply by being women in a largely male environment. However, they often specifically reminded the men of their mothers, sisters, and wives, providing a touch of home to the patient far away from his family. In some cases, the severely ill or dying patient was comforted by the hallucination that a visiting woman was actually his dear relative. Visitors of either sex might sit with the sick, wounded, and dying, providing companionship, praying, reading the Bible, and sharing spiritual consolation.

For the patients who were not in desperate straits, visitors tried to provide entertainment of various kinds. They might read to the patients or sing for them. Generally the visitors did whatever they could to encourage and help men undergoing a tedious convalescence.

Probably the best known of hospital visitors was Walt Whitman who, by his own estimation, spent time with or gave small gifts to 80,000–100,000 patients in the Washington, D.C., hospitals between the end of 1862 and the end of the war in 1865. He later published accounts of his service. Although often labeled as a nurse, Whitman was actually a volunteer visitor.

President Abraham Lincoln and his wife Mary visited hospitals in Washington, D.C., together and separately, on a number of occasions. The President also visited soldiers in field hospitals at Antietam, Maryland and at City Point, Virginia, always speaking to the patients individually and shaking the hands of those who were able to do so. In addition to personal visits, the First Lady sent much fruit and other food to the hospitals, working with some other women to provide Christmas dinner as well. She also sent flowers from the White House conservatory to brighten the wards.

Although some of the most detailed accounts of hospital visitors survive for Washington, D.C., there are numerous other references in diaries, letters, and newspapers in both the North and the South indicating that men and women, as well as some young people, of all regions did their best to cheer their sick and wounded soldiers and provide them with such delicacies and necessities as they could.

Glenna R. Schroeder-Lein

See also: *Family Life and Gender Roles*: United States Sanitary Commission (USSC); *Religion and Belief*: United States Christian Commission (USCC); *Science and Technology*: Hospitals; Nursing

FURTHER READING

Adams, Lois Bryan. *Letter from Washington, 1863–1865*. Edited by Evelyn Leasher. Detroit, MI: Wayne State University Press, 1999.

Schroeder-Lein, Glenna R. *The Encyclopedia of Civil War Medicine*. Armonk, NY: M.E. Sharpe, 2008.

Schroeder-Lein, Glenna R. " 'H.G.': A Medical History of James M. Taylor of the 96th Illinois Infantry." *Journal of Illinois History* 15 (Spring 2012): 21–40.

Schroeder-Lein, Glenna R. *Lincoln and Medicine*. Carbondale: Southern Illinois University Press, 2012.

Whitman, Walt. *Memoranda During the War*. Reprint ed. Boston: Applewood, 1990 (1875).

HOUSEHOLD ENTERTAINMENT

Families on the Civil War home front faced countless hardships. With husbands, fathers, sons, brothers, and friends away at war, families were deprived of their loved ones and often had little news of their whereabouts or health. In the South, this crippling hardship was compounded by numerous shortages of food and consumer goods. Southerners had to deal with the Union blockade of Confederate ports and the relative underdevelopment of Southern industry compared to the burgeoning industrial economy supplying Northern troops and households with the necessities of life and war. Enslaved African Americans in the South were placed in an even more difficult position by the Civil War. Forced to continue working, enslaved people suffered from the same deprivations as their white masters while they anxiously awaited the conclusion of the conflict that would decide their future. Left with little to do but wait and worry, families on all sides of the conflict occupied their time with a number of household entertainments. Reading, writing, music, games, and crafts filled the time and offered a brief escape from the harsh realities of war. These activities also served an important social function, affording important opportunities for civilians to bond, cope, and organize for mutual support.

Reading was by far the most popular form of household entertainment during the Civil War. High literacy rates and the rapid growth of the antebellum publishing industry created a strong reading culture in the years before the war. After American publishing and the writing profession both came to prominence in the 1820s, Americans enjoyed an expanding market that offered works in numerous categories. Religious works were perennial favorites; Americans enjoyed reading the Bible, religious tracts, and sermons. Periodicals and newspapers were also extremely popular. Americans had long been able to subscribe to local and national newspapers, and they also enjoyed magazines like the political journal *Harper's Weekly* and *Godey's Lady's Book*, which offered fashion guidance, sewing and needlepoint patterns, sheet music, short stories, and articles.

Just as newspapers and magazines kept readers informed about the war, fiction offered readers a chance to put it out of their minds. Victor Hugo's *Les Miserables* (1862) was the most popular novel of the period, but James Fenimore Cooper, Ann Radcliffe, Sir Walter Scott, Charles Dickens, and Harriet Beecher Stowe—author of the divisive *Uncle Tom's Cabin* (1852)—were favorites as well. Readers did not stop with high-brow literature, however. Dime novels, first published in 1860, offered escapist fantasies, detective stories, and frontier tales at a low price to readers across class lines.

When the war began, Northern readers continued to enjoy a strong publishing market. Southerners faced an immediate shortage of new reading material. Long dependent on Northern industry for books, magazines, publishing equipment, and paper, Southerners were forced to reread and share the books they already owned. Many Southern newspapers went out of business for lack of newsprint and type. Despite these differences in the market, however, civilians on both sides of the conflict took part in reading clubs that allowed them to socialize and work with their hands while others took turns reading aloud. Reading thus served important individual and social functions during the war. It offered readers news of the war, ways to support it in social gatherings, and, when it became too much to bear, an escape from its seemingly endless hardship. Books, newspapers, and magazines circulated from home to camp, home to home, and hand to hand during the Civil War.

Music was also a popular diversion. Pianos were important furnishings in middle- and upper-class homes, and even Southern piano stores continued to operate during the war. A thriving sheet music industry fed the insatiable musical appetites of Northerners and Southerners during the conflict. The Civil War produced more popular songs than any other conflict in American history; in addition to enduring songs like "Dixie" (1860) and "The Battle Hymn of the Republic" (1862), Americans sang "The Battle Cry of Freedom" (1862), "God Save the South" (1861), and hundreds of other songs. Music was a prominent part of social gatherings for rich and poor, free and enslaved. It offered both emotional release and opportunities to bond with others; singing groups staged concerts in private homes to raise funds for war relief and other philanthropic functions. Similar to reading clubs, singing groups allowed families, friends, and soldiers to unite and pass the time while supporting the ongoing war effort.

When civilians were not reading or singing, they might play parlor games, pass the time with arts and crafts, or just visit and talk. Card games were ancient favorites, but commercial board games like the "The Mansion of Happiness" (1843), designed to teach Christian virtue to children, were more recent inventions. Checkers, chess, cribbage, and tangrams were also popular diversions. Needlework of all sorts was an important and pleasing pursuit for many that united necessity and entertainment. Pattern books and magazines featuring sewing patterns sold briskly, and sewing offered women both economic opportunities and a way to support the soldiers. Similar to reading clubs and singing groups, too, sewing circles were significant social groups where women could grieve, bond, and organize.

Social gatherings were part of an elaborate culture of etiquette and entertainment that cemented class bonds. Etiquette required a social call at least once a year—frequently much more often—and visitors often left calling cards for separate members of the family. Calling rituals persisted throughout the war, and lively visitors could fill hours in conversation. Even in the South, where the declining military fortunes of the Confederacy magnified the difficulties of the war, civilians attended "starvation parties" without food or refreshments. Socialization was not limited to the well-to-do. Americans of all classes countered the worry, loneliness, and boredom of the Civil War with numerous forms of entertainment in the home.

Books, music, games, and crafts allowed them to combine individual and social pursuits while continuing to build and cement tight bonds of family and friendship.

Christopher B. Crenshaw

See also: *Arts*: "Battle Hymn of the Republic"; "Dixie"; *Harper's Weekly*; Literature, Northern; Literature, Southern; Music, Nonmilitary; Newspapers, Northern; Newspapers, Southern; Poetry; Serial Novels; Quilts; *Uncle Tom's Cabin* (1852); *Clothing, Fashion, and Appearance: Godey's Ladies Book*; Sewing Societies; *Family Life and Gender Roles*: Slave Families; *Food and Drink*: Food, Shortages; *Housing and Community*: Slave Quarters; *Recreation and Social Customs*: Hospitality; Leisure Time; Parlors

FURTHER READING

Faust, Drew Gilpin. *Mothers of Invention: Women of the Slaveholding South in the American Civil War*. Chapel Hill: University of North Carolina Press, 1996.
Rogers, William Warren. *Confederate Home Front: Montgomery During the Civil War*. Tuscaloosa: University of Alabama Press, 1999.
Varhola, Michael O. *Life in Civil War America*. Cincinnati, OH: Family Tree Books, 1999.
Volo, Dorothy Denneen, and James M. Volo. *Daily Life in Civil War America*. Westport, CT: Greenwood Press, 1998.

IMMIGRANTS

During the antebellum era, European immigration to the United States reached record heights. The number of foreign-born Americans doubled between 1850 and 1860. 13.2 percent of Americans listed in the 1860 Census were born abroad: 4,138,697 out of a total population of 31,443,321. Consequently, newly arrived Americans from many nations served in Civil War armies and navies. Exact percentages are impossible to obtain, but perhaps as many as one quarter of the Union's soldiers, and as much as 45 percent of its naval personnel, were born outside the United States. Estimates of the foreign-born portion of the Confederate Army run from around 5 percent to slightly higher.

Most Civil War era immigrants came from northern Europe; large-scale migration from eastern and Southern Europe came after the war. In 1861, the largest numbers of new arrivals were from Germany and the British Isles, particularly Ireland. The majority of other immigrants came from elsewhere in Europe or from Canada. A few Asian or African-born men served, mainly in the Union Navy. Consuls from several foreign nations served their countrymen in the United States.

1862 photo by Alexander Gardner of a group of soldiers from the Irish Brigade while at Harrison's Landing, Virginia. Many immigrants fought for the Union during the Civil War, some in units made up primarily of their countrymen from Europe. Immigration during the nineteenth century was primarily to the Northern states, so the Union's military force had more immigrants than did the Confederacy's. (Library of Congress)

As a courtesy to their respective nations, the Union unofficially accredited consuls who served in the Confederacy.

Military or naval service offered work for newly arrived or unemployed immigrants, and offered an easier path to adjusting to life in their new country. Although immigration to the United States fell during the war, the Union actively encouraged recruiting efforts in Europe and among immigrant ships arriving at Castle Garden in New York. In general, immigrants were loyal to the Union because their attachments were with their new nation as a whole, rather than the sectional feelings held by native-born citizens.

Germans, many of whom settled in the Midwest, were the most numerous immigrant group in the Union Army. They were often referred to by native-born Americans as "Dutch," a corruption of the German word "Deutsch." The loyalty of German immigrants to the Union and their opposition to slavery were instrumental in preventing Missouri from joining the Confederacy. The next largest group of immigrants was the Irish, who were concentrated in large eastern cities. New York enlisted the largest numbers of Irish soldiers from any state. About one fifth of the sailors in the Union Navy had been born in Ireland; one tenth were English; and smaller numbers came from those born in Canada, Scandinavia, and France.

The majority of immigrants, 86.6 percent, settled in the free states. This numerical dominance in one section resulted from the different labor systems in the North and South. Southern slavery left few job openings for newly arrived unskilled laborers or trained craftsmen. About one quarter of a million people in the slave states, or only about 5 percent of the population, were born outside the United States. In the South, immigrants were heavily concentrated in port towns.

About 40 percent of the population of New Orleans, the Confederacy's largest city, was foreign-born. Louisiana contributed the largest number of non-native soldiers to the Confederate Army.

Immigrants served as soldiers and commanders during the Civil War. For example, 45 Union generals (about 8% of the total), including 12 each from Germany and Ireland, were born outside the United States. In part, promoting immigrant officers helped encourage enlistments of foreign-born troops, easing the North's need for military conscription. In contrast, only about 2 percent of Confederate generals were of foreign birth. However, two members of the Confederate cabinet were born abroad: Secretary of the Treasury Christopher Memminger was born in Germany; and Judah Benjamin, who held multiple cabinet posts, had been born in the British Virgin Islands.

Soldiers belonging to the most numerous immigrant groups, the German and Irish, found themselves especially stigmatized by native-born Americans and mocked for their accents and customs. European immigrants who practiced Catholicism faced additional prejudice as a result of their religion. Many Southerners believed that the foreigners made up a majority of the Union forces, and saw them as hired mercenaries.

Most foreign-born soldiers were scattered piecemeal throughout the armies, but there were numerous companies and regiments that were almost exclusively made of immigrants from a particular background. Several units carried regimental flags of Irish green, decorated with Irish patriotic symbols such as harps. The Scots heritage of the 79th New York Highlanders showed in the regiment's full dress uniforms, with kilts, sporrans, and glengarry caps. Among the Confederates, the 1st Louisiana was said to include soldiers of 37 different nationalities. A small but colorful contingent of immigrants seeking adventure arrived to fight in the Civil War. German aristocrat Heros von Borcke served on the staff of Confederate lieutenant general J.E.B. Stuart. A veteran of several European wars, soldier of fortune Colonel Sir Percy Wyndham, served with the Army of the Potomac.

Both navies recruited large numbers of foreign-born mariners. Experienced sailors were needed to supplement the thousands of landsmen inducted into the navy, and naval pay was better than that offered by the army. Many a Union vessel's crew was one third or more foreign-born. For example, the CSS *Shenandoah*, which circumnavigated the globe, included Australians and Pacific islanders. Most of the foreign-born crewmen of these European-built Rebel ships were recruited abroad and never saw the Confederate States. Sailors from Ireland, England, and other European nations also formed a substantial part of the crew of Confederate blockade runners.

Early in the war, foreign nationals were exempt from conscription, but naturalized citizens found themselves subject to the draft. Immigrants formed a major source of exempted men who hired themselves out as substitutes for drafted men.

DIFFICULTIES WITH GERMAN SOLDIERS

In January 1862, General Henry W. Halleck wrote to President Lincoln regarding unrest among regiments of German American soldiers in Halleck's command, the Department of Missouri. At the heart of the discontent was General Franz Sigel, who was widely popular in the German American community and who had been instrumental in convincing many young Germans to enlist. At the Battle of Wilson's Creek on August 10, 1861, Sigel led an ill-considered flanking move that contributed heavily to the defeat of Union forces. Relieved of his command by Halleck, Sigel resigned his commission, an action that caused a great uproar among the German units in Missouri and within the German American community generally. In the following excerpt from Halleck's letter, the general explains the situation regarding Sigel and the Germans.

> The difficulty with the Germans results from two causes: 1st [lack of pay]; 2d, they are continually tampered with by designing politicians in and out of service . . . to serve particular ends. A part of the scheme is the story of the ill-treatment of General Sigel, which is without the slightest foundation. All these difficulties are being satisfactorily arranged. A firm and decided course will end them forever. Any yielding on the part of the Government will only create new difficulties and give rise to new demands. Being a German myself by descent, I know something of the German character, and I am confident that in a few weeks, if the Government does not interfere, I can reduce these disaffected elements to order and discipline.

FURTHER READING

U.S. War Department. *War of the Rebellion: A Compilation of the Official Records of the Union and Confederate Armies.* Series I. Vol. VIII, p. 827.

A Confederate law of January 1864 subjected all males from the ages of 18 to 45 to the draft, without reference to place of birth. Believing that the urban poor were unfairly targeted by conscription, Irish immigrants were heavily involved in sparking the Draft Riots that swept New York City in July 1863.

David A. Norris

See also: *Arts*: Flags, Confederate; Flags, United States; *Economy and Work*: Factory Workers, Northern; Slavery; Urban Life, Northern; Urban Life, Southern;

Politics and Warfare: Camp Life; Draft Riots and Resistance; Enlistment; Morale; *Recreation and Social Customs*: Holidays; *Religion and Belief*: Catholicism

FURTHER READING

Efford, Alison Clark. *German Immigrants, Race, and Citizenship in the Civil War Era.* New York: Cambridge University Press, 2013.

Halloran, Fiona Deans. "Patriotism, Preparation, and Reputation: Immigrants in Battle and on the Home Front in the American Civil War." In Lisa Tendrich Frank, ed. *Civil War: People and Perspectives.* Santa Barbara, CA: ABC-Clio, 2009, pp. 77–94.

Lonn, Ella. *Foreigners in the Confederacy.* Reprint ed. Chapel Hill: University of North Carolina Press, 2001 (1940).

Lonn, Ella. *Foreigners in the Union Army and Navy.* Reprint ed. Baton Rouge: Louisiana State University Press, 1969 (1951).

Ural, Susannah J., ed. *Civil War Citizens: Race, Ethnicity, and Identity in America's Bloodiest Conflict.* New York: New York University Press, 2010.

MANHOOD, NORTHERN

Most social scientists and biologists agree that the ideas of "masculine" and "feminine" exist only as a social and cultural construct. Although sex, in a strict biological sense, refers to the differences in physical anatomy, gender refers to a complex set of cultural norms, assumptions, and inventions that shape social roles. A social construct like manhood is not inherited in the genetic code; rather, an individual male uses, learns, and absorbs his understanding of manhood from the larger society. What is construed as "masculine" or "feminine" will vary between social groups and over the course of time. Moreover, even in the same society definitions of manhood can vary depending on class, race, ethnicity, age, and region. Hence, masculinity and femininity are not universal, timeless constants. Historians, anthropologists, and sociologists interested in the evolution of male identity throughout American history have looked at how men view women and children, how men develop the awareness of their male self, and how male identity changes in conjunction with larger social, economic, and culture trends.

Having helped found the American Republic in the late eighteenth century, Thomas Jefferson held as ideal a republican citizenry composed of the rural yeomanry, small-scale craft artisans, and independent shopkeepers. White men constructed both their political worth and their social identity within this socioeconomic order. In the first half of the nineteenth century, however, the rise of the industrial marketplace, particularly in the North, had an enormous impact on how men constructed their social roles. With each passing decade a larger percentage of men in the North found themselves working for wages in the urban industrial and commercial centers. Fewer men were masters of their economic fate, either as owners of independent farms or as self-employed artisans, craftsmen, and shopkeepers. The economic order on which white manhood rested shifted in response to the fundamental transformation of the modes of production.

During the antebellum period, the ideal of "self-made manhood" rose to prominence within the broader historical developments of the nineteenth century. By the time of Jefferson's death in 1824, the rise of the market economy resulted in an increasing number of male wage laborers. Simultaneously, the westward territorial expansion of the United States afforded to many white men a high degree of social and geographic mobility. In the political realm, the expansion of democratic participation in the Jacksonian era demolished the close communal ties, guild associations, and small-town civic loyalties of late eighteenth-century Jeffersonian America.

Still, within this new economic order a great deal of social mobility was available to white men. Whereas in old Europe social classes were rigid and identities more fixed, in the emerging industrial economies of the Northern United States the essence of a man's identity rested less on the circumstances of birth—that is, the socioeconomic conditions of his origins—and more on his ability to rise up in society through luck, ambition, and talent. In the early days of the American Republic, in a pre-industrial era, manhood was about the inner self; by the end of the nineteenth century, the notion of manhood emphasized the acquisition of possession and property as the means to rise up from one's humble roots.

The new class of male wage laborers in the growing cities of the North often harbored hostility toward African Americans, women, and immigrants. White men perceived these social groups as rivals who threatened the exclusive preserve of professions once held exclusively by white men. Manhood came to be defined as something of a zero-sum game. Advances made by women, blacks, and immigrants in the socioeconomic order were perceived as a threat by many white men in the urbanizing centers. Supporting women's suffrage or legal equality meant diminishing the perceived rights and privileges men felt as their entitlement. Equality of the sexes necessarily meant a reduction in the worth and meaning of manhood.

Antebellum masculinity celebrated both men's capacity for violent insurrection and their ability to behave as civilized gentlemen. Thus, two versions of manhood competed in the Victorian era. On the one hand, Americans looked to the hard-drinking, gambling, womanizing male figure as the epitome of manhood. This vision of manhood was a counterweight to the notion that education and "soft" urban living had made Northern men enervated and effeminate. On the other hand, the sober, responsible, dutiful son or husband was also held up as the ideal model of manly conduct. Both models of masculine behavior propelled many Northern men to enlist during the war. The aggressive bar-brawler saw the war as an outlet for hyper-masculine aggression and state-sanctioned violence.

The respectable family man, on the other hand, also enlisted but out of a different set of impulses. In Victorian America, men felt they had a duty to protect the national government that provided them with constitutional liberties and privileges. Manhood, by this definition, involved a reciprocal moral obligation between male citizens and the democratic government.

For both groups of men, manhood compelled a display of courage and physical stamina in defense of both individual honor and the nation's survival. Hence, to prove one's self a man meant for many Northern men a trip to the enlistment office. The eagerness of raw recruits to prove themselves in battle grew out of their concept of manhood as intrinsically linked to one's ability to defend the government under which they lived. Notions of manliness equated fear with feminization and cowardice. Furthermore, the recent Mexican-American War helped accentuate the already preexisting dichotomy that cast men as citizens and defenders of the state and women as the recipients and beneficiaries of male protection. Men who refused to fight were traitors to both their sex and the country.

During the war, about 150,000 African American ex-slaves, joined by another 50,000 free blacks of the North, took up arms on behalf of the Union cause. Through their military service, these black men sought to assert their manhood and claim the rights that only white men could previously claim. Among these rights that African American men fought for were the right to independent legal standing, the right to own property, the right to rise up the social ladder, and the right to head the household as husbands and fathers without the presence of overseers and slaveholders.

Middle-class whites of the North, though they never constituted the majority of the population during the course of the nineteenth century, nevertheless managed to exert a lasting and, in many ways, permanent cultural influence on the broader discourses that dominated American life and society. However, the years after the war would show once again how conceptions of masculinity and manhood were intrinsically linked to changes in society. Postwar models of masculinity would come under challenge by increasing numbers of women entering the public sphere, the second wave of European migration, and the new class of newly freed blacks.

Long Bao Bui

See also: *Family Life and Gender Roles*: Free Blacks; Honor; Immigrants; Manhood, Southern; Slave Families; Womanhood, Northern; Womanhood, Southern

FURTHER READING

Dubbert, Joe L. *A Man's Place: Masculinity in Transition*. Englewood Cliffs, NJ: Prentice-Hall, Inc. 1979.

Frank, Stephen M. "'Rendering Aid and Comfort': Images of Fatherhood in the Letters of Civil War Soldiers from Massachusetts and Michigan." *Journal of Social History* 26:1 (Autumn 1992): 5–31.

Kimmel, Michael S. *Manhood in America: A Cultural History.* New York: Oxford University Press, 2006.

McPherson, James M. *For Cause and Comrades: Why Men Fought in the Civil War.* New York: Oxford University Press, 1997.

Rotunda, E. Anthony. *American Manhood: Transformations in Masculinity from the Revolution to the Modern Era.* New York: Basic Books, 1993.

Stauffer, John. "Embattled Manhood and New England Writers, 1860–1870." In Catherine Clinton and Nina Silber, eds. *Battle Scars: Gender and Sexuality in the American Civil War.* New York: Oxford University Press, 2006, pp. 120–139.

Wyatt-Brown, Bertram. *Yankee Saints and Southern Sinners.* Baton Rouge: Louisiana State University Press, 1985.

MANHOOD, SOUTHERN

The white masculine culture of the American South in the Civil War era involved two dominant ethics: honor and religious piety. Honor prioritized the public recognition and defense of masculine claims to reputation and authority. It also emphasized private, self-reflective masculine evaluations of honor status. White male claims to authority rested on their claims to honor, and those claims involved both these individual self-conceptions and public reputations. Even the most trivial social intercourse became vital in these men's incessant attempts to define and defend personal and public honor. Honor governed male interactions with each other and—by proxy—between their households, dependents, and subordinates, male and female, white and black. Disorder at home undermined personal honor, which threatened public disgrace. All had to be guarded against to uphold the social order, peacefully if possible, violently if necessary.

The South's honor culture ensured that a peculiar version of masculinity prevailed in both its public spaces and its private homes. It upheld a rigidly hierarchical view of society: one which placed white men of wealth at the top and rendered dependent white males, women, and African Americans subservient to elite white male authority. A major facet of this masculine honor culture was its performative nature, its tendency to encourage white men to wear many masks in their coded and ritualized correspondence and confrontations with one another. This ritual was most vividly displayed in the formal duel. However, such honor and violence was not reserved for social elites alone. Lower-class Southern men exerted and defended their honor according to more virile expectations and with more brutal results like brawling and eye gouging. Southern yeomen and middle-class merchants and professionals bridged the social gap by aspiring to and adapting forms of elite honorable restraint while shunning lower-class "barbarity."

The personal pursuit and public defense of that Southern honor could be genuinely heart-rending for men at all social levels. But it could also assume false pretences as these men sought to shape their public reputations without serious self-reflection. Honor put Southern men of all classes in uneasy tension with themselves and their role in society. Many felt vulnerable, prone to self-doubt and fearful of public shame, both of which put them on the defensive in private life and public affairs. It caused others to mask their insecurities through humor. As a whole, Southern honor promoted both passion and restraint, as its coded ritual and language shaped the discourse and behaviors of white men throughout the Civil War era South.

Religious piety emphasized moral self-reflection and encouraged believers to curb excessive pride and passion. The American South has long been viewed as the "Bible Belt" of the nation, and Protestant evangelicals played a prominent role in fastening that moniker upon the region, beginning with the "Second Great Awakening" (1800–1805). These Protestant evangelicals—Baptists, Methodists, and Presbyterians especially—took the lead in proselytizing the Southern backcountry. Their emphasis on the conversion experience lent these revivals an unprecedented emotional fervor. As a result, a pervasive spirituality had enveloped the region by 1810 and continued to grow in its geographic reach and cultural influence into the antebellum years. The religious piety that emerged from this transformation sought to instill a sense of the spiritual—the eternal—in believers' daily lives. It could lead them to shun worldly matters for spiritual ones, but it could also prompt an attempt to purify their temporal lives that they might more effectively serve spiritual ends. A moral concern was ever-present and produced a tension between private spirituality and social stewardship, between moral self-reflection and public moral reform, between passivity and crusade. Within the South's masculine culture, this religious piety, to a degree, operated as a check on the more hedonistic and anarchic aspects of honor.

White Southern men in the Civil War era did not simply pick and choose between various aspects of honor and religious piety; they inextricably linked both in their minds and applied both in their daily lives. Beginning in the 1830s and increasing as the sectional crisis intensified and the Civil War approached, the honor creed came to capture piety, creating a wrathful ethic of "righteous honor." Most white Southern men believed self-mastery was the key to achieving this righteous honor. As a result they prioritized self-control when faced with various forms of vice—sensual and sexual lust, alcoholic indulgence, wanton violence, and unrestrained racial exploitation—all of which they saw as especially prevalent temptations within Southern slavery. Self-mastery, they believed, would lead to proper mastery of enslaved people by ensuring righteous honor became the guiding principle of their peculiar institution. Righteous honor was thus the cornerstone of white Southern manhood: it purportedly upheld white supremacy in the racial order; upheld white male authority in the patriarchal order; and in so doing promoted stability in the social order. Righteous honor became the ethic in which the South would make war.

Their experience of war—as soldiers and civilians—would alter that ethical ideal. Rampant death, dismemberment, and the demolition of the Southern social order were the prices white men paid for staking their future authority—over the South's racial and patriarchal hierarchies—on secession and war. From the outset they had conceived of the conflict as a test of their honor, their faith, and their manhood. They had continually looked for signs that these ideals were holding firm against the Union military onslaught. Impending military defeat led them to ambiguous conclusions regarding the effectiveness of their ideals. For some, defeat conspicuously revealed the immorality of Southern ideologies; righteous honor and self-mastery had failed them. For others, these ideals remained stalwart but Southern men themselves had failed to live up to them, so military defeat was the predictable result. Most white men probably accepted both conclusions in varying degrees according to shifts in the postwar social landscape.

Thus the same ethical ideal that enabled white Southern men to make war would also help them to make sense of defeat, and to remake themselves, their households, and their society in the face of the new realities brought on by emancipation and Reconstruction. Most of these men gradually determined to pick up the pieces in the wake of the war's physical and psychological destruction. What emerged—the "New South" and the "Lost Cause"—would both be profoundly shaped by the twin ethics of "self-mastery" on the one hand, and "righteous violence" on the other. As federal Reconstruction ended and white Southern men "redeemed" their state governments, they whitewashed the public memory of the Civil War and Reconstruction through the "Lost Cause." They reasserted white supremacy through legal disfranchisement, as well as the segregation of—and extralegal violence toward—Southern blacks. All were supposed to point to a more prosperous future in a more economically diverse "New South." The ethical ideals of righteous honor, self-mastery, and manhood reflected and promoted these changes.

James Hill Welborn III

See also: *Economy and Work*: Rural Life, Southern; Slaveholders; Slavery; Urban Life, Southern; *Family Life and Gender Roles*: Honor; Manhood, Northern; Patriarchy; Womanhood, Southern; *Housing and Community*: Nationalism, Confederate; *Politics and Warfare*: Morale; Secession; *Religion and Belief*: Evangelicalism; Lost Cause; Methodism; Presbyterianism; Religious Revivals

FURTHER READING

Berry, Stephen W., II. *All That Makes a Man: Love and Ambition in the Civil War South.* New York: Oxford University Press, 2003.

Carmichael, Peter S. *The Last Generation: Young Virginians in Peace, War, and Reunion.* Chapel Hill: University of North Carolina Press, 2005.

Friend, Craig Thompson, ed. *Southern Masculinity: Perspectives on Manhood in the South Since Reconstruction.* Athens: University of Georgia Press, 2009.

Friend, Craig Thompson, and Lorri Glover, eds. *Southern Manhood: Perspectives on Masculinity in the Old South.* Athens: University of Georgia Press, 2004.

Mayfield, John. *Counterfeit Gentlemen: Manhood and Humor in the Old South.* Gainesville: University Press of Florida, 2009.

Welborn, James Hill, III. "Drinkin', Fightin', Prayin': The Southern Male in the Civil War Era." Doctoral dissertation, University of Georgia, 2014.

Wyatt-Brown, Bertram. *Southern Honor: Ethics and Behavior in the Old South.* New York: Oxford University Press, 1982.

MIDWIFERY

Midwifery is the traditionally female role of attending women before, during, and after childbirth. Knowledge for this practice was passed down through generations, usually from mothers to daughters. In addition, attendance at parturition, or giving birth, was considered proper only for women. Birth was understood to be a natural process, and a nineteenth-century midwife assisted in a birth with as little intervention as possible. Unless problems occurred, she was there only to facilitate. Midwives were also called accoucheurs.

The medicalization of the birth process began in the middle of the nineteenth century signaling a slow trend away from traditional female midwifery. Only men could become doctors because women were considered intellectually and emotionally incapable of becoming educated in the field of medicine. Elizabeth Blackwell the first woman to graduate from an American medical school, New York's Geneva Medical College in 1849, was not the typical doctor of her time. Men trained in birthing were called male or man midwives until the term "obstetrician" was coined to professionalize the care of pregnant women and create a term that differentiated their methods from those of a midwife. Although doctors had medical and scientific instruction, they had no hands-on training with birth in medical school, and were not very capable at delivering babies. In the mid-1850s, "demonstrative midwifery," where medical students could watch a live birth, was first introduced, but it was not widely used as its propriety was controversial. The customary modesty concerns in the nineteenth century only added to the awkwardness of men in the birth chamber. Male doctors were only allowed eye contact with the patient. A sheet covered women in labor, and the doctor reached under the sheet to examine the woman with his hand that was lubricated with lard or oil. He maintained eye contact only with the woman, never looking under the covers as she gave birth.

Traditional midwives were often poor and uneducated. Midwifery was unregulated, and there were no standard operating procedures. Although the newly formed American Medical Association proposed standards in 1847, they would not be accepted before the 1870s. Midwifery was a social and traditional role, and it was considered improper for men to be present at a birth. The midwife assessed the progress of birth, including dilation, contractions, and breaking water. Midwives were trained to be patient and to allow the birth to proceed naturally even if it took a long time. As parturition was not considered an illness, obstetricians were not considered necessary. Hastening the process was frowned upon.

Dr. William Dewees (1768–1841), professor of obstetrics in Philadelphia, wrote a manual for midwives in 1824 that stressed nonintervention. Samuel Gregory began a campaign against male midwives in 1848 when he established the Boston Female Medical College to formally educate midwives. They earned certificates, not medical degrees. Arguments for male midwives were often based on the image of women as frail and emotional, whose proper role was domesticity and motherhood.

Midwives were responsible for setting up the birthing room, including providing clean linens to keep the bed and the delivering mother dry. The presence of appropriate female friends was recommended to cheer the woman through labor and to avoid the need for pain medication. Neither the pregnant woman's mother nor unmarried women were considered acceptable in this role. Although some women were encouraged to lie down as delivery approached, in rural areas sitting was more common. If a male midwife was attending, lying near the edge of a bed with knees drawn was the preferred position because it was the most modest as less of the woman's body was exposed. Sarah Josepha Hale, editor of the influential and popular *Godey's Lady's Book*, opposed the presence of men in a lying-in room as detrimental to a woman's chastity, delicacy, and character.

The first sign of impending delivery was sinking of the fetus, now known as "lightening," followed by discharge of mucus. Labor pains came in stages. Early pains, called "grinding" pains, came from dilation contractions. Later "bearing down" pains arose from expulsive contractions. Obstetrician Dr. Charles D. Meigs (1792–1869), who opposed the use of anesthesia and intervention, believed that the two types of pain could be determined because women in the early stage squeezed or twisted objects, while in the later stages they pulled. Midwives often attached towels on bedposts for women to grasp during labor. Use of anesthesia was new during the Civil War, but its use during childbirth was discouraged because the pains of labor and birth were seen as morally desirable for the romanticized image of woman as pure, spiritual, and modest. The use of pain relievers was also frowned upon.

Midwives were able to reach into the uterus to determine if a baby was in the right position for birth, and knew how to cut the umbilical cord safely. They were responsible for washing and wrapping the newborn and checking its vital signs. Midwives generally did not use instruments such as forceps, and surgeons would be called in for problem births. Midwives might use ergot (a fungus found on rye) to hasten the expulsion of the placenta or speed up labor, but ergot had harmful side effects. Puerperal fever was a side effect, often fatal, of childbirth, caused by a resistance to or ignorance of the need for hand-washing so germs were easily spread. Post-delivery, female midwives would care for the mother and the newborn. If there was not a live birth, they would bind the mother's breasts with herbal and homemade remedies to stop lactation.

Women were neither educated in nor prepared for childbirth. The use of corsets and waist stays remained despite movements against such fashion as detrimental to a woman's health. By about 1830, middle- and upper-class urban women were turning to doctors for what they considered short safer deliveries. Walter Channing (1876–1876), Harvard College professor of obstetrics, opposed female midwives because he saw male-midwifery as a way to generate more income from patients. If an obstetrician successfully delivered a baby without complications the family would be more likely to turn to that doctor for other treatments. Eventually, childbirth was viewed as a complicated medical procedure requiring a doctor's intervention, and female midwifery declined.

Jane Brodsky Fitzpatrick

See also: *Clothing, Fashion, and Appearance: Godey's Lady's Book*; *Family Life and Gender Roles*: Childbirth; Cult of Domesticity; Motherhood; Womanhood, Northern; Womanhood, Southern

FURTHER READING

Donegan, Jane B. *Women & Men Midwives: Medicine, Morality and Misogyny in Early America*. Westport, CT: Greenwood Press, 1978.

Litoff, Judy Barrett. *American Midwives, 1860 to the Present*. Westport, CT: Greenwood Press, 1978.

Wertz, Richard W., and Dorothy C. Wertz. *Lying-In: A History of Childbirth in America*. New Haven, CT: Yale University Press, 1989.

MOTHERHOOD

The most important occupation for a married woman, after serving as devoted wife to her husband, was the role of mother.

Young women spent their late adolescent years and early 20s searching for a suitable partner, and then spent their married years bearing and raising children. For women on the eve of the Civil War, motherhood was a significant personal achievement, and family served as the core of her social and economic fabric during this time period. Most couples attempted to begin their brood as soon as they married, and most women expected to bear children until they reached menopause or death. Most rural Southern families wanted many children to serve as labor on the family farm, companionship in a place of rural isolation, and a sign of status.

Similar to their white counterparts, enslaved women spent the majority of their adult lives bearing and raising their own children, as well as serving as a significant parental role in the lives of their white owner's children and in the lives of other children in the enslaved community. As did all mothers, enslaved black women felt a connection to their children. However, slavery made motherhood bittersweet because enslaved children were considered property and therefore subject to the whims of their masters.

Northern middle-class women bore fewer children than did women in the South. Rapid urban industrialization, along with Victorian social ideas, altered Northern women's views on childrearing. The home became the mother's sphere and she focused her attention on nurturing and educating her children so that they might grow into moral and virtuous adults. During the Civil War though, overall conception rates among American women declined dramatically as couples made efforts to prevent pregnancies due to the effects of the conflict.

As the Civil War continued, the mother's role as caretaker did not subside nor diminish. Rather, the conflict provided many mothers with a sense of anxiety as they worried about their older sons who left to enlist in the war effort. Concern for the safety of their sons' lives certainly affected each soldier's mother, but Southern and Northern mothers differed on their commitment to the conflict. The majority of elite Southern women strongly supported the Confederate cause and rarely discouraged their adult sons or husbands from enlisting. Many Northern women, on the other hand, found it difficult to watch their sons enlist and sometimes objected to their involvement as they were afraid of the potential danger that might harm their child. Southern women worried too, but saw their sons as necessary defenders of the Confederacy, whereas Northern mother generally experienced a sense of loss within their domestic sphere. Southern mothers did, however, fear for the safety of their daughters during the conflict as they faced potential danger without the protection of a father or brother.

Many elite women took their children out of their homes and became refugees with family and friends throughout the South in an effort to circumvent any potential peril. Less affluent mothers in the South remained on their family farms and took responsibility for their productivity as well as for their young children.

Northern mothers believed it was their duty to nurture and educate their children to become virtuous and moral citizens. As the Civil War gained traction and caused disruption within families, these mothers witnessed their authority and influence diminish. Eventually, Northern mothers put their domestic values and skills to use by supporting the war effort in their respective towns, as nurses and within politics.

As the conflict continued and took increasing numbers of men away from home, families did not increase in numbers as quickly as they had before the conflict. Letters between husbands and wives reveal their apprehension at conceiving during this period and many women attempted to prevent pregnancies by abstinence. Raising young children during wartime, along with losing older children at the hands of the war, proved tremendously difficult for mothers waiting at home. Despite the war, both Southern and Northern mothers continued with their roles as caretakers and continued to impart lessons of virtue, responsibility, and morality through correspondence with their sons and daughters.

Enslaved women's motherly roles differed substantially from those of white women. Enslaved women were encouraged and expected to procreate. Their children would expand the work force and offered economic benefits to their masters. The connection between mother and child developed within the enslaved community, but the realization that a child or mother might be sold at any time placed the family in a precarious situation. Despite this reality, enslaved women retained protective feelings toward their young and held out hope that they might eventually remove themselves from slavery. In cases where mothers or children were sold apart at auction and separated, enslaved children usually found a maternal support system with other nurturing enslaved women.

Enslaved mothers experienced further hardship throughout the war as they took on increased responsibilities in the home and in the fields, particularly as enslaved men were conscripted into the Confederate Army or escaped to freedom behind Union lines. However, most enslaved women understood the potential significance of the Civil War. They realized that the possibility of freedom meant that they might reconnect with loved ones that had been sold away. Furthermore, the prospect of freedom meant that they would never lose their children again. Despite recognizing this possibility, many enslaved mothers remained on their owners' land.

Amber Surmiller

See also: *Economy and Work*: Rural Life, Northern; Rural Life, Southern; Urban Life, Northern; Urban Life, Southern; *Family Life and Gender Roles*: Childbirth; Courtship and Marriage; Slave Families; Womanhood, Northern; Womanhood, Southern; Young Women; *Housing and Community*: Refugees

FURTHER READING

Jabour, Anya. *Scarlett's Sisters: Young Women in the Old South*. Chapel Hill: University of North Carolina Press, 2007.

McMillen, Sally G. *Southern Women: Black and White in the Old South*. Baton Rouge: Louisiana State University Press, 1990.

Mintz, Steven. *Domestic Revolutions: A Social History of the American Family*. New York: The Free Press, 1998.

Ott, Victoria E. *Confederate Daughters: Coming of Age During the Civil War*. Carbondale: Southern Illinois University Press, 2008.

Silber, Nina. *Daughters of the Union: Northern Women Fight the Civil War*. Cambridge, MA: Harvard University Press, 2005.

PATRIARCHY

Patriarchy is a social system in which men are entitled to positions of power, authority, and influence that women are largely excluded from. Traditionally, the father or the eldest male is considered the head of the household, and lines of descent are traced through the male line, placing them at the center of social organization. Although patriarchy in American history is largely understood in linear terms, moving from rigid patriarchal hierarchy to increasing egalitarianism, patriarchal structures are far more complex and have actually risen and fallen in prominence at different times in the United States due to shifts in demographic, economic, religious, cultural, ideological, and geographical forces.

To better understand the occasionally paradoxical evolution of patriarchy that took place in the nineteenth century, it's helpful to consider how it differs in contrast to some aspects of traditional patriarchy in colonial and eighteenth-century America. A traditional patriarch devoted himself to leading his family and serving his community. In previous centuries, it was unquestioningly expected that a woman would transition directly from being under her father's authority to being under her husband's authority. It was also customary in previous centuries for a father to actively participate in his children's upbringing, which included making decisions about his offspring's occupation as well as whom they were allowed to court and marry. Because it was typical for fathers to wait until death before handing over the legal title of their property to their sons, children were kept dependent until they reached middle age.

Although these systems were not entirely done away with by the nineteenth century, there were certain modifications. In antebellum America, for example, young women experienced a period of comparative freedom from subjection to a male figure when they temporarily worked outside of the home before marriage.

Also, the subtle erosion of certain aspects within patriarchal dominance began when men experienced the loss of control over land due to steep increases in population. Plots became too small to be farmed for profit, and with the loss of land value younger generations sought alternative sources of capital in a variety of occupational choices, such as business and factory work, that took them away from the home, all of which contributed to waning paternal control.

This steady forward movement away from the farmland toward a more commercial and industrial economy was the primary cause for the massive shifts in patriarchal structure during the nineteenth century. Prior to the turn of the century, women had actively participated in the business of farming, assisting their husbands by managing accounts and looking after apprentices and journeymen. Even wives of lawyers and doctors were intimately involved with their husband's profession, as it was common for these occupations to be practiced at home as well. Women also became active producers in commerce by manufacturing goods for sale.

However, the beginning of the nineteenth century witnessed a growing distinction between household and workplace as farmland disappeared and men had to seek work outside of the home. This change formed a new middle-class ideology that reorganized family roles around the idea of sexual difference, giving rise to sharply contrasting gender roles in culture and language that had not existed earlier. The public sphere of the business world inhabited by men was seen as an external space apart from the interior, private sphere of domesticity occupied by women. The father's role increasingly became solidified as protector and provider, whereas the mother's role was confined to the domestic and consisted of childrearing and housework, which developed into ideals of womanhood stressing nurturer and devoted or obedient housewife. Furthermore, the home was increasingly seen as a space for men to relax in after a hard day's work, the environmental conditions of which also came under the duties of a responsible wife. Nothing speaks more directly to this new ideal than Coventry Patmore's famous poem published in 1854 entitled "The Angel in the House," which depicts the Victorian ideal of the patient and sacrificing housewife. The sharp sexual division of labor even reorganized farming families; although both husband and wife had previously worked side by side in productive wage-earning activities, the farmhouse was now considered separate from the labor activities of the farm itself and now operated with the aid of paid farm laborers.

An unforeseen outcome of this sexual division of labor was the use of a new gendered language when describing familial relationships. For example, a woman was traditionally considered both the wife and mistress of a household where the term "mistress" was a title describing a wife's duty to oversee servants, apprentices, and journeymen. However, the term mistress was eventually replaced by "Mrs."

with the husband's name appended; in this linguistic manner, a woman's identity was wholly subsumed by her husband's. However, masculine identity underwent some difficult changes as well. With a new emphasis on men to earn money and material possessions outside of the home, the demands and pressures to keep up with the rapidly changing economic conditions and technological advancements of the nineteenth century proved to be overwhelming. To cope, many turned to the consumption of alcohol, which more than doubled in the first decades of the 1800s.

Another powerful influence on patriarchy during antebellum America was the Second Great Awakening, a Protestant revival movement that enrolled millions of new members. The revivalists placed great emphasis on the family as bearers of morality, and they advocated for the ideal Christian man: a father whose role was to serve as the family's spiritual and moral leader, to educate and discipline his children, and to take an active interest in the lives of his family members. Men who subscribed to this evangelical conception of fatherhood developed close companionship within their families but there were plenty within the population who defined themselves in opposition to it, as rates of abandonment and divorce also increased in the first half of the century. Despite the revivals, the widening space between home and the workplace steadily reduced the overall involvement fathers had with their families post–Civil War. This change was especially evident in the cities, where male-exclusive organizations and forms of recreation became more commonplace as an alternative to returning to domestic life, and American masculinity became progressively identified with a man's profession.

The nineteenth century, despite being unquestioningly dominated by men, did have a few female voices that began to challenge the hidden assumptions of patriarchy. Most notably, Margaret Fuller published an essay in July 1843 in the American magazine the *Dial* entitled, "The Great Lawsuit. Man Versus Men: Woman Versus Women," which was later expanded and republished under its more recognizable title, "Woman in the Nineteenth Century." Fuller's thesis centered on the cultivation of the individual and illustrated the effect that upbringing and environment had on a woman's ability to reason, the creation of so-called feminine qualities, and the underlying sexism apparent in common language.

Laura L. S. Bauer

See also: *Economy and Work*: Factory Workers, Northern; Factory Workers, Southern; Landowners; Rural Life, Northern; Rural Life, Southern; Slaveholders; Slavery; Urban Life, Northern; Urban Life, Southern; *Family Life and Gender Roles*: Courtship and Marriage; Cult of Domesticity; Manhood, Northern; Manhood, Southern; Motherhood; Womanhood, Northern; Womanhood, Southern; Young Men; Young Women; *Housing and Community*: Slave Life; *Religion and Belief*: Evangelicalism; Religious Revivals; *Science and Technology*: Factories

FURTHER READING

Davidoff, Lenore, and Catherine Hall. *Family Fortunes: Men and Women of the English Middle Class*. New York: Routledge. 1987.

Frank, S. M. "Rendering Aid and Comfort: Images of Fatherhood in the Letters of Civil War Soldiers from Massachusetts and Michigan." *Journal of Social History* 26 (1992): 5–31.

Kann, Mark E. *The Gendering of American Politics: Founding Mothers, Founding Fathers, and Political Patriarchy*. Westport, CT: Praeger, 1999.

Kann, Mark E. *A Republic of Men: The American Founders, Gendered Language, and Patriarchal Politics*. New York: New York University Press, 1998.

Miller, Pavla. *Transformations of Patriarchy in the West: 1500–1900*. Bloomington: Indiana University Press, 1998.

Mintz, Steven. *A Prison of Expectations: The Family in Victorian Culture*. New York: New York University Press. 1983.

Mintz, Steven, and Susan Kellogg. *Domestic Revolutions: A Social History of American Family Life*. New York: Free Press. 1988.

Volo, James M., and Dorothy Denneen Volo. *Family Life in 19th-Century America*. Westport, CT: Greenwood Press, 2007.

SLAVE FAMILIES

Throughout the Civil War era, enslaved families endured separation and coercion as well as the denial of legal recognition and protection. Within a dense extended kinship network, enslaved people forged bonds that mediated the detrimental effects of the domestic slave trade, harsh labor, physical violence, and sexual exploitation. The existence, resilience, and persistence of black families contradicted slavery as an institution that defined humans as property and identified enslaved people as slaveholders' subordinates.

Slaveholders' financial interests dictated the ability of enslaved families to remain intact during the domestic slave trade. The sale, gift, or division of estates often separated spouses and orphaned children. One historian estimates that during the decades preceding the Civil War, out of two-thirds of a million interstate slave sales, about 25 percent destroyed a first marriage and 50 percent decimated a nuclear family. Temporary and permanent separation denied spouses the opportunity to live together, share responsibility for childrearing, and engage in a sexual relationship. Because slave traders and buyers often grouped new mothers with their children during sale as part of a bargain, nursing babies saw the best chance of remaining with their mothers.

Enslaved families exhibited great adaptive potential and resiliency through the creation of an extended kinship network based on community obligations.

Photograph of five generations of a slave family in Beaufort, South Carolina, in 1862. Despite enslavement African Americans maintained family ties and formed extended kinship networks with the members of their community. Naming children for relatives enabled enslaved people to maintain emotional ties to their families even when family members were sold away or died. (Library of Congress)

Because separation, sale, and labor divisions destabilized the nuclear slave family, enslaved people did not always idealize or imitate the monogamy and patrifocality of white nuclear families. Many African Americans saw kinship as an array of flexible and negotiable social relationships among people unrelated through blood or marriage. Matrifocality, single parenthood, abroad marriages, multigenerational households, single- and mixed-gender dwellings, in addition to monogamous marriages and nuclear households, all represented common slave family experiences. Grandparents, other relatives, or non-kin often "adopted" newcomers and assumed the responsibility for childrearing and provided nurture, education, socialization, material support, and recreation when possible. Some enslaved people forged kinship ties through shared interests in resources like animals, clothing, food, furniture, and money. Customs like naming children for absent relatives enabled enslaved people to maintain emotional ties to their families.

Within their limited legal and social status, enslaved people developed standards for intimate marital and sexual relationships. They entered into long-lasting faithful relationships, though some also committed adultery and ended relationships. Contrary to white social norms, many enslaved people lived together prior to marriage and did not condemn premarital pregnancy. Soon after conceiving a child, enslaved couples took marital vows. Laws did not recognize slave unions, but enslaved couples needed the consent of their masters to marry or "jump the broom." Even though slave marriages presented incentives to slaveholders, including the possibility of slave births and deterrence of runaways, the union's permanency depended on the couple's prospects for living and working together.

To serve practical needs, slaveholders usually granted permission for abroad marriages, or marital unions between enslaved people on different plantations. Although larger slaveholdings promised few benefits to masters who granted permission for abroad marriages, smaller slaveholdings could lack suitable numbers of partners for enslaved people. Masters sometimes granted enslaved couples permission to visit one another across short distances, but they risked reprisal during illicit nighttime reunions. During the final years of the Civil War, some enslaved people took advantage of the opportunity to hold formal ceremonies and register their long-standing marriages. Between 1864 and 1865, white clergymen who accompanied the Union Army into Mississippi and northern Louisiana conducted marriage rites for thousands of enslaved couples.

Marriage did not shield enslaved women from the nonconsensual sexual advances of white men. White slaveholders and overseers could force married and unmarried enslaved women to engage in sexual relationships that resulted in pregnancy. Children born from interracial sexual encounters between enslaved women and white men inherited the slave status of their mothers.

Although enslaved women received little physical protection, they remained at the center of the life of their families. The dual roles of slave and mother presented a set of circumstances peculiar to African American women. Although enslaved families depended on women to raise children and keep families intact, the everyday realities of enslaved labor inhibited the ability of women to fully prioritize family needs. The multiple demands on enslaved women anchored them to the home and community, a situation that raised few opportunities for temporary or permanent escape. Although enslaved women professed loyalty to mistresses when forced to serve them as domestics, their true allegiance belonged to their own communities and families. With the onset of the Civil War, rumors of freedom led many enslaved women to work less and claim greater personal time and authority over themselves and their families. Although some enslaved women chose to leave their owners after years of suffering and witnessing abuse, others found that extended family ties made escape to safety within Union lines too difficult.

Slaveholders interfered in enslaved children's lives through disciplinary action, parental displacement, and forced labor. Although laws granted slaveholders the ability to shape and supervise the conditions under which children grew to adulthood under bondage, slaveholders largely proved unwilling to assume responsibility for the childrearing of slaves. Enslaved parents encouraged slaveholders to provide resources that would ensure the health, safety, and survival of their children, yet they also understood that such a bargain posed a challenge to their parental duties. Although slaveholders wished to perpetuate the asymmetry of the master-slave relationship that would deny children a sense of self, enslaved parents wanted to expose children to examples and lessons of fortitude within the extended kinship network.

Despite the painful loss of separation, enslaved people created new families, accentuated community bonds, and maintained emotional ties to missing relatives. At the risk of severe punishment and sale, many enslaved people sought to make contact with those from whom they had been separated. The extended kinship network that characterized the enslaved family during the Civil War era provided a blueprint for the creation of communities after Emancipation.

Justin Isaac Rogers

See also: *Economy and Work*: Plantations; Rural Life, Southern; Slavery; *Family Life and Gender Roles*: Courtship and Marriage; Motherhood

FURTHER READING

Berlin, Ira, and Leslie S. Rowland, eds. *Families and Freedom: A Documentary History of African-American Kinship in the Civil War Era*. New York: The New Press, 1997.

Camp, Stephanie M. H. *Closer to Freedom: Enslaved Women and Everyday Resistance in the Plantation South*. Chapel Hill: University of North Carolina Press, 2004.

Fox-Genovese, Elizabeth. *Within the Plantation Household: Black and White Women of the Old South*. Chapel Hill: University of North Carolina Press, 1988.

Glymph, Thavolia. *Out of the House of Bondage: The Transformation of the Plantation Household*. New York: Cambridge University Press, 2008.

Gutman, Herbert G. *The Black Family in Slavery and Freedom, 1750–1925*. New York: Vintage Books, 1976.

Johnson, Walter. *Soul by Soul: Life Inside the Antebellum Slave Market*. Cambridge, MA: Harvard University Press, 1999.

Kaye, Anthony E. *Joining Places: Slave Neighborhoods in the Old South*. Chapel Hill: University of North Carolina Press, 2007.

King, Wilma. *Stolen Childhood: Slave Youth in Nineteenth-Century America*. 2nd ed. Bloomington: Indiana University Press, 2011 (1995).

Penningroth, Dylan C. *The Claims of Kinfolk: African American Property and Community in the Nineteenth-Century South*. Chapel Hill: University of North Carolina Press, 2003.

Schwartz, Marie Jenkins. *Born in Bondage: Growing Up Enslaved in the Antebellum South*. Cambridge, MA: Harvard University Press, 2000.

Stevenson, Brenda E. *Life in Black and White: Family and Community in the Slave South*. New York: Oxford University Press, 1996

West, Emily. *Chains of Love: Slave Couples in Antebellum South Carolina*. Urbana: University of Illinois Press, 2004.

Williams, Heather Andrea. *Help Me to Find My People: The African American Search for Family Lost in Slavery*. Chapel Hill: University of North Carolina Press, 2012.

UNITED STATES SANITARY COMMISSION (USSC)

The United States Sanitary Commission was a civilian organization formed to provide relief to the sick and wounded soldiers of the Union Army during the Civil War. It was not a government institution so it depended on the efforts and donations of private citizens. As the war progressed, it became one of the largest and most successful private aid organizations in the country, proving itself largely competent and efficient in helping Union soldiers from 1861 to 1865.

Neither side was ready for the great number of casualties caused by the Civil War. Organizations within the military, such as the Medical Bureau of the War Department, were small, understaffed, and unprepared. Battles in which tens of thousands of men were killed and wounded became common. Conditions in soldiers' camps were often unclean and ridden with disease. The combination of these factors led to the sick and wounded often depending on the care and charitable contributions of individuals and volunteer organizations. The idea for the creation of the USSC came about the summer following the fall of Fort Sumter to Confederate forces and was endorsed by President Abraham Lincoln on June 13, 1861. Officially known in government records as the "Commission of Inquiry and Advice in respect of the Sanitary Interests of the United States," it quickly established headquarters in Washington, D.C., and eventually opened numerous branches throughout the North.

Several influential individuals lent their efforts to the Sanitary Commission during the Civil War. One of the most notable and well known was Frederick

Photograph of United States Sanitary Commission wagons leaving Washington for the front in the last days of the war. Formed by civilians in 1861, the USSC raised money for the Union war effort, provided clothing, blankets, food, and other supplies to the soldiers, created mobile hospitals and recovery centers, and sent nurses to volunteer in hospitals. Women formed the bulk of the USSC's volunteers. (Miller, Francis Trevelyan and Robert Sampson Lanier, *The Photographic History of the Civil War*, vol 7, 1911)

Law Olmsted, the landscape architect of New York City's Central Park. Acting as secretary general with his headquarters in the capital, Olmsted began recruiting volunteers and personally inspecting conditions in camps. His observations of the Union Army early in the war strengthened his belief that the government was unprepared and that the services of his organization would be greatly needed. Under the direction of the Sanitary Commission, volunteers gathered and stockpiled supplies in depots where Olmsted determined future battles would be fought. In its early stages, the Sanitary Commission overcame many challenges to become successful. One of the most significant difficulties was the opposition it faced from medical personnel in the Union Army. Olmsted remedied the situation by working closely with army medical staff and by impressing upon Sanitary Commission personnel the necessity for cordial and respectful relations. Although he would resign his position in 1864, his work reflected the efforts of the organization, energetic and efficient. His organizational abilities and herculean efforts allowed for the Sanitary Commission, with its numerous branches and wide range of activities, to be the force that it was in the Civil War.

The activities of the Sanitary Commission during the war were wide in scope. Near the fields of battle, volunteers and staff provided comfort and care to wounded soldiers. Cooperating with the Union Army, the Sanitary Commission converted steam ships and trains into mobile hospitals and created a mobile ambulance corps to better treat the wounded. In army camps, inspectors working for the Sanitary Commission offered advice to officers and enlisted men on everything from maintaining a clean water supply to cooking. On the home front, female volunteers collected money and donations of badly needed supplies, such as bandages and medicine. Sanitary Commission volunteers organized numerous fund-raisers including "sanitary fairs," dances, and auctions. The volunteers' efforts were successful; in California alone, the USSC raised more than $1.2 million by the end of the war. Another valuable service provided by the Sanitary Commission was helping soldiers transition from the battlefield to their homes. The Union Army often discharged wounded soldiers soon after treatment, although many were still incapable of caring for themselves, unable to finds the means to travel home, and unable to collect their pay. To address this problem, the Sanitary Commission created "lodges" where discharged soldiers could recover from their wounds. While there, volunteers would ensure that their discharge papers were fully processed, that they received their pay and, when fully recovered, that they were given a train ticket home. By the end of the war, the impact of the Sanitary Commission's activities greatly improved the lives of countless Union soldiers while also providing new opportunities to its volunteers.

Women were some of the most active and enthusiastic volunteers to serve in the Sanitary Commission during the Civil War, and they made up the majority of the tens of thousands of workers upon whom the organization depended. Women undertook many of the Sanitary Commission's activities, including sewing uniforms, collecting supplies, fund-raising, and most importantly, caring for wounded soldiers. It is in this role in which the women of the Sanitary Commission found the most opportunity, many working outside the home for the first time. Well trained and dedicated, the group's nurses so impressed the Union Army Surgeon General William Hammond that in 1862 he ordered all military hospitals to have staffs comprised of at least one-third female nurses. Within the Sanitary Commission and the Union Army, female nurses, such as Louisa May Alcott, performed admirably under much stress and difficult conditions. Despite the fact that the majority of nurses in the Civil War were actually male, it was the war that transformed nursing into a female-dominated profession, one of the many legacies created by the Sanitary Commission.

By war's end, the USSC had raised $25 million for its causes and had opened over 7,000 branches throughout the country. It was of immense benefit to the Union Army and its soldiers, countless numbers of whom depended upon the charity of the organization at one point or another during the war. The success of the Sanitary Commission is clear; in the Confederacy, where no such large-scale, well-organized group existed, the rate that soldiers died of wounds and disease was significantly higher than it was in the North. After aiding soldiers in transitioning out of the military and back to their homes, the group was disbanded in May 1866.

Justin Riskus

See also: *Arts*: Letter Writing; *Clothing, Fashion, and Appearance*: Personal Hygiene; Sewing Societies; Shortages, Clothing; *Economy and Work*: Urban Life, Northern; *Family Life and Gender Roles*: Womanhood, Northern; *Recreation and Social Customs*: Fairs and Bazaars; *Science and Technology*: Disease; Hospitals; Nursing; Transportation, Medical

FURTHER READING

Attie, Jeanie. *Patriotic Toil: Northern Women and the American Civil War*. Ithaca, NY: Cornell University Press, 1998.

Giesberg, Judith. *Army at Home: Women and the Civil War on the Northern Home Front*. Chapel Hill: University of North Carolina Press, 2009.

Giesberg, Judith Ann. *Civil War Sisterhood: The U.S. Sanitary Commission and Women's Politics in Transition*. Boston: Northeastern University Press, 2000.

Leonard, Elizabeth D. *Yankee Women: Gender Battles and the Civil War*. New York: W.W. Norton & Company, 1994.

Mugridge, Donald H. "The United States Sanitary Commission in Washington, 1861–1865." *Records of the Columbia Historical Society, Washington, D.C.* Vol. 60/62: 134–149.

Slavicek, Louise Chipley. *Women and the Civil War*. New York: Chelsea House Books, 2009.

Stevenson, Elizabeth. "Olmsted of F Street: The Beginnings of the United States Sanitary Commission." *Records of the Columbia Historical Society, Washington, D.C.* Vol. 49: 125–136.

Varhola, Michael J. *Everyday Life During the Civil War*. Cincinnati, OH: Writer's Digest Books, 1999.

WIDOWS, CONFEDERATE

The American Civil War created an unprecedented number of widows in the South, many of them young wives who had been married only a short amount of time before their husbands' deaths. Between 1861 and 1865, approximately three million men left for war; 750,000 men died. As a result, 200,000 white women throughout the nation became widows within four years. For many Confederate widows, as for many women in the South, the war was an extremely close and personal experience, as battles and armies brought death, destruction, and shortages into their states, their communities, and, for some, their backyards. Given all that they had sacrificed for the Confederacy, Confederate widows played an important role in supporting the war effort and memorializing it after the conflict.

When men left for war, the ways in which they could meet their demise were nearly innumerable—disease, prisons, bullets, even lightning strikes and bee stings took men slowly or suddenly. Before the war, a wife was expected to sit at her husband's deathbed, holding his hand, and ministering to him after a long, fulfilling life. This type of death, the Good Death, changed during the Civil War as men died often far from home and among strangers. As part of the grieving process, most wives wanted to know the circumstances and details surrounding their spouses' deaths. A well-written condolence letter allowed a widow to imagine herself next to her husband's deathbed if he died in a hospital, or at his side if he died on the field. Because Southern casualty reporting was inconsistent, however, a woman was often at the mercy of the men who fought alongside her husband to learn not only the details of his death, but even that the death had occurred.

Confederate widows' responses to the news of death were as diverse as the widows themselves. From shock to denial, depression to acceptance, wives came to terms with their new identities as widows in different ways. The amount of time this process took varied tremendously as well. Some women felt disoriented by the news, some were consumed by frantic grief, and others were resigned calmly to the designs of their Maker.

No matter the response, one thing was certain: the widow was expected to play a certain social role. The Civil War altered antebellum mourning rituals tremendously, impacting both clothing customs and condolence letters. One contributing factor to this change was that the war created widows in higher numbers than ever before in American history. Widowhood was more prevalent and more visible in towns, especially Southern towns, which had not one widow, but many. Unlike the antebellum period, during the Civil War so many women wore black that it often seemed that the entire South was cloaked in nighttime shadows.

The inability to purchase proper mourning garb plagued women of lower classes. Especially during the economic hardships of 1863–1865, mourning was a luxury that these women could not afford. Silk black dresses, heavy veils, and other features of antebellum mourning were expensive. With supply shortages and greater demands in the South, the materials became even more expensive and harder to find. Though they were priced out of respectable mourning rituals, lower-class women often did the best they could to mimic these customs, even if it meant dyeing the only clothes they owned in black ink.

The large number of young widows in their 20s and 30s also affected mourning rituals and expectations. While premature and sudden death certainly occurred in the antebellum period, the extent to which the Civil War killed young men astounded Southern communities. In addition, because these women were often newlyweds in their childbearing years, the war created an unprecedented number of widows who were pregnant or still nursing infants. In a time when the average woman gave birth to eight to ten children in her lifetime, it is not surprising that the Civil War created so many widows of this type.

Although the younger age of widows would change many aspects of their mourning experience, it did not impact every aspect of widowhood. Religious sentiments continued to dominate nearly every letter written to a Confederate widow. Like antebellum condolence letters, most correspondents genuinely attempted to comfort a widow with the notion of reunion in the hereafter.

The Civil War also gave Southern widows an entirely new task to complete: get their husbands' bodies home. The idea of a body resting far from home, or worse, in enemy soil, was unacceptable. The body was important because graves were sacred sites in the nineteenth century. Once a woman had a place to mourn her husband, her mourning could really begin.

Confederate nationalism demanded that war widows remember their late husbands both honorably and often. Etiquette required women to mourn for two and a half years. The pressure placed on widows to remember husbands stemmed from a fear that amid soaring death tolls, soldiers would be forgotten. Ideally, her devotion would not only continue, but also increase. Wartime condolence letters also urged widows to remain loyal to the cause that their husbands died defending, especially in the South.

Some widows tried to live up to the ideals their communities stressed. Soldiers often recorded stories and encounters that reinforced this image of the saintly and dedicated Southern widow. But for some widows, it was harder to achieve the ideal even if they chose to try. Grief plagued widows in different degrees and at different times. Some were younger than others and some had barely tasted marriage before it was over. Grief-stricken widows sometimes struggled with resignation to their situation. Some widows chose to flirt and remarry. Most people sanctioned remarriage after the respectable amount of time had passed, but at a time of war, a hasty remarriage suggested that the loss of the husband was unimportant. Southern society especially could not and would not accept the idea that all their sacrifices and bloodshed had been for nothing. Mourning and moving on should not be an easy, painless process and happy, hurried marriages suggested otherwise, and were discouraged.

In sum, the ideal Confederate widow wore black, mourned for a minimum of two and a half years, resigned herself to God's will, focused on her children, devoted herself to her husband's memory, and brought his body home for burial. These messages of ideal wartime widowhood, coming from condolence letters, husbands, literature, and newspapers, permeated all of American society. But in the end, it was up to the Confederate widow to interpret all of these messages, live up to her prescribed role, and navigate her way through mourning. The Civil War changed the prescription of widowhood, but widows often decided for themselves which elements of the role they would perform. As a lived experience, widowhood changed.

Angela Esco Elder

See also: *Clothing, Fashion, and Appearance*: Mourning Clothes; *Family Life and Gender Roles*: Courtship and Marriage; Motherhood; Widows, Union; Womanhood, Southern; Young Women; *Housing and Community*: Cemeteries; *Politics and Warfare*: Casualties; *Recreation and Social Customs*: Etiquette, Advice Manuals; *Religion and Belief*: Burial; Death; Mourning

FURTHER READING

Faust, Drew Gilpin. *This Republic of Suffering: Death and the American Civil War*. New York: Random House, 2008

Gross, Jennifer Lynn " 'And for the Widow and the Orphan': Confederate Widows, Poverty, and Public Assistance." In Lesley J. Gordon and John C. Inscoe, eds. *Inside the Confederate Nation: Essays in Honor of Emory M. Thomas*. Baton Rouge: Louisiana State University Press, 2005, pp. 209–229.

Hacker, J. David. "A Census-Based Count of the Civil War Dead." *Civil War History* 57:4 (2011): 306–347.

Kenzer, Robert. "The Uncertainty of Life: A Profile of Virginia's Civil War Widows." In Joan E. Cashin, ed. *The War Was You and Me: Civilians in the American Civil War*. Princeton, NJ: Princeton University Press, 2002, pp. 112–135.

Wood, Kirsten E. *Masterful Women: Slaveholding Widows from the American Revolution Through the Civil War*. Chapel Hill: University of North Carolina Press, 2004.

WIDOWS, UNION

Thousands of Civil War soldiers who died left behind wives and families. Estimates of Civil War dead have grown over the last several years, rising from approximately 618,000 to 750,000 men. The deaths of many of these soldiers resulted in the widowhood of thousands of women. Estimates place Union women widowed immediately by the war at around 100,000; that number increased as war wounds led to mortality in the postbellum era. Union widows had to learn to accept death, mourn, and move on. They became part of a large cohort of women left alone to raise children and support themselves.

In a pattern repeated in later conflicts, particularly in World War II, many couples married shortly before the groom had to join his regiment. Numerous Union brides were thus quite young and had only a short experience with marriage before they faced the potentially long years of widowhood. Many had experienced a few years of marriage and had some small children; others were pregnant when their husbands died. Regardless of the length of their marriage or whether or not they had produced children, widows had to rely on family, whatever small savings they may have had, and eventually the government for financial assistance.

Family connections were especially important for financial support of widows. During the nineteenth century, there were few jobs available to women. Some jobs existed only during wartime as women replaced men in clerical and government jobs. Many jobs available to women paid little. In addition, for many women of the middle- and upper classes, taking a job was something they could not do while maintaining their status and respect.

Before the Civil War, most women anticipated long

The Soldier's Memorial by Currier and Ives, 1863, shows a woman in mourning dress visiting the tomb of Civil War soldier. Widowhood shaped the lives of many Northern women; at the end of the Civil War approximately 100,000 Union women had been widowed. (Library of Congress)

lives with their husbands. In an ideal world, husbands would face death resolutely, confident in their faith and a marital reunion in the afterlife. These men would accept their fate after a well-lived life or an illness bravely faced. This way of dying a "Good Death" was desired by all. However, war did not always afford the possibility of a traditional Good Death. Indeed, most men who died in the course of war did so suddenly on the field, or with prolonged agony. Stories abound of men left to die on the front lines calling for wives and mothers, as reality sharply challenged the pre-battle self-images as entirely courageous and stoic soldiers until passing. Men groaned in hospitals, victims of infection, gangrene, and fever. Surrounded by chaos rather than family, men died in ways their wives found especially hard to conceptualize and accept.

Bridging this gap between battlefield death and home front widows were letters from fellow soldiers, superiors, and nurses, all who wrote to wives to inform them as to how their husbands had died. These letters brought women as close as they might get to their husbands' deathbeds as the writer recounted each man's final moments before he perished. A small consolation to grieving widows, the letters often assured them as best they might that husbands died Good Deaths, brave, calm, and faithful at the end. In other cases, the letters merely relayed the particulars of a man's death, so a wife did not wonder how her husband had passed. It is unknown if widows of black soldiers received the benefit of detailed death letters, as most surviving records are from their white counterparts.

Widows who could afford to do so purchased mourning attire—a full wardrobe in black or other suitably dark colors. The customary mourning period was two and a half years. Some women, however, remarried earlier, perhaps for love, perhaps out of financial necessity. As a result, the concept of the flirty widow was a popular one during the war.

Beginning in 1862, the federal government legislated pensions for Union veterans and dependents of soldiers who had either died in battle or as a result of the war. Confederate widows and orphans did not qualify for federal benefits. On average, the initial pension payment was $8 a month for dependents of privates. Civil War pensions totaled some $5 billion and widows comprised one in six of the recipients by the early 1880s. The government modified pension policy in the decades following the war, adding further payments for dependent children, changing the rate of pay, and permitting lump sum payments to those who had not filed when their husbands first died. Remarriage negated pension claims.

The initial challenge in getting a widow's pension was in proving that the husband's death was war-related. This detail was simple for husbands killed in action, but trickier for claims that later deaths were based on wartime injuries. After 1890, the government abolished the death-by-war requirement and allotted all Union widows, regardless of her husband's cause of death, $12 per month. Both prior to and after 1890, women had to prove they had been married to a soldier, which was not always an easy task because of sporadic records. The Pension Bureau certified claims agents to help dependents and soldiers navigate the system, file claims, and petition for redress if they were removed incorrectly from the rolls.

Claims agents were especially important for African American widows, who were granted rights to dependents' pensions in 1866. Many former slaves had fought and died for the Union, and their widows faced a difficult process made more challenging by poverty and the experience of slavery. Proving marriage was difficult, because slave marriages were not filed with local governments and the Pension Bureau's definition of marriage did not mesh with the forced practices of those who had been enslaved. Claims agents gathered witnesses and presented testimony to help clients who lacked paperwork. They also filled out the requisite forms for many previously enslaved widows and poor whites, as they were frequently illiterate and thus could not do so without help.

The last Union widow, Gertrude Janeway, died in 2003. A teenager when she married a veteran in his 80s in 1927, she collected her widow's pension until she died.

Jennifer Cote

See also: *Clothing, Fashion, and Appearance*: Mourning Clothes; *Family Life and Gender Roles*: Widows, Confederate; *Religion and Belief*: Death; Eulogies; Mourning

FURTHER READING

Brimmer, Brandi C. " 'Her Claim for Pension Is Lawful and Just': Representing Black Union Widows in Late-Nineteenth Century North Carolina." *Journal of the Civil War Era* 1:2 (June 2011): 207–236.

Elder, Angela Esco. "Civil War Widows." *The Essential Civil War Curriculum*. Virginia Center for Civil War Studies at Virginia Tech. http://www.essential.civilwar.vt.edu/assets/files/ECWC%20TOPIC%20Widows%20Essay.pdf. Accessed August 1, 2014.

Faust, Drew Gilpin. *This Republic of Suffering: Death and the American Civil War*. New York: Random House, 2008.

Hacker, J. David. "A Census-Based Count of the Civil War Dead." *Civil War History* 57:4 (December 2011): 307–348.

Holmes, Amy E. " 'Such Is the Price We Pay:' American Widows and the Civil War Pension System." In Maris A. Vinovskis, ed. *Towards a Social History of the American Civil War*. New York: Cambridge University Press, 1990.

WOMANHOOD, NORTHERN

From the start, the Civil War challenged American society's definition of womanhood in the North and in the South. For decades, historians marginalized Northern women preferring to focus on the trials and tribulations experienced by women in the war-torn South. A number of recent studies, however, have revealed Northern women as active participants in the conflict and in the changing social and economic structure of the North. Driven by necessity in the absence of men, women learned new skills and took on unfamiliar responsibilities in an effort to maintain stability at home. Although few women understood the revolutionary nature of their actions, their wartime activities defied a popular ideology, the "Cult of Domesticity," which relegated women to the home. Although women proved their competence as laborers, clerks, nurses, organizers, and even as soldiers, the end of the war threatened to confine women to purely domestic roles once more.

As men rallied to enlist following the attack on Fort Sumter, women united forming charitable societies and organizations with missions to supply soldiers with

Civil War portrait of Union nurse Clara Barton. The Civil War opened up new opportunities for women and many, like Barton, became nurses or government clerks. Others took factory jobs, made and collected supplies for soldiers, raised money for Union troops, and ran farms and family businesses. (Library of Congress)

uniforms and other necessities. These efforts launched what would become the United States Sanitary Commission (USSC). Although led primarily by men, women formed the backbone of the USSC. Women raised funds, collected supplies, nursed the sick and wounded, cooked meals, and performed other duties. Women employed by the federal government performed similar duties at distant battlefields, hospitals, or camps. A new class of working women emerged as vacant or newly created factory jobs became available. Similarly, in Washington, young women, eager to support the cause and to earn money, became clerks in understaffed government offices. Known as government girls, these women earned 50 percent less than their male counterparts. In 1865, the government recognized the value of all women and authorized the employment of African American women in general hospitals as cooks or nurses.

During the Civil War Clara Harlowe Barton (1821–1912), who would later found the American Red Cross, volunteered on battlefields and in hospitals organizing first aid efforts, delivering mail, and cooking for the soldiers. Former slave Harriet Tubman (1820–1913) not only risked personal safety by guiding runaway slaves on the Underground Railroad, but she also served the Union Army as spy. In 1865, Dr. Mary Edwards Walker (1832–1919), Union spy and army surgeon, became the first female Congressional Medal of Honor recipient. Others such as Sarah Emma Edmonds (1841–1898) enlisted in the army disguised as men. While serving with the Second Michigan Volunteers as Frank Thompson, Edmonds served as a soldier, a nurse, and a spy. After the war, her 1865 memoir sold thousands of copies. Barton,

Edmonds, and Walker represent the thousands of unidentified women who served as soldiers, spies, nurses, cooks, laundresses, clerks, and fund-raisers during the war.

At times, female relatives and children followed the armies marching south. Camp followers, although frowned on by the military, provided men with some of the comforts of home such as clean laundry and cooked food. Emerging modern military principles allowed for better control of camp followers through government employment. Young women seeking adventure, marriage prospects, or financial gain also followed soldiers. More difficult to control than soldiers' families, prostitutes spread venereal disease in the field and in occupied areas crippling armies. Although few women witnessed the war from the front lines, mothers, sisters, daughters, wives, and sweethearts constantly occupied soldiers' thoughts. Before battle, men entrusted each other with messages and mementos to deliver to loved ones at home in the event of their deaths. Countless letters and memoirs recount a dying soldier's last words calling for his mother, sister, or wife.

Many abolitionists viewed women's rights as synonymous with African American rights. Activists lobbied for an end to slavery and for universal equality. Harriet Elizabeth Beecher Stowe (1811–1896) captured the injustices of slavery in her novel *Uncle Tom's Cabin* (1852). Accused of intensifying the slavery debate, Stowe became one of the most well-known and controversial Northern women of the period. African American women in the North, including those born free and those transplanted from slaveholding states, aided in and often led the antislavery movement before and during the war. Slaves who escaped to the safety of the North knew the horrors of enslavement and often had relatives still in bondage. After 1863, African American women watched husbands, brothers, sons, and sweethearts march south with United States Colored Troops Regiments. Late in the war, the Freedmen's Bureau employed white and black women as teachers in newly established schools in the South. These women faced great opposition for aiding in the education of African Americans, an illegal practice in the antebellum South.

Although nineteenth-century mourning practices, lack of adequate medical care, and high rates of infant mortality made death intimate family affairs, the Civil War challenged traditional coping mechanisms. The changing nature of warfare and the sheer volume of deaths made identification and transport home of bodies difficult or nearly impossible in many cases. Unable to see and prepare bodies for burial, women struggled to accept deaths reported through letters and newspapers. Some denied what they believed to be false reports for months or years, remaining confident that a husband or son would return after the war. Others coped with their grief through mourning attire, one of the few mediums of expressing loss available. Popular women's magazines such as *Godey's Lady's Book* standardized mourning wardrobes and appropriate grieving periods based on a woman's relationship to the deceased. The war transformed mourning from intimate to communal as women experienced and expressed grief collectively through memorials, days of remembrance, or published works. After the death of her sweetheart Elizabeth Stuart Phelps (1844–1911) began writing *The Gates Ajar* to cope with her grief and to console other women experiencing loss. Women also experienced tremendous emotional pain and uncertainty when unprecedented numbers of men returned home horribly wounded or disabled.

Following the war, Northern women continued to devote their efforts to establishing order, to caring for those in need, and to rebuilding their lives.

Krista K. Castillo

See also: *Arts: Uncle Tom's Cabin* (1852); *Clothing, Fashion, and Appearance: Godey's Lady's Book*; Mourning Clothes; *Economy and Work*: Camp Followers; Factory Workers, Northern; Prostitutes; Rural Life, Northern; Urban Life, Northern; *Family Life and Gender Roles*: Aid Societies; United States Sanitary Commission (USSC); Widows, Union; Womanhood, Southern; Young Women; *Politics and Warfare*: Abolitionists; Female Combatants; Freedmen's Bureau; *Religion and Belief*: Mourning; *Science and Technology*: Nursing

FURTHER READING

Cutter, Barbara. *Domestic Devils, Battlefield Angels: The Radicalism of American Womanhood, 1830–1865*. DeKalb: Northern Illinois University Press, 2003.

Faust, Drew Gilpin. *This Republic of Suffering: Death and the American Civil War*. New York: Vintage Books, 2008.

Giesberg, Judith Ann. *The U.S. Sanitary Commission and Women's Politics in Transition*. Lebanon, NH: University Press of New England, 2006.

Quarles, Benjamin. *The Negro in the Civil War*. Boston: Da Capo Press, 1989.

Richard, Patricia L. *Busy Hands: Images of the Family in the Northern Civil War Effort*. New York: Fordham University Press, 2003.

WOMANHOOD, SOUTHERN

Southern womanhood was an ideological set of expectations and proscriptions devised largely by the Southern elite to guide women's and young girls' appropriate behavior, beliefs, and appearance. These guidelines also served as a way to reinforce gender roles and patriarchy, or men's position of power in society. At the same time, it gave women a particular and often revered role in their households and in Southern society at large.

Women in the South were expected to conform to a set of characteristics associated with the ideal woman. These guidelines originated in the nationwide early American ideal of Republican Motherhood. The ideal Southern woman demonstrated intelligence, charm, grace, and virtue. In addition, women were admired for their modesty, moral character, and industry and were often educated in subjects such as music, dancing, drawing, and foreign languages—frequently French. All of these characteristics were meant to prepare an elite white Southern woman to be the perfect helpmeet for her husband and the ideal moral instructor for her children, a principle often referred to as Republican Motherhood.

Southern women and girls often found guidelines and expectations for "true woman-

Photograph of two young women wearing printed dresses and necklaces in front of painted backdrop showing a plantation. Southern women, especially those of the planter class, were expected to be charming, intelligent, graceful, and pious. Their roles were designed to support those of the men in their family, although they had some control over the domestic sphere. (Library of Congress)

hood" in magazines, advice and etiquette manuals, and literature, including domestic fiction, a genre devoted to exploring and defining womanhood. Women looked to these print sources for images of the latest fashions, advice for finding a spouse and maintaining a household, and a plethora of other concerns deemed feminine.

Southern womanhood ideology defined who could and could not be considered womanly and feminine, and it depended on showing racial and class superiority. Like its Northern counterpart the ideal of Southern womanhood was difficult, if not impossible, to attain for most women, which was part of its appeal for elite women. Its guidelines helped to keep poor whites, immigrants, as well as free and enslaved African Americans from reaching true womanhood, allowing white, elite women to keep their privileged status.

Unlike Northern womanhood, Southern womanhood rested on the household work and field labor completed by enslaved people; thus, owning enslaved

African Americans proved to be an integral part of Southern womanhood. By the 1840s and especially in the 1850s, the standards of the Southern lady dictated that slaveholding women should treat their enslaved workers with benevolence and kindness. However, slaveholding women did not always comply with these expectations and sometimes exhibited violent behavior toward the enslaved people. In addition, unlike Northern women, Southern women did not frequently participate in large-scale, public reform movements of the 1840s and 1850s.

The Civil War challenged and altered Southern womanhood in very significant ways. It forced women to act in roles they often had no experience with or felt uncomfortable performing. As husbands, brothers, and sons left home to fight in the war, women had to conduct plantation business, protect themselves, and discipline slaves, among many other things. Women's behavior during the war often defied the norms of antebellum Southern womanhood because of necessity. They gained more public roles than they had before and they sometimes became the main breadwinner for their families. By the latter part of the war, these women often did so without material goods that helped them maintain their elite status. Food shortages, civil unrest, an overwhelming amount of death and loss, and severe economic instability plagued the South and forced women to rethink their role in the household and in public.

Several occupations challenged images of innocent, demure womanhood more than others. Nursing became a way for many women to serve the Confederacy, but it forced women to be in close, intimate contact with strange men, something that did not conform to traditional feminine values. Many young elite women flocked to cities—Richmond in particular—for government jobs that placed them in office spaces with strange male supervisors, which also challenged ideals of womanhood. Moral uprightness was a prerequisite for both of these jobs and some elite men and women still found these jobs unacceptable for young women.

Not all of women's activities undermined traditional Southern womanhood. In fact, some actually bolstered and reinforced existing expectations and only expanded women's roles slightly. Fund-raising efforts such as tableaux as well as sewing battle flags, officers' sashes, bandages, and other goods provided women with a feminine endeavor that allowed them to maintain their status as ladies.

Following the Civil War, women and men tried to make sense of their new world that did not include slavery. Many elite Southern women had to complete household chores that enslaved people had done for them before the war. A great number of women lost husbands, brothers, and children in the war and had to process the overwhelming amount of death that surrounded them. In addition, the death of a significant portion of young and middle-aged men created a male void in Southern society, leading to a forced change in gender ideology. This void also created an unusual number of unmarried women of marriageable age. Additionally, the war left many women as widows, which forced them to piece their lives back together without male guidance or oversight from a husband.

These significant demographic and cultural changes also spawned a new type of Southern womanhood. This new womanhood combined antebellum femininity with a new value for self-reliance, self-sacrifice, and resilience, in part because many families faced economic hardship following the war. Women also gained a more public role by memorializing Confederate soldiers and the dead by decorating graves, organizing memorial parades and celebrations, and eventually founding Ladies' Memorial Associations across the South.

See also: Arts: Diary Writing; Letter Writing; Literature, Northern; Literature, Southern; *Macaria; or, Altars of Sacrifice* (1864); Serial Novels; *Clothing, Fashion, and Appearance*: Sewing Societies; *Economy and Work*: Government Girls; Plantations; Rural Life, Southern; Slaveholders; Treasury Girls; Urban Life, Southern; *Family Life and Gender Roles*: Aid Societies; Courtship and Marriage; Cult of Domesticity; Divorce; Honor; Manhood, Southern; Motherhood; Patriarchy; Widows, Confederate; Womanhood, Northern; Woman Order (General Order 28); Young Women; *Food and Drink*: Food Riots; *Housing and Community*: Nationalism, Confederate; Refugees; *Politics and Warfare*: Rape and Sexual Assault; *Recreation and Social Customs*: Dances and Balls; Etiquette, Advice Manuals; Fairs and Bazaars; Hospitality; Leisure Time; *Religion and Belief*: Mourning; *Science and Technology*: Education, Southern; Nursing

Katherine Brackett Fialka

FURTHER READING

Farnham, Christie. *The Education of the Southern Belle: Higher Education and Student Socialization in the Antebellum South*. New York: New York University Press, 1994.

Faust, Drew Gilpin. *Mothers of Invention: Women of the Slaveholding South in the American Civil War*. Chapel Hill: University of North Carolina Press, 1996.

Fox-Genovese, Elizabeth. *Within the Plantation Household: Black and White Women of the Old South*. Chapel Hill: University of North Carolina Press, 1988.

Frank, Lisa Tendrich. " 'Between Death and Dishonor': Defending Confederate Womanhood During Sherman's March." In Lisa Tendrich Frank and Daniel Kilbride, eds. *Southern Character: Essays in Honor of Bertram Wyatt-Brown*. Gainesville: University Press of Florida, 2011, pp. 116–127.

Ott, Victoria. *Confederate Daughters: Coming of Age During the Civil War*. Carbondale: Southern Illinois University Press, 2008.

WOMAN ORDER (GENERAL ORDER 28)

Union military authorities issued General Order 28, commonly referred to as the "Woman Order," in May 1862 during the occupation of New Orleans. When white Southern female residents insulted and harassed his troops, Major General Benjamin F. Butler proclaimed that women who continued to behave in such a manner would be treated as prostitutes. The order caused much controversy and marked the beginning of stricter Union occupation policies across the South.

New Orleans was the largest and most diverse city in the Confederacy. Although slaveholding, upper-class Confederates dominated the city government in the first year of the war, the bulk of the population consisted of immigrants, African Americans, and poor whites, most of whom were less enthusiastic about slavery and secession than the elites. When a combined Union naval and ground force moved to capture the crucial port city in April 1862, a local female noted that Confederate women seemed to be the only residents who were not afraid. Although several prominent ladies presented the city council with a petition urging that New Orleans not surrender, Union forces quickly captured the weakly defended city. Butler and 2,500 troops took control on May 1.

Image from July 12, 1862, issue of *Harper's Weekly* portraying New Orleans women both before and after Butler's General Order 28, often referred to as the "Woman Order." Designed to control New Orleans' hostile female population, the Woman Order stated that any women who treated Union soldiers rudely would be treated as prostitutes. The order provoked outrage from men and women throughout the Confederacy. (Library of Congress)

Union invasions of Southern territory such as New Orleans marked a turning point for local women. As enemy troops took control, women had to face the invaders alone, for their able-bodied male relatives had mostly fled when the city fell. Although some Confederate women felt betrayed by this desertion, they also determined to resist the invaders as best they could. Across Louisiana and the Confederacy, Confederate women insulted, snubbed, and refused to cooperate with the Federals.

In New Orleans, the women's struggle was also fueled by class resentment. Butler—a prewar lawyer and politician who had built a reputation as a campaigner for workers' rights—cultivated goodwill among the lower classes by giving away free food and hiring locals for public works projects. As a result, the wealthier residents were left to resist the occupation on their own. The upper-class women of New Orleans, feeling abandoned on all sides and released from the restraint expected of their sex and station, launched a campaign of intimidation as soon as the Federals marched in.

Much of the women's behavior—such as moving to avoid having to walk past Union soldiers on the street or flamboyantly turning their backs on them—was merely insulting, but some of it was abusive and humiliating. Women cursed the Northerners, dumped chamber pots and slop buckets on their heads from windows above, and threw garbage at them as they passed. On May 15, a colonel reported to Butler that a "very well-dressed and respectable-looking" woman had spit in his face as they passed each other on the sidewalk, and the general decided that he had to stop the provoking behavior before his men struck back. That day he issued General Order No. 28:

> As the officers and soldiers of the United States have been subject to repeated insults by the women (calling themselves ladies) of New Orleans, in return for the most scrupulous non-interference and courtesy on our part, it is ordered that hereafter when any female shall by word, gesture, or movement insult or show contempt for any officer or soldier of the United States she shall be regarded and held liable to be treated as a woman of the town plying her avocation.

Butler later explained that the directive was intended for his own men as well as for the women. The troops were supposed to ignore the insults just as they would the advances of prostitutes; the women, meanwhile, were threatened with imprisonment should they continue their harassment.

This subtlety was lost on many people, however. The "Woman Order" quickly became a lightning rod for controversy. Confederates interpreted it as a license from Butler to his soldiers to rape women. The general gained the nickname "Beast Butler," and the Confederate government and private citizens placed bounties on his head. In the North, reaction was also initially negative, but when it became apparent that no soldiers were actually brutalizing women, this changed to widespread support for Butler and his administration.

The Woman Order had an immediate effect in New Orleans. Although Confederate women were shocked and insulted by what it implied, they toned down their words and actions. Butler's troops arrested very few white women and did not rape any. In addition, the general placed several prominent Confederate families under protection. Meanwhile, his policies as military governor improved city sanitation and provided for the poor. In December 1862, however, President Abraham Lincoln removed Butler from command of the Department of the Gulf. The British and French governments had criticized the Woman Order and Butler's heavy-handed treatment of European officials in New Orleans, and Lincoln fired the general to keep them from entering the war on the Confederate side. Butler's replacement, General Nathaniel P. Banks, adopted a much more lenient style of rule. Consequently, rebellious behavior by Confederate sympathizers in New Orleans quickly resumed and became more overt than it had been previously.

The Woman Order had a wide-ranging legacy. Butler's decision to clamp down on female dissent demonstrated that Union forces needed the cooperation of Southern women to control occupied territory. The order also helped to begin a new, more forceful era in Union military rule. Confederates and their supporters celebrated the women of New Orleans as heroines. At the same time, they vilified "Beast" Butler, and his reputation has never fully recovered from the Woman Order controversy.

William D. Hickox

See also: *Economy and Work*: Prostitutes; *Family Life and Gender Roles*: Cult of Domesticity; Womanhood, Southern

FURTHER READING

Ash, Stephen V. *When the Yankees Came: Conflict and Chaos in the Occupied South, 1861–1865*. Chapel Hill: University of North Carolina Press, 1995.

Butler, Benjamin F. *Private and Official Correspondence of Gen. Benjamin F. Butler During the Period of the Civil War*. Edited by Jesse Ames Marshall. 5 vols. Norwood, MA: Plimpton Press, 1917.

Faust, Drew Gilpin. *Mothers of Invention: Women of the Slaveholding South in the American Civil War*. Chapel Hill: University of North Carolina Press, 2004.

Grimsley, Mark. *The Hard Hand of War: Union Military Policy Toward Southern Civilians, 1861–1865*. New York: Cambridge University Press, 1995.

Long, Alecia P. "(Mis)Remembering General Order No. 28: Benjamin Butler, the Woman Order, and Historical Memory." In Lee Ann Whites and Alecia P. Long, eds. *Occupied*

Women: Gender, Military Occupation, and the American Civil War. Baton Rouge: Louisiana State University Press, 2009, pp. 17–32.

Morgan, Sarah. *The Civil War Diary of Sarah Morgan.* Edited by Charles East. Athens: University of Georgia Press, 1991.

YOUNG MEN

Young men's transition from youth to manhood played a central role in the national imagination during the Civil War. In the North, images of young men heading off to the front to "see the elephant" saturated popular publications and educational materials. More than just a colorful euphemism for enlistment, "seeing the elephant" also signaled achieving manhood through battle. And though the average enlistment age for the Union and Confederate armies was between 25 and 26, more than 20 percent of Civil War soldiers were men under 18.

In the North, young men's enlistment meant that many schools had to replace their male teachers with educated women, who entered the classroom in record numbers. Though boys under 16 could enlist with parental permission, they rarely reached the front lines. Instead, these boys were often assigned to "domestic" duties such as carrying water, cutting hair, assisting in the kitchen, ferrying mail, or transporting supplies. If they made it to the front, young men served as surgeons' assistants or musicians. Musicians played an essential role in lifting morale, communicating orders in battle, and setting the tempo for the march; these young men were also romanticized as national mascots in popular media.

Arriving at the Union camps, young men entered a realm dominated by racial, religious, and class-based conflicts about what it meant to be a man. For those who came of age during the religious tent-revivals of the mid-nineteenth-century, manliness was displayed through service to God and country. For those born into wealthier families, it was tied to gentility, a complex notion involving social decorum, cleanliness, dress, moral fiber, and emotional restraint. In the period surrounding the Civil War, it was believed that wealth and comfort had made upper-class men soft, and enlistment provided young men of this background an opportunity to harden themselves in battle as their social status allowed them to secure positions of authority.

For young Union soldiers of all upbringings, camp was a place where one's manliness was marked by cleanliness, physical prowess, alcohol consumption, and gambling. Cleaning habits communicated discipline and moral refinement, and many units had a mandatory once- or twice-a-week bathing requirement that would have been unusual for rural youth for whom bathing meant washing one's face and arms in public basins. Manliness was also measured by one's physical build, and muscular tone demonstrated manly vigor while bulk was seen as brutish or vulgar.

Soldiers showed off their physical prowess in games like "slack sheet," in which a naked man stood on a sheet while two soldiers tried to pull him off his feet while onlookers jeered and made bets. Drinking and gambling were morally and religiously divisive during this period, and these activities would have been acceptable for rural and working-class men, but they were thought unbecoming of refined, upper-class men. In the rare incident that a dispute about one's manliness got out of hand, soldiers occasionally dueled to defend their honor.

Though many aspects of manly honor were tied to social status, they were also affected by race and country of origin. For young African American men, enlisting in the Union Army provided a paradoxical opportunity to serve their country even as they endured the many inequalities of military life. African American soldiers were often placed in noncombat roles to free white soldiers for battle. When African American units did see battle, they were deployed in dangerous positions that resulted in proportionately higher casualty rates. African American losses were amplified by the Confederate policy of killing or enslaving African American soldiers rather than taking them prisoner. However, the war afforded young African American men an opportunity to improve their education, as the officers of their regiments were usually college graduates and schoolteachers.

Like their African American counterparts, many young immigrant men initially viewed the Civil War as a chance to gain financial security and a foothold in public life. Though foreign-born soldiers made up 20 to 25 percent of the Union Army, their enlistment dwindled steadily as the war wore on. Young immigrant men often found the stark inequalities of civilian life mirrored in the camps. And, like their African American counterparts, immigrant units were assigned to deployments that resulted in disproportionately higher casualty rates than those of their white peers born in the United States.

Definitions of white manhood in the South were heavily influenced by anxieties concerning African American manhood, which would linger long after the war was over. Young men from plantation-owning families were likely to witness the violent management and exploitation of the enslaved firsthand, and their manliness would have been measured by their emulation of this practice. There was no specified enlistment age for the Confederate Army, and many young white men occupied positions similar to those in the North, though some would also have fought in guerrilla units with looser formations and less disciplinary oversight.

The disruption of the war afforded many of the enslaved an opportunity to escape to freedom in the North, and many young men underwent this journey only to enlist and head South again with the Union Army. Though the Confederate Army struggled to incorporate the enslaved into military ranks, the Confederacy saw enlistment of Mexican, German, Irish, and Polish immigrants. For those young, white Southern men who stayed home, it fell to them to manage farms and plantations amid this atmosphere of uncertainty. And, though many Southerners assumed that Union soldiers would spare female civilians and children, many young men were overtaken by Union troops who sacked and burned their homes and plantations, or converted them into military outposts and hospitals.

For young men on all sides of the conflict, the Civil War marked a significant shift in the ways Americans understood manliness, especially with regard to race, class, and social status. The war brought many of these young men into contact with social customs they would not have encountered otherwise, and it birthed divisions in racial, national, and social notions of manliness that would continue to echo into the next century.

Daniel Lanza

See also: *Arts*: Music, Military; *Clothing, Fashion, and Appearance*: Men's Dress, Confederate Civilian; Men's Dress, Union Civilian; Personal Hygiene; Uniforms, Confederate; Uniforms, Union; *Economy and Work*: Factory Workers, Northern; Factory Workers, Southern; Rural Life, Northern; Rural Life, Southern; Urban Life, Northern; Urban Life, Southern; *Family Life and Gender Roles*: Childhood and Adolescence, Northern; Childhood and Adolescence, Southern; Free Blacks; Honor; Immigrants; Manhood, Northern; Manhood, Southern; Womanhood, Northern; Womanhood, Southern; Young Women; *Food and Drink*: Moonshine; Spirits; Tobacco; *Politics and Warfare*: Camp Life; Enlistment; *Recreation and Social Customs*: Gambling; *Religion and Belief*: Religious Revivals; *Science and Technology*: Education, Northern; Education, Southern

FURTHER READING

Foote, Lorien. *The Gentlemen and the Roughs: Manhood, Honor, and Violence in the Union Army*. New York: New York University Press, 2010.

Kantrowitz, Stephen. "Fighting Like Men: Civil War Dilemmas of Abolitionist Manhood." In Catherine Clinton and Nina Silber, eds. *Battle Scars: Gender and Sexuality in the American Civil War*. New York: Oxford University Press, 2006, pp. 19–40.

Kimmel, Michael S. *Manhood in America: A Cultural History*. New York: Free Press, 1996.

Marten, James Alan. *Children for the Union: The War Spirit on the Northern Home Front*. Chicago: Ivan R. Dee, 2004.

Tendrich Frank, Lisa. "Bedrooms as Battlefields: The Role of Gender Politics in Sherman's March." In LeeAnn Whites and Alecia P. Long, eds. *Occupied Women: Gender, Military Occupation, and the American Civil War*. Baton Rouge: Louisiana State University Press, 2009, pp. 33–48.

Volo, Dorothy Denneen, and James M. Volo. *Daily Life in Civil War America*. Westport, CT: Greenwood, 1998.

YOUNG WOMEN

Young women of all backgrounds and classes faced difficulties during the Civil War. The transition to womanhood in the nineteenth century was marked by finishing school for young white women whose families could afford it or working outside the home for girls from poorer backgrounds. Young enslaved women began working long hours in the field or plantation. Marriage completed the passage to adulthood. War disrupted all of these activities during a crucial period in young women's lives.

Although the war took place mainly in the South, it profoundly affected the lives of all young women, including those in the North. Many experienced intense bouts of patriotism like that of Fanny Pierce, who insisted that if she were a man, she would find a gun and join the Union Army. Although Pierce never enlisted, some young women did. Others encouraged men to enlist by refusing to be courted by men who remained at home. Middle- and upper-class white young women contributed to the war through work in soldiers' aid societies by knitting garments, assembling boxes of supplies, and making homemade goods to sell in fund-raising fairs. Others became nurses, taught schools for freed slaves, or worked for the federal government. The majority of young women lived on farms, and their workload increased when men went off to fight. Poorer young women helped their families by beginning jobs in factories and mills or as domestic servants.

In the North, young African American women had fewer job opportunities than did their white counterparts. In addition, the pay that their soldier relatives received was less than that of white soldiers. Some young women participated in societies to aid African American soldiers and freedpeople. Others became involved in public campaigns for freedom and equality. For example, Charlotte Brown, a young African American woman from San Francisco, protested laws common in the North that prohibited blacks from riding streetcars.

The increasing visibility of young women of all classes worried many politicians and officials who feared that disruptions to women's home life might cause them to become sexually promiscuous or turn to prostitution. Officials established temporary housing and placed young women in jobs to keep them off the streets. Even so, some Northern young women still managed to experience new freedoms during the war.

Many young women in the South experienced the conflict firsthand. For white elites, defeat of the Confederacy threatened their family's wealth and position in society. Thus, many wealthy white young women wholeheartedly served the cause in soldier's aid societies. They made uniforms, knit socks, rolled bandages, and hosted performances to raise money for the war. The South's young women also displayed their patriotism by wearing the Confederate battle flag on their clothes, singing rebel songs, and wearing homespun. Some disguised themselves as men to enlist as soldiers, while others served as spies for the Confederate Army.

The war brought further changes to Southern young women's lives when some parents sent their daughters to boarding schools or to live with relatives away from the conflict. As supplies grew scarce and Confederate currency lost value, some young women took jobs as teachers, governesses, or treasury girls. When slaves left plantations, elite young women also helped with the housekeeping and cooking. Despite these circumstances, many young women clung to the ideals of their privileged social positions, hoping to marry wealthy men and live leisurely after the war.

Less wealthy white young women faced many wartime difficulties. The daughters of small farmers struggled to cope with high prices, scarce supplies, and the loss of male relatives to the army. Confederate soldiers and officials took their horses, mules, livestock, and supplies to feed soldiers. As the Union Army occupied more areas of the Confederacy, soldiers took what little was left of food and other supplies. Harriet McGee, a 15-year-old young woman from Virginia, watched as Union soldiers took all her family's clothes, linens, and curtains to use in an army hospital. Armies destroyed the houses, farms, and cities of those without the money to flee to safer areas, leaving many poor young women and their families wandering the countryside penniless and starving. Although local and state officials attempted to distribute aid to the needy, by the end of the war there was little these governments could do to ease citizens' suffering.

War increased the workload of enslaved young women. Making homespun cloth, growing food, and caring for farm animals was vital to the Confederate war effort. When wartime shortages plagued the Confederacy, slaves' clothing and food allowances became even smaller. Some owners, desperate to keep their slaves, forcibly separated enslaved youngsters from their families and took them to Arkansas or Texas. In spite of these hardships, young enslaved women undermined their master's control by working slowly or refusing to work. Although most remained on the plantation, some ran away to the Union Army. The crowded contraband camps established for escaped slaves by Northern troops often lacked food, shelter, and other necessities. Although some soldiers treated the young freedwomen decently, others stole their belongings and some physically or sexually assaulted them. Although they faced some of the worst conditions during the conflict, the war changed young enslaved women's lives dramatically. Through a series of national laws, they gained their freedom and some basic human rights, such as the freedom to marry.

The war had some common effects on all young women. Over 600,000 soldiers and 50,000 civilians died, so most young women experienced some form of loss. Conflict raged within families and communities as the war divided relatives and neighbors between Confederates and Unionists. It painfully separated many young women from their beaux or fiancés, and young people resorted to letter writing to continue their relationships. War increased religious fervor among many young women, who observed national days of fast and prayer, entreating God to keep their relatives safe and petitioning for success on the battlefield or for a peaceful end to the conflict. The end of the war brought many emotions to the forefront. Elite slaveholding young women mourned the passing of plantation life, while young freedwomen responded with exuberant celebration or merely by leaving their former houses of bondage.

Laura Mammina

See also: Clothing, Fashion, and Appearance: Homespun; Sewing Societies; *Economy and Work*: Camp Followers; Government Girls; Impressment; Prostitutes; Rural Life, Northern; Rural Life, Southern; Slavery; Treasury Girls; *Family Life and Gender Roles*: Aid Societies; Childhood and Adolescence, Northern; Childhood and Adolescence, Southern; Courtship and Marriage; Slave Families; United States Sanitary Commission (USSC); Urban Life, Northern; Urban Life, Southern; *Housing and Community*: Refugees; *Politics and Warfare*: Espionage; *Recreation and Social Customs*: Fairs and Bazaars; Sanitary Fairs; *Religion and Belief*: Death; *Science and Technology*: Disease; Education, Northern; Education, Southern; Nursing

FURTHER READING

Attie, Jeanie. *Patriotic Toil: Northern Women and the American Civil War*. Ithaca, NY: Cornell University Press, 1998.

Clinton, Catherine, and Nina Silber, eds. *Battle Scars: Gender and Sexuality in the American Civil War*. New York: Oxford University Press, 2006.

Edwards, Laura F. *Scarlett Doesn't Live Here Anymore: Southern Women in the Civil War Era*. Urbana: University of Illinois Press, 2004.

Frank, Lisa Tendrich. "Children of the March: Confederate Girls and Sherman's Homefront Campaign." In James Marten, ed. *Children and Youth During the Civil War Era*. New York: New York University Press, 2012, pp. 110–124.

Giesberg, Judith. *Army at Home: Women and the Civil War on the Northern Home Front*. Chapel Hill: University of North Carolina Press, 2009.

Jabour, Anya. *Scarlett's Sisters: Young Women in the Old South*. Chapel Hill: University of North Carolina Press, 2007.

Ott, Victoria. *Confederate Daughters: Coming of Age During the Civil War*. Carbondale: University of Southern Illinois Press, 2008.

Schwartz, Marie Jenkins. *Born in Bondage: Growing Up Enslaved in the Antebellum South*. Cambridge, MA: Harvard University Press, 2000.

Silber, Nina. *Daughters of the Union: Northern Women Fight the Civil War*. Cambridge, MA: Harvard University Press, 2005.

Whites, LeeAnn, and Alecia P. Long, eds. *Occupied Women: Gender, Military Occupation, and the American Civil War*. Baton Rouge: Louisiana State University Press, 2009.

FOOD AND DRINK

INTRODUCTION

Nineteenth-century Americans had to reshape their expectations about food during the Civil War. Popular food items became scarce during the war as did methods to prepare and preserve food. For example, salt and flour were difficult to find during wartime.

As they had in the antebellum years, different groups of people had different food habits. People in the North and the South depended on different local staples for their diets. Native Americans ate food that was specific to their region and culture as well. Similarly, African Americans ate foods that were sometimes reminiscent of traditional African meals. During the war and in the antebellum years Americans in the North and South used gardening, hunting, and fishing to supplement their meals.

Despite the upheavals of wartime, mealtime etiquette was still observed by many people, North and South. These rules of the table helped keep in place the hierarchy of the family and allowed some semblance of order. In addition, families still tried to serve normal meals, finding substitutes for meats, coffee, flour, sugar, and other antebellum staples. The gardens that some kept outside helped provide wartime Southerners and Northerners with food for their tables when wartime inflation on food got out of control.

Cookbooks and recipes changed during the war years to reflect shortages and the desire for foods that had been common in peacetime. As a result, many wartime cookbooks, newspapers, and magazines contained recipes for coffee substitutes as well as for breads made without flour or other staples that became scarce during the war. Salt, too, was in short supply during the war, so Confederates had to find other ways to preserve food.

Food and drink often united people. Families gathered around the table to eat together. Taverns also brought people together, although these places were primarily the domain of men. Moonshine, spirits, and other alcoholic beverages were enjoyed in taverns and homes.

Severe wartime shortages led to food riots in several Southern cities in 1863. The most famous bread riot occurred in Richmond, Virginia, in April 1863. A group of working women marched to the Virginia Capitol to talk to the governor about their need for help; when he would not talk to them, they took to the streets to demand food to feed their families. In the process, many smashed the windows of government warehouses, grocery stores, and mercantile stores, taking bread and other foodstuffs.

During the Civil War, troops on the move foraged for food to supplement their rations. Soldiers often had to prepare their own food and eat whatever rations were issued. Most soldiers were issued hardtack and had to find ways to make it palatable.

COFFEE

Coffee consumption was reduced during the Civil War as the Union government levied a 4-cent duty on imported beans and blockaded Southern ports, preventing the Confederacy from receiving any coffee. Until the war, coffee production had actually dwindled, undercut by years of low prices, as consumer demand slowly grew. With the huge price hikes caused by the war, producers redoubled their efforts. For example, in 1861, Brazilian coffee increased to 14 cents a pound then rose to 23 cents as the war continued, then finally 42 cents before reverting back to 18 cents when the war ended. Since the U.S. Army was a major purchaser of such coffee, each Union victory propelled trade and increased prices. By 1864, the Union was purchasing over 40 million pounds of green coffee beans.

The Civil War gave soldiers a permanent taste for coffee, usually taken black. Union troops had coffee; Confederate soldiers had to make do with substitutes at best. Each Union soldier's daily allotment included one-tenth of a pound of green coffee beans that amounted to about 36 pounds per capita. Coffee was a traditional food beverage for generations of drinkers but in the nineteenth century, it was not a beverage that was consumed regularly by the poorer segments of American society. However that changed when the Civil War began and coffee drinking suddenly became a new and pleasurable experience for soldiers from all backgrounds. Both armies lacked decent cooks so food served to the troops tended to be bland and boring, mainly some form of bread, with coffee to wash it down. One result of this type of meal was that soldiers quickly grew to love their coffee; it was usually available to every Billy Yank (Union) and Johnny Reb (Confederate), as the common foot soldiers were called.

Because ground coffee could go stale quickly, soldiers preferred to carry whole beans and grind them as necessary. Each company cook carried a portable grinder while a few Sharps carbines were designed to hold a coffee mill in the buttstock of the gun, so that the soldier could always carry his grinder with him. Another method was to store ground coffee, mixed together with a soldier's sugar ration, in a small cloth pouch carefully secured in a haversack.

The value of coffee to the average soldier was mentioned frequently in soldiers' letters home and other types of correspondence of the Civil War. In his 1888 memoir of military service, *Hardtack and Coffee*, Union Army soldier John Billings, a veteran of the 10th Massachusetts Volunteer Artillery, considered coffee a "Godsend" to invigorate him.

Another coffee vendor had a different type of tribute. According to Robert Porter, Sergeant William McKinley, then Commissary Sergeant and member of Company E, Twenty-Third Ohio Volunteer Infantry Regiment and later U.S. president, was present during the battle of Antietam, near Sharpsburg, Maryland, on September 17, 1862, in the rear of the front lines with the unit wagon train and supplies. As the men of the regiment rushed into battle before dawn, McKinley pulled together a work detail, commandeered a couple of mule-drawn wagons, one of which was reportedly a mobile field kitchen, and transported hot coffee into the battlefront. In 1903, a monument to William McKinley and his front-line coffee service was dedicated on the Antietam Battlefield, with an inscription that notes that McKinley "personally and without orders served hot coffee and warm food to every man in the Regiment, on this spot, and in doing so had to pass under fire." Another part of the same monument shows McKinley, hot cup of coffee in hand, with shells bursting all around him.

On the home front, the situation was much different. Union soldiers' families did not have as much access to coffee, mostly from lack of supply, as did their men on the battlefield. However, the shortage of coffee was even more severe in the Confederate States where the U.S. Navy's blockade of the Southern ports stopped supplies such as coffee from ever reaching the intended consumers. Another factor contributing to the coffee shortage in the South was the lack of money. The depreciation of Confederate currency was well underway by the second year of the war, with increasingly worthless paper money as legal tender. Out of necessity, the poverty-stricken, undernourished Confederate civilians and soldiers had to drink coffee substitutes such as dandelion roots, sugar cane, parched rice, cotton seed, sweet potatoes, wheat, beans, corn, rye, okra, peanuts, acorns, and chicory. In the war-torn South, real coffee was so scarce that it cost $5 a pound in Richmond, Virginia, and one Atlanta jeweler used coffee beans instead of diamonds in breast pins. Even in New England, where coffee drinkers had better access to the beverage, it was costly as well, so many substitutes found a market in the North, often with endorsements from well-known people.

When the war ended and the soldiers returned home, they brought with them the custom of drinking coffee and the practice of sharing it. The tradition continues

SOUTHERN COFFEE RECIPES

Because coffee was an import, the federal blockade of Confederate ports caused a severe coffee bean shortage in the South as the war progressed. Southern soldiers and civilians had to use their ingenuity to devise drinkable coffee substitutes from a wide variety of other commodities, such as peas, burnt corn, peanuts, potatoes, chicory, and even acorns. Writing in the November 5, 1861, issue of the *Natchez Daily Courier,* Doctor A. Poitevan described the following recipe for a substitute coffee:

> If, therefore, the blockade should continue, and the importation of coffee is rendered impracticable, it would be very natural that the use of acorn coffee, mixed with the genuine should become universal. The poor would find it equally a source of economy and a valuable remedy; and soldiers in camp would be less exposed to diarrhea, one of the most terrible evils that can exist in an army. In order to prepare this coffee, the acorns must first be roasted in an oven. The hard outer shell is removed, and the kernel is preserved, which, after being roasted, is ground with ordinary coffee.

> On November 7, 1861, an Atlanta newspaper, the *Southern Confederacy,* offered another alternative coffee recipe: "Take sweet potatoes and after peeling them, cut them up into small pieces about the size of the joint of your little finger, dry them either in the sun or by the fire, (sun dried is probably best) and then parch and grind the same as if coffee. Take two thirds of this to one third of coffee to a making. Try it, not particularly for its economy but for its superiority over any coffee you ever tasted."

although memory of how America's coffee drinking habit traces its origin to the American Civil War has faded from public memory.

Martin J. Manning

See also: Food and Drink: Hardtack; Substitutes, Food and Drink; Tea

FURTHER READING

Banks, Mary, Christine McFadden, and Catherine Atkinson. *The World Encyclopedia of Coffee: The Definitive Guide to Coffee, from Simple Bean to Irresistible Beverage.* London: Lorenz, 2005.--

Billings, John D. *Hardtack and Coffee, or, The Unwritten Story of Army Life.* Lincoln: University of Nebraska Press, 1993 (1887).

Jacob, Heinrich E. *Coffee: The Epic of a Commodity.* Short Hills, NJ: Burford Books, 1998.

Lynch, Fredric C. "Civil War Soldiers Made Coffee America's Drink." Unpublished paper prepared for the Sons of Union Veterans of the Civil War. http://www.landrethseeds .com/newsletters/Volume%205/Issue%207%20-%20Part%20VII%20The%20 Period:%201860–1870/Article-Coffee%20is%20America's%20Brew-Landreth%20 10–10.pdf. Accessed August 1, 2014.

Pendergrast, Mark. *Uncommon Grounds: The History of Coffee and How It Transformed Our World.* Rev. ed. New York: Basic Books, 2010.

Porter, Robert P. *Life of William McKinley, Soldier, Lawyer, Statesman.* Cleveland: The N.G. Hamilton Publishing Co., 1896.

Tucker, Catherine M. *Coffee Culture: Local Experiences, Global Connections.* New York: Routledge, 2011.

Ukers, William H. *All About Coffee.* Avon, MA: Adams Media, 2012 (1922).

Weinberg, Bennett Alan, and Bonnie K. Bealer. *The World of Caffeine: The Science and Culture of the World's Most Popular Drug.* New York: Routledge, 2001.

Wild, Antony. *Coffee: A Dark History.* New York: W.W. Norton, 2005.

Wiley, Bell I. *The Life of Billy Yank: The Common Soldier of the Union.* Updated ed. Baton Rouge: Louisiana State University Press, 2008.

COOKBOOKS AND RECIPES

During the Civil War, food supplies were limited for everyone in the South, and many of the foods available were of poor quality. The North's blockade on Southern ports, in effect for most of the war, limited the South's ability to import food. Additionally, even though the South was a largely agricultural region, its railroad networks were underdeveloped, and the inhabitants were unable to transport foodstuffs to locations in need. To make matters worse, Northern troops quickly destroyed Southern agricultural fields and railroads. Northern troops also seized Southern salt mines in Virginia and Louisiana, appropriating the resources for their own use. These wartime issues hindered Southern cooks' ability to preserve meat and can vegetables. Moreover, Southern cooks at home felt it was their duty to provide what food they could from their homes to the needy Confederate troops, foods such as coffee, milk, cornbread, soup, and sometimes cakes and pies. By the first years of the war, items such as bacon, butter, coffee, and flour quickly became scarce. The industrialized North avoided food shortage problems because it had a well-developed transportation system and had begun to develop a regional canning industry, which allowed the preservation of foods that might otherwise quickly spoil in wartime conditions. These preserved foods were then transported to citizens and soldiers. The North's agricultural land was largely unscathed by the war.

These wartime situations affected cooking, especially for Southerners, and cooks often had to modify recipes, called "receipts" during the nineteenth century, by substituting for ingredients that had become scarce. In 1863, a publishing house in Virginia produced *The Confederate Receipt Book: A Compilation of Over One Hundred Receipts, Adapted to the Times.* This is the only cookbook known to have been published in the South during the war. Foodstuffs in shortest supply were butter, salt, meat, and leavening, so recipes such as those in *The Confederate Receipt Book* included instructions on how to preserve meats without the use of salt and how to bake breads without yeast. Rice, molasses, and cornmeal were common substitutions in many recipes.

The cookbook also instructed cooks about how to make coffee from ground acorns that had been roasted in bacon fat. Roasted okra seeds were another substitution for coffee beans. Many of the wartime recipes instructed cooks on how to continue to create baked goods, which were popular in the South; few of the recipes were for vegetable side dishes cooked from fresh vegetables, to which many Southerners had an aversion and which may have been hard to obtain during the war. Sometimes, the creators of these wartime recipes gave them patriotic names, such as Confederate Cake, Secession Bread, and Hampton Ginger Bread—after South Carolina's General Wade Hampton.

Before the war, wealthy Southerners—plantation owners and urbanites—ate a diet that differed from the diet of their poorer, rural counterparts. Poor Southerners' diets consisted mainly of pork and corn, but occasionally included chicken, wild game, sweet potatoes, field peas, and greens. These foods of the rural poor also composed the diet of enslaved African Americans. Wealthier Southerners, on the other hand, had the ability to buy more expensive foods such as wheat flour, rice, sugar, butter, beef, fresh seafood, and Irish potatoes, which often eliminated their need for and consumption of local foods. However, as conditions worsened during wartime, the food crisis affected even wealthy Southerners, who were reduced to eating less expensive foods that could be obtained locally, the previous diet of the rural poor and enslaved people. These affluent Southerners learned to re-create popular and fashionable, high-society antebellum dishes such as oysters by combining green corn with beaten eggs and flour. They also learned to replace sugar in their desserts with sorghum, watermelon syrup, or persimmons, and to replace wheat flour with rice flour.

Although many Southerners had to deal with extreme food shortages, those at home in the North had food surpluses. As a result, Northerners rarely needed to substitute foods or create new recipes during the war. Northern cooks continued to cook traditional and popular Northern favorites such as chicken pie, fish chowder, clam chowder, Boston baked beans, brown bread, plum pudding, Boston cream cakes, and mincemeat.

Soldiers on both sides of the war staved off hunger by eating salt pork and hardtack, a nonperishable very hard, flat cracker or biscuit, made from unleavened flour, water, and sometimes salt, which had been dried after being baked. Many soldiers fried their hardtack with their pork and bacon fat making a dish they called skillygalee. Food rations for Confederate troops were meager, especially late in the war, and often consisted solely of corn bread and rotting beef, which was regularly absent. In 1861, in place of beef, the commissary general recommended substituting a combination of rice and molasses. By 1864, mule meat substituted for beef for the Southern troops. Sometimes, Confederate rations included bacon, molasses, and peas.

Even though they sometimes experienced hunger, Union troops' rations were usually adequate, and they received what the Confederates would have considered luxuries. The War Department even produced a cookbook entitled *Camp Fires and Camp Cooking; or Culinary Hints for the Soldier: Including Receipt for Making Bread in the "Portable Field Oven" Furnished by the Subsistence Department* to be distributed to the Union military to increase their health and comfort. The recipe for "Commissary Beef Stew" called for a stew of fresh beef—an uncommon ingredient on the battlefield—potatoes, and vegetables, thickened with flour. The typical diet of Union soldiers consisted of pork or beef, which was usually salted or boiled for preservation, salt, vinegar, dried fruits and vegetables when available, coffee, and sugar. Yet, they, too, faced substitutions. One such item that appeared in the rations for Northern troops was coffee, which was actually a substitution for tea. Up until the Civil War, Americans preferred to drink tea; however, perhaps due to its use as a substitute during the war, coffee became the preferred drink of Americans after the war.

Tiffany Hensley

See also: *Economy and Work*: Rural Life, Northern; Rural Life, Southern; Urban Life, Northern; Urban Life, Southern; *Family Life and Gender Roles*: Womanhood, Northern; Womanhood, Southern; *Food and Drink*: Coffee; Food, African Americans; Food, Native Americans; Food, Northern; Food, Shortages; Food, Soldiers; Food, Southern; Food, Upper Classes; Food Riots; Kitchens; Salt; Substitutes, Food and Drink; Taverns; Tea; *Housing and Community*: Boarding Houses; *Politics and Warfare*: Camp Life; *Science and Technology*: Cooking Techniques

FURTHER READING

The Confederate Receipt Book: A Compilation of Over One Hundred Receipts, Adapted to the Times. Richmond, VA: West & Johnson, 1863.

Davis, William C. *A Taste for War: The Culinary History of the Blue and the Gray*. Mechanicsburg, PA: Stackpole Books, 2003.

Robertson, James I., Jr. *Soldiers Blue and Gray*. Columbia: University of South Carolina Press, 1988.

Spaulding, Lily May, and John Spauldin, eds. *Civil War Recipes: Receipts from the Pages of Godey's Lady's Book*. Lexington: University of Kentucky Press, 1999.

Varhola, Michael J. *Everyday Life During the Civil War*. Cincinnati, OH: Writer's Digest Books, 1999.

Volo, Dorothy Denneen, and James M. Volo. *Daily Life in Civil War America*. Westport, CT: Greenwood Press, 1998.

FOOD, AFRICAN AMERICANS

The food African Americans consumed during the Civil War reflects the legacy of transatlantic slavery. Enslaved African Americans and freedmen all created unique cuisines by combining elements from the different cultures they encountered. After blacks migrated from West Africa to North America in a European colonial slave system, their consumption synergized West African, Caribbean, and European food traditions and adapted to available ingredients. Enslavement and poverty limited many African Americans' access to ingredients before the 1860s, and fluctuating scarcity during the war years impacted the diets of all Americans. African Americans prepared the ingredients using techniques developed both in Africa and in the Americas. Diverse African ethnic heritage and American regional agricultural variances contributed to the creations of many different African American foods by the dawn of the Civil War. These different cuisines shared a multicultural and multicontinental heritage, and they served to provide sustenance despite limitations in ingredients.

African American food began evolving before Africans crossed the Atlantic. West Africa, the ethnic homeland of most African Americans in the mid-nineteenth century, experienced a culinary transformation following both the Columbian Exchange and increased trade with Europe. For example, pork, introduced by the Portuguese, became a desirable delicacy in the non-Muslim parts of West and Central Africa before the sixteenth century. The Igbo and Hausa-speaking people, whose progeny would later be enslaved and sold on the mid-Atlantic coast, began planting corn and sweet potatoes alongside indigenous crops. These African people incorporated the non-indigenous foods into their diets using traditional African cooking techniques. For example, African women in the Congo ground corn to make bread in the same way they had previously prepared millet bread. When slave traders brought Africans to North America, enslaved Africans were already familiar with most available foods.

In addition to cooking techniques, Africans introduced some ingredients to North America that contributed to the development of African American cuisine.

Slave ships brought black-eyed peas from West Africa in their ration holds as a source of protein for those on board. Enslaved people in the southeastern United States grew African-native okra to supplement their rations on plantations. African American cooks adapted the African ingredients to use with available American ingredients and created hybrid cuisines. When former slave Mary Scranton of Texas recalled the "chicken 'r' shrimp 'r' meat" gumbo of her youth, the food she remembered was not unlike the stews and soups that Igbo-speaking people ate in the Biafra region of Nigeria. Scranton used whatever protein she could procure to flavor her okra-thickened soup. Combining the African and American ingredients created unique hybrid foods that were uniquely African American.

African American cuisines developed as a response to limited access to certain foods and ingredients. Enslavement, poverty, and wartime shortages determined the ingredients that African American cooks could utilize. Adaptability remained an important culinary tool for both free and enslaved African Americans. On the plantation, owners stingily rationed vegetables and provided slaves with inferior cuts of meat. Enslaved people adapted to their condition by growing personal or communal gardens, and by hunting, fishing, and stealing from neighboring farms to supplement their diets. When preparing foods, enslaved people developed cooking techniques to flavor the leftover cuts of meat provided by their masters. In the pork-heavy South, African Americans began smoking, pickling, and barbequing leftover scraps of ham from a plantation's big house to improve their taste. African American cooks on South Carolina's Sea Islands heavily seasoned their soups and stews with red pepper to make them more palatable and delicious. Mid-nineteenth century-African American cuisines were peasant foods, developed from necessity and adapted to provide flavorful sustenance.

The adaptability of African American cookery proved advantageous during wartime shortages. Blockades and plundering armies created a food scarcity, especially in the South. Both blacks and whites suffered from want, but there is some evidence that blacks fared better than their white counterparts. Booker Washington suggested that since enslaved people were unaccustomed to luxury items, shortages of coffee and sugar had little impact on them. When the war interrupted their food systems, African Americans simply adopted the use of other ingredients. Because they had grown accustomed to creating meals from cheap or meager ingredients, many African American cooks created a black market economy of selling their wares to deserters and hungry soldiers for a profit. Both the North and the South desired the skills of the adaptable black cooks; they found employment on both sides during the war. African American food traditions survived the war because the African American cooks already knew how to adapt to shortages.

Still, the war brought suffering and famine to some African Americans. As Northern armies advanced through the South, pillaging soldiers often left nothing on plantations for the enslaved people to eat. Former Mississippi slave Ann May recalled that the invading Yankees killed all the livestock and stole the flour and sugar. In another instance, a recently discharged black soldier from Tennessee wrote to the Secretary of War requesting immediate aid for the hungry families of African American soldiers. Although African Americans were often able to overcome wartime food shortages, those who lived in close proximity to the conflict faced hunger.

African Americans did not share a common diet during the war years. Different geographic locations yielded distinct black cultures and foods. Historians note that when the Union Army adjusted its rations to include more pork and corn bread for its black regiments, African American soldiers from the South invited the changes, while their counterparts from the North preferred beef and wheat bread. Even within the same region, African American diets varied between locations. In the rice-growing regions of the Carolinas and Louisiana, rice was a black dietary staple, while African Americans ate corn in cotton- and tobacco-producing regions. Not surprisingly, seafood entered African American diet on the coast. Several unique African American cuisines existed in the nineteenth century, but they remained unified by a common food tradition and the legacy of adaptability.

Ryan Hall

See also: *Economy and Work*: Camp Followers; Impressment; Plantations; Slavery; *Family Life and Gender Roles*: Free Blacks; Slave Families; *Food and Drink*: Food Shortages; Gardens; Salt

FURTHER READING

Berlin, Ira, Joseph P. Reidy, and Leslie S. Rowland, eds. *Freedom's Soldiers: The Black Military Experience in the Civil War*. New York: Cambridge University Press, 1998.
Covey, Herbert C., and Dwight Eisnach, ed. *What the Slaves Ate: Recollections of African American Foods and Foodways from the Slave Narratives*. Santa Barbara, CA: ABC-CLIO, 2009.
Graydon, Nell S. *Tales of Edisto*. Orangeburg, SC: Sandlapper Publishing, 1955
Opie, Frederick Douglas. *Hog & Hominy: Soul Food from Africa to America*. New York: Columbia University Press, 2008.

FOOD, NATIVE AMERICANS

The Civil War affected the food supplies and eating habits of many Native American tribes. When the Civil War began, Americans were in the middle of a campaign to win the West. Even though the Civil War drew troops out of frontier regions and hindered white migration to the West, Indian conflicts with whites continued. The war affected Native Americans in myriad ways, and tribes responded in equally varied ways. Sometimes, their experiences during the war affected their subsistence.

The Civil War affected the subsistence of the Navajo. Before and for a time after European contact, the Navajo had been a nomadic people who subsisted by hunting, gathering, and raiding other peoples, both Indian and European. However, after contact with the Spanish, they adopted many Spanish practices, including farming. They grew crops such as corn, pumpkins, sunflowers, and beans. They also adopted the Spanish practice of sheep herding, and sheep became a significant part of their culture, lifestyle, and diet, which allowed them to move away from raiding. In addition, the Navajo continued to participate in raiding expeditions, often stealing enemy livestock, especially in retaliation against the Mexicans who often entered Navajo territory to raid Navajo settlements for Indian slaves. At the start of the U.S.-Mexican War in 1846, the United States established sustained relations with the Navajo when American military officials promised protection to Mexicans and Anglo-Americans from raiding Indians, including the Navajo. Out of this agreement began a complicated relationship between the Navajo and the United States, one that continued to affect the Navajo and their subsistence practices during the American Civil War.

In the spring of 1862, Confederate troops had moved out of Navajo territory, and the Union Army had moved in. The commander of the Union troops focused on controlling the Indians in the area, including the Navajo. The plan was to move the Indians to a location 300 miles east so that the United States could better observe and control the Indians' actions. When the Navajo refused to leave, the Union troops initiated a campaign to destroy Navajo territory, including fields and orchards, and to seize property, including livestock. By March, many of the Navajo were starving, and the Union began forcefully removing the Indians east to Bosque Redondo in the Pecos River Valley, an episode the Navajo call the "Long Walk." There, the Navajo faced terrible conditions because of infertile soil and inadequate supplies.

The Dakota Sioux in Minnesota were also negatively affected by circumstances precipitated by the American Civil War. At this time, the Dakota Sioux were semi-sedentary, living in one place for most of the year. They hunted buffalo and raised crops for food. They ate plants including plums, currants, beans, camas bulbs, and turnips. They ate animals including beavers, rabbit, deer, and antelope. They also depended on the federal government for money, in the form of annuity payments, to buy food supplies from local traders. Their chief, Little Crow, had chosen to accommodate the United States and white settlement in their lands by signing treaties and selling Dakota Sioux territory to the United States. In return, the United States agreed to pay them a sum at particular intervals. However, the United States had not fulfilled its responsibilities as stipulated in these deals and had not delivered the payment on time. Their crops had failed in 1861, and by early 1862, the Dakota Sioux were facing starvation. Because of these conditions, in 1862, Little Crow's people convinced him to lead them into war against the American settlers in their territory, a war termed the "Great Sioux Uprising" by the United States. The United States retaliated, capturing approximately 1,700 Sioux, trying 400, and executing 38 at Mankato, the largest public hanging in American history.

Some Indians were involved more directly in the American Civil War, and this also affected their food supplies. The Caddos in Indian Territory grew beans, squash, pumpkins, and sunflowers and hunted waterfowl, bears, deer, and sometimes buffalo. However, at the time of the American Civil War, they were already suffering from the depredations of Texans and from Kiowa and Comanche raids. Union troops were initially posted nearby the Caddo, but when they moved, the Caddos felt it necessary to ally with the Confederacy in 1861. Many Caddos felt that the Confederacy could not or would not protect them so they moved to Kansas. There they allied with Union troops; however, this move did not provide a better situation than they had in Indian Territory. They were starving at their settlement at the mouth of the Little Arkansas River. Many continued to migrate looking for a more stable existence, and the Caddo population declined significantly during the American Civil War.

The Cherokee Indians were also involved directly in the American Civil War. After Indian removal, the Cherokee had rebuilt their society in Indian Territory. Most Cherokees had small farms, raised small herds of livestock, and had gardens and orchards. Corn was an important part of their diet. Many of these small farmers retained much of the traditional Cherokee culture and language. However, a small, slaveholding elite increasingly dominated Cherokee national affairs. Many of these people were sympathetic to the sentiments of the Confederacy in the years leading up to the American Civil War. Other Cherokees, who organized as the Keetoowahs, felt that siding with the South threatened Cherokee lifestyle and autonomy. Initially hoping to remain neutral, Cherokee chief John Ross eventually signed a treaty with the Confederacy in 1861. However, Union troops defeated the Confederates in Arkansas in 1862 and marched on Indian Territory. Union troops arrested Ross and took him back east, but he used the opportunity to reestablish the tribe's relationship with the United States. Yet, many Cherokees still remained committed to the South, and in Ross's absence, civil war broke out among the Cherokees. Farms and plantations were destroyed leaving the Cherokee nation practically in ruins. The Cherokee also lost a significant proportion of their population during this time.

After the Civil War, Americans felt that conquering the West would bring the nation back together. American efforts to do this further disrupted Indian subsistence as American settlers gained control of increasingly more territory that Indians used for subsistence, such as buffalo hunting. Over time, American settlement replaced Indian buffalo hunting with American cattle ranching in the West, a practice the West is often known for today.

Tiffany Hensley

See also: *Food and Drink*: Kitchens; *Religion and Belief*: Native American Religions; *Science and Technology*: Cooking Techniques

FURTHER READING

Abel, Annie Heloise. *The American Indian in the Civil War, 1862–1865.* Lincoln: University of Nebraska Press, 1992.

Confer, Clarissa. *The Cherokee Nation in the Civil War.* Norman: University of Oklahoma Press, 2012.

Cunningham, Frank. *General Stand Watie's Confederate Indians.* Norman: University of Oklahoma Press, 1998.

Hatch, Tom. *The Blue, the Gray, and the Red: Indian Campaigns of the Civil War.* Mechanicsburg, PA: Stackpole Books, 2003.

Hauptman, Laurence M. *Between Two Fires: American Indians in the Civil War.* New York: Free Press, 1995.

Mihesuah, Devon. *Recovering Our Ancestors' Gardens: Indigenous Recipes and Guide to Diet and Fitness.* Lincoln: University of Nebraska Press, 2005.

FOOD, NORTHERN

The type of food Northerners ate during the Civil War depended on a number of factors, including an individual's wealth and region. Immigrant ethnic groups, including those from Germany, England, and Ireland, heavily influenced mid-nineteenth-century cuisine in the North. There were also differences between what urban dwellers and those in the country typically ate. People in cities purchased much of their food from various stores, while those in rural areas grew much of their own. Some items, such as pork and bread, were ubiquitous, while particular dishes such as fish chowder or chicken pie, as well as fruits and vegetables varied from one region to the next. If they could afford it, most Northern families kept their kitchen stocked with staples including flour, salt, sugar, tea, coffee, and vinegar. Although the Civil War affected food prices and availability, it did not cause the severe shortages in the North that existed in the South.

The existence of extensive railroad networks and industrial meatpacking centers such as Chicago and Cincinnati, in addition to the large number of family farms, meant that civilians in Northern states had access to a steady supply of meat for the duration of the war. Pork was most popular, as hogs were not difficult to raise and feed, and their meat was easily preserved and palatable. Bacon and ham were widely consumed for breakfast, lunch, and dinner. In rural areas, hogs were important to family farms as they provided a convenient source of meat as well as a source of lard, valued for its many uses. It could be substituted for butter, used for frying, and used to keep eggs throughout the winter.

Northerners also consumed relatively large amounts of beef, sometimes preserved (as in salt beef) or eaten fresh (as in steaks and roasts). By the 1860s, iceboxes were common in households and people used ice harvested in the winter to keep perishable goods below spoiling temperatures. In this way, fresh meat could be kept longer and did not always require preservation.

Other varieties of meat were eaten on a smaller scale. Some Northerners, mostly in rural areas, kept chickens, which could be eaten fresh or kept for their eggs. Eggs were mostly eaten fried or hard boiled, but they could also be pickled in vinegar to make them last. Those in the country supplemented their diets by hunting a variety of game, including duck, pheasant, turkey, and deer. In coastal areas and by lakes and rivers, the consumption of fish and other seafood was common, and included crab, lobster, bass, catfish, and pike. Shellfish, particularly oysters, were extremely popular at the time and were eaten fresh, pickled, or smoked.

Along with meat, bread was a staple of Northern diet. The woman of the household often prided herself on the bread she baked at home. Northerners also consumed other varieties of baked goods, such as biscuits or the occasional cake or pie. Sugar, a necessity for Northern families, was used not only for baking and as a sweetener, but also for preserving fruits and vegetables in jellies, jams, and sauces. In addition, Northerners used other sweeteners, such as maple syrup (mostly in the Northeast) or honey. Candy was a popular treat; young and old Northerners alike consumed a number of homemade or store-bought varieties that included rock candy, peppermint sticks, jelly beans, and taffy.

The availability of fruits and vegetables depended on the season. Apples were by far the most common and widely eaten fruit in the North. Others, such as pears, plums, and cherries, were enjoyed and often cultivated by families on farms or in small garden plots in cities. Those who could gathered berries and mushrooms in the countryside. Throughout the winter, vegetables such as potatoes, beets, cabbage, carrots, and turnips were stored in root cellars and barrels, sustaining families with additional nutrition. Peas, corn, and beans were often dried and used in soups and stews. At this time, many regional varieties of fruits and vegetables existed but were available fresh only locally. To make these items transportable or savable, people turned to canning. Canning was used to preserve all types of seasonal vegetables and fruits. Foods such as sauerkraut or catsup—the name used for any sauce made from vegetables and fruits; tomato and mushroom catsups were popular—could then be enjoyed throughout the year.

As with fruits and vegetables, rural households had more access to dairy products than did urban households. Creameries existed in the North to provide urban populations with milk, butter, and cheese, but most rural families kept at least one dairy cow or two for their own benefit. The widespread consumption of milk did not become common until the latter part of the nineteenth century.

Popular beverages in the North included hot tea and coffee, sweetened drinks such as lemonade or cider, and water. Water, however, became easily contaminated in the urban areas. Northerners also consumed significant quantities of beer and hard liquor, mostly whiskey. Some commercial or homemade soft drinks also existed, notably sarsaparilla.

The Civil War era marked an important milestone regarding the ways Americans prepared and consumed food. Canned goods and dehydrated products, such as "desiccated vegetables," became common and were in great demand by the Union Army during the war. Valued for their shelf life, consistent taste, and convenience, prepared canned goods such as Van Camp's Pork and Beans or Borden's Condensed Milk quickly became well-known, popular products in Northern kitchens. These items became particularly prevalent in the kitchens of urban families who worked long hours in factories. Another reason for the rise in popularity of prepared food was that Union veterans, accustomed to canned rations provided by the army, continued to consume them upon returning home.

Although the war had an effect on prices and, in some areas, availability, shortages affected Northern civilians far less than it did their Southern counterparts. In addition, during home front campaigns such as General William T. Sherman's march through Georgia and the Carolinas, Union troops lived off of the food that they encountered along their route. They feasted on fresh fruits and vegetables from the fields as well as on the meat and other items they found in wealthy Southern homes. Thus, food was an important weapon for the North, which could adequately supply its population with a variety of foodstuffs while many people in the South struggled to feed their families.

Justin Riskus

See also: *Family Life and Gender Roles*: Immigrants; *Food and Drink*: Coffee; Cookbooks and Recipes; Food, African American; Food, Native American; Food, Shortages; Food, Soldiers; Food, Southern; Food, Upper Classes; Food Riots; Foraging; Gardens; Hunting; Kitchens; Moonshine; Salt; Spirits; Substitutes, Food and Drink; Tea; *Science and Technology*: Railroads

FURTHER READING

Billings, John D. *Hard Tack and Coffee: The Untold Story of Army Life*. Williamstown, MA: Corner House, 1973.

Spaulding, John, and Lily May. *Civil War Recipes: Receipts from the Pages of Godey's Lady's Book*. Lexington: University Press of Kentucky, 1999.

Slavicek, Louise Chipley. *Women and the Civil War*. New York: Chelsea House, 2009.

Stanchak, John. *Civil War*. New York: Dorling Kindersley, 2000.

Varhola, Michael J. *Everyday Life During the Civil War*. Cincinnati, OH: Writer's Digest Books, 1999.

FOOD, SHORTAGES

In the Civil War, food was a critical component of wartime strategy, and food shortages weighed heavily on the minds of leaders, generals, soldiers, and civilians. The North, where ports remained open and industry could aid agriculture, did not experience crippling food shortages, though wartime prices rose with inflation. Citizens and soldiers in the Confederacy, however, increasingly suffered from food shortages as the war lengthened, often nearing famine by the end of the war. The reasons for this Southern shortage of food were numerous, including the blockade by the North, shortages of key goods and resources that were not produced locally, a lack of trade, and a poor transportation infrastructure.

When the Civil War began, Confederate prospects in food production may not have appeared particularly grim. In terms of livestock, Southern states had double the ratio of hogs to people as that of Northern states and an even greater superiority of cattle to people. Much of the South boasted prime agricultural land which some thought could make the Confederacy self-sufficient. The South produced more corn than did the North and virtually monopolized the production of rice and dominated in the production of beans and peas. If the land devoted to producing cotton and tobacco were to be converted into producing foodstuffs, the position of the South was even better.

Nevertheless, this Southern strength in agriculture was deceptive. Southerners depended on the Border States for transporting agricultural goods and acquiring other key foodstuffs. As a result, President Abraham Lincoln's success in keeping the Border States in the Union cut off a key market for the South. Missouri possessed more cattle than any state in the Union, except for Texas, and the loss of Missouri deeply hurt the Confederacy. Even though the South possessed greater numbers of hogs and cattle, the size of Southern livestock was reported to be small, or "bony," "lanky," and "scrubby." The Confederacy's relatively primitive rail network also made it difficult to move needed supplies around, and the loss of Vicksburg, Mississippi, in July 1863 effectively cut off the western Confederacy from the rest of the South.

More advanced technology aided the crops and livestock in the Union. Superior breeding techniques in the North meant that its cattle tended to be substantially larger than Southern cattle and consequently produced more meat for consumption. Agriculture changed substantially during this time as well. Northern farmers discovered the benefit of more industrialized farming, using devices such as drills, harrows, and reapers to produce greater harvests. In the Confederacy, manual labor proved inefficient in increasing the amount of food available, especially as the numbers of available laborers dwindled. The Confederate Army drafted white men and, and at the same time enslaved men were impressed by the Confederate Army, ran away, or found freedom with Northern soldiers. Across the South basic farm implements such as scythes and plows suffered from wartime shortages, as new equipment could not be made or was in short supply. Tools began to wear out after several years of continuous use.

To combat the food shortages, Confederate officials tried to induce farmers and planters to give up growing cotton and tobacco and switch to the production of food products. First the government appealed to the patriotism of those involved as it encouraged them to grow foodstuffs. When that proved insufficient, individual states began to legislate limits on cash crops that could be cultivated. Arkansas established a limit of two acres of cotton cultivation per farmhand, whereas Alabama imposed a tax of 10 cents a pound over 2,500 pounds per farmhand.

Food shortages also resulted from wartime shortages of preservatives. Prior to the war, the South had largely depended on England for salt, an item critical for the preservation of meats. The few salt sources in the South were located on the coast and subject to capture by the North, whose navy encircled the coast. The blockade cut the South off from foreign markets; the only supplies that came in were from those blockade runners that managed to elude Northern ships. Shortages of salt led to the spoilage of meat and the inability to stockpile food for future use.

Northern leaders were aware of the vulnerability the South had to disruptions of food supplies, and they focused in on this weakness. Northern raiders captured what livestock they could to feed Union troops and incapacitate Southern ones. Later, as Northern armies advanced through some of the prime agricultural land of the South, soldiers made every effort to leave nothing behind for their enemies to eat. Philip Sheridan's invasion of the Shenandoah Valley and William Tecumseh Sherman's march through Georgia and the Carolinas both included orders for soldiers to form foraging parties, destroy mills and other infrastructure wherever the population was hostile, and "appropriate" whatever field animals they might require. Union troops could thereby operate without supply lines as they existed on seized livestock and grain they denied to Confederate soldiers and civilians.

The cumulative effect was a slow tightening of screws on the Confederacy, whose people became first underfed and then malnourished. Confederate officials "impressed" produce and foodstuffs for the war effort, producing shortages in areas that were otherwise untouched by the war. Areas under siege, such as Vicksburg, saw appalling food shortages; shortly before the city capitulated, one woman reported seeing rats for sale in a butcher's window. Meat quickly disappeared from many menus and was replaced by fish, but even this was not enough to meet the shortfall. President Jefferson Davis claimed that he saw no reason for not eating rats, claiming that they would be "as good as squirrels."

Confederate citizens did the best that they could to improvise. Coffee, tea, and sugar disappeared from markets early in the war, and many people did what they could using chicory as a substitute for coffee and sorghum as a sweetener. Due to the lack of dairies, butter was in short supply. In response, citizens began using oil from sunflower seeds as a substitute. Peanuts came to be consumed in great quantities during this time and were frequently used in desserts. Despite their ingenuity, however, too many families went to bed hungry, and this lack of food had a profoundly negative effect on the war effort. Some Confederate soldiers deserted in response to their families' complaints of impending starvation.

In 1863, food riots broke out around the Confederacy. The largest bread riot took place in Richmond, Virginia, where hundreds of women stormed the shops on Main and Cary Streets and seized necessities such as bacon, flour, shoes, and candles. The governor called in the Public Guard to bring the city under control. Similar riots took place in urban centers in Georgia, Louisiana, Tennessee, Alabama, and North Carolina.

Zeb Larson

See also: *Economy and Work*: Impressment; Rural Life, Southern; Urban Life, Southern; *Food and Drink*: Food Riots; Salt

FURTHER READING

Gates, Paul W. *Agriculture and the Civil War*. New York: Alfred A. Knopf, 1965.
Massey, Mary Elizabeth. *Ersatz in the Confederacy*. Columbia: University of South Carolina Press, 1952.
Wiley, Irvin Bell. *The Life of Johnny Reb*. Baton Rouge: Louisiana State University Press, 1978.

FOOD, SOLDIERS

The food of Civil War soldiers changed based on the time of year, location, and preferences of the individuals. Although many hoped that their eating habits would not change or would improve during their time in camp, they often faced shortages and had to make do with the natural resources surrounding them.

Food consumption in the armies reflected the dining habits of the American people in the nineteenth century. Food was cooked in a wood burning stove or fireplace; meats were usually boiled, fried, or roasted. Fresh fruits and vegetables were common, as were bread, cakes, and pies. Certain types of food were more predominant in one region, such as beef, wheat, and apples in the North, and pork, rice, and peaches in the South. In addition, potatoes were a common food staple in the North, while corn was a predominant food item in the South. Coffee and tea were popular hot beverages throughout the nation.

The common soldier's diet in both armies during the Civil War consisted of bread, meat, and vegetables. In addition, soldiers consumed coffee as their main

Photograph of Union soldiers gathered around a log hut company kitchen in 1864. The common soldier's diet in both armies during the Civil War tended to focus on bread, meat, and vegetables. Both armies supplemented their meager supplies with foraging and impressment. (National Archives)

beverage. The large armies relied on animal transport to move cannons and supply wagons. These animals, numbering about 60,000 to support an army of 100,000, had to be fed as well. The requirements to feed these armies required a certain level of standardization and a specified amount of food per man (and animal) per day. Each soldier ate about three pounds of food every day; the animals generally ate 10–20 pounds of feed daily.

At the beginning of the war, while encamped for any period of time, food supplies were predictable and fresh food was supplied through purchases, barter, or impressment of food from local farmers. Armies brought along herds of hogs, sheep, or cattle to be slaughtered to provide soldiers with fresh meat. During campaigns and while on the march, fresh food was often difficult to obtain. The soldiers had to rely on nonperishable food that the army had purchased from contractors, who were not always honest in representing their products to the government. The soldiers were provided meat, usually preserved in salt or pickled. The process of preserving meat tended to be haphazard, and many a soldier received an inedible lump of "salt horse" or pickled pork. Union soldiers received bread in the form of 9–10 uniformly shaped rectangles of a wheat-flour mixture called hardtack. The only way it could be eaten was to break it up (often with the butt of a rifle) and put it in coffee, soup, or water. Union troops made what they called "skillygallee," which was fried salt pork and hardtack soaked in water.

Confederate soldiers ate captured hardtack, but their bread ration was usually a little over a pound of cornmeal. Confederates made "coosh," a mixture of cornmeal, water, and bacon, or cornmeal biscuits. Both armies made "slapjacks" when flour was available. They mixed the flour with cold water and fried it in grease. Coffee was part of the ration throughout the war for Union soldiers; it rapidly became scarce in the Confederate camps. Sassafras tea was common as was coffee made from peas, rye, acorns, or chicory, which made a less-than-satisfying substitute. Soldiers relied on coffee (or its substitute) as an essential part of life. The coffee was served over an open fire, scalding hot, and very strong. Coffee was an important trading item for tobacco between Union and Confederate soldiers during times when the armies faced each other in entrenchments or across rivers.

Hardly any of the soldiers who came into the army had cooking skills. In the camps, soldiers were expected to pool their individual rations into communal meals. These meals often consisted of whatever was at hand and could fit in a pot. They were not always very satisfying or filling and were often the source of sickness. Units usually had cooking pots and utensils carried in the supply wagons, but over time individual soldiers began to carry cooking items. Soldiers had learned through hard experience that the wagons often arrived long after the men had set up camp for the night. Few veterans were without a knife, fork, tin cup, and spoon; some carried their own pans and pots or a skillet for cooking. The bayonet was used far more as a cooking implement than as a battle instrument. It had many uses as a skewer, a potholder, or a candleholder. The monotonous diet of bread and meat led to vitamin deficiencies and even scurvy. The Union Army began to supply its soldiers with desiccated vegetables—dried carrots, turnips, parsnips, and other unidentifiable greens—that could be added to soups and stews. The soldiers renamed the unappetizing material "desecrated vegetables."

As the war progressed, Confederate soldiers received fewer and fewer items in their rations. Winters were especially hard. Lacking rail transportation and with few usable roads, it was nearly impossible to move the tons of supplies necessary to feed the army and its animals. Soldiers commonly received one-fourth of their normal rations, 2–3 ounces of meat and a cupful of meal; other days there was nothing to eat. In early spring, soldiers scoured the woods and fields near the camps for wild onions: it was the only fresh vegetable available. Soldiers wrote home asking for corn or potatoes, and expressed their yearning for milk, butter, and fresh meat.

The armies often broke camp with orders for the soldiers to carry three day's full rations in their haversacks. This ration varied with conditions, but it usually meant some form of salt meat, flour, hominy, meal, rice, or hard bread (hardtack), sometimes supplemented with dried beans, peas, or desiccated vegetables. Coffee, sugar, molasses, and salt were also provided. The men would eat when they could, usually during intermittent breaks during the march, or while camped for the night. On these marches, fresh meat would be distributed when possible, but these rations would have to be immediately cooked and eaten when received or jerked (dried over a low fire) during the night. The soldiers often had little time to prepare food prior to battle, usually brewing coffee and swallowing down whatever could be easily collected from their haversacks.

During the 1864 Union campaigns in the Shenandoah Valley and in Georgia and the Carolinas, Northern soldiers ate well. Their orders allowed them to forage for food from Southern farms and plantations. Soldiers recorded their delight at the bountiful meals of sweet potatoes, peaches, chicken, turkey, beef, honey, syrup, and other local delicacies.

Keith Dickson

See also: *Economy and Work*: Impressment; *Food and Drink*: Coffee; Food, Northern; Food, Southern; Food Shortages; Foraging; Hardtack; Salt; Substitutes, Food and Drink; Tea; *Politics and Warfare*: Camp Life; *Science and Technology*: Disease

FURTHER READING

Billings, John D. *Hardtack and Coffee: The Unwritten Story of Army Life*. Glendale, NY: Benchmark Publishing Corp., 1970.

Davis, William C. *A Taste for War: The Culinary History of the Blue and Gray*. Mechanicsburg, PA: Stackpole Books, 2003.

Sheehan-Dean, Aaron. *The View for the Ground: Experiences of Civil War Soldiers*. Lexington: University Press of Kentucky, 2007.

Wiley, Bell Irvin. *The Life of Billy Yank: The Common Soldier of the Union*. Baton Rouge: Louisiana State University Press, 1978.

Wiley, Bell Irvin. *The Life of Johnny Reb: The Common Soldier of the Confederacy*. Baton Rouge: Louisiana State University Press, 1978.

FOOD, SOUTHERN

During the nineteenth century, food played a pivotal role in the cultural underpinnings of Southern society and it dramatically influenced the Civil War's military and domestic front. Southern food's importance manifested itself in the assimilation process between European and African traditions, the dynamics among white and black Southerners, and the Confederacy's hardships. Food affected the behavior of all Southerners during the Civil War.

Most foods that modern Americans consider to be distinctly "Southern"—okra, pork barbeque, cornbread, or fried chicken, just to name a few—resulted from combinations of the Columbian Exchange, African culinary methods practiced by enslaved people, and economic circumstance. Wealthy planters dined on a widespread assortment of greens, corn, beans, rice, game, seafood, birds, and pork. However, it was enslaved African Americans who prepared a majority of planters' meals and did so by combining their traditional cooking techniques with New and Old World crops that grew well in the American South's climate and soil.

Although slaveholders enjoyed this European, American, and African culinary assimilation, they usually fed their enslaved Africans a monthly ration of only corn meal, "fat pork," and sometimes molasses. Because this apportionment often left them hungry and malnourished, enslaved people supplemented their own diets by cultivating small garden plots containing fruits and vegetables, raising hogs, hunting and fishing for rabbits, squirrels, possum, and catfish, or by stealing from their master's stores. Enslaved African Americans exhibited exceptional skill in cooking even the worst quality of foodstuffs. For example, cooking cheap, tough, and fatty cuts of meat over low temperatures for a long period of time breaks down the connective tissues and tendons and produces moist and flavorful meat commonly known as barbeque. Poor white yeoman, who, due to a lack of financial income, also needed ways of cooking inexpensive meals, often ate the same types of foods as enslaved people but had much more time to dedicate to larger portion sizes and a more balanced diet.

Food acted as a cog in the wheel of sustaining the institution of slavery and Southern society's paternalistic organization. Elite planters often hosted large barbeques for white yeoman from their local communities. More than simply paying for a yeoman's food and drink for the day, slaveholders often promised poor whites the use of their enslaved laborers during especially busy times of the year or offered the use of costly wagons and carriages during the harvest so yeoman could transport their crops to market and consequently provide for their families. In these ways, non-slaveholding whites depended on the institution of slavery for their own livelihood. It further contributed to their sense of superiority over blacks and reinforced their privileged societal position based on skin color. Elite planters also used electioneering techniques at these barbeques to guarantee political power within their communities. Slaveholders invited their preferred candidates to rally voters during barbeque festivities in an effort to buy votes through favors. Poor whites associated benefits from generous slaveholders, their enhanced societal status, and their ability to participate in a market economy with the political candidates on display at elites' barbeques. More than sustenance, Southern food—and the cultural exchanges surrounding it—was crucial in maintaining the South's steadfast dedication to a slave society.

Enslaved African Americans used food to gain status in their own communities and to negotiate a better working relationship with their masters. In addition to breaking tools, feigning illness, running away, or utilizing violence to achieve better working conditions, some slaves who raised their own gardens and livestock sold surplus foodstuffs for cash. With this income, enslaved people purchased clothing, home goods, culinary delicacies, extra rations, or in some instances, their own or their families' freedom. Those enslaved individuals fortunate enough to have the opportunity to raise their own foodstuffs and motivated enough to save those goods for market or share them with their fellow bondsmen often gained status in their community. Similarly, enslaved men and women who supplemented their families' diet by hunting, gardening, or theft enjoyed a privileged status in their families. A working knowledge of growing, storing, and selling food served as a defense against the evils of enslaved life.

Food held an even higher stature in Southern society after the Confederate States of America marched to war against the Union. Hunger proved to be a formidable enemy for the rebel soldier. Confederate troops tightened their belts due to limited rations as early as July 1861 and went days or weeks at a time without prescribed rations by the end of the war. In letters written home to loved ones, soldiers depicted gruesome scenes of famine: a chronic deficiency of vegetables; substituting mule, dog, and rat meat for pork or beef; livestock relegated to eating wood; and near starvation. The common Confederate soldier ate cornbread and spoiled beef more than anything else and often foraged for sustenance. The Confederacy's failure to adequately feed its troops did not stem from a lack of foodstuffs—the South successfully converted enough cotton fields to edible crops to feed its own armies during the Civil War. However, the Union's surmounting control of Southern transportation and distribution networks—specifically railroads and rivers—through military victories in the western theater and an increasingly effective naval blockade, coupled with a shortage of salt, other preservatives, and suitable packaging materials left most Southern food to rot at railroad depots or warehouses before it found the mouths of those in need.

Starting in 1864, the Union strategy of attrition directly involved destroying Southern food and it largely succeeded. Furthermore, the pinch in foodstuffs dramatically impacted the Confederacy's home front. The South's civilian population faced just as many food shortages as its soldiers and also confronted an astronomical inflation of prices. The inability of the Confederate government to feed its own population caused women to instigate food riots, soldiers to desert the army to protect their homes, and ultimately assisted in crumbling federal power from within the Confederacy itself. In many ways, Southern food influenced the creation, preservation, and downfall of Southern society before 1865.

Andrew William Fialka

See also: *Economy and Work*: Impressment; Landowners; Plantations; Rural Life, Southern; Slaveholders; Slavery; Urban Life, Southern; *Family and Gender Roles*: Slave Families; *Food and Drink*: Food, African Americans; Food, Native Americans; Food, Northern; Food, Shortages; Food, Soldiers; Food, Upper Classes; Food Riots; Foraging; Gardens; Hardtack; Hunting; Kitchens; Salt; Substitutes, Food and Drink; Tea; *Housing and Community*: Slave Life; *Politics and Warfare*: Blockades; Morale; *Religion and Belief*: Fast Days

FURTHER READING

Blassingame, John W. *The Slave Community: Plantation Life in the Antebellum South.* New York: Oxford University Press, 1972.

Dupre, Daniel. "Barbeques and Pledges: Electioneering and the Rise of Democratic Politics in Antebellum Alabama." *The Journal of Southern History* 60:3 (August 1994): 479–512.

Genovese, Eugene D. *Roll, Jordan, Roll: The World the Slaves Made.* New York: Random House, 1972.

Steinberg, Ted. *Down to Earth: Nature's Role in American History.* New York: Oxford University Press, 2002.

Wiley, Bell Irvin. *The Life of Johnny Reb: The Common Soldier of the Confederacy.* Baton Rouge: Louisiana State University Press, 1978.

FOOD, UPPER CLASSES

The Civil War affected the diets of the upper classes to varying degrees. For some wealthy people in the North and West, wartime food price inflation served as a minor inconvenience. In the South, blockades, agricultural impressment, and reduced agricultural output dramatically affected the elites' diets. In general, the wealthiest elites suffered less from wartime shortages than the common folk, the poor, and the enslaved people, but some, especially planters nearest to the fighting, faced starvation. For those Americans whose wealth survived intact, the Civil War's impact on diet persisted; although old foodways returned following Reconstruction, the war's legacy changed what the wealthy ate and how they procured food.

Technological and infrastructural advances in the decades preceding the war facilitated long-distance food transportation in the immediate antebellum period. By 1860, people in Michigan could purchase fresh oysters from the Gulf of Mexico, and those in Georgia could purchase midwestern beef and wheat flour. The wealthy quickly grew accustomed to foods produced hundreds or even thousands of miles away. In the decades leading to the war, the industrialization of American cities created an elite class of businessmen in the North who were economically removed from food production. Likewise wealthy planters in the South abandoned the ideal of subsistence agriculture to focus on profitable cash crops like cotton and sugar. As a result, by the start of the war, the wealthiest Americans ceased to produce what they ate. Instead, they purchased foods that sometimes traveled great distances.

The Civil War interrupted American foodways in three ways. First, blockades and trade embargos prevented traders from moving food across the country. Second, certain items became unavailable on both sides of the conflict as the two governments diverted food to their armies. Third, some places, especially in the South, lost significant food production when armies conscripted agricultural labor and farms were managed poorly. The result was that food prices inflated dramatically, and some foods disappeared from the diets of the wealthy. In the North, wealthy people simply paid more and transitioned to industrially produced foods to maintain their prewar diet, but in the South, this shift was not always possible.

Even before the war began, the Confederate government recognized the challenge of feeding its citizens if trade with the North became interrupted. When Union general Winfield Scott's Anaconda Plan blockaded Southern ports, the diets of the wealthy were immediately impacted. Before the war, the elites in both the North and South enjoyed expensive wheat flour, sugar, butter, Irish potatoes, beef, and poultry. When shipments of these luxury staples stopped arriving from the North, wealthy Southerners needed to immediately adapt to eat the cheaper, locally raised corn, sweet potatoes, and pork of the regular folk. Although wealthy planters had plenty of the cheap staples, even these items were sometimes hard to come by for Southern urban elites as the Confederate government struggled to transport food within its borders. The blockades had little impact on the foodways of the Northern elites, though. The Anaconda Plan impeded the transportation to the South of the luxury staples, but not the production of these goods in the North.

Both the Union's and Confederacy's need to feed their armies impacted the diets of the wealthy. Meat, wheat, and dairy farmers in the Midwest produced high yields through the war years and produced enough to satisfy both the Union Army and Northern civilians. The North industrialized food production to mobilize the rations for soldiers. However, the advancement in food preservation and transportation benefitted civilian foodways as well, and before long, even wealthy Northerners consumed packaged and canned goods. The Confederacy could not keep up in the struggle to feed its troops. Production of food crops was low, and the South did not have the infrastructure to industrialize production. To overcome this problem, the Confederate government took drastic measures by instituting impressment for food. Confederate agents confiscated a mandatory 10 percent of certain crops for the war effort. Impressment depleted civilian food supplies and inflated prices, affecting Southerners of every economic strata.

Southern elites actually caused some Southern food shortages; despite inflated prices and the urging of the Confederate government to grow food, wealthy planters continued to grow cash commodities during the war. In Georgia, female civilians rioted for bread and soldiers starved while planters continued to use their land to produce cotton for export. Even when they did grow corn, planters preferred selling it to higher-paying whiskey distillers instead of contributing it to food stockpiles. Low food production on plantations dropped even lower when the Confederacy conscripted men away from the fields. Low agricultural yields inflated food prices dramatically. By January 1863, wholesale price indexes were seven times higher than at the beginning of the war. Even the wealthiest felt the impact of inflation that they partially caused.

In areas that experienced food shortages, the wealthy adapted their diets by substituting locally produced ingredients for unavailable foods. In the South, elite women viewed these dietary substitutions as a way to contribute to the war effort. While their husbands, fathers, and sons fought for the Confederacy, the women exchanged recipes as part of their civic duty. Wealthy Southerners continued to prefer breads and baked goods over vegetables during the war years, a problem since most wheat, yeast, and potash came from the North. To overcome shortages of ingredients, elite Southern women invented recipes like the patriotically named "Secession Bread," which called for rice or corn flour and corn cob "yeast."

The war's legacy on the foodways of wealthy Americans is twofold. First, industrialized food production facilitated even more long-distance food transportation than before the war. Elites in all sections of the country still ate midwestern wheat flour and beef as they did before the war, but after the war, the luxury staples became even more accessible. Second, wealthy Americans, especially in the South, gained a fondness for the corn bread, lard, molasses, and cheap cuts of pork that they consumed during the lean years of the war. Food that people ate from necessity became the food that people desired.

Ryan Hall

See also: *Economy and Work*: Impressment; Plantations; Rural Life, Northern; Rural Life, Southern; Urban Life, Northern; Urban Life, Southern; *Food and Drink*: Food, Shortages; Food Riots; *Housing and Community*: Refugees; Sieges; *Politics and Warfare*: Blockades

FURTHER READING

Burroughs, Frances M. "The Confederate Receipt Book: A Study of Food Substitution in the American Civil War," *The South Carolina Historical Magazine* 39:1 (January 1992): 31–50.

Smith, Andrew F. *Starving the South: How the North Won the Civil War*. New York: St. Martin's Press, 2011.

Williams, Teresa Crisp, and David Williams. " 'The Women Rising': Cotton, Class, and Confederate Georgia's Rioting Women." *Georgia Historical Quarterly* 86:1 (Spring 2002): 35–49.

FOOD RIOTS

Between March and April 1863, more than a dozen food riots erupted across the Confederacy. Across this two-month span, Confederate soldiers' wives organized a highly disciplined series of armed protests, participating in one of the most dramatic political expressions by Confederate women during the war. The food riots forced the Confederate government to provide support to women on the home front and fundamentally changed the relationship between Confederate women and the local, state, and federal governments.

Confederate bread riots as depicted in May 23, 1863, issue of *Frank Leslie's Illustrated Newspaper*. Between March and April in more than a dozen cities, desperate Confederate women protested food shortages and inflation. (Library of Congress)

In 1863, the Confederate government faced several crises, many of which focused on the food supply. The Davis administration struggled to field, feed, and equip the Confederate Army, as it simultaneously worked to maintain support for the war on the home front. As the Confederate government increased its demands on poor Southern families and pulled more men and supplies away from their homes and into the army, the burdens of war fell increasingly on women on the home front. Soldiers' inadequate wages, taxation, conscription, monetary policy, and other issues related to the ability of Southern women to support themselves during the war coalesced into the politics of subsistence. Throughout the war, poor families bore the brunt of the Confederate government's attempt to fend off Union forces. Slaveholding planters increasingly found ways to avoid military service, keep their property, and avoid taxation, which increasingly made poor Southerners wary of the Confederate government's loyalties. The breaking point came in early 1863 when the Davis administration issued a 10 percent tax on agricultural goods. This tax drove many soldiers' families past the point of subsistence toward starvation and precipitated the tumult of March and April.

Southern civilians ultimately turned to the only means of protest available. At least one dozen riots erupted in cities across the Confederacy. Soldiers' wives rioted in Atlanta, Georgia; Salisbury, North Carolina; Mobile, Alabama; Macon, Georgia; Petersburg, Virginia; and at least five other Southern cities. The biggest of all the riots occurred in Richmond, Virginia, on April 2, when 300 women marched through the streets of the Confederate capital and procured food and other essential supplies. Mary Jackson, whose son served in the Confederate Army, organized the protest. Jackson recruited soldiers' wives from the city and surrounding counties to protest the exorbitant food prices and the inadequate governmental support for soldiers' families. The women held a meeting at the Belvidere Baptist Church on Oregon Hill on April 1, to plan the riot. In an attempt to peaceably find a solution to their problems, the group of 300 women marched to the governor's mansion and demanded a meeting the following day, but they were turned away. The women then made their way to the city's market and demanded that local merchants sell their goods for the low prices guaranteed by the Confederate government. Once again, the women's demands were not met. After their initial efforts failed, the women broke into speculators' shops, looted them at gunpoint, and procured wagons to transport the goods to working-class sections of the city and countryside. All of the food riots followed the Richmond pattern of an organized public protest, the use of violence, and the procurement of goods to support soldiers' wives' subsistence.

In a direct response to the food riots, city and state governments expanded the public welfare provided for soldiers' families. At the local level, city governments expanded social services for the families of soldiers. In Mobile, Alabama, the city council appropriated $15,000 in poor relief and created the Citizen Relief Committee to procure food to sell to the indigent at reasonable prices. Similarly, in Richmond, Virginia, the city appropriated $20,000 for the families of soldiers. Several states also supplemented local governments and provided poor relief for the first time. Governor Joseph Brown of Georgia provided property tax exemptions, free salt, and free corn to soldiers' families. The Georgia state legislature also appropriated $2.5 million in 1863, $6 million in 1864, and $8 million in 1865, to provide relief for soldiers' families. The North Carolina state legislature distributed $20 million over the course of the war to help county governments support soldiers' families. State and local relief efforts directly addressed the issues raised by the women who participated in the food riots.

President Jefferson Davis's administration supplemented state and local relief efforts. Although the federal government did not provide direct welfare relief, they did alter several wartime policies to alleviate the stress on soldiers' families. The Davis administration revised the conscription legislation so that those slaveholders who were previously exempted from mandatory service had to grow food for the government. In North Carolina, for example, the Confederate government demanded that growers supply three-fourths of their of the corn crop to governmental agencies. As the Confederate government's supply of food increased, it distributed food to the most destitute counties. In 1864, the Confederate legislature exempted families with less than $500 in property from the 10 percent tax on produce to help assuage the pressures on poor families. These efforts did not provide direct relief, but they did alleviate much of the pressure that soldiers' families faced as their husbands, sons, fathers, and brothers fought for the Confederate cause.

By 1865, the relationship between Southern women and the government had fundamentally changed, in part as a result of the food riots. Although the Confederacy denied full citizenship rights and suffrage to women, the government listened to their complaints. Despite their inability to constitutionally participate in the political process, by participating in protests like the food riots, soldiers' wives flexed their collective political muscle, repudiated Confederate policies, and forced the government to address their needs. As hundreds of thousands of Southern men remained at and left for the front lines, their wives demanded the government provide adequate support for their subsistence as part of the contractual obligation between Southern citizens and the Confederate government.

Brandon T. Jett

See also: *Economy and Work*: Factory Workers, Southern; *Family Life and Gender Roles*: Cult of Domesticity; Womanhood, Southern; Young Women; *Food and Drink*: Food, Shortages

FURTHER READING

Amos, Harriet E. "All Absorbing Topics: Food and Clothing in Confederate Mobile." *Atlanta Historical Journal* 22: 3–4 (Fall/Winter 1978): 17–28.

Chesson, Michael V. "Harlots or Heroines? A New Look at the Richmond Bread Riot." *Virginia Magazine of History and Biography* 92:2 (April 1984): 131–175.

Escott, Paul. "The Moral Economy of the Crowd in Confederate North Carolina." *Maryland Historian* 13 (Spring/Summer 1982): 1–18.

McCurry, Stephanie. *Confederate Reckoning: Power and Politics in the Civil War South.* Cambridge, MA: Harvard University Press, 2010.

Rable, George C. *Civil Wars: Women and the Crisis of Southern Nationalism.* Urbana: University of Illinois Press, 1989.

FORAGING

Foraging, the taking of food and supplies from the surrounding countryside by soldiers, plagued civilians of both sides during the Civil War. Soldiers foraged to supplement monotonous or nonexistent rations, as well as to inflict punishment and revenge on enemy populations. Adding to farmers' losses, hostile troops often destroyed what they could not take with them. Although foraging was most prevalent when armies passed through or occupied enemy territory, civilians often found that their own troops were a menace as well.

Foraging was considered a legitimate practice, but one to be conducted under military rules. Unauthorized foraging encouraged straggling, undermined

1865 image of Sherman's Union troops foraging in South Carolina during his campaign. Soldiers on both sides foraged to supplement their food supply and to punish the enemy. (Library of Congress)

discipline, and weakened the army, and such illicit activity could descend into looting and pillage. According to regulations, foraging was to be conducted by parties of soldiers officially detailed from regiments or brigades for such a purpose, under officers' supervision. Property seized by foraging parties was to be accounted for and turned over to the army commissary or quartermaster departments, to be distributed as fairly as possible.

Civilians had little recourse when their food was taken by enemy troops. Officers in charge of foraging parties could issue receipts for confiscated property. Such receipts could be submitted to army officials who issued vouchers for repayment if the claimants could prove their loyalty. "Disloyal" claimants would receive nothing. Damage claims for military seizure of food and other property from Southerners who claimed to be Unionists were filed for decades after the war.

Early in the war, some Union officers tried to limit taking provisions from the civilian population, to keep from turning loyal Southerners into rebels. As the war continued and grew more bitter, foraging was excused and was even considered a legitimate method of weakening the Confederate war effort. In regions with loyal elements, the Union Army might issue a call for farmers to voluntarily bring in provisions in exchange for payment, before they dispatched foraging expeditions to take what was needed.

Despite regulations, it was common for soldiers to forage on their own account. A band of soldiers might slip out of camp at night, obtain what they could, and hide their plunder to consume later. In practice, officers tended to overlook illicit foraging, as long as their soldiers were present for duty when needed.

Once an army marched through or camped in an area, civilian food stores were soon exhausted. If armies settled down for extended periods, foraging and theft were so prevalent that many farmers found it pointless to plant crops, and soldiers found little or nothing to take. Scarcity of foodstuffs forced official as well as clandestine foragers to search far from camp, placing them in danger of capture by the enemy.

Cavalrymen had the best opportunities for foraging. Patrols and raids took them into places previously unvisited by hostile troops, where there was abundant food for the taking. Picket duty, marches, and transfers gave the infantry some chance of successful foraging; artillerymen's prospects were limited by their more restricted movements. Naval personnel, if serving in the rivers or sounds of the South, had opportunities for foraging ashore.

Commonly seized items included bacon, hams, and corn meal, as well as live poultry, hogs, and cattle. Gardens and orchards were stripped of all manner of fruits and vegetables, and forage was taken for army horses and mules. Many foragers avidly hunted for alcohol and tobacco. Soldiers also seized horses and mules, using them to pull farm wagons, carts, and carriages loaded with provisions. Foragers also dismantled rail fences to burn in campfires, and seized straw for their bedding.

By subsisting in large part on local food, an army could travel faster than one that carried all of its supplies in burdensome wagon trains. During Sherman's March in late 1864 and early 1865, foraging was used as a weapon of war as well as to provision the army. Usually each regiment had a permanent foraging squad, made of one man from each company. Their orders stated that farms would be emptied of nearly all provisions, but soldiers were not to enter private homes, and some portion of a family's food was to be left to the family to eat. Troops would destroy any captured firearms, as well as farm implements and tools. All horses, mules, and vehicles were to be taken. Empty wagons in the forefront of Sherman's army were detached for loading with captured food and forage, and then dropped back to join the supply train in the rear.

Self-appointed foragers in Sherman's March were called "bummers." Spreading far into the countryside, the bummers engaged in many skirmishes with Confederate cavalry and in effect formed a screen of patrols to protect the main column. Without military restrictions, bummers also committed many acts of plunder, arson, and other crimes. Seen by the enemy as mere criminals, a number of captured bummers were hanged by Confederate troops. Legitimate foraging parties carried signed orders to protect them against being treated as robbers.

Because most of the fighting happened in Confederate territory, Confederate foraging in the Union states was limited to a few events such as the Antietam and Gettysburg campaigns. Most foraging by Confederates was done in Southern territory. An 1863 impressment law allowed the Confederate Army to seize provisions and livestock for military use. Farmers were paid, but at official prices that were poor compensation for their losses. Failures in the supply system often left Southern troops short of food, and the resulting hunger and resentment pushed soldiers into illicit foraging.

A benign aspect of foraging was collecting blackberries, persimmons, and other wild edibles. Beginning in the spring of 1863, detailed soldiers of the Army of Northern Virginia gathered fresh wild onions, garlic, and sprouts to relieve shortages of fresh vegetables that contributed to scurvy among Confederate troops.

David A. Norris

See also: *Economy and Work*: Impressment; Plantations; Rural Life, Northern; Rural Life, Southern; *Food and Drink*: Gardens; Spirits; Tobacco

FURTHER READING

Billings, John D. *Hardtack and Coffee: The Unwritten Story of Army Life*. Reprint ed. Lincoln: University of Nebraska Press, 1993 (1887).

Campbell, Jacqueline Glass. *When Sherman Marched North from the Sea: Resistance on the Confederate Home Front*. Chapel Hill: University of North Carolina Press, 2003.

Frank, Lisa Tendrich. *The Civilian War: Confederate Women and Union Soldiers during Sherman's March*. Baton Rouge: Louisiana State University Press, 2015.

Kennett, Lee. *Marching Through Georgia: The Story of Soldiers and Civilians During Sherman's Campaign*. New York: Harper Collins, 1995.

GARDENS

Gardens of the Civil War period, in both the North and the South, largely reflected inherited English ideas of beauty and function. Nineteenth-century garden designs and plantings ranged from the purely aesthetic to the practical and pragmatic, with clearly demarcated spaces for each: cottage and cutting gardens, areas for the cultivation of vegetables and medicinal plants, and "sitting" or "viewing" gardens. Early gardens were typically arranged formally, often in geometric and concentric patterns, and designed with an eye to creating distinct rooms, with architectural plants such as trees and hedging used to demarcate the boundaries between sections.

Interest in gardening is reflected in the number of popular nineteenth-century books devoted to the subject such as Thomas G. Fessenden's *The New American Gardner, Containing Practical Directions for the Culture of Fruits and Vegetables, Including Landscape and Ornamental Gardening* (1845), and Mrs. S. O. Johnson's *Every Woman Her Own Flower Gardener* (1871). Even books with a political agenda and little ostensible focus on gardens or gardening carried surreptitious information on the subject. For example, landscape designer and social critic, Frederick Law Olmsted, who designed New York's Central Park, wrote *The Cotton Kingdom* in 1861 as a commentary on the slave economy. Within the book he found space to extol the particular beauties of Southern gardens. Gardening journals such as the *Soil of the South, A Monthly Journal Devoted to Agriculture, Horticulture, and Rural and Domestic Economy;* as well as the *Southern Cultivator;* the *Southern Agriculturalist*; *Gardening Magazine*; the *Magazine of Horticulture*; and the *Horticulturalist* all tended to be less political, and more instructive.

The British influence on American gardening may also be seen in individual gardeners, botanists, horticulturalists, garden writers, and gardeners who continued to shape American gardens and horticultural practices. Thomas Affleck (1812–1868), originally from Dumfries in Scotland, studied agriculture in Edinburgh, Scotland, before immigrating to America. He soon became an agricultural writer for the *Western Farmer and Gardener* in Cincinnati (1840), established the prominent "Southern Nurseries" in Mississippi as well as the later "Central Nursery" in Texas, and published *Affleck's Southern Rural Almanac and Plantation/ Garden Calendar* in the 1850s. Likewise, Englishman David Landreth (1752–1836) began the first seed business in America in Philadelphia in 1786, sold seeds propagated from plants sent back from the Lewis and Clark Expedition in 1804, and maintained a branch office in Charleston, South Carolina, until April 1862.

The continued British influence on American gardening was also propagated in the writings, design, and plantings of prominent American horticulturists and landscape architects. Landscape designer and editor of the *Horticulturist*, Andrew Jackson Downing, cowrote the extremely popular and highly influential *Cottage Residences* in 1842, borrowing romantic ideas of pastoral design and the relationship of architecture to landscape from the English author, John C. Loudon.

Gardens on either side of the Mason-Dixon line prior to the Civil War were often laid out in formal patterns. Plans designed in 1850–1860 for Parterre Gardens in Savannah, Georgia, were based on perfectly proportioned geometric shapes centered on circular, or ovoid, central planting beds with clearly demarcated walks from which to access, and appreciate, the plantings. Similarly, the 1840s plan for a "Persian Rug" garden at Henry Wadsworth Longfellow's garden in Cambridge, Massachusetts also reflects a complex, symmetrical, and formal garden design patterning, and is centered on a small central circle encased in a broad, swirling circle, with mirrored patterned beds on either side.

A second aspect of formal gardening was the planting and maintenance of tree avenues. In the South, live oaks (*Quercus virginiana*), lime flower trees (*Tilia europaea*), elms (*Ulmus compestris*), horse chestnuts (*Aesculus hippocastanum*), and the eastern red cedar (*Juniperus virginiana*) often lined plantation avenues. Magnolias (*Magnolia grandiflora*) were common avenue trees for city dwellings. Although a less common feature in Northern Gardens, tree avenues lined stately country homes in the Hudson Valley, New York, and before city residences in Philadelphia and Boston. Northern gardens typically used hedging plants such as box (*Buxus sempervirens*) and acacias (*Acacia farnesiana*) instead of stately trees for these avenues.

Although garden design remained largely static during the Civil War period, the postbellum era of Reconstruction saw a blossoming of interest in more romantic, and less formal, garden designs. This change in part reflected new English ideas of nature and mankind. It also showed Americans' embracing of visions of the frontier and interest in national landscape vistas. Not only were domestic gardens loosened from their formal, symmetrical patterns, but also plantings reflected a more studied abandon. Individual trees with expression were used to provide interesting shape and texture to the landscape rather than formal lines used to delineate it. In addition, postwar gardens tended to meander, gently enfolding the visitor, rather than directing and determining his or her path.

The nineteenth century saw the beginning of commercial seed and plant propagation and marketing. Nurserymen such as William Brackenridge of Philadelphia and Joseph Breck of Medfield, Massachusetts, as well as commercial producers of garden seeds such as the Shaker community at New Lebanon, New York, offered ornamental flowers such as roses, camellias, bluebells and bleeding hearts, chrysanthemums, and lily of the valley, alongside vegetables and fruits such as cabbages, brussels sprouts, lettuces, peas, pumpkins, yams, green beans, strawberries, gooseberries, raspberries, and currant bushes.

Changes in domestic planting habits occurred during the Civil War period, particularly in the South. These changes reflected the shifting demands and needs of the populace, particularly in terms of the increased use of domestic land for the production of utility crops in gardens. The correspondence of Southern families during the war regularly highlighted the impact of the war on food and medicine availability. For example, from Salem, North Carolina, Howell Hobbs noted the scarcity of foods in an 1861 letter to his daughter, Eudora. Hobbs wrote of planting radishes, lettuce, peas, cabbages, squashes, "snaps," cucumbers, and tomatoes. Others wrote of the lack of medicines, particularly the absence of quinine, due to Union blockades. The lack of access to regular medical preparations meant that Southerners regularly and specifically resorted to homegrown medicines such as boneset (*Eupatorium perfoliatum*), heal-all (*Prunella vulgaris*), pot marigold (*Calendula officinalis*), and the opium poppy (*Papaver somniferum*).

Bruna Gushurst-Moore

See also: Economy and Work: Agriculture; Impressment; Plantations; Rural Life, Northern; Rural Life, Southern; *Food and Drink*: Food, Shortages; *Science and Technology*: Medicine, Practice of

FURTHER READING

Cothran, James R. *Gardens and Historic Plants of the Antebellum South*. Columbia: University of South Carolina Press, 2003.
Leighton, Ann. *American Gardens of the Nineteenth Century: "For Comfort and Affluence."* Amherst: University of Massachusetts Press, 1987.
Otis, Denise. *Ground for Pleasure: Four Centuries of the American Garden*. New York: Harry N. Abrams, 2002.

HARDTACK

Hardtack, a plain flour-and-water cracker measuring about three inches square and half an inch thick, was the most common food that the U.S. government issued to its soldiers and sailors during the Civil War. Unappetizing, monotonous, and hated by the troops, hard bread—as it was officially called—nevertheless became a mainstay of armies in the field.

At least on paper, Union soldiers were the best-fed troops in the world. In August 1861 the army set each man's daily ration at one pound and six ounces of soft bread or flour or one pound of hard bread (in addition to other items). Hardtack, being long-lasting, cheap, and easy to produce, was much more common than soft bread. Troops stationed in forts or permanent camps had their meals prepared by company cooks, and they rarely ate hardtack unless there was no fresh bread available. In the field, however, each soldier ideally received 9 to 12 crackers per day along with salt pork, coffee, and sugar.

Quartermasters often issued several days' rations at once in preparation for a campaign, and this caused problems for men who ate them up immediately to lighten their load. Soldiers often drew rations for multiple days at a time; however, they typically had a difficult time stretching the rations to last the allotted period.

Hungry troops addressed this problem by "foraging"—that is, begging or stealing food from local civilians. Officers were not issued rations and had to buy their own food. Although supplying their own food meant that officers frequently ate well, there were occasions when a desperate officer had to ask his enlisted men for a couple of hardtack.

Although hardtack was extremely durable, this quality also made it very difficult to eat. Many described it as tasteless and difficult to chew. Soldiers in the field tried many different tricks to make hardtack edible. One of the most common methods was to drop crackers in coffee so that the liquid would soften them. Some pieces, however, were so hard that they refused to soften after a full day of soaking. Another popular method was to make a sandwich with two pieces of hardtack and a slice of raw salt pork.

Soldiers would cook their hardtack when time permitted. Soaking hardtack in water and then frying it in pork fat produced a dish that the men called "skillygalee." If the crackers were crumbled before soaking, the resulting meal was "hellfire stew," while "lobscouse" was the name given to hardtack and pork mixed in a pot with anything else available. It took experienced soldiers no more than half an hour to prepare their coffee, pork, and hardtack in the field. Each man cooked his meals in a group made up of him and a few comrades called a "mess." Sailors aboard naval ships had cooks to prepare their food, but they also ate together in messes.

Hardtack was everywhere during the war. It was a common sight to see hundreds of boxes marked "Army Bread" stacked in small mountains at a military supply base. Occupying U.S. authorities in the South supplied hard bread and other military rations to black laborers, freed slaves, war refugees, and other destitute civilians. One group of Union soldiers used the crackers to build a path through their camp, while others sent pieces home as souvenirs. Southern trains, meanwhile, carried hardtack to feed passengers and crew. The Confederate Army issued its men cornbread or meal, and hungry Southern soldiers eagerly acquired Yankee crackers whenever possible to fend off starvation or the monotony of their own rations.

In the days before the advent of strict food safety laws, government officials often let boxes of hardtack sit in warehouses or outside in the weather for long periods. This meant that by the time it reached the soldiers, it might be moldy and infested with weevils. Quartermasters did not usually give soldiers moldy hardtack, but had to distribute it even when infested with weevils. Unsanitary conditions and an unbalanced diet of hard bread and meat—which troops sometimes ate for months at a time—caused thousands of cases of scurvy and intestinal ailments.

Jokes about the hardness and durability of hardtack abounded. Soldiers called the plain wafers "sheet iron crackers," "cast-iron biscuits," "worm castles," and "teeth-dullers." They could be loaded into guns and shot at the enemy, it was said, or used to build fortifications. Men claimed that hardtack boxes marked "B.C." (Brigade Commissary) indicated the date of manufacture. There were many instances in the field, however, when hardtack was all that saved soldiers from starvation. During the siege of Chattanooga in late 1863, some Union troops were reduced to half of a cracker apiece per day. When supplies gave out during the Wilderness Campaign the following year, hungry men yelled "hardtack!" at passing generals. On such occasions, soldiers ate available hardtack with relish, weevils, and all.

Hardtack remained a staple item in U.S. Army field rations up to and during World War I. The unsavory crackers also retained notoriety in Civil War lore for many years after the conflict, with one veteran titling his account of soldier life *Hardtack and Coffee*.

William D. Hickox

See also: *Politics and Warfare*: Camp Life; *Food and Drink*: Coffee; Food, Soldiers; *Science and Technology*: Disease

FURTHER READING

Billings, John D. *Hardtack and Coffee: The Unwritten Story of Army Life*. Reprint ed. Lincoln: University of Nebraska Press, 1993.

Bircher, William. *A Drummer-Boy's Diary: Comprising Four Years of Service with the Second Regiment Minnesota Veteran Volunteers, 1861 to 1865*. St. Paul, MN: St. Paul Book and Stationery Co., 1889.

Bull, Rice C. *Soldiering: The Civil War Diary of Rice C. Bull, 123rd New York Volunteer Infantry*. San Rafael, CA: Presidio Press, 1977.

Davis, William C. *A Taste for War: The Culinary History of the Blue and the Gray*. Mechanicsburg, PA: Stackpole Books, 2003.

Wiley, Bell Irvin. *The Life of Billy Yank: The Common Soldier of the Union* Reprint. Baton Rouge: Louisiana State University Press, 1978.

Wiley, Bell Irvin. *The Life of Johnny Reb: The Common Soldier of the Confederacy*. Reprint. Baton Rouge: Louisiana State University Press, 1978.

HUNTING

In the 1860s, men hunted for subsistence, market, or sport. Although most families supplemented their diets with wild game, hunting allowed poor, rural families to meet vital nutritional needs, introduce variety into monotonous diets, and gain valuable goods to sell or trade. Hunters, almost all of whom were men, gained social advantages along with the practical benefits of meat and skins. Hunting met practical needs for poor families, but for men from all socioeconomic positions, hunting served as a demonstration of masculinity and helped reinforce the hunter's position as head of the household. Through hunting, men gained admission into a community of social peers and demonstrated their ability to provide for their dependents, social subordinates, or community.

In the United States, traditional land use practices meant that anyone with access to undeveloped land was able to hunt. For much of the nineteenth century, restrictions limiting access to private property applied primarily to the developed portions of an owner's land. Undeveloped forests or fields, even when privately owned, acted as a public commons from which anyone could harvest wildlife, gather wood, or forage edible plants. In addition, the law did not recognize ownership of wildlife until a hunter killed the animal, at which point the game became the property of the hunter. When hunters were actively pursuing game, they even believed that they had the right to cross into the developed areas of someone else's property. Some areas of the United States enacted game laws to protect wildlife populations from depletion as early as the seventeenth century, but these first laws were largely unenforced. Beginning in the 1840s, elite hunting clubs lobbied for laws restricting hunting access to certain groups, limiting the number of animals that hunters could kill, and placing restrictions on access to private property, but most states did not implement these types of restrictions until the decades following the Civil War. Throughout the 1860s, law and tradition ensured that hunting remained open to everyone with access to undeveloped land.

Free men and enslaved people alike expected the right to hunt on undeveloped land. Many slaveholders believed hunting made their enslaved people more compliant while supplementing rations with additional protein. Slaveholders thought they were granting slaves a privilege when they permitted them to hunt pest animals like raccoons and opossums, but enslaved men regarded hunting as a right, not a privilege. They hunted even when slaveholders discouraged or forbade hunting.

For enslaved African Americans to hunt successfully, they had to overcome barriers that free men did not face. During daylight hours, work dominated slaves' lives. In addition, laws prohibited enslaved people from owning guns. Due to these restrictions, slaves adopted hunting practices that offered the greatest reward for the least effort and met the challenge of hunting without firearms. They often hunted animals like raccoons and opossums, which slaveholders considered pests and which were active at night, when slaves had greater control over their own time. Among the enslaved community, a proven hunting dog was a particularly valuable asset. Raccoons often fought viciously when cornered, making a well-trained hunting dog essential for successful hunting. Working at night, the hunters and dogs would pursue the quarry and trap the opossum or raccoon in a tree. Hunters with guns shot the animals that their dogs treed, but slaves relied on their dogs for both the chase and the kill. The hunter climbed the tree, shook the animal loose, and the dogs waiting below dispatched the quarry.

Regardless of race, all men who depended on hunting for food or income used hunting practices that maximized their chances of success. For small game like rabbits and squirrels, hunters erected snares, traps, or deadfalls. Once set, these devices required little time or attention; the hunter simply returned regularly to collect his game and reset the trap. Hunters occasionally laid traps for large game by placing sharpened spikes behind fences along known deer runs, but hunters pursuing large game usually stalked and shot their quarry. One widely practiced method was fire or torch hunting, in which hunters carried hot coals in a pan or an aloft torch with a reflector positioned behind so that the light was directed away from the hunters. The bright light made deer easy targets for hunters, who could locate deer by the reflection of the animals' eyes as the animal stood mesmerized by the light. Men who hunted purely for pleasure and sport disdained fire hunting and derided fire hunters as "pothunters," lower-class hunters who resorted to unsportsmanlike tricks to fill their stew pots. Middle- and upper-class hunters may have criticized fire hunters, but the practice was effective; even sport hunters who criticized the practice occasionally admitted to resorting to fire hunting when frustrated in their efforts to take down a deer.

Many hunters supplemented their income by selling or trading excess game, but hunters who killed large quantities of game could earn their livelihood by selling game for market. Large numbers of game animals rarely survived in populated areas, so dedicated market hunters typically worked in the West or isolated regions of the East that were poorly suited for agricultural settlement. Market hunters often worked on commission or salary for wholesalers, who distributed goods to urban game merchants, milliners who decorated fashionable hats with fur and feathers, and other markets. Market hunters strived to take as much game as quickly as possible. To sport hunters, market hunting threatened the population of game animals by encouraging wasteful slaughter, which in turn left little or no game available for sport hunting.

The reasons men hunted and the methods they employed differed depending on their race and class, but for all hunters, the act of hunting was closely associated with concepts of manliness and masculinity. Whether men added meat to the sparse diet of the slave quarters or proudly displayed trophy animals, hunters demonstrated their ability to meet the obligations of their sex and class by providing and caring for their dependents.

Jama McMurtery Grove

See also: *Family Life and Gender Roles*: Manhood, Northern; Manhood, Southern; *Recreation and Social Customs*: Sport Hunting

FURTHER READING

Giltner, Scott. "Slave Hunting and Fishing in the Antebellum South." In Dianne D. Glave and Mark Stoll, eds. *"To Love the Wind and Rain": African Americans and Environmental History*. Pittsburgh: University of Pittsburgh Press, 2006, pp. 21–36.

Herman, Daniel Justin. *Hunting and the American Imagination*. Washington, DC: Smithsonian Institution Press, 2001.

Marks, Stuart A. *Southern Hunting in Black and White: Nature, History, and Ritual in a Carolina Community*. Princeton, NJ: Princeton University Press, 1991.

Tober, James A. *Who Owns the Wildlife?: The Political Economy of Conservation in Nineteenth-Century America*. Westport, CT: Greenwood Press, 1981.

KITCHENS

American kitchens during the Civil War were much like kitchens throughout the country during the prior decades. Like today, the kitchen was important for all Americans. In rural households, the kitchen acted not only as a place of food preparation and consumption, but also as a meeting place and a place of entertaining and family time. For middle class or wealthy families in urban areas, the kitchen played a smaller role, and was mostly a place of food preparation as parlors and dining rooms acted as places of consumption and entertainment. In the South, many middle- and upper-class households maintained kitchens and cookhouses that were separate from the main household. This location served to isolate the house from fires and to keep cooking-related heat out of the house during the hot summer months. In the urban centers of the North, kitchens were built at the back of the house or in basements.

Although the items of a household kitchen could vary depending on the region and the wealth of the occupant, kitchens in general contained many of the same staples and appliances. The center of the Civil War era kitchen was the wood or coal burning cookstove or range. Cookstoves and ranges were a fairly new addition to the American kitchen and had only come into widespread use during the 1850s. Before this advance, Americans cooked in a hearth. A cooking range was a large, brick-set iron appliance. Stoves were completely cast iron and took up less space in a kitchen. Ranges were typically larger than cookstoves, and could accommodate the cooking of a number of dishes at one time. Some ranges also had a "hot closet" below the oven, which could keep dishes warm. Sizes varied depending on the size and the wealth of the household. By the 1860s, many urban houses were using coal as fuel for their stoves or ranges, while rural people continued to use wood. As the kitchen was the center of the household for many, the kitchen stove or range became the center of attention because it provided warmth and sustenance.

Women prepare food in the kitchen of the Philadelphia Citizens Volunteer Hospital during the Civil War. Industrial kitchens like this one were designed to feed large numbers of people and had to adapt to the available supplies and food. Home kitchens during the war varied based on the size and wealth of a household. (Library of Congress)

Sinks also became a staple of nineteenth-century kitchens. Kitchen sinks were made of iron, soapstone, or granite, encased in a wooden structure. Although in the 1860s some poorer people in rural areas still had to carry water into the kitchen, much of the urban middle and upper class had water pumped into their kitchens.

By the 1860s, kitchen utensils, which had previously been handcrafted or forged, were often machine made and manufactured in large quantities. Each household's utensils depended on the wealth of a family. Kitchen utensils could be made of cast iron, wood, and sometimes sheet metal or tin. The typical kitchen of the middle-class American—such as in the homes of doctors and lawyers—during the 1860s contained cookware that was usually made of cast iron or tin.

Like earlier kitchens, kitchens of the 1860s had a wide variety of accessories. Members of the middle class had oil cans, a candle box, a funnel, an egg boiler, various scoops and dippers, a colander, as well as bread and cake boxes. Many middle-class households possessed a number of wooden and earthenware kitchen utensils and accessories. Typical wooden items included a breadboard, spice boxes, and a salt box. Earthenware jars with lids for pickles, butter, and salt and variously sized baskets for gathering fruit, vegetables, and eggs were also often present. In addition, the 1850s and 1860s saw an explosion in the number of kitchen contraptions and utensils that were earlier considered to be novel.

These included cast-iron peach parers, lemon squeezers, nutcrackers, graters, and other devices. Rotary egg beaters were also introduced during this period. Another novel contraption was the ice-cream freezer, first invented in 1864.

Most cookware—pots and pans—was made of heavy forged iron, cast iron, tin, or copper. Copper pots and pans were more expensive than others and usually only found in the kitchens of the middle and upper class. The usual kitchen contained various large pots and pans such as an oval fish kettle, multiple and differently sized saucepans, many skillets, a waffle iron, a toasting iron, bread pans, and a tea kettle. Household kitchens of the middle class had a much wider variety of items, and often included tin cake and pie pans.

Kitchen furnishings in the nineteenth century were similar to those of earlier periods. Many Americans used large cupboards to store pots, pans, and other kitchenware. Kitchens also had a small table located next to the sink, which was used for preparing food prior to cooking. Larger kitchens for the wealthier or for larger families had more worktables and cupboards than those of poorer families.

Army camp kitchens during the Civil War were much different from civilian kitchens. Union Army soldiers and quartermasters were typically much better provisioned than their Confederate counterparts were. Federal authorities issued troops a number of items, including kettles, mess pans, and coffee pots. Usually kettles were made of tinned sheet iron. Union troops used large iron mess pans to serve food. Soldiers on both sides used their cookware for multiple purposes, as mess pans were used to cook food and as washbasins. Sometimes Confederate soldiers would build stoves into the side of hills. When they marched, soldiers used mules to carry camp cooking equipment. In many circumstances, soldiers on both sides only used a few small items that they could carry. On both sides, soldiers often left camp cookware behind in hasty movements of camps. Confederate troops frequently lacked cookware and eating utensils. This shortage resulted both from neglect by the Confederate administration and, as the war progressed, from rampant shortages in the South.

Tiffany Hensley

See also: *Economy and Work*: Rural Life, Northern; Rural Life, Southern; Urban Life, Northern; Urban Life, Southern; *Family Life and Gender Roles*: Womanhood, Northern; Womanhood, Southern; *Food and Drink*: Coffee; Cookbooks and Recipes; Food, African Americans; Food, Native Americans; Food, Northern; Food, Shortages; Food, Soldiers; Food, Southern; Food, Upper Classes; Food Riots; Substitutes, Food and Drink; Taverns; *Housing and Community*: Boarding Houses; *Politics and Warfare*: Camp Life; *Science and Technology*: Cooking Techniques

FURTHER READING

Carlisle, Nancy, Melinda Talbot Nasardinov, and Jennifer Pustz. *America's Kitchens*. Boston: Historic New England, 2008.

Harrison, Molly. *The Kitchen in History*. Oxford, UK: Osprey Publishing, 1972.

Plante, Ellen M. *The American Kitchen*. New York: Facts on File, 1995.

Volo, Dorothy Denneen, and James M. Volo. *Daily Life in Civil War America*. Westport, CT: Greenwood Press, 1998.

Wilson, Bee. *Consider the Fork: A History of How We Cook and Eat*. New York: Basic Books, 2012.

MEALTIME ETIQUETTE

Mealtime etiquette played an important role in nineteenth-century culture. Many etiquette books of the time stressed the importance of mealtime etiquette. The primary audiences for these books were the upper class, wealthy American ladies and gentlemen. The working class, poor, soldiers, and emancipated slaves would have performed varying degrees of these manners depending on their exposure to etiquette nuances and their financial means. Americans believed that manners and social grace distinguished a lady or gentleman from those of the lower classes. As a result, they believed that proper etiquette ought to be practiced at home daily and not just when in the company of others. An individual who was clumsy and ill-rehearsed in manners during mealtime would be seen as someone who only had "company manners," evidence of lower-class status.

Proper mealtime etiquette included adequately preparing the dining room for guests. Civil War era Americans with the means to plan lavish dinners for friends went to great lengths to ensure that the atmosphere promoted conversation and digestion. Homes that could afford to do so would carpet their dining rooms to help muffle the sound of their free or enslaved servants' feet as they served dinner. Owners of homes without servants would likewise want to carpet their dining rooms in an effort to quiet creaking floorboards as well as to mirror the practices of wealthier homes. In addition, rooms where guests would be eating or conversing needed to be well lit. Some etiquette books of the period claimed that light was essential to the digestive process, and that light should be both soft and fill the room. Chandeliers were the preferred method of lighting because they did not give off a distracting, unpleasant glare. In addition, proper table furniture included slightly elevated, high-backed dining chairs with no armrests and, ideally, a footstool for each guest's comfort.

During the Civil War era the Russian plan of table setting became the earmark of wealth and society at the American table. The degree of elegance of this setting varied depending on the status, season, and occasion for the dinner. For wealthy families, this setting began with a white damask tablecloth over the table covering. Any lamps, candles, or decorations placed on the table could not hinder eye contact between any parties present at the meal. A work of art would be placed in the middle as a centerpiece that allowed all guests a common point of conversation. On each side of the centerpiece bouquets of flowers or, for elegance, small table fountains could be added. The rest of the table would be covered with the dessert to admire throughout the meal. Glasses for wine were placed above the silverware to the right of the plate; napkins could be folded into designs and put on the plate or they could simply be folded neatly and placed on the plate. Either servants, usually no more than two, would move around the table to serve the food to each guest individually, or the food would come out to the guest already plated.

The menu and number of courses served to guests during the nineteenth century depended entirely upon the season, the guests' and host's preferences, and the resources of the host of the meal. Meals followed a predictable pattern of drinks and courses but part of the pleasure of the meal was in the presentation and variety in courses.

The flow of the meal would depend upon the number of courses and the menu. One constant in formal dining was that each meal would begin with soup. The purpose of the soup was to aid in digestion by starting the digestive process with liquids before moving to solid food. For this reason, broth-based soups were preferred because thicker soups were thought to clog the digestive track and hamper diners' appetites. After the soup, the menu typically moved from light to heavy—both in terms of heartiness and richness of flavor—and ended with the dessert, the richest and thickest component of the meal.

Mealtime etiquette also included rules on table behavior. Guests waited in the sitting room or parlor for dinner to be announced. Once the host announced dinner, men would escort women to the table and then wait for all of the women to be seated before taking their seats. As a sign of respect, any time a lady entered the room or rose to leave the table all the men at the table stood up.

Once at the table, there were several points of etiquette for both men and women in regards to the serving and eating of the meal. Meals centered on the pleasure of company and the enjoyment of food rather than on sustenance and satiety. Most etiquette books reminded men and women of the importance of utilizing the right utensil for each course, taking small bites, chewing quietly with the mouth closed, and maintaining polite conversation. Etiquette books also reminded guests that food directly correlated to the host's hospitality. As a result, it was seen as incredibly rude to eat too quickly or too slowly, decline a dish, or ask for seconds. A host would always offer seconds but a polite guest knew to decline them. Formal mealtime was an opportunity for a host to show hospitality and for a guest to be appreciative, never taking advantage of the generosity shown by the host or hostess.

Megan M. Gallagher

See also: *Economy and Work*: Rural Life, Northern; Rural Life, Southern; Urban Life, Northern; Urban Life, Southern; *Family Life and Gender Roles*: Honor; Manhood, Northern; Manhood, Southern; Womanhood, Northern; Womanhood, Southern; *Food and Drink*: Food, Upper Classes; *Recreation and Social Customs*: Etiquette, Advice Manuals; Etiquette, Rural Manners; Etiquette, Urban Manners; Parlors

FURTHER READING

Habits of Good Society: A Handbook for Ladies and Gentlemen. New York: Carleton Publishers, 1865.

Hartley, Cecil B. *The Gentlemen's Book of Etiquette and Manual of Politeness: Being a Complete Guide for a Gentleman's Conduct in All His Relations Towards Society*. Boston: G.W. Cottrell Publisher, 1860.

Hartley, Florence. *The Ladies' Book of Etiquette and Manual of Politeness: A Complete Hand Book for the Use of the Lady in Polite Society*. Boston: G.W. Cottrell Publisher, 1860.

MOONSHINE

Applied generally, the name "moonshine" referred to any variety of corn whiskey privately and illegally distilled. Though moonshine is known by other names as well, Tennessee white and hooch, for instance, and even though its origins in the United States began during colonial times in western Pennsylvania by Scots-Irish immigrants, or Ulstermen, it is most often associated with Appalachia after Reconstruction. The name "moonshine" dates to the seventeenth century, and represents a derivation of the term "moonrakers," or English smugglers who attempted to evade the excise tax on alcohol and royal tax collectors by working at night. After ratification of the Constitution, the Washington administration levied an excise tax on whiskey, provoking a rebellion of western frontier farmers. Thus began the American chapter of the tension between illegal distillers and "reveneuers."

By the Civil War, the federal government had re-imposed the excise tax on whiskey and tobacco to help finance the war effort. As Union troops swept through the states of the Confederacy, they provided a lucrative market for both legal and illegal whiskey merchants. Most of the legal distillers lived in Northern states and enjoyed the option of procuring a license to sell directly to Union troops. Indeed, Union officers encountered little in the way of limits on access to alcohol. Enlisted troops, on the other hand, were permitted access to alcohol only under heavily regulated conditions while on duty, and though the army discouraged alcohol use, it did little to prevent soldiers from procuring alcohol while on leave. As such, Union soldiers learned to be quite crafty about the manner in which they procured and consumed alcohol. Sometimes soldiers requested whiskey for medicinal purposes while in camp, and sometimes they smuggled illegally procured whiskey into camp using butter jars with the butter smeared on the outside of the jar to mask its true contents. In other cases smuggling alcohol into the camp was achieved by using the muzzle of the rifle, which could hold approximately one pint of alcohol.

Legal commissary whiskey could prove quite expensive during the Civil War period. In Fredericksburg, Virginia, Union troops, who were paid only $13 per month, were known to pay up to $10 per gallon for legal whiskey. As expensive as it was, some troops took to acquiring it from local taverns or from civilian distillers in occupied areas who still remained outside the reach of the revenuers. In some cases, soldiers worked out deals with local purveyors for prices well below the price of commissary whiskey. In others, soldiers simply took provisions of "moonshine," illegally distilled whiskey. Soldiers even engaged in foraging expeditions with the expressed intention of conducting economic warfare when their true intention was to procure moonshine.

Before the war, distillers of whiskey in what would become the Confederacy crafted spirits for small-scale use. During the war, as Union troops occupied more Confederate territory, Southerners hid their stills from foraging Union troops and created lookout networks from within family units. They sometimes sold to sutlers, or licensed merchants who sold wares directly to the army but who purchased the moonshine illegally. These sutlers then sold moonshine clandestinely from within their licensed operation. These exchanges often became elaborate ploys that involved code words and networks from within the ranks of the army itself; soldiers would ask for an obscure product and subsequently be sent to an alternate location, usually the back of the wagon, tent, or temporary store. In this way, moonshiners avoided interacting with the soldiers and sutlers avoided paying the tax on whiskey. On other occasions, they established relationships with the soldiers themselves whereupon prices were negotiated through only a few trusted participants. This practice of hiding stills deep within mountain communities and seeking to avoid the revenuers through kinship lookouts continued into Reconstruction.

The economic relationship between moonshiners and Union troops took on a mythic quality during Reconstruction. Whereas Yankee troops sometimes took moonshine without paying for it, this behavior was the exception rather than the rule. After all, moonshiners sought out Yankee markets, though it might mean retribution from local militias or regulators. Distillers made a comparatively good living producing moonshine within an incredibly difficult economic context. Nevertheless, after the war, moonshiners went from being considered virtual traitors to heroes as they successfully branded their economic self-interest in evading revenue men as a heroic form of resisting Yankee tyranny during Reconstruction.

Reconstruction governments maintained the excise taxes on whiskey, as the costs of postwar governing continued to mount. The Revenue Bureau of the Treasury Department was transformed after the Civil War from merely collecting revenue into becoming a virtual police agency whose agents were armed and who sometimes engaged in shootouts with moonshiners to more actively engage in revenue collection. Southern Democratic candidates, such as Zebulon Vance of North Carolina, campaigned in opposition of the revenue laws that served as a symbol of Yankee oppression. Such campaigning benefitted moonshiners in two ways. For one, it drove up the price of untaxed whiskey creating a lucrative market for distillers. The federal government estimated that up to 10 million gallons of moonshine were produced and sold by 1896. More importantly though, such campaigning made folk heroes out of distillers and branded an image that endured for decades after the Reconstruction and well beyond World War II.

Moonshine's unregulated and underground production led to creative and questionable techniques of production that sometimes led to unexpected and harmful effects. Most distillers used fractional distillation, and the circumstances behind its production sometimes produced deleterious effects on consumers and distillers alike. Moonshine gained a reputation for sometimes causing temporary blindness resulting from the presence of large quantities of methanol. Also known as wood alcohol, it contains a toxin that directly attacks the optic nerve. In addition, heating the yeast, corn husk, and water mixture sometimes caused explosions.

Mark A. Panuthos

See also: Economy and Work: Sutlers; *Family Life and Gender Roles*: Manhood, Northern; Manhood, Southern; *Food and Drink*: Spirits; Taverns

FURTHER READING

Johnson, Burt. *American Moonshine: The History of Illegal Liquor in the American South.* Minneapolis: University of Minnesota Press, 2002.

Peine, Emelie K., and Kai A. Schafft. "Moonshine, Mountaineers, and Modernity: Distilling Cultural History in the Southern Appalachian Mountains." *Journal of Appalachian Studies* 18 (Spring–Fall 2012): 93–112.

Ramold, Steven. *Baring the Iron Hand: Discipline in the Union Army.* Dekalb: Northern Illinois University Press, 2010.

The Science and History of Moonshine. http://www.instituteofman.com/2011/08/24/the-science-and-history-of-moonshine/. Accessed August 1, 2014.

Wiley, Bell Irvin. *The Life of Billy Yank: The Common Soldier of the Union Army.* Baton Rouge: Louisiana State University Press, 2008.

SALT

Salt was a valuable commodity during the Civil War. A necessary part of the human diet, salt was also required for preserving meat and keeping livestock healthy. In addition, in antebellum America, fresh eggs were packed in rock salt to cushion them during shipping. Salt was also used to preserve butter, to treat hides intended for tanning, and to make some household dyes. In the U.S. Army and in most civilian references, a bushel of salt weighed 50 pounds.

Before the war, salt was so inexpensive that most people took it for granted. Antebellum salt consumption was estimated at approximately one bushel per person. Imported salt, much of it brought in as ballast cargo in British vessels, accounted for about 17 million bushels annually. In addition, Americans produced approximately 12 million bushels domestically. Much domestic salt was produced at inland works drawing from prehistoric deposits, usually in the form of brine drawn from salt marshes, or from salt water pumped from shallow wells. New York's salt industry was the largest in the United States in 1860, producing over seven million bushels annually.

Except in Virginia, the South produced relatively little salt before the war. After the Union blockade began in 1861, limited amounts of salt arrived in steam blockade-runners. However, Union blockaders seized numerous schooners laden with salt along the Southern coast. As a result, the Confederacy's national and state governments fostered public and private efforts to establish new sources of salt, and tried to restrict speculators from manipulating its price.

Important Southern salt manufacturing regions such as West Virginia's Kanawha Valley and Louisiana's Avery Island were also lost to Union forces, further tightening supplies across the Confederacy. Critical shipments of Confederate salt came from Saltville, in the southwest Virginia mountains. The supply there was abundant enough to permit North Carolina, Georgia, and Alabama to establish salt works, and Confederates worked to protect this resource. Confederate troops repulsed a Union attack on Saltville on October 2, 1864. A later raid by Major General George Stoneman destroyed the salt works on December 20 and 21, 1864. Other significant inland salt sources were located in Alabama and Texas. Some small rural salt licks—naturally occurring deposits of salt—scattered across the South also yielded salt for livestock.

Another major source of Confederate salt was the sea. However, because Union forces occupied or continually besieged much of the South's coast early in the war, salt from these sources was not readily available. Salt making continued in Confederate-held coastal regions, with the highest output coming from Florida as well as from southeastern North Carolina and Texas.

In coastal salt works, brick furnaces boiled brine in large shallow iron pans of various sizes, approximately four by six feet or larger, but only about five or ten inches deep. One authority estimated that boiling 10,000 gallons of seawater yielded nearly 32 ½ bushels of salt, at a cost of one cord of wood to 4 ½ bushels of salt. Concentrating the brine by solar evaporation before boiling it saved fuel. Wooden sheds covered the salt pans and reservoirs to prevent dilution by rainwater. Some works used windmills or steam engines to pump water.

Crystallized salt was shoveled into troughs, allowing some of the remaining water to drain out. The salt was then scraped off, bagged, and sold. The sale of wet salt, which could lose a fifth of its weight during shipment, was a frequent cause of complaint during the Civil War.

Salt works located near the ocean were particularly vulnerable to Union naval raids. Plumes of smoke in the daytime and the glow of furnace fires at night betrayed their locations. Enemy warships frequently bombarded the Confederate salt works and launched hundreds of raiding parties that captured laborers, burned or destroyed sheds and equipment, and dumped finished salt into sounds or creeks.

Salt makers found some safety from the Union Navy by leaving the ocean for the sounds and tidal creeks, although more fuel was needed to boil the less saline water. Quakers were permitted to labor in the salt works in lieu of military service, and other workers were exempted from conscription.

Before the war, salt was available in large sacks for one half cent per pound, or less. During the war, the price of salt soared in the Confederacy, temporarily reaching $1.50 per pound in Richmond when speculators took advantage of the attacks on the Saltville mines late in 1864.

A ration of salt was issued to Civil War soldiers. For most of the war, Union soldiers received 3 ¾ pounds of salt per day, divided among 100 men. Rations changed based on shortages and the locations of the troops. In addition, meat provided for the troops was usually heavily treated with salt for preservation. Curing one thousand pounds of pork required around two bushels of salt.

In the South, the shortage of rail and wagon transportation made getting fuel and supplies for salt works and sending out the salt almost impossible at times. Labor, teams and wagons, food and forage, and even sacks and barrels for salt were in short supply. Many salt makers gave up and got out of the business.

Civilians desperate for salt often dug up earth from under their smokehouses. Salt accumulated over the years could be extracted by dissolving the dirt in water, and boiling it. Some people filtered the brine through sand or straw. The resulting salt was regarded as useable, although it was usually described as dark in color because it was stained by traces of soil.

Newspapers printed hints for conserving salt. The most common suggestions involved cutting meat into very thin strips and drying it, or mixing saltpeter or wood ashes in the salt used for curing bacon or hams. Another suggestion, for people living near the coast, was using seawater for cooking.

Due to high prices and scarcity, some Southern state governments distributed free or reduced-price salt to indigent families of Confederate soldiers.

David A. Norris

See also: *Arts*: Newspapers, Northern; Newspapers, Southern; *Economy and Work*: Rural Life, Northern; Rural Life, Southern; Urban Life, Northern; Urban Life, Southern; *Food and Drink*: Food, Shortages; *Religion and Belief*: Quakerism; *Science and Technology*: Railroads

FURTHER READING

Leconte, John. *How to Make Salt from Sea-Water*. Columbia, SC: The Governor and Council, 1862.

Lonn, Ella. *Salt as a Factor in the* Confederacy. Tuscaloosa: University of Alabama Press, 1965.

Williams, Isabel M., and Leora H. McEachern. *Salt: That Necessary Article*. Wilmington, NC: Historical Society of the Lower Cape Fear, 1973.

SPIRITS

Distilled alcohol was widely enjoyed, reviled, regulated, and smuggled during the Civil War. In army camps, liquor was both a source of relaxation and a cause for serious disciplinary problems. Excessive alcohol use was a problem for both sides, but was perhaps worse for the Union, because wartime shortages made it more difficult for Confederate soldiers to obtain illicit liquor.

In the antebellum United States, a temperance movement had been growing in strength since the 1830s. Several Northern states, beginning with Maine in 1846, had passed laws restricting alcohol. Annual alcohol consumption had dropped to about 2 ½ gallons per capita for people of drinking age by 1860, about one third of the rate in the 1820s.

Despite prohibitionist sentiment, alcohol use was common in the nineteenth century. Almost every town across the United States had drinking establishments, usually referred to as saloons rather than as taverns. Whiskey was by far the most preferred type of distilled liquor, but brandy, rum, and flavored cordials were also popular. Bitters were concoctions of herbs and alcohol; touted as medicine, they also were served as drinks in saloons. Popular nondistilled alcoholic drinks included beer, wine, and apple cider.

The U.S. Army halted its daily spirit ration to enlisted men in 1832, but the U.S. Navy continued a daily allowance of one gill (four ounces) for enlisted men. Still referred to as grog, as the Royal Navy had long called its ration of watered-down rum, the U.S. Navy spirit ration was usually American-made whiskey. Aboard ship, liquor for naval rations or medical use was kept in a secure room called a spirit locker. Spirit rations were doled out mixed with water at scheduled intervals, under the supervision of petty officers and armed marines.

At the instigation of temperance advocates and reformers, the Union Navy abolished its spirit ration as of September 1, 1862. Hundreds of kegs of naval whiskey were then sold at auction or turned over to medical use. Sailors and marines received an extra five cents a day in pay in lieu of the alcohol allotment. The roughly $1.50 a month was in effect a raise of about 8 to 10 percent in enlisted men's pay. Officially, the Confederate Navy kept daily ration of one gill of spirits or half a pint of wine until the end of the war.

Naval officers still had access to liquor and wine aboard ship, and army officers could keep private supplies or buy whiskey from the commissary department. Although some generals such as "Stonewall" Jackson and J. E. B. Stuart were known abstainers, many officers on both sides were accused of drunkenness on duty or even on the battlefield. General Ulysses S. Grant was dogged by rumors of excessive drinking.

Although now recognized as a depressant, alcohol was considered a stimulant or tonic by physicians in the 1800s. Laudanum, a mixture of alcohol and opium, was used as a painkiller and a treatment for dysentery. Other medicines such as quinine were often given in whiskey. Doctors prescribed whiskey, brandy, wine, eggnog, or other alcoholic beverages for patients suffering from wounds, shock, fevers, or nearly any other condition. Alcohol might be administered in great quantity. One Union soldier in a St. Louis army hospital was prescribed 36 ounces of brandy a day. The Confederate Army's Medical Department determined by 1865 that it needed over 600,000 gallons of alcohol per year. Hospitals often ran short of alcohol supplies due to medical needs as well as theft, and especially in the Confederacy, administrators appealed to the public for donations.

Army and navy officers issued special servings of liquor to men suffering from fatigue or exposure to harsh weather, or after and even during combat. Captain John Worden of the USS *Monitor* issued his men two ounces of whiskey during their battle with the ironclad CSS *Virginia* at Hampton Roads on March 9, 1862. Survivors saved from the sea after the sinking of the CSS *Alabama* by the USS *Kearsarge* in 1864 were also issued whiskey.

With new soldiers crowded into army camps and away from their families and the social restrictions of home, excessive drinking led to misconduct, disobedience, desertion, crime, and health problems. Many commanders worried about the effect of alcohol on their troops. In 1862 Major General George B. McClellan deplored drunkenness as a vice, asserting that eliminating alcohol in the military would undoubtedly aid the U.S. army and be like adding 50,000 fighting men. Despite the concerns of the leadership, army regulations that prohibited drinking in camp were not valid in civilian establishments. As a result, the Confederacy declared martial law in some cities such as Richmond to prevent soldiers from getting drunk while off duty.

The smuggling of alcohol by enlisted personnel was a perennial problem in the Civil War armies. Sutlers were prohibited from selling alcohol in army camps, but such regulations were often evaded. Alcohol might be purchased from local civilians, or even shipped to camp in express packages hidden inside mislabeled jars or cans, loaves of bread, or roast chickens. In the field, soldiers seized liquor when capturing enemy supply depots or while looting civilian homes.

Luxury items that took up valuable space on blockade runners included imported brandy, gin, rum, wine, and sherry. Imports of alcohol through the blockade for private use were prohibited early in 1864, but often continued because of demand.

To conserve food, most Confederate state legislatures prohibited the distillation of alcohol from corn or grain, other than supplies made for military use. The Union taxed alcohol rather than restricting its manufacture.

Illicit whiskey could be made from appalling ingredients, with additives such as turpentine, coal oil, and chewing tobacco mixed in for flavor or color. Southern newspapers printed numerous recipes for beer and wine made from locally available ingredients such as fruits and berries, often using molasses in place of sugar for fermentation. Common slang terms for liquor included "oil of gladness," "forty rod," "bust-head," "blue ruin," "tanglefoot," and "pop-skull."

David A. Norris

See also: *Arts*: Newspapers, Northern; Newspapers, Southern; *Economy and Work*: Sutlers; *Food and Drink*: Moonshine; Taverns; Tobacco; *Politics and Warfare*: Blockades; Camp Life

FURTHER READING

Wiley, Bell Irvin. *The Life of Billy Yank*. Reprint ed. Baton Rouge: Louisiana State University Press, 1990.

Wiley, Bell Irvin. Reprint ed. *The Life of Johnny Reb*. Baton Rouge: Louisiana State University Press, 1990.

SUBSTITUTES, FOOD AND DRINK

Particularly in the Confederacy, the Union blockade, inflation, the breakdown of the transportation system, and the disruption of agriculture by the war created shortages of many types of food and drink. Shortages were aggravated by the lack of food processing facilities in the South. Southerners replaced numerous missing items in their diets with substitute ingredients during the war.

By 1861 Southern agriculture had moved sharply toward growing cash crops, mainly cotton, instead of food. Most American wheat was grown in the Union and in the Border States. As a result, white flour became very scarce and expensive in the Confederacy. Most wartime Southern bread was made from cornmeal, but some households baked bread with flour made from rice or cow peas. Cooked pumpkin mixed with the dough helped stretch supplies of meal or flour. Potatoes found their way into bread as well as pie crusts.

With coffee imports practically cut off by the blockade, rye coffee was the most popular substitute. Already in use in antebellum America by frugal families, rye coffee was also used by some Northerners during the war, because it was more affordable than real coffee beans. Also substituted for coffee were concoctions made from chicory; corn, peas, peanuts, or okra seeds; dandelion roots; acorns; cotton seeds; or chopped and dried sweet potatoes. The seeds or other ingredients were variously dried in the sun or scorched on a stove. Once dry they were ground in a coffee mill, or with a mortar and pestle, and then boiled as if they were coffee beans. Coffee made from alternatives, with or without a trace of the real product, came to be called "Confederate coffee." Most of these versions were unsuccessful on their own, but they helped to stretch a small but expensive supply of real "Rio" or "Mocha" coffee. Some Confederate newspapers claimed that substitute coffees were healthier than the original. However, there was also some debate in the Northern as well as the Southern press over the safety of rye coffee, which some authorities believed was toxic.

During wartime, imported tea could be replaced with herbs or wild plants such as blackberry or raspberry leaves, sage, mint, or sassafras root. Yaupon, a coastal shrub with leaves that contain caffeine, was also used to make tea.

Sugar also became scarce in the Confederacy during the war, particularly in the East after the July 4, 1863 fall of Vicksburg and the Union control of the Mississippi River. Sorghum became the primary replacement for sugar. Also called "Chinese sugar cane," sorghum was introduced in the South during the 1850s. The sorghum stalks were crushed to extract a sweet juice, which was then boiled down into a form of molasses called "long sweetening." This syrup sweetened rye coffee and tea substitutes. It was also baked into cakes and pies and used to make jelly or preserves. Sorghum seeds were ground into flour, and crushed stalks were used as livestock feed.

Other sugar substitutes were not as widespread. For example, honey was appreciated but could not be produced in enough quantities to take the place of sugar. In the Appalachians, limited amounts of sugar were made from maple sap. Watermelons and figs also yielded sweet syrups. Because of the scarcity of sugar and other supplies, some Southern families stopped having desserts during the war; even if some form of sugar was available, necessities such as butter or flour might not be. Peach leaves replaced vanilla flavoring. At Christmas, peanuts, local fruit, walnuts, and popcorn stood in as treats for children in place of stick candies and baked delicacies.

Sometimes suggestions for food substitutes were impractical. If no cream was available for coffee, alternatives included beaten egg whites mixed with a little butter or wheat flour, but these ingredients might also be in short supply. Before the war, much of the South's butter was imported from the North, and many families were not used to churning their own butter.

The hunting of squirrels, opossums, and other small game could supplement farm-raised meat, although civilians found it difficult to obtain ammunition. Fish and shellfish eased shortages of beef and pork, although Union control of the coasts and major rivers and transportation constraints limited the preservation and shipment of fish. More desperate measures were used to replace meat. Occasionally, vendors were hauled into court for passing off dog meat as beef or pork. Some soldiers and civilians trapped at the Siege of Vicksburg in 1863 resorted to eating rats or mule meat. Accounts also mention Civil War prisoners of war, of both sides, being so hungry as to consume rats.

Household tips for cooking, while reducing or replacing hard-to-get ingredients, were common items in Confederate newspapers. Numerous recipes appeared for making bread, cakes, biscuits, and pancakes out of unusual supplies.

Wartime food production from farms and home gardens was limited by the scarcity of seeds. Francis Peyre Porcher's influential 1863 *Resources of the Southern Fields and Forests* recommended hundreds of wild native plants that could be harvested for medicinal use or to replace garden produce. Dried pumpkin replaced dried apples; the starchy roots of Jerusalem artichokes took the place of potatoes; and dried persimmons served as dates.

The Confederate government tried to keep corn and grain from going into whiskey, and much alcohol was impressed for military medical use. Southern distillers made whiskey from sweet potatoes, rice, sorghum seeds, or other available ingredients. Beer was brewed from persimmons, and all sorts of fruits and berries were made into wine, or distilled into brandy. When apples were unavailable, vinegar was made from beets, molasses, and blackberries.

Ingenuity, patriotism, and necessity pushed Confederates into trying countless substitutes for food and drink. Few alternatives were truly successful. Such attempts eased life to a degree in the Confederacy, but could not solve the serious problems with food production and distribution that afflicted the South.

David A. Norris

See also: Economy and Work: Sutlers; Urban Life, Northern; Urban Life, Southern; *Food and Drink*: Coffee; Cookbooks and Recipes; Food, Northern; Food, Shortages; Food, Soldiers; Food, Southern; Food, Upper Classes; Foraging; Gardens; Hardtack; Hunting; Kitchens; Moonshine; Salt; Spirits; Tea; *Housing and Community*: Refugees; Sieges; Slave Life; *Politics and Warfare*: Bombardments; Camp Life; Morale; *Science and Technology*: Cooking Techniques; Disease

FURTHER READING

Confederate Receipt Book: A Compilation of Over One Hundred Receipts, Adapted to the Times. Richmond: West & Johnson, 1863.

Davis, William C. *A Taste for War: The Culinary History of the Blue and the Gray*. Mechanicsburg, PA: Stackpole Books, 2003.

Massey, Mary Elizabeth. *Ersatz in the Confederacy: Shortages and Substitutes on the Southern Homefront*. Reprint ed. Columbia: University of South Carolina Press, 1993.

TAVERNS

By the eve of the Civil War, the tavern had evolved into a uniquely American institution. Though European taverns predated those in America by several centuries, taverns in the United States provided space for everything from hospitality for travelers and locals to political meetings, weddings, receptions, and dens for a variety of different vices. Whereas tavern ownership in Europe fixed the proprietor to a moderate social station, in the United States taverns vaulted proprietors into positions of local power and influence. Tavern patrons varied from those who needed

1862 Mathew Brady photograph of soldiers standing outside Taylor's Tavern, near Falls Church, Virginia, during the Civil War. Nineteenth-century American taverns served alcohol and food to travelers and locals and hosted political and social events as well as illicit activities. (Library of Congress)

a location for special events to those who sought an escape from the oppression of the various reform movements that defined the late antebellum period.

The term "tavern" itself connoted an establishment that provided alcohol and other activities defined as taboo by the rise of antebellum evangelicalism. Previously, the terms "tavern" and "inn" were used synonymously to refer to a boarding establishment that also offered food and drink. During the colonial period and beyond, inn patrons usually expected a place to spend the night, procure food, and imbibe in alcoholic beverages. Any American home might function as an inn, as it was common for travelers to seek individual homes for shelter from the elements. In such cases, property owners may or may not have sought payment for remuneration of services and it was quite common for them to seek only enough to cover basic costs. Hospitality on the part of local homeowners derived from notions of pride, honor, and reputation. In essence, an inn by the late eighteenth and early nineteenth centuries might be any building, whether a place of business or a private home, where travelers sought room, board, food, and drink. Some homeowners were thus "innkeepers" only reluctantly, while others earned their livelihoods in that manner.

By the 1830s, the number of inns in the United States had grown owing in large measure to American westward expansion. As such, states increasingly regulated the industry so that only professional inns could advertise on wooden signage at public embarkation points, and professionalism was defined as a function of the amount and type of services rendered. As a general rule, inns were defined as places that profited from the boarding enterprise (though states set maximum boarding rates), that provided food, that offered "systematic" entertainment, and that secured a license from local political authorities. Many states also mandated that inn owners be of sound moral character; some states even required regular church attendance by inn owners. Barkeeps were required by law to prevent drunkenness at their establishments. The physical layout of an inn had evolved to provide a separated, if not completely separate, space for the bar apart from main areas of congregation. Such layouts were especially common in the Midwest as western expansion accelerated and because tavern construction was newer.

Northerners and midwesterners were more likely to frequent taverns than were Southerners. This owed primarily to the larger number of urban areas in the Northeast and the function of midwestern cities as points of embarkation during the gold rush and migration westward. In the South, the issuance of dry laws by the state legislatures plus the relative dearth of urban areas rendered drinking in the South, especially among the lower orders, largely a private affair. To be sure, alcohol distribution and consumption was a central activity in taverns, but taverns also functioned as points of dissemination of news, arenas for political debate and antiquarian story-telling, forums for civic and political activities, venues for courtroom proceedings, and dens for practitioners of illicit activities. A number of tavern owners rose to political heights as a function of owning the central meeting point in town. In the days before scientific poll-taking, political party hacks took the pulse of local patrons on a variety of political issues by engaging them in conversation and debate. Territorial courts sometimes used taverns as the venue to hear cases and render verdicts. And of course, as antebellum reforms spread across the Northern states and into the South and Midwest, activities like card-playing, gambling, shaving in public, and cigar smoking increasingly moved "underground" to the tavern. Itinerant preachers also sought room, board, and audience at taverns where it has been recorded that preachers both plied their trade attempting to convert sinners and on occasion enjoyed drink and company of locals at the bar.

Taverns grew from farmhouses that occasionally took in travelers to boarding houses with farms attached to provide room and food as a fully functional business unto themselves. Most taverns provided similar fare for their customers. They served meals three times daily, provided beds with varying degrees of comfort and privacy, distilled and served whisky made locally from corn and/or rye, and provided entertainment of varying degrees of quality. Some taverns, especially those located within heavily trafficked cities and towns, often hired "hawkers" to utilize both positive and negative means of advertising for their tavern. Sometimes, hawkers promoted the virtues of the tavern they worked for, extolling the comfort of the beds, quality of the entertainment and food, and hospitality of the owners. On other occasions, they would tout the lack of quality of their competitors and often lie about vacancy at competitor taverns.

Until civilization destroyed the habitat of deer, venison was ubiquitously served at taverns. In the age before refrigeration, most taverns maintained small farms to provide for food products for their patrons. Pigs reproduced frequently and provided bacon and pork, whereas chickens supplied an almost daily source of eggs. Food was mass-produced and served at regular intervals. Cooks would signal meals were ready by ringing a triangular bell and patrons would have limited time to get down to the dining hall on a first-come, first-served basis. Different foods would be boiled or cooked together, such as pork with turnip-tops served with aged butter and warm salad. Sanitation norms were far from regulated and reports indicate that livestock often populated areas of service, animal dung often polluted areas around the kitchen (which was usually detached from the main service areas), mosquitoes and other pests flew freely around dining and service areas, and bed linens were used as table cloths without having been laundered.

Service tables, also known as tables d'hote, were quite diverse in terms of patrons. The relatively well-to-do sat with commoners, politicians, constituents, men and women, middle class, and day-laborers. Conversation was loud and cacophonous and where there were no spittoons, guests spit their tobacco juice onto the floor.

Freight trains rendered the traditional function of the tavern obsolete. After the Civil War, rail travel whisked travelers to their points of destination much more quickly and began to provide accoutrements like dining and sleeping cars. The advent of cheap newspapers eroded the role of taverns as news centers and increasingly state legislatures allowed taverns to serve drink without also providing food. This served to undercut the table d'hote with its democratic seating arrangements and regular meal times.

Mark A. Panuthos

See also: *Economy and Work*: Urban Life, Northern; Urban Life, Southern; *Food and Drink*: Coffee; Kitchens; Mealtime Etiquette; Moonshine; Salt; Spirits;

Tea; Tobacco; *Housing and Community*: Boarding Houses; Voting; *Recreation and Social Customs*: Gambling; Hospitality; Political Speeches; *Religion and Belief*: Reformers; Traveling Preachers; *Science and Technology*: Railroads

FURTHER READING

Lathrop, Elise. *Early American Inns and Taverns*. New York: Tudor Publishing, 1926.

Lender, Mark Edward, and James Kirby Martin. *Drinking in America: A History*. New York: Free Press, 1982.

Rorabaugh, W. J. *The Alcoholic Republic: An American Tradition*. New York: Oxford University Press, 1979.

Yoder, Paton. *Taverns and Travelers: Inns of the Early Midwest*. Bloomington: University of Indiana Press, 1969.

TEA

When Northern and Southern soldiers or civilians consumed tea during the Civil War, they usually did so for medicinal purposes, although in high culture circles, especially in the North, afternoon tea ceremonies enjoyed a brief comeback during Queen Victoria's reign.

By the eve of the Civil War Americans much preferred coffee to tea. Prior to the American Revolution tea consumption in the colonies amounted to more than 1,462,000 pounds per year, between the 900,000 pounds smuggled into the colonies and the 562,000 pounds purchased legally from the British East India Company. Multiple theories explain the decline of tea popularity ranging from the patriotic and symbolic to the practical and to the chemical. Tea played a central role in fomenting the Revolution. John Adams referred to it as "Traitors Tea." In addition, coffee came from South American countries rather than India or China and was therefore less expensive. At any rate, coffee rations were standard issue to federal troops during the war and coffee was in high demand among Confederate troops.

Regionally, teas consumed during the Civil War era acquired peculiar and distinctive characteristics. By the early years of the nineteenth century, cold teas called "punches"—which usually consisted of green teas, as well as indigenous and fragrant flora like gardenias, azaleas, and camellias—were popular among the wealthier segments of Southern plantation society. By the 1830s, primitive refrigeration units called "ice boxes" were developed, which enabled the ready availability of cold water. Although ice boxes were relatively rare, iced sweet teas proved particularly refreshing, especially considering the nature of Southern agricultural labor. This early forerunner of modern-day Southern sweet tea varied by region and usually contained alcohol. Logistical difficulties on campaigns made sweet tea consumption a rare treat during the Civil War for Confederate troops, even for the officer corps.

After the war the varieties of popular tea that developed differed from wartime teas. Postwar teas usually consisted of black teas, no alcohol, and sugar cane or syrup added during the process of boiling the water. These types of tea all predated the introduction of tea leaves infused through a strainer. Owing to its geographic isolation such tea consumption continued primarily in the ricelands of South Carolina and Georgia, which centered in Charleston and Savannah, the "camels hump" of Virginia, a small portion of Maryland, and in the southern portion of Louisiana, centered in New Orleans. Family records show monthly purchases of large quantities of tea in these regions, and given the nature of the planter lifestyle, they would have had ample time to enjoy the full English tea ceremony. Confederate defeat in the Civil War, and the harsh realities brought on by Reconstruction, contributed to the end of this tradition in the South. During Reconstruction, sweet tea consumption, although different in composition from its earlier forebears, proved a popular beverage because it was inexpensive to make and provided a flavorful reminder of days gone by.

The South's enslaved blacks continued to use African folk remedies as the war approached. Although by the mid-nineteenth century, they likely no longer retained accurate knowledge of African folk remedies or had access to the same roots and herbs used in traditional African folk remedies, some African plants used for herbal remedies were successfully introduced into North America and cultivated through the generations. Enslaved Africans often combined, when possible, these herbs with indigenous roots and plants which when combined with boiling waters produced a tea-like beverage. Whatever the degree of authenticity for these African herbal remedies, white Southerners believed that their enslaved population retained such knowledge of herbal tea remedies and relied on them for medicinal purposes. Although the actual remedial effects of such teas are questionable, in the absence of manufactured medicines and the relative paucity of medical knowledge, there was little in the way of alternatives. For instance, slaves boiled corn shucks to make a medicinal tea that would be used to address hives, cotton seeds to make a tea to cure chills and fever, jimson weed for stomach aches, and mixed fennel with corn shucks to cure malaria. In addition, they used feverfew to concoct a purgative tea. Sassafras root, a common herb throughout the eastern United States, provided a multifaceted elixir that slaves used as a blood cleanser and Northerners used it as a treatment for syphilis, rheumatism, and as a general pain reliever. Masters and overseers observed enslaved African Americans drinking the hot excess liquid from boiled vegetables, which they considered as a hot "tea" beverage and while it did not necessarily cure anything specific, it did contain nutrients from the vegetables and thus produced a nineteenth-century health beverage.

In the North, where the climate was colder, warm, nonmedicinal tea consumption continued in some circles, especially during the reign of Queen Victoria. Afternoon tea parties, largely out of practice in the United States since the Revolution, witnessed something of a comeback by the late 1830s. During the Civil War, Union soldiers overwhelmingly preferred coffee to tea though they too sought medicinal teas for a variety of ailments. In addition, when campaigning in the South, Union soldiers often sought the services of black herbalists for cures.

Tea consumption increased during and after the Civil War in the Northern states. In fact, the predecessor of the Atlantic and Pacific Grocery chain owed its initial growth to forays into the coffee and tea markets by founder George Gilman in 1850. By 1863, the original business, Gilman and Sons had become the Great American Tea Company, and expanded to five stores in New York City. Eventually, the store grew into a grocery chain the Great Atlantic and Pacific Tea Company, later known as A & P.

Mark A. Panuthos

See also: *Economy and Work*: Slavery; *Food and Drink*: Coffee; Substitutes, Food and Drink; *Science and Technology*: Medicine, Practice of

FURTHER READING

Covey, Herbert C. *African American Slave Medicine*. Lanham, MD: Lexington Books, 2007.

Genovese, Eugene D. *Roll Jordan Roll: The World the Slaves Made*. New York: Vintage Books, 1972.

Graham, Joe S. "Folk Medicine." *Handbook of Texas Online*. Texas State Historical Association. http://www.tshaonline.org/handbook/online/articles/sdf01. Accessed November 24, 2013.

TOBACCO

The cultivation and use of tobacco was prevalent in the United States leading up to and during the Civil War. This popularity was particularly true in the South, where tobacco was grown on large plantations as well as in small plots, and was an important part of the economy. From 1861 to 1865 tobacco was widely used, enjoyed, and culturally accepted by soldiers and civilians on both sides.

Prior to the Civil War, the growth of tobacco contributed to the ongoing debate concerning the spread of slavery in new territory acquired by the United States. On large plantations, enslaved labor was prevalent in the cultivation of this labor-intensive crop, and growers supported its extension into new territory acquired by the United States in the 1800s. It is estimated that on the eve of the Civil War, nearly 350,000 enslaved African Americans were being used to grow tobacco in the South, mostly in the states of Virginia, North Carolina, and Tennessee. The demand for tobacco during the Civil War was high, and

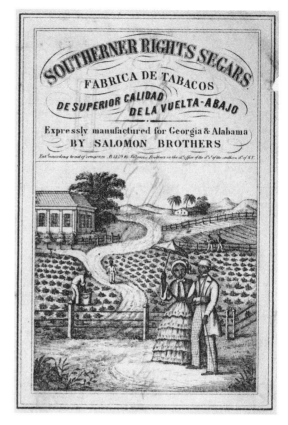

Antebellum "Southerner Rights Segars" label depicting idealized view of slavery and plantation life. Tobacco proved to be one of the South's most profitable and labor-intensive crops, and its cultivation frequently depended on enslaved labor. (Library of Congress)

the economies of the North and South struggled to provide this popular product to their respective militaries and civilian populations despite the war.

Tobacco was a labor-intensive crop that often utilized enslaved labor when produced in mass quantities. Most households in Border and Southern States, however, grew small plots for personal use and for trade. Once mature, the leaves of tobacco plants were gathered and dried in sheds by air or heat. Leaves were later rolled into cigars, "plugs" (compressed and sweetened rolls of tobacco leaves), or shredded into pipe tobacco. The type of tobacco plant and the soil it was grown in could affect its quality and taste, and many strands of tobacco became popular and were spread throughout the country by soldiers after the war.

During the Civil War, tobacco use among soldiers and civilians was ubiquitous. Indeed, tobacco use was widespread throughout the country before the war and dated back to Native Americans and European colonies in the New World. Americans in the Civil War era used tobacco in many ways, the most prevalent were chewing and smoking, mostly in the form of pipes and cigars. Tobacco was often chewed in "plugs," which released flavor and nicotine, as well as copious amounts of spit. Spittoons, containers into which tobacco chewers were supposed to spit, were widely placed inside buildings, including some churches. Pipes—made from corncobs, clay, animal bone, wood, or even metal—were most commonly used for smoking. Cigar smoking was popular but more expensive. Other forms of tobacco usage included snuff—dry, powdered tobacco "dipped" between the gums and cheek or snorted through the nose—and cigarettes, which were introduced to the United States from England around 1860.

War greatly disrupted tobacco production in the North and South thus making it harder for civilians to obtain it. It was easier for soldiers to obtain tobacco during wartime than it was for civilians. Confederate troops were constantly fighting on Southern soil, where plantations were common. Supplying soldiers with tobacco was easier to do and was one of the few plentiful rations provided to Confederate armies. Union soldiers fighting in the South often pillaged tobacco products from Confederate owned farms and warehouses. When tobacco could not be found, Union soldiers commonly took advantage of lulls in fighting to trade with the enemy. It was quite common for Union troops to trade coffee, which was plentiful in the North, with Confederates for tobacco, which was plentiful in the South. For many soldiers, tobacco was one of the few luxuries available. Soldiers' diaries and letters home included numerous positive references to tobacco use as well as requests that family send them more. The Union and Confederate governments realized the popularity of tobacco among soldiers and did their best to ensure soldiers had access to it. By the end of the war, soldiers fighting for the North and South were given tobacco rations when available.

Heavy fighting in tobacco-producing Southern states such as Virginia, North Carolina, and Tennessee severely interrupted the trade and limited its availability throughout the country. In addition, the Confederate government sought to limit the amount of tobacco farmers could grow during the war, hoping to alleviate a serious shortage of foodstuffs for soldiers. To feed demand in the North, tobacco production shifted to states under Union control. Numerous cities benefitted, such as Louisville and New York City, which embraced and greatly profited from processing tobacco for consumption. However, the war in the South meant that tobacco was more difficult to come by and more expensive for the civilian populace, particularly in the North.

The use of tobacco during the Civil War was often divided by class and gender. Chewing tobacco and smoking it in pipes was more common in rural areas, while cigar smoking was more popular among the well-to-do. This difference applied to soldiers as well. Enlisted men were more likely to chew and smoke

TOBACCO USE BY SOUTHERN WOMEN

Union solders often commented on the heavy use of tobacco by Southerners. Of particular interest to Northern soldiers was the widespread use of tobacco by Southern women. In this letter Illinois soldier Charles Wills disdained Confederate women in Alabama's use of chewing tobacco.

I went to the nearest house to camp today, to beg a little piece of tallow. . . . I sat down by a fire in company with three young women, all cleanly dressed, and powdered to death. Their ages were from 18 to 24. Each of them had a quid of tobacco in her cheek about the size of my stone inkstand, and if they didn't make the extract fly worse than I ever saw in any country grocery, shoot me. These women here have so disgusted me with the use of tobacco that I have determined to abandon it. (Wills, 215)

Wills also commented on the use of snuff by Southern women, telling his family of the following experience he had while serving in Iuka, Mississippi.

Snuff-dipping is an universal custom here, and there are only two women in all Iuka that do not practice it. . . . Sometimes girls ask their beaux to take a dip with them during a spark. I asked one if it didn't interfere with the old fashioned habit of kissing. She assured me that it did not in the least, and I marveled. (Wills, 99)

FURTHER READING

Wills, Charles W. *Army Life of an Illinois Soldier*. Washington, DC: Globe Printing Company, 1906.

pipes, which were easy to carry, lasted longer than cigars, and cost less money. Officers were more likely to afford and smoke cigars. An average soldier in the Union Army made approximately $13 per month; cigars cost anywhere from 5 to 20 cents each. By this measure, an expensive cigar cost a regular soldier a half day's pay. Tobacco use among women was less common than it was among men, and was relegated to different forms. More Southern women used tobacco than did their counterparts in the North, often in the form of snuff, which was placed in the cheek. According to accounts, many Northern soldiers were taken aback by the sight of the tobacco-spitting Southern women they encountered during the war.

Although tobacco was widely used by people on both sides, there were those who realized the ill effects of tobacco usage. Some medical personnel derided its use, complaining about the uncleanliness of spit and smoke in camp. There also existed numerous social organizations that attempted to dissuade soldiers from using tobacco, often with little success. By the time the war ended, Americans were still using tobacco in large numbers and would continue to do so well into the next century.

Justin Riskus

See also: Clothing, Fashion, and Appearance: Personal Hygiene; *Politics and Warfare*: Camp Life; *Recreation and Social Customs*: Leisure Time

FURTHER READING

Gottsegen, Jack J. *Tobacco: A Study of Its Consumption in the United States*. New York: Pitman Publishing, 1940.

Hahn, Barbara. *Making Tobacco Bright: Creating an American Commodity, 1617–1937.* Baltimore: Johns Hopkins University Press, 2011.

Kulikoff, Allen. *Tobacco and Slaves: The Development of Southern Cultures in the Chesapeake, 1680–1800*. Chapel Hill: University of North Carolina Press, 1986.

Lord, Francis A. "That 'Wonderful Solace,' Virginia Tobacco in the Civil War." *Virginia Calvacade* 20:4 (1971): 36–47.

Quigley, Paul D. H. "Tobacco's Civil War." *Southern Cultures* 12:2 (Summer 2006): 53–57.